ACCIDENTAL ACTIVISTS

Mark Phariss, Vic Holmes, and Their Fight for Marriage Equality in Texas

by
David Collins

Foreword by Evan Wolfson and Julian Castro
Number 8 in the Mayborn Literary Nonfiction Series

University of North Texas Press
Mayborn Graduate Institute of Journalism
Denton, Texas

10 9 8 7 6 5 4 3 2 1

Permissions:
University of North Texas Press
1155 Union Circle #311336
Denton, TX 76203-5017

The paper used in this book meets the minimum requirements
of the American National Standard for Permanence of Paper for
Printed Library Materials, z39.48.1984. Binding materials have
been chosen for durability.

Library of Congress Cataloging-in-Publication Data

Collins, David, 1945 June-
   Accidental activists : Mark Phariss, Vic Holmes, and their fight
for marriage equality in Texas / by David Collins ; foreword by Evan
Wolfson and Julian Castro.
      p. cm. – (No. 8 in the Mayborn Literary Nonfiction series)
   Includes bibliographical references and index.
   ISBN-13 978-1-57441-692-3 (cloth : alk. paper)
   ISBN-13 978-1-57441-703-6 (ebook)
   1. De Leon, Cleopatra—Trials, litigation, etc. 2. Texas—Trials,
litigation, etc. 3. Phariss, Mark—Trials , litigation, etc. 4. Holmes,
Victor—Trials, litigation, etc. 5. Same-sex marriage—Law and
legislation—Texas—Cases. I. Title. II. Series: Mayborn Literary
Nonfiction ; no. 8.

   KF229 .D45 C65 2017
   DDC 346.7301/68–dc23
                       2017017751

*Accidental Activists: Mark Phariss, Vic Holmes, and Their Fight for
Marriage Equality in Texas* is Number 8 in the Mayborn Literary
Nonfiction Series

The electronic edition of this book was made possible by the support
of the Vick Family Foundation. Typeset by vPrompt eServices.

For Mark Phariss and Vic Holmes who set aside their fears and rose to challenge injustice in Texas;

For Cleopatra DeLeon and Nicole Dimetman, equal in courage, who walked with them in the legal battles that ensued;

For the nearly six-hundred couples nationwide, plaintiffs in same-sex marriage cases since 1970;

For the countless private attorneys, law firms, and legal groups who supported them in their pursuit of the fundamental right to marry—including the American Civil Liberties Union, GLBTQ Legal Advocates & Defenders, Lambda Legal, and the National Center for Lesbian Rights.

Contents

Foreword by Evan Wolfson and Julian Castro vi

Author's Preface x

Introduction   Reluctant Rebels . . . but Rebels with a Cause   1

Chapter 1   Growing Up Absurd   13

Chapter 2   Should We? Or Shouldn't We?   61

Chapter 3   The First Blast of the Trumpet   98

Chapter 4   The Battle of New Orleans, Part I Opening Salvos: Louisiana and Mississippi   144

Chapter 5   The Battle of New Orleans, Part II Texas Engages   164

Chapter 6   Crossing the Threshold   198

Chapter 7   Justice That Arrives Like a Thunderbolt   235

    Photos

Chapter 8   Backlash in Texas   293

Chapter 9   Married at Last, Deep in the Heart of Texas   304

Table of Cases   330

Endnotes   332

Bibliography   356

Index   369

Foreword

On June 26, 2015, more than four decades of struggle and engagement, combat and persuasion, activism and conversation culminated in a Supreme Court ruling affirming the freedom to marry for all Americans, including same-sex couples like Vic Holmes and Mark Phariss, whose story David Collins recounts with impressive empathy in this book. More than a million gay people have legally married in the United States, and a super-majority of Americans (more than 60 percent!) support the freedom to marry and are proud that our country lived up to its promise and became —through all that hard work and hope, battling and belief—a more perfect union.

How did this historic transformation and triumph happen?

Well, four decades of work means it didn't happen overnight. The climax in the Supreme Court of course means it took lawyers, litigation, and hundreds of plaintiffs like Mark and Vic. It also took battles in state legislatures and in Congress, millions of conversations and millions of dollars raised and invested. It took courageous elected officials and determined constituents helping to push them and create space in which they could rise. It took many organizations and allies; it took a movement, a strategy, and a campaign, Freedom to Marry.

And it took We, the People—everyday Americans willing to trust that others could rise to fairness. People willing to share their stories, engage in conversations and persuasion, provide both information and an appeal to shared values, the heartfelt truths of our lives. Conversation is the chief engine of change in a country like America, and as the book sums it up so well, we needed "accidental activists" willing to:

> Lead good and productive lives, tell your stories, engage the people around you, but do so quietly, in conversational terms. Respect those who

stand opposed, give them time and the psychological space they need to grow, to discover their better selves and to become supporters.

This essential engagement worked. It created space for business and labor, voices of faith and advocates for children, political leaders and former opponents to open their hearts and minds and move. It created space for the political successes and litigation victories that hard work delivered and that cumulatively created the climate for triumph in the Supreme Court.

LGBT Americans have won the freedom to marry in law, but, of course, the marriage conversation has only just begun to penetrate some parts of the country, some communities, including, yes, some in Texas. The freedom to marry remains the gift that keeps on giving. By giving more and more people the chance to hear the stories, see the joy and needs of their fellow Americans, the power of the marriage conversation continues to build greater understanding of gay and transgender people. Greater visibility and showing shared values increases empathy and adds momentum to the urgent work still ahead. That work includes ending discrimination and exclusion in other important arenas such as employment, housing, education, and places of public accommodation such as businesses and, yes, even bathrooms.

It includes making sure that people's actual lived experience is good— not just the laws, but their actual lives: Young people growing up safe, accepted, and free to dream big. Older people finding support and facilities for care without being forced back into the closet because of who they are and whom they love. All Americans free and equal and able to pursue happiness in every state, every community.

And it includes defending our country's hard-won gains against efforts to divide Americans, demean communities, undermine progress, or roll back the clock.

In 2014, on the day Judge Orlando Garcia heard arguments in *DeLeon v. Perry*, the case Mark and Vic and another courageous couple, Cleopatra DeLeon and Nicole Dimetman brought against Texas, we partnered on an op-ed in *The San Antonio Express News*. We wrote:

The moral question on the table is, do we treat others as we would want to be treated? Aren't we all striving to follow the Golden Rule without succumbing to divisiveness and discrimination? Aren't we all God's children? We think that most Americans, and most Texans, would agree: The answer is a resounding yes.

The discussion around dinner tables is about the right to marry—not what churches can or cannot do. Churches and other religious institutions will always be free—as they are now—to decide whom they want to marry. Religious freedom, like equal protection and the freedom to marry, is a bedrock constitutional principle of this great country. But the government should not [discriminate]. Like the majority of Americans nationwide…we believe in individual responsibility and the pursuit of happiness, and know that freedom means freedom for all.

Accidental Activists is the touching story of Mark and Vic's love and commitment, a moving account of their willingness to work and fight to defend America's values. David Collins captures the couple's talk of family and of their fears, traces the difficulties they confronted, and stirringly conveys the determination that carried them through difficult moments, the ups and downs of facing a big No from so many parts of society and turning it not just into a Yes, but an I Do.

As we move through 2017 and into the future, America faces some tough times, domestic as well as foreign threats. Once again too many in power are falling far short of the values and promise that make America great. Once again, we are all called to take action to get our country back on track, much as Mark and Vic and millions like them had to do at a time when winning the freedom to marry was dismissed as appalling or laughable, dangerous and doomed.

David Collins calls Mark and Vic "accidental activists," but as Aristotle said long ago, "The ideal man bears the accidents of life with dignity and grace, making the best of circumstances."

It took hope, clarity, and tenacity to win the freedom to marry—and all of us must now step up and meet the challenges of this moment to defend our Republic and fight against bad policies, bad politics, bad politicians. We must all be activists now—and must do so with trust we can win, not cynicism; belief that others can rise, not despair; commitment to America's constitutional and moral values, not surrender. This book offers lessons for effective action, and it offers hope. That is the start of winning. That is what is needed now.

Julian Castro

Evan Wolfson

Julian Castro was Secretary of Housing and Urban Development and the Mayor of San Antonio. Evan Wolfson was founder and president of Freedom to Marry.

Author's Preface

By at least one way of reckoning, this book began in the fall of 1978 at Westminster College in Fulton, Missouri. When classes began that year, I was a newly tenured, newly promoted Associate Professor of English determined that the world would, or at least should, share my love of Shakespeare. But as I walked in the still intense heat of August from my office to the room where I would meet my first class of the semester, I was thinking less about Shakespeare than about making the world safe for English grammar, about the importance of pre-writing and the link between clear thinking and clear writing. The students waiting for me had signed up for ENG 104 Academic Writing, a required course few students in those days escaped. Another year had begun, my thirteenth year teaching in one or another college or university. I knew from long experience that great hopes, great expectations, great joys, and no doubt a few disappointments would follow.

Just over twenty faces looked up as I entered the classroom and took the place traditionally left for the instructor at the head of the large oval table that reached nearly to the four walls. In the next academic year, Westminster would admit its first-ever class of women, but in the fall of 1978 the faces that turned expectantly toward me belonged exclusively to young men. Introducing myself, searching their faces as I talked about what would come, I looked for distinguishing marks that would help me to associate names with faces. Only one really stood out, a function of his light-skinned, freckled face topped by a shock of red hair that drew the eye. His name, I would soon learn, was Mark Phariss.

In those long-ago days before the fabled "Gentleman's C" became the "Gentleman's B," and evolved later into the "Gentleman's A," few students in Academic Writing at Westminster earned more than a "C" on their first essay.

Most improved steadily as the semester wore on, but that first experience was intended as a shot across the bow, a sign to incoming students that standards in college would be considerably higher than what most had experienced in high school. The real test was how any given student would react to his lower-than-expected grade.

When I returned the first set of essays that fall, Mark Phariss looked at his and found among the comments at the end the standard "C." Alarmed, perhaps a little angry—he had graduated fifth in his high school class of almost 600 and had never seen a "C" on any academic exercise—he made his way to my office the next day. Already a history buff, he had chosen Westminster in part because Winston Churchill had delivered his famous "Iron Curtain" speech there in 1946, in part because its unusually low faculty-student ratio promised an opportunity to work closely with faculty. A generous scholarship had made his enrollment possible and he was determined that nothing would endanger that scholarship. Rather than grouse about unreasonable demands, he chose to take advantage of that low faculty-student ratio and stopped by to see what he needed to do to improve his writing. That day he passed the first test by which faculty measure students.

We talked that afternoon and many afternoons after that. I came quickly to realize that Mark was the student every professor dreams of: smart, serious, hard-working, and yet funny. I was impressed, so much so that two years later when I sat on a committee charged with choosing the recipient of the Cranshaw Scholarship, Westminster's most prestigious award for study abroad, I convinced my colleagues that the coveted prize should go to Mark. I must have impressed him as well since he quickly got over the disappointment of that first "C." Semester after semester, he appeared in one or another of my classes. We got to know each other well—or so I thought. I learned a great deal about Mark's family, about his life in Oklahoma, about his ambition for a life in the law. What I didn't learn then, or for many years to come, was that Mark was gay.

One of the great virtues of small liberal arts colleges like Westminster is that faculty-student friendships often grow into life-long friendships—and that happened with Mark and me. After four years he sailed off to law school at Vanderbilt, settled in San Antonio to practice law, moved on and up in the legal profession—but always he came back to Westminster. Whenever he did, he sought me out and our conversations picked up where they had left off. When Facebook came along our interactions became more frequent. I retired at the end of May 2013, and in the winter before that another alum organized a banquet to celebrate my forty years of service at Westminster. Mark was one of half-a-dozen all-time favorite students I insisted be invited to that celebration. I knew by then that Mark was gay, knew that he was already working to defend the rights of gays and lesbians in Texas. Still, my knowledge was incomplete. I had no idea how far he was willing to take the battle.

Within six months of my retirement, the story told in this book began in earnest. Toward the end of October 2013 Mark posted on Facebook that he and his partner, Vic Holmes, together with Cleopatra DeLeon and Nicole Dimetman, had filed suit against Texas. Mark and Vic wanted the right to marry, denied them by statutory and constitutional law in Texas. Nicole and Cleo wanted their legal marriage, performed in Massachusetts, recognized in Texas. For a year I followed Mark and Vic's posts and comments closely, reading what they sent, commenting on occasion, sending words of encouragement when that seemed necessary. Though separated by hundreds of miles—as many miles as separate Missouri and Texas—I celebrated with Mark and Vic and Cleo and Nicole when a decision from the Federal District Court for the Western District of Texas declared Texas's bans against same-sex marriage unconstitutional. I grieved with them when the Fifth Circuit Court of Appeals delayed and delayed again in setting a date for oral arguments on Texas's appeal. Though on occasion Mark or Vic would raise the lid and I was able to catch in their comments a glimpse of what they were feeling, most of what I read that first year was merely informative.

But in the fall of 2014 something changed. Where occasional posts about marriage equality had once been balanced by other posts—photos of and stories about their travels or their beloved beagles, artful photographs of wildlife or wild places they had visited, family pictures from long ago and warm vignettes of family life in the present, celebrations of or laments for the fortunes of the Oklahoma Sooners football team, always rising or falling—in October and November as the struggle for marriage equality in Texas and across the nation heated up most posts focused on new developments in the struggle he and Vic had joined. Four and five posts a day, sometimes six and even seven, the drumbeat summoning supporters to prepare for a decisive battle had clearly begun.

When on November 20, 2014, Mark posted an announcement from the Fifth Circuit Court of Appeals—they had at last set January 9 as the date for oral arguments in the Texas case—I sent a private message congratulating Mark and Vic on their courage and promising whatever support I could offer from a distance. Unable to shake entirely my old role as Professor of English—the habits of forty years die hard—I added the usual injunction to "write it all down." "I hope you're keeping a journal," I told Mark, "since this is going to make a great book."

Minutes later, Mark messaged me. "Are you busy?" he asked. "Can I call you?" We talked that afternoon as we had talked so often before. Mark had only one question: "Why don't *you* write the book?" I hadn't been the first to suggest a book about his and Vic's still-developing story, Mark told me. At first they had dismissed the suggestion. What had they done, they wondered, what could they do that would be of interest to a general audience? But as the number of people imagining a book grew, their minds had changed. My suggestion had come in a fortunate hour. Moreover, Mark knew my writing and trusted me.

I had other projects in hand, had begun revising a series of essays published over the years in literary magazines for publication as a collection. That done, I had planned to finish a book of walking tours of sites in Paris made famous by American writers who lived and wrote there from the end of the First World War to the present. And I had already roughed out a novel set in Paris. I had projects aplenty. But the idea of writing about marriage equality, of telling the story of the struggle for same-sex marriage through the lives of two ordinary men who, finding themselves at a crossroads, found as well the courage to move along the road no one in Texas had yet dared to follow, was compelling. I talked with Jean, my wife; we flew to Texas to learn more.

That weekend we met Vic, came to understand at least a bit of why Mark loved him, and learned the outlines of his story: very different from Mark's, but no less compelling. Jean and I had long numbered other gay men and lesbians among our friends. They had talked with us about the indignities so often heaped on people in the LGBT community, problems with jobs, housing, families. Some had shared difficult coming out stories. But listening to Mark and Vic speak of homophobia in the legal profession, in the armed services, in Texas—much of it condoned and even encouraged by law—brought home the need for change in a whole new way.

I was hooked. Their story needed to be written and deserved to be written well. But as we talked our way through the weekend, questions arose, at least in my own mind. Would my heterosexuality be an issue? Could a straight man write effectively about the experience of two gay men fighting for what I had taken for granted my entire life, the right to marry the person they loved most in all the world? Was my experience too "different"? The more I thought, the more I came to see my perspective as an advantage—a two-fold advantage. Though I hadn't lived the lives Mark and Vic had lived, couldn't identify *entirely* with them, I realized quickly that what seemed in one moment an obstacle appeared in the next as an advantage. My perspective would enable me to stand at once "inside" and "outside," to tell the whole story in a way they could not. More important, perhaps, I knew that a writer's job is to enter into the lives of other people—some villains, some heroes, some sympathetic, some condemnable, some projections of the author's self, some very different—and to make the reader feel what they feel. That I had done before and knew I could do again.

That weekend I wondered as well about "difference." Mark and Vic knew full well that not everyone in the LGBT community was of one mind about the desirability of marriage. As Cleve Jones writes in *When We Rise*, the debate that began in the late 1960s continues still. "Each [generation] has employed a different vocabulary," he suggests, "but the issue remains essentially unchanged: are we a queer and distinct people, with revolutionary potential born from our experiences—or are we really just like everyone else except for what we do in bed."[1] Though Mark and Vic recognized, even sympathized with the opposing view, they had come down on the side of marriage—likeness over difference. As boys and young men, "difference" had been thrust upon them, a razor-sharp blade that inflicted a thousand cuts. They had struggled to create authentic selves, struggled to achieve what in *Romer v. Evans*, *Lawrence v. Texas*, and *United States v. Windsor* Justice Anthony Kennedy refers to consistently as "personhood," too often denied to gays and lesbians. In their eyes marriage was an important signifier, a cultural *rite de passage* that signaled social acceptance: two members of the community had come together as one in the ultimate expression of love and commitment.

Not everyone in the gay community, Mark and Vic recognized, may want to marry, but they were determined that, as a recognition of their essential humanity, the opportunity ought to be available for those who do. Moreover, they recognized that choosing likeness over difference, choosing to fight for the right to marry, brought with it an additional advantage. As Justice Breyer would point out the day *Obergefell* was argued, "the Constitution and Amendment Fourteen does say you cannot deprive a person of liberty, certainly of basic liberty, without due process of law; and that to take a group of people where so little distinguished them from the people you give liberty to . . . [and not] let them participate in this basic institution, that violates the Fourteenth Amendment."[2] The right to marry wasn't the beginning of the struggle for gay rights; it wouldn't be the end. But for Mark and Vic the right to marry was an important way-station on the road to full equality—and the likely road there ran through likeness.

Listening as Mark and Vic talked of their lives, of the plans they hoped to make real, I recognized that we were not different in any meaningful way. If as a straight man I had not experienced all that they had experienced, could not identify *entirely* with them, I could identify with them in all that mattered: the desire to be recognized as an autonomous human being with inalienable rights, part of a larger community. By the time I boarded a plane to return to Missouri I knew how I would spend the next year or so.

Writing the story Mark and Vic had lived since birth—and continued to live as I watched—sent me on a great adventure, a personal voyage of discovery. That first weekend I recorded hours and hours of conversation. For two years I talked almost daily with one or both men; we exchanged countless e-mails and text messages as I discovered what I did know, what I didn't know, and worked to fill in the gaps, reaching always not just to record, not just to understand, but to feel their experience and, I hope, to enable the reader to do the same. I combed through e-mails between lawyers and plaintiffs, read briefs and court decisions that introduced me to a whole new vocabulary. I read widely—and I hope, well—plunging for hours into books that would provide background for the still-developing story of their lives as gay men and their challenge to Texas. As the battle for marriage equality in Texas and across the nation developed, I combed the *New York Times, The Washington Post, The Advocate* and the gay press generally for relevant stories. I watched as Mark and Vic and their friends on Facebook reacted to each victory, each loss.

I traveled with Mark and Vic to New Orleans when the Fifth Circuit Court of Appeals heard *DeLeon v. Perry*. I watched and listened the night before at the Cathedral Creative Studies as Mark and Vic, Cleo and Nicole, together with plaintiffs from Louisiana and Mississippi, told their stories and reached out to support each other. I accompanied them to Washington, D. C. as the fight for marriage equality entered its final phase, listened with them as Evan Wolfson, the godfather of same-sex marriage, and Valerie Jarrett, one of President Obama's most trusted aides, spoke encouragingly to plaintiffs in same-sex marriage cases from around the country, sat with them in the Supreme Court the next day as Mary Bonauto and Solicitor General Donald Verrilli argued for their rights in *Obergefell v. Hodges*. When they married at last in Frisco, Texas, I was there, watching, listening, still working my way, chapter by chapter, toward a book that would do justice to their story. The parallel story of Nicole and Cleo, co-plaintiffs in *DeLeon v. Perry*, a different but no less compelling story, deserves its own book.

Encouraged by Ron Chrisman, director of the University of North Texas Press, I submitted a chapter from the still-developing manuscript— *Accidental Activists: Mark Phariss, Vic Holmes, and their Fight for Marriage Equality in Texas*—to the 2016 book manuscript contest sponsored by the Frank W. and Sue Mayborn Foundation and awarded at the Mayborn Literary Nonfiction Conference. The judges smiled on my efforts. At the Conference in late July *Accidental Activists* won first place—and a contract for publication with the University of North Texas Press. In mid-September I sent the completed manuscript to the press; by December I had the readers' reports in hand and had begun to revise. At the end of January 2017 I returned a new, much-improved version to the press. And as I worked through the months between September and January, the election of Donald Trump as president of the United States turned the world in which Mark and Vic married upside down.

No one had imagined that winning the right to marry would end forever the debate over gay rights. Three weeks to the day before the Supreme Court heard oral arguments in *Obergefell,* Michelangelo Signorile's *It's Not Over: Getting Beyond Tolerance, Defeating Homophobia, and Winning True Equality* appeared in bookstores. "Imagine a group of people," he asked in the spring of 2015, "who have spent decades—generations, centuries—in fear, invisibility, silence."

> Now imagine that, in a matter of a few short years, everything seems to change. At what feels like light speed, they make momentous gains. The world begins to open its arms to them in ways they had never thought possible. The experience is powerful, exhilarating, spellbinding even.

But beneath the glittering surface, Signorile warned readers, LGBT and straight allies alike, there lurks "a reality more treacherous than many . . . imagine." We have arrived, he claimed, at "a dangerous moment" in which "victory blindness" imperils recent gains.[3] A year and more later at the White House Pride Reception in June 2016, President Obama sounded the same note. Don't Ask, Don't Tell had been repealed; the Matthew Shepard Hate Crimes Bill had been signed into law; LGBT Americans had won the right to marry. But progress, he warned, isn't "inevitable . . . History doesn't just travel forward; it can go backwards if we don't work hard."[4]

Though in the summer of 2016 even dyed-in-the-wool optimists recognized that the fight for equality was far from over and were inclined to listen to the prudent voices advising caution, few imagined that in the November elections Republicans would retain control of the House *and* the Senate—and that Donald Trump would win the presidency. Suddenly, the possibility that history could—and would—move quickly backward seemed not just possible but probable. Though Trump claimed during the campaign that he was not anti-LGBT, he chose as his running mate Governor Mike Pence, the man who signed and stubbornly defended SB 101, the toxic Religious Freedom Restoration Act that shattered Indiana's "open for business" reputation. Senior staff picks and nominees for Cabinet positions sent a similar message.

Steve Bannon, poised to take up residence in the West Wing as Trump's Chief Strategist and Senior Counselor, telegraphed his attitude toward gay rights when as chairman of Breitbart News he passed on stories with titles like "Gay Rights Have Made Us Dumber, It's Time to Get Back in the Closet" and "Day of Silence: How the LGBT Agenda Is Hijacking America's Youth." Betsy DeVos, Trump's pick for Secretary of Education, claimed during her confirmation hearings that paperwork listing her for seventeen years as vice-president of the Edgar & Elsa Prince Foundation—a generous donor to anti-LGBT groups like Focus on the Family and the Family Research Council—was the result of a "clerical error," but few were convinced. Ben Carson, Trump's choice for Housing and Urban Development, denied during the campaign that gay rights are civil rights, asserted that being gay is a choice, and compared gay sex to bestiality. Most frightening of all was Senator Jeff Sessions, Donald Trump's nominee to lead the Department of Justice, whose long and well-documented history opposing minority rights shed doubt on his pledge to defend gay rights. As the attorney general of Alabama in 1996 he turned to an unconstitutional state law in an attempt to keep the Southeastern Lesbian, Gay, Bisexual College Conference from meeting at the state's flagship university. As a U.S. senator he voted for a constitutional ban on same-sex marriage, against repealing Don't Ask, Don't Tell, and against expanding hate crimes legislation to include protections for the LGBT community, positions so consistently extreme that in 2014 the Human Rights Campaign inducted him into its Hall of Shame.

Most frightening, perhaps, in June 2015 Sessions joined with thirty-three other senators to co-sponsor the First Amendment Defense Act, designed to shield people who asserted religious beliefs as their reason for refusing to serve LGBT Americans from prosecution, a bill so broadly written that it could be used to deny not just everyday services, but employment, housing, and even medical care. As Donald Trump moved closer to the Oval Office, Texas Senator Ted Cruz and Utah Senator Mike Lee renewed the threat, announcing that they planned to reintroduce the First Amendment Defense Act, and the president-elect vowed to sign the bill into law when it reached his desk—promises made despite the fact that in June 2016 federal district court Judge Carlton W. Reeves had declared Mississippi's nearly identical law, HB 1523, the Religious Liberties Accommodations Act, unconstitutional. That all mention of LGBT Americans disappeared from the White House website within minutes of Trump's inauguration confirmed for many the dangers of the new administration.

Worse, even, than Donald Trump's staff and cabinet picks were his announced plans for appointments to the Supreme Court. As a candidate, he promised to choose justices in the mold of the recently deceased Antonin Scalia, an unwavering conservative famous for his opposition to gay rights. Shaped by advisors at the Heritage Foundation and the Federalist Society, the short list of candidates announced in the first week of Trump's presidency—Judge William Pryor (11th Circuit U.S. Court of Appeals), Judge Neil Gorsuch (10th U.S. Circuit Court of Appeals), and Judge Thomas Hardiman (3rd Circuit U.S. Court of Appeals)—promised a world of trouble. Opponents seized quickly on William Pryor—as early as 2005 when President George W. Bush nominated him to the 11th Circuit, Kenneth Cathcart, Executive Director of Lambda Legal at the time, called him "the most demonstrably antigay judicial nominee in recent memory"—as an indication of the legal philosophy the new president wanted to elevate to the Supreme Court.[5] As attorney general of Alabama when *Lawrence v. Texas* (2003) came before the Court, Pryor had submitted an amicus brief that left little doubt about his attitude toward the LGBT community.

Drawing a line between what is to be permitted for heterosexuals as opposed to homosexuals, he argued in favor of Texas's conclusion that "*homosexual* sodomy may have severe physical, emotional, psychological, and spiritual consequences" from which "Texas's citizens need to be protected" (emphasis added). Denying the immutability of sexual orientation—gays and lesbians, he asserted, did not possess "some feature of their personhood that they cannot immediately control"—Pryor argued against the recognition of a suspect class and, consequently, against a higher level of scrutiny. Were the Court to hold in favor of "a constitutional right that protects 'the choice of one's partner,'" he concluded, the same rights would "most logically extend to activities like prostitution, adultery, necrophilia, bestiality, possession of child pornography, and even incest and pedophilia"—the all-too-familiar litany of guilt by association. Texas, Pryor argued, had every right to raise its voice against the idea "that homosexuality is harmless and does not expose both the individual and the public to deleterious spiritual and physical consequences."[6]

President Obama's warning that hard work would be required to prevent the erosion of LGBT rights played out as well in Texas where, emboldened by the course Donald Trump had set for the nation, Republicans launched new attacks. Though aware that North Carolina's HB 2 had resulted in economic losses totaling nearly $400 million, Lieutenant Governor Dan Patrick and State Senator Lois Kolkhorst introduced SB 6, The Texas Privacy Act, a "bathroom bill" that roughly mirrored HB 2 in its assault on transgender Texans. That Texas's most influential business lobby, the Texas Association of Business, quickly condemned the bill—estimates of economic losses ranged from $964 million into the billions—was reassuring, but for LGBT Texans faced with the prospect of beating back waves of discriminatory bills in yet another legislative session, SB 6 induced a kind of pre-traumatic stress disorder. That feeling was compounded when, after ruling decisively in September 2016 (8-1) against hearing *Parker v. Pidgeon*, an attempt by two men in Houston to narrow the reach of *Obergefell v. Hodges* by denying spousal benefits to same-sex couples, the Supreme Court of Texas—an elected body made up of nine elected justices, all Republicans—bowed to political pressure after the November elections, and agreed to take the case.

With the accession of Donald Trump to the presidency, the world of LGBT Americans and straight allies concerned for their rights has darkened. New threats seem to arise every day. But this book is a snapshot of another time, the time when Mark Phariss and Vic Holmes, two men in love who wanted to marry, joined with Cleo DeLeon and Nicole Dimetman to lead the fight for marriage equality in Texas and helped to light the darkness. It is a celebration of love, of marriage, and perhaps most of all, of a new level of equality recognized in the right to marry.

* * *

Thinking of the many people who reached out with aid and counsel in the two years it took me to research and write this book, my mind turns— as it often does—to Shakespeare, in this instance to Sebastian's apology in *Twelfth Night*:

I can no other answer make but thanks,
And thanks; and ever thanks; and oft good turns
Are shuffled off with such uncurrent pay;
But were my worth as is my conscience firm,
You should find better dealing.

So many have done so much, and I realize in setting out to acknowledge their help that the best I can offer is but "uncurrent pay," payment of a sort that cannot pay the debt. And yet . . .

First thanks must go to the subjects of this book, Mark Phariss and Vic Holmes, who endured hours of interviews in person and on the phone, who answered countless sometimes repetitive e-mails, who in the course of remembering came too often face to face with memories that brought them to tears. At the end of his struggles for the crown of France, Henry IV had to sacrifice a bit of himself for what he considered the greater good, famously asserting that "Paris is worth a mass." I can only hope that at the end of their struggles Mark and Vic think that the sacrifices they have made, sacrifices that have made possible the book that tells their story, were worth the pain they endured.

Next to Mark and Vic, thanks are due to the lawyers, not just the team at Akin Gump that saw *DeLeon v. Perry* through the courts, but the hundreds of lawyers around the country who litigated case after case in the battle for marriage equality, and to the judges at every level of the state and federal judiciary whose decisions over time prepared the way for the Supreme Court's affirmation of marriage equality in *Obergefell v. Hodges*. Reading the lawyers' briefs and the decisions handed down by enlightened judges buoyed my spirits at times when the darkness seemed to have crept too close.

To Evan Wolfson and Julian Castro I owe thanks for their generous foreword, an acknowledgement of the good that has come to pass and a call to arms that looks ahead to the work that will preserve and expand the rights of LGBT Americans. Their words have reminded me why I wanted to write this book.

I will be forever grateful to Ron Chrisman, the director of the University of North Texas Press who has believed in this book since he first read the proposal and has guided me so kindly and so well as I worked to finish and revise the text, and to George Hodgman and Casey Charles whose combination of praise and constructive criticism after reading the manuscript enabled me to move beyond my early drafts.

I owe a debt of gratitude to the many friends who have listened patiently as I talked my way through the difficult patches that are inevitable in a long project or who offered guidance after reading parts of the manuscript.

Special thanks must go, however, to Cathy Hill Morrison, once my student, now my friend, no stranger in her own writing to controversial topics, who read and commented on the developing manuscript, read it again at the end when the pieces had come together. And to my lifelong friend, Sam DiSano, who as the hearing officer for the Rhode Island Department for Children and Their Families in the early 1980s ruled in favor of two women who had been denied the right to adopt because of their sexual orientation—and stirred more than a little controversy. An attorney, Sam was the first to read the "legal chapters" and offer advice, the first to read and comment on the completed manuscript.

Most of all, however, I owe thanks to my wife, Jean—proofreader *par excellence*, my first and best critic in writing as in all things. Her ability to see the text from the point of view of one not completely immersed in the history of marriage equality has helped me to fill in gaps that might otherwise have confused the "average reader." She has encouraged me, pushed me, calmed me, and, as she has done for forty-eight years, brought out what is best in me.

For so much help from so many quarters, I am grateful beyond words. What faults remain are mine. I ask only that you think of me at the end of my labors as you would think of Shakespeare's Prospero at the end of *The Tempest*:

> Now I want
> Spirits to enforce, art to enchant,
> And my ending is despair,
> Unless I be reliev'd by prayer,
> Which pierces so, that it assaults,
> Mercy itself, and frees all faults,
> As you from crimes would pardoned be,
> Let your indulgence set me free.

Introduction

Reluctant Rebels . . . but Rebels with a Cause

To be nobody-but-yourself — in a world which is doing its best, night and day, to make you everybody else — means to fight the hardest battle which any human being can fight; and never stop fighting.

—E. E. Cummings, *A Poet's Advice to Students*

"**Y**ou're kidding, right?"

Mark assured her, politely, that he was *not* kidding. Not at all.

The clerk at the license bureau in the Bexar County Courthouse in San Antonio paused for a few seconds before responding to Mark's request for a marriage license, unable quite to believe what had just happened. She glanced quickly at her co-worker, a silent plea for help. Seconds more passed before she was able to find her voice and reply.

"I'm sorry, we don't do that here," she stammered. "We don't marry same-sex couples."

The few words she spoke, though quiet and polite, would soon echo across Texas, an active front in America's culture wars.

* * *

Home for Mark Phariss and Vic Holmes lies on a quiet street in an upscale section of west Plano, Texas. Theirs is the kind of neighborhood where well-tended front yards are unbroken by driveways, where imposing, two-story facades are punctuated by oversized windows that carry natural light inside, where roof lines have been sculpted to be architecturally interesting. Inside, their home is no less impressive. In the two-story foyer, backed by an open staircase that rises to a spacious loft on the second floor, a gleaming baby grand piano beckons guests to sit and play. If you're lucky enough to be invited inside, chances are better than good that Mark and Vic's beloved beagles—Betsy, Abby, and Jake—will come skidding along the wooden floor from the cozy den where they usually hold court, happy to add their welcome.

From the wall of the dining room to the right of the entrance, more beagles watch over new arrivals—Winston, Churchill, and Clementine—these from paintings by San Antonio artist Pauline Howard of dogs Vic and Mark loved and cared for that have left this world. Elsewhere the walls are heavy with artwork Mark and Vic have brought back from their extensive travels, the tabletops thick with photographs of family and friends they want to hold close. Comfortable, inviting, their home is a refuge, the kind of space that tempts a body to relax, to settle in for a quiet talk with friends or loved ones, for a long afternoon or evening curled up with a good book. It's an idyll, a bit of the American dream made incarnate.

But on the third of October 2013 words like "quiet" and "refuge" were the farthest things from Mark's and Vic's minds. By the time they rose, two hours and more before the sun, Mark had been tossing and turning for hours, worried about what lay ahead. Granted, the desire to get an early start on the day's work, coupled with the necessities of Vic's hour-long commute to Fort Worth, had long ago made waking in the hours before dawn a habit. But as they moved quietly through their routine this morning, even earlier than usual, each knew that the day spreading before them would be unlike anything they had ever experienced.

In October 2013 same-sex marriage was legal in twelve states and the District of Columbia, but Texas was emphatically not among the twelve. Reluctant rebels, but very much rebels with a cause, Mark and Vic were determined to change that. Together for more than sixteen years, deeply in love, they wanted nothing more than any other couple longing to spend the rest of their lives together, caring for each other in sickness and in health, sharing the joys and the occasional sorrows that life brings. They wanted for themselves the dignity and liberty so many others in Texas take for granted. They wanted the freedom to marry the person they loved most in all the world in the state they call home.

Nothing more, but certainly nothing less.

Letting the dogs into the backyard, Mark stared into the darkness and blinked as the already warm air struck his face. Nervous about the day to come, he found in the heat and darkness an apt metaphor for what lay ahead. A student of literature in his undergraduate days, Mark steadied himself with a favorite passage from Mark Twain: "Twenty years from now, you will be more disappointed by the things you didn't do than by the ones you did do. So throw off the bowlines. Sail away from the safe harbor. Catch the trade winds in your sails." He could just as well have brought to mind the familiar lines of Jacques's speech on the seven ages of man in *As You Like It*, one of Shakespeare's many comedies about the troubled road to marriage:

All the world's a stage,
And all the men and women merely players;
They have their exits and their entrances,
And one man in his time plays many parts.

Months earlier, in mid-July, Mark and Vic had resolved that in the next few hours they would play a role neither had ever foreseen, certainly not a role for which either had ever prepared. Today they planned to return to San Antonio, the city where they met and shared their first date, where they fell in love, where they first lived together. Back on that familiar ground where, ironically, other Texans had fought for liberty, they planned to rise above their own fears and to ask their fellow Texans to do the same. They knew, of course, that the laws of Texas—layers and layers of laws including a statute to amend the Family Code passed in 1973, the "mini-DOMA" enacted in 2003, and a constitutional amendment approved by voters in 2005—were stacked against them. And yet, they were determined to mess with Texas, to apply for a marriage license they knew would be refused to a gay couple.

Never mind that both men had led exemplary lives, that they had embraced the promise of America, had worked hard and given back in public service more than was given to them, that their lives to date had been in many ways the incarnation of the American Dream. Mark—whose lineage includes Britton Willis, a grandfather five generations back who left his home to fight against tyranny in the American Revolution and an uncle, similarly distant, who in 1814 stood with Andrew Jackson at New Orleans when a ragtag army of Americans drove the British to the sea—had been the first in his family to earn a college degree. A 1982 graduate of Westminster College in Fulton, Missouri, a 1985 graduate of the Vanderbilt University School of Law, by the fall of 2013 Mark had lived and worked for almost thirty years in Texas—San Antonio, Addison, Dallas, and Plano—where he had risen to become a successful and much-respected corporate attorney, Assistant General Counsel at Expert Global Solutions, Inc., a 1.5-billion-dollar-revenue business process outsourcing company in Plano.

Year by Texas year, Mark looked for and found ways to give back to the community, quietly accumulating thousands of *pro bono* hours working for civic organizations. A plaque on a shelf in the den upstairs honors him as a "Founder, San Antonio Sports Foundation" (known now as San Antonio Sports) which he served as *pro-bono* general counsel while working on projects like the AAU Junior Olympics (1989), the Olympic Festival (1993), and the NCAA Final Four (1998). During his years in San Antonio, he served in the same capacity for the 2007 Pan Am Games Local Organizing Committee and the San Antonio Bowl Association (which organizes the Alamo Bowl). After moving to Plano, he accepted a place on the Board of Directors of the Family Place in Dallas, a refuge for victims of domestic violence, and the Board of Directors of Team SA Endowment which funds San Antonio Sports.

Vic, who traces his ancestry in part to Cherokee Indians who survived the infamous Trail of Tears, had enlisted in the United States Air Force immediately after graduating from high school in 1988. In the nearly twenty-three years he served his country, Vic moved as his orders dictated—San Antonio for basic training, Wichita Falls for training as an optometry tech, and then on to duty stations in Sacramento, Dayton, San Antonio (again), San Diego,

Biloxi, Little Rock, and Wichita Falls (again). By the fall of 2000 when he finished his physician assistant residency in San Diego, he had earned an undergraduate degree from the University of Nebraska the hard way—taking a course here, another there, as his duties allowed—and a promotion to second lieutenant. Five years later, he added a Master's Degree in Physician Assistant Studies, also from the University of Nebraska. He rose steadily through the ranks, step by careful step, from airman basic to commissioned officer, retiring as Major Victor Holmes in 2010 to accept a position at the University of North Texas Health Science Center where he works as a Physician Assistant and an assistant professor in the Department of Physician's Assistant Studies.

Like Mark, Vic has spent his life looking for ways to give back. From 2004 to 2010 he served as a member of the House of Delegates, the policymaking body of the American Academy of Physician Assistants. From 2004 to 2008 he served as well on the Board of Directors of the Society of Air Force Physician Assistants (SAFPA). Elected president of SAFPA, he restructured the group, created a web site, and helped increase both membership and attendance at the annual conference by 200 percent. Stationed in 2009 at Sheppard Air Force Base in Wichita Falls, he led the base's Holocaust Remembrance Services earning commendations from the Dallas Holocaust Museum, the Wichita Falls Jewish community, and his commanding officer. Newly arrived at the University of North Texas, looking as usual for new ways to serve, he started a home healthcare program for children and adults with physical and mental disabilities, patients whose special needs would be better served in a more familiar, more comfortable environment.

Never mind that as sons and brothers, as uncles and great-uncles and friends, they have done more than anyone could reasonably expect, reaching out time and time again to offer emotional and even financial support. When his brother, Greg, fell into a slump after a painful divorce, Mark took him to Paris to cheer him up. When his twin sister, Marsha, fell on hard times after divorcing her first husband, Mark sent her a monthly check for years, more when special needs arose. Later, realizing that costs might make college unaffordable, Mark offered financial help to his nieces and nephew. Vic too has reached out to help his parents and siblings financially, even to the extent of helping one of his siblings purchase a home. Together they have trave-led with Mark's great-nephews, life-changing trips that would not otherwise have been possible. Ironically, in the summer of 1984 Mark reached out to comfort a friend from law school who would eventually stand against the right of gays and lesbians to marry in Texas. Hearing of the freak accident that had paralyzed Greg Abbott—a burst of wind uprooted an oak tree that fell across his back—Mark flew to Abbott's bedside in Houston, a gift of books in hand, to offer what consolation he could.

Never mind that by the fall of 2013 public opinion in favor of allowing gays and lesbians to marry had shifted with a velocity that surprised even the most ardent advocates of equality. Ten years earlier an ABC News/*Washington Post* poll had revealed that only 37 percent of registered voters nationally, a minor-ity too easily dismissed, supported same-sex marriage. Fifty-five percent stood opposed. By the middle of March 2013, in the week before the Supreme Court was to hear arguments in *United States v. Windsor* and *Hollingsworth v. Perry*, the landscape had changed dramatically.[1] Fifty-eight percent of registered voters in an ABC News/*Washington Post* poll released that week, a significant majority, agreed that gay and lesbian couples should be able to marry. An even higher number of those polled, 64 percent, felt that the legal status of gay marriage "should be decided for all states on the basis of the U. S. Constitution" rather than by allowing the voters of each state to stake out their own positions.

Three months later, a poll conducted by the Pew Research Center indi-cated that 72 percent of adults across the United States, regardless of their own position on same-sex marriage, believed that legal recognition of same-sex marriage was inevitable. But Texas is in many ways "another country," and Texans a different breed of cat. Though support for same-sex marriage in Texas had been trending upward for years, the rate of change through October 2013 had been glacial. A University of Texas/*Texas Tribune* poll conducted in June 2013 revealed that only 39 percent of registered voters approved. And on the matter of states' rights, few Texans were willing to yield so much as an inch. In October 2013 nothing about marriage equality seemed certain in Texas.

Dressing for the day, Mark and Vic opted for "business casual," but they found it hard to be casual about what lay ahead. Despite the depth of their love for one another, the long list of their accomplishments, the positive movement of public opinion, markers that would in any other context be reassuring, Mark and Vic knew full well that when they stood before a clerk in San Antonio to ask for a marriage license none of that would matter. Their complexity as human beings, the fullness of the selves they had developed over decades of living and learning and loving, would be reduced in the eyes of the law to a single marker: "gay men." Driving that morning to Love Field—remarkably, both men were so focused on what lay ahead that neither gave a moment's thought to how perfectly their point of departure aligned with the purpose of their trip—Mark and Vic had time to think about what they wanted most: to be legally married in Texas, to be together for the rest of their lives. Checking in with the airline, making their way through security, waiting for their flight to take off, every circumstance, every public moment that morning conspired to drive Mark and Vic more and more deeply into their own thoughts. Beyond the certainty of refusal and the pain that would bring, neither knew exactly what was going to happen in San Antonio.

Both were nervous, perhaps even a little jumpy at the prospect of what lay ahead. Pressed together in the crowded cabin of the plane, they talked quietly of their plans. Three or four times Mark pulled from the pocket of his sport jacket the script he had prepared, worried that he would forget something important. When the flight arrived at last at the San Antonio International Airport, Frank Stenger-Castro, a friend of Mark's from his days as a young attorney in San Antonio, was waiting to drive them to the Bexar County Courthouse. Mark and Vic breathed a little more easily. The presence of a third person, the sound of another voice, would provide a welcome diversion. The drive into town would be quick, and the ordeal of applying for a license, the indignity of being refused, would be over even more quickly.

Walking between the parking garage and the Cadena-Reeves Justice Center, the three men found little to lift their spirits. The Cathedral of San Fernando, stunning gothic arches that lead the eye upward, massive stone buttresses that anchor it to the ground, a venerable landmark in San Antonio, served only to remind them how tenaciously the Catholic Church was fighting against same-sex marriage. One Texas freedom fighter, Jim Bowie, was married inside; some claim that the charred remains of another, Davy Crockett, lie buried there. But neither Mark nor Vic made the connection with their own quest for freedom and they passed the old church without comment. At Dolorosa Street—its name an ominous echo of the Via Dolorosa, the "Way of Sorrows" or the "Way of Pain" Christ walked on his way to Golgotha—they caught a glance of the fortress-like Bexar County Courthouse on the left. A massive block of red sandstone, Romanesque in style with its rounded, weight-bearing arches, it looms threateningly over anyone approaching the intersection. The shorter of its two unequal towers, square and squat, looks to have been pressed back to earth as it tried to rise. Mark distracted himself from looking too closely by talking excitedly with Frank about the lawsuit that would follow; Vic took refuge in what was natural, a green anole on one of the trees that caught his eye as they passed. Where, he wondered, would that lizard go when temperatures dropped?

Crossing Dolorosa Street, they turned right toward the entrance of the Cadena-Reeves Justice Building—red sandstone accents, but built mostly with a light stone that brightens the façade—and passed through the arched entry, sheltered by a roof above. Ironically, Mark thought as they passed through security and made their way along the hallway to the Paul Elizondo Tower where the Marriage License Department was located, the building in which he and Vic would be denied a license to marry had been designed by the architectural firm of Henry Muñoz, a true philanthropist, an award-winning architect, a friend—and a gay man.

In the hall just outside the license bureau, Clayton Matheson, an attorney with Akin Gump Strauss Hauer & Feld LLP, was waiting. Mark and Vic had not been the only ones worried about what might happen when two gay men applied for a marriage license. The clerks, employees of County Clerk Gerry Rickhoff who had long ago declared his support for same-sex marriage, would almost certainly behave professionally. But what if others were present, a roomful of people with deep-set objections to same-sex marriage inclined to express their disapproval physically? There had been talk of videotaping Mark and Vic's first skirmish with Texas's ban on same-sex marriage to provide visual proof they had been refused a license. In the end everyone involved settled on the presence of an impartial witness who could help if things got out of hand. Outside the office, Mark and Vic ran through the script one more time; every move had been choreographed.

Entering the office, Mark and Vic were relieved to discover that they were alone but for two women sitting behind the counter. Vic stopped a few feet short of the barrier. Mark stepped forward and greeted the woman to his right. "We're here for a marriage license," he told her. Smiling, he handed over his and Vic's passports, their drivers' licenses, the application for a marriage license, and sixty-six dollars in cash. He was on script.

Accepting Mark's documentation and payment, the woman smiled back. "Where is your fiancée?" she asked. "Your fiancée has to be here with you."

"Right here," Mark replied, turning toward Vic. Smiling, Vic gave a little wave so there would be no doubt where she should turn her eyes.

"You're kidding, right?"

Mark assured her with a polite "No, ma'am," that he was *not* kidding. Not at all.

Paying attention for the first time, the second woman looked in shock at her coworker. Vic had no trouble reading the look on her face—could this really be happening? Dumbfounded, the women exchanged a quick glance. Neither seemed quite sure what to do. After a long pause, two beats, three beats, maybe four, the first woman broke the awkward silence. "We don't do that here," she stammered. "We don't marry same-sex couples." She handed the passports, the licenses, the application, and the cash back to Mark.

Still on script, Mark showed both women a printed copy of the requirements for marriage licenses posted on the Bexar County website. He pointed out that nowhere did the information provided on-line indicate that only opposite-sex couples could marry, only that both parties had to be over eighteen years of age.

"Well," the first woman said, "we don't do that here in Texas."

"Would it help," Mark asked, "if we were to get married out-of-state and return later to get the marriage license?"

"No," the women replied almost in unison.

Mark and Vic thanked them for their trouble and left, Frank Stenger-Castro and Clayton Matheson close at their heels. The public ritual necessary to push Texas toward marriage equality had been enacted; what had to be done had been done.

Back in the hallway, the four men gathered to collect their thoughts. "It was a predictable event," Vic suggested, "with a predictable script and we followed through." For the most part that was true. But in two things Mark and Vic had been surprised. They had, as expected, been treated respectfully even as they were refused a marriage license; but they had not expected to be treated sympathetically. Mark remembers that "There was no sense of disgust or disapproval. It was completely pleasant." One of the women had even apologized for turning them down. "I'm sorry," she said as they left. It was a human gesture as much appreciated as it was unexpected, a moment both men would hold close in darker days to come. They were surprised as well at how completely unprepared the County Clerk's Office seemed to be for their visit. More than three months had passed since the *Windsor* decision had been handed down; they had assumed that other same-sex couples would have applied for marriage licenses, at the very least that the staff would have been prepped for the inevitable moment. But as Mark would point out later, "They were taken completely by surprise and really had no clue what to say."

Only one thing, it seemed, had been left undone. Mark and Vic had applied for a license and been refused. Two others had witnessed the moment. But what of the women who had refused to issue a marriage license—what were their names? The attorneys at Akin Gump Strauss Hauer & Feld who would soon file a complaint in the federal court for Western District of Texas might need to name names. And so Mark returned to the room to determine who was who. What he saw when he went back was a harbinger of things to come. The woman with whom he had spoken was on the phone talking in hushed tones, and the moment he reappeared she looked up, guiltily. "I'll call you back," she whispered into the receiver. As Mark would remark later, "It was as though I had caught her with her hand in the cookie jar!" He had no idea who she was calling—the County Clerk, Gerry Rickhoff, or perhaps the Attorney General, Greg Abbott? Clearly, wheels had begun to turn and the game was afoot. At Mark's request the women gave, even spelled their names—Janette Santibanez and Lilah Gonzalez. He wrote their names on a slip of paper and passed it to Frank who would pass it to their attorneys at Akin Gump. The long paper trail—complaints, motions, judicial rulings, requests to lift stays, amicus briefs—that would in the months to come stretch as far as the Supreme Court had begun.

With time on their hands before the return flight to Dallas, Mark, Vic, and Frank headed to the cafeteria for a bite to eat and a moment to relax after the stressful scene played out at the license bureau. Sitting in a booth at the center of the packed room, they talked for a few minutes about what had happened and, most important, about the lawsuit soon to follow. Until, that is, Mark began to feel that they were talking too loudly, that people around them were listening to their talk of marriage and wondering what had happened. "We need to talk more softly," he counseled. Ever the lawyer, he was worried about tipping off the Office of the Attorney General or, worse yet, the press. Privileged communication overheard in a public place could, he knew, lead to a loss of attorney-client privilege. And if the Attorney General's office were to get wind of their plans before a lawsuit was filed, lawyers for the State could try to get a pre-emptive order, pick a conservative judge, and ask at trial for a declaratory judgment that Texas's ban on same-sex marriage was constitutional. Though less convinced that people were listening, Vic was sufficiently concerned about security that all three lowered their voices. Within a few minutes they were on their way to the airport.

By the time Mark and Vic landed in Dallas, Neel Lane, the attorney who would lead the team at Akin Gump in suing the State of Texas, had been briefed on the morning's activities. "Our first challenge," he told *Law360*, "was the one that any civil rights case has, which is that you're championing the rights of a minority group that isn't politically powerful enough to secure its own right. And it was particularly true with this case because the entire political structure of Texas, including the governor, the attorney general and every statewide official who had gone on record was opposed to marriage equality."[2] He was spoiling for a fight and preparing for a long legal battle.

Back in Dallas, Mark and Vic headed off to work, an attempt to return to the reassuring routine of their everyday lives. "This wasn't the only thing I had to do in my life. I had a clinic to run. I had lesson plans to get done,"

Vic thought in summing up the morning. "That was anti-climactic" he would tell friends later, remembering how completely uneventful the morning had seemed, how much he had hoped that those first few hours of the struggle to bring marriage equality to Texas were an indication of how the months to come would unfold.[3]

Even then the new, eventful "normal" that would mark their lives for the next year and a half was rushing toward them.

Chapter 1

Growing Up Absurd

Go. There's a journey out there beyond what any of us know, daring and illuminating once taken, for once taken it takes you. Not so much down some path or road as from one chamber of the heart to another, one way of seeing to another, where the old definitions of "productive citizen" and "progress" mean nothing . . . these are troubled times, and for some, hard times. But they are not end times. Many great problems and challenges lie ahead. It's not your job to solve them all, but it is your responsibility to be aware, to come together and take problems as best you can, and at the same time enjoy the beauty of this world, celebrate it, restore it, share it, and make it better one day at a time. You don't have to be anything you're not; instead, be everything you are.

—Kim Heacox, *Rhythm of the Wild: A Life Inspired by Alaska's Denali National Park*

Climbing into his car for the short drive to the home of Chris Hammet and Keith Stanford, Mark Phariss was looking forward to an evening with friends but expecting nothing out of the ordinary. Less than ten blocks, less than two miles, barely time to think two thoughts. No great adventure, just another day in the thus far uneventful spring of 1997—and that was okay.

Chris was a radiologist in the Air Force Reserve, Keith, an ophthalmologist in the Army Reserve. A couple for three years, they were throwing a birthday party for a mutual friend. Mark was pretty sure that, as was so often the case, he'd know everyone there.

As he walked up the short driveway and into the house, Mark had no idea he was minutes from meeting the love of his life, Vic Holmes. One look, one brief conversation and he was smitten, a classic case of love at first sight. The one person Mark didn't know—handsome, beautiful smile, eyes that twinkled when he laughed—was suddenly the only one who mattered.

Vic, not so much. He didn't know the hosts, had been invited to the party by chance through a medical connection: Mark Reid, a doctor he met online who just happened to be the birthday boy. Vic was dating someone at the time, had a date that night in fact, and planned to stay only a few minutes. Ironically, he had come very close to not showing up at all. Drove by several times, but kept missing the house, a bit hidden behind trees. He had very nearly driven on. Settling in at the party, Vic chatted with a few people—forty-five minutes, perhaps an hour—moving constantly from group to group as Mark followed, hoping to make an impression and trying not to be too obvious. Tired of fending off the mosquitos, having stayed long enough to be polite, Vic sought out Chris and Keith one more time, thanked them, and left.

Luckily, Mark knew nothing about Vic's personal life—knew he had a date that night, but not that he was in a relationship. Unwilling to watch as Vic walked out of his life, Mark got his phone number from a friend.

* * *

The path that brought Mark to that first meeting with Vic had not been easy. By the age of six—years before he had words to express what he felt—he knew he was attracted to other boys. But as he moved through childhood, adolescence, and eventually into young adulthood, he read the cultural signs—sometimes consciously, sometimes absorbing the message by osmosis. And every sign said "No, don't go there." Year by year, understanding more and more the heavy price to be paid for being gay, he struggled to admit the reality of his sexual orientation, even to himself. He struggled as well to keep the truth about himself from others.

Mark had barely entered elementary school when his parents and siblings first warned him that intense emotional ties between boys were taboo. Walking home from his second grade classroom the day his best friend announced that his family was moving to another side of town, Mark began to cry. When he explained the reason for his tears, his mother, his twin sister, and his older brother looked at him, Mark remembers, "as though I was nuts."[1] From then on he understood the male code to which he was expected to subscribe. Boys don't get too close to other boys; they certainly don't cry on parting from other boys. Mark's father, born in 1921 and a George Wallace conservative, had old-fashioned ideas about masculinity: he didn't change diapers, he didn't cook, he didn't do dishes. Men were to be tough, to fight when necessary as he had done in the Second World War. Women were to be "feminine"; no woman could ever be vice-president, let alone president.

Though he grew up in Oklahoma where conservative values seep from the ground like oil, Mark caught a break early on. His mother was deeply religious—she rose before dawn to read the Bible, saw to it that Sunday school and services were a regular part of her children's lives—but by the time Mark was old enough to remember, his parents had joined St. Paul's Methodist Church, a progressive congregation whose young, educated minister, the Rev. John Reskovac, preached an enlightened version of Christianity. The fundamentalist threats of hellfire and damnation that darkened the lives of so many gays and lesbians born in the Sooner State did come into Mark's life at the annual revivals to which his mother took the children, but she was always careful to temper the fiery preachers they heard there with her own more humane vision. When at the age of twelve Mark and his twin sister, Marsha, spread the word to children in the neighborhood that they were sinners bound for hell, their mother quickly put a stop to their misguided evangelism. You'll bring more people to Christ, she told them, by the way you live your own lives and treat others than you will by threatening them with damnation. The lesson his mother taught that day Mark never forgot.

And yet, the anti-gay message found its way eventually into his head, seepage from the general culture. Mark was just a few months shy of his fourteenth birthday when in October 1973 the local paper, the *Lawton*

Constitution, reported on a study by Eugene Leivitt and Albert Klassen on attitudes toward homosexuality—and what he read disturbed him.[2] Two-thirds of those surveyed considered homosexuality "very obscene and vulgar"; almost 50 percent saw in homosexuality "a corruption that can cause the downfall of a civilization." Fully a third thought homosexuals should be jailed.[3] Though the minister at St. Paul's was enlightened, Mark knew that in 1972 the larger church had added a new line to its *Book of Discipline*. "The practice of homosexuality," it read, "is incompatible with Christian teaching."[4]

When friends from school stayed the night in Mark's early years, or when he stayed with friends, they would occasionally experiment sexually. "Each time I had physical contact," Mark remembers, "I was wracked with guilt. Even when there was no physical contact, I was wracked by guilt because I wanted it so badly." Born into a world in which he was ill-equipped to live, Mark suffered at night, alone with his thoughts. "Late at night, in bed by myself, I'd cry myself to sleep. I'd pray for God to make me straight or, if He couldn't, to take me in my sleep." Like many another trapped between worlds, he thought of taking his own life. But though his prayers went unanswered, he somehow turned away from death. "Each morning I'd wake up, still very much alive, still very much attracted to men."[5]

Through high school, through college, through law school and beyond, Mark was painfully aware that he would be ostracized were anyone to discover, even to suspect, that he was gay. He struggled to maintain a double life, perpetually guilty of bad faith, of denying who he was. When a few beers at a pool party in the summer between his eighth- and ninth-grade years led to co-ed streaking across nearby fields, he worked hard to disguise the fact that he was more interested in the boys running next to him than the girls. In high school he kept his interest in men under a tightly fitted cover made possible by occasional dates with young women. Offers of sexual favors from a few who wanted to draw his attention went unanswered. Though he carefully perpetuated the illusion that he was interested in girls, his seeming interest extended no further than a polite good-night kiss.

Ever more aware that his sexual orientation set him apart from his classmates, Mark realized as a teenager that cultural warnings to the LGBT community were flying thick and fast. Classes had barely begun in the fall of 1975 when he pulled the September 8 copy of *Time* from the mailbox and found himself face to face with Leonard Matlovich, the first openly gay man ever to appear on the cover of a national magazine. Celebrated in the LGBT community for challenging the ban on gays in the military, Matlovich was discharged from the Air Force a month later. For four years appeals kept the case alive until in September 1980 he accepted a cash settlement—and the case was still very much on Mark's mind as he filled out college applications. Worried about money, his father urged him to join an ROTC program to help with expenses. Worried about being dishonorably discharged, about being tossed into a jail at Fort Leavenworth, about never being able to find a job, Mark refused—joking defensively with his father about what a terrible soldier he would make, inclined as he was to ask "why?" when told what to do.

Just a year and a few months after the Leonard Matlovich story broke, Mark was knocked on his heels again by Anita Bryant's vicious Save Our Children campaign in Florida. As the sixties gave way to the seventies and the counterculture spread across the country, as the sexual revolution changed behaviors, the LGBT community in Miami had found itself less and less marginalized. Until, that is, January of 1977 when the Dade County Commission passed an ordinance prohibiting discrimination in employment, housing, and public services based on sexual orientation and the Reverend William Chapman, pastor of the Northwest Baptist Church, railed against it from the pulpit, rallying the congregation to bring a quick end to the Age of Aquarius. Chosen to lead the opposition, Bryant set out to convince voters by whatever means, fair or foul, that homosexuals were immoral, promiscuous, and specifically, an immediate danger to children. "If homosexuals are allowed to change the law in their favor," she asserted in a classic attempt to create guilt-by-association, "why not prostitutes, thieves, or murderers?" And again, "Some of the stories I could tell you of child recruitment and child abuse by homosexuals would turn your stomach."[6]

The anti-discrimination ordinance in Dade County was repealed in June, a reversal approved by an overwhelming majority of voters; the repeal of similar protective ordinances in St. Paul, Minnesota; Wichita, Kansas;

and Eugene, Oregon, followed. Seventeen-years-old, a soon-to-be high school senior living in Lawton, Oklahoma, Mark watched in horror, realizing that Anita Bryant's hate had sprung from roots in the home state they shared. He shuddered anew in January 1978 when Mary Helm, a state senator, brought the lies on which the Save Our Children campaign was founded to Oklahoma. Determined to drive gays and lesbians from public school classrooms, she introduced a bill that that would allow administrators to refuse to hire or to fire teachers for "advocating, soliciting, imposing, encouraging or promoting public or private homosexual activity." Helm's bill passed by overwhelming margins—88 to 2 in the House of Representatives, unanimously in the Senate—and was quickly signed into law.[7] "It was a very frightening time for me," Mark recalled nearly forty years later, "17 years old and living in Oklahoma, to realize that I was gay in a society that did not accept me. The only sensible thing to do seemed not to be gay."[8]

Deaths in the family while Mark was in his teens—an uncle died of a heart attack, his older brother in a tragic motorcycle accident—drove home the fragility of life and intensified his sense of alienation. "I didn't think anyone would love me if they knew I was gay," he wrote of those unsteady years; "I realized that I could die at any time, unloved."[9] To get by he threw himself into activities of every sort, worked to excel at all the things "normal" kids do. In grade school he played football, but gave it up in junior high to focus on academics. He joined the Boy Scouts, earned the Scouts' God and Country award, and rose quickly to Eagle Scout; he was inducted into the Order of the Arrow and rose to become Lodge Chief and a Vigil Honor Member. Whatever sage chose his Indian name—*Wischiti*, "the busy one"—understood him well. He played trumpet in the junior high school band and served as its drum major in his ninth grade year; through elementary school, junior and senior high he studied piano privately. In high school he joined the student government and spent four busy years on the debate team, managing in his senior year to place fifth in the state with debate partner, Mike Carnahan. He was selected for the National Honor Society and chosen to attend Boy's State. His "free time" after school was taken up with work, sometimes at more than one job, to help pay for his activities.

And yet, no matter how hard he worked to project the image of the all-American boy whose multiple talents left him without a care, Mark's world through high school was repeatedly shaken by people who seemed to have peered behind the curtain he had so carefully set in place. Like most adolescent boys, he regarded "fag" and "queer" as the worst insults anyone could hurl at him, their power to demean multiplied many times over by the secret he was trying to keep close. But in a crowded hallway after lunch one day in junior high, a boy from his neighborhood, a boy Mark had regarded as a friend, called him out. "Faggot!" he shouted, and his tone left no doubt that he was serious. To do nothing, Mark thought, would be unacceptable, an admission of his deeply concealed truth. When the two squared off after school—to save face Mark had challenged his much larger antagonist to a fight—the other boy picked him up and slammed his head into the concrete driveway. Lying on his bed at home, stars still whirling about, his head throbbing as he waited for the aspirin he had swallowed to take effect, Mark understood that the pain he was feeling was in fact a dark promise, a first taste of the violence that would follow were the wrong people to learn he was gay.

Like anyone in junior high or high school, Mark was acutely aware of his school's social hierarchy, acutely aware of how quickly and for what fantastic reasons people rose or fell in popularity. Part of the "in-crowd," at the very least on its periphery, he feared he'd be cast into the outer darkness were anyone to discover he was gay. Though he lost the fight with the boy who called him a "faggot," standing up to the bully was enough to stop any open talk. No one ever again called him "faggot" or "queer" to his face. But other disconcerting signs continued. On several occasions Mark invited Robert "Butch" Shanklin, a straight friend who quarterbacked the football team at their junior high, to spend the night. Sometimes Butch would turn down the invitations outright; sometimes he'd accept and then cancel at the last moment. Something, Mark knew, was wrong, but he couldn't be sure what. Worse yet, he was afraid to ask for fear of the answer that might come back. Did Butch suspect the truth about his sexual orientation? If so, would he share his suspicions with others? Not until years later did Mark discover how justified his boyish suspicions has been. Butch admitted his suspicions, admitted that he feared what his father would do to him if he spent the night and Mark did turn out to be gay—one of the cultural messages that stuck with Mark through the years.

In high school Mark discovered to his dismay that even a small, spontaneous act of kindness could raise questions. Scooping ice cream at Baskin Robbins in the summer of 1976, he refused payment one day when his partner on the high school debate team, Mike Carnahan, stopped by with his father. "My treat," Mark said as he handed their ice cream cones across the counter. That was all it took for Mike's father to suggest to his son that Mark was gay—and for Mark to panic at how easily he seemed at times to betray the secret of his inner life.

College was a frenetic repeat of what already seemed a double-time schedule. Mark joined a fraternity, Beta Theta Pi, and played an active role. He volunteered as a Big Brother and served on the Honor Commission and as a member of the Student Foundation; he was elected to the Student Government Association as a representative. He worked as a Student Academic Counselor and as a tutor/researcher for the Department of English. And despite the wealth of extra-curricular activities, he excelled as a student, winning the college's most prestigious scholarship for study abroad in his sophomore year, ultimately graduating *magna cum laude*. "I loved my years as an undergrad," he says looking back, "but I regret that I could never be myself. That had to be buried very deep."[10]

And for good reasons.

When in the fall of 1978 Mark enrolled at Westminster College in Fulton, Missouri was still reeling from a gay rights controversy that had erupted seven years earlier at the state university in Columbia. Endorsed by the Student Senate and by a student-faculty committee, Gay Lib, a largely gay student group, petitioned the university in 1971 for formal recognition that would allow them to meet on campus. And President C. Brice Ratchford vetoed their application. "Homosexuality," he argued "is generally treated in the state of Missouri as a socially repugnant concept as is evidenced by criminal statutes." About the legal ramifications at least he was correct. Missouri law at the time mandated a two-year prison term for anyone convicted of what the statute described as "the detestable and abominable crime against nature."

When Gay Lib appealed the president's decision and the Board of Curators ordered hearings in Jefferson City, Missouri's anti-gay sentiments were confirmed—some wondered "whether orgies were standard homosexual practice"—and the president's veto was upheld.[11] Year by year, the resulting lawsuit wound its way through the courts. In June 1976 the student petitioners lost at the district court level; in September 1977 Gay Lib's right to meet on campus was affirmed by the Eighth Circuit Court of Appeals. Not until the following December, eight months before Mark was to begin college just twenty miles away, was the issue at last resolved when the Supreme Court refused to hear the case, thereby upholding the decision of the appellate court. And many in mid-Missouri—where Little Dixie Lake sits just off the most direct road between Westminster College and the University of Missouri—were not pleased. On April 20, 1978, the night the students in Gay Lib marched from the Ecumenical Center to the Student Union for its first on-campus meeting, a disapproving crowd of fraternity boys pelted them with water balloons, rotten food, and rocks. "Faggots die. Faggots die," they screamed; "Off this campus. Off this campus."[12]

Mark's life at Westminster was better. Much better. But Mark's first roommate, outed when someone read a paper he wrote for a sociology class, moved from the room and chose to leave the college quietly the next year. He and Mark continued to be friends, continued to meet for an occasional game of chess, but Mark knew that spending too much time with him would draw suspicion. Worse still, fearing for his own safety, Mark had to listen as a fraternity brother from Amarillo bragged on occasion of going home and rallying friends to beat up "queers." Though at times he wasn't sure who he wanted most to fool—the people around him or himself—he worked desperately to draw attention from the truth of who he was. He was trying to be straight, dating women, even experimenting sexually with them. The all-American boy who did it all, who did it better than anyone else, couldn't possibly be gay.

The three years Mark spent at Vanderbilt University Law School (1982–1985) were mostly a happy time—more academic success, more new friends who would become lifelong friends. But storm clouds massing on the cultural horizon tempered Mark's happiness. Messages signaling middle-America's almost militant homophobia—it seemed to Mark at times not *a* hallmark, but *the* hallmark of our puritanical culture—continued to pour in. James Dobson's Family Research Council—designated a hate group by the Southern Poverty Law Center in 2010 for its virulently anti-gay stance—was founded in 1981 and incorporated in 1983. Speaking to a rally of the Moral Majority on July 4, 1983, in Cincinnati, Jerry Falwell railed against the "gay plague" sweeping America," payback for what he called a "perverted lifestyle." "AIDS," he proclaimed, is "the judgment of God. You can't fly into the laws of God and God's nature without paying the price."[13]

In the summer of 1984, hoping to gain a little real world experience of the law before plunging into his third and final year of law school, Mark clerked at Matthews & Branscomb, a prominent San Antonio firm. Unaware that Mark was gay, one of his mentors shared a story—and provided Mark with a real world lesson about what a gay man in the field of law could expect. Three years earlier, Hap Veltman, a downtown real-estate developer very much out of the closet as a gay man, had asked the firm to represent him in a legal battle with Valero over the continued operation of one of his businesses, The San Antonio Country, then the city's premier gay bar. At a meeting to discuss the case, one of the senior partners brought the discussion to a quick end: "This firm," he asserted, "will not represent a God-damned cocksucker."[14] Looking ahead to a lifetime practicing law, Mark was shattered.

Increasingly frustrated with the double life he felt forced to lead, unable to talk with law-school classmates about his deepest thoughts and feelings, Mark went with friends one evening in the fall of 1983 to see Barbra Streisand's *Yentl*—and found in the lead character the comfort of a kindred spirit. The storyline—a young Jewish woman disguises herself as a man in order to study the Talmud, refusing to be limited by the expectations of the culture into which she had been born—seemed a variation of his own story and affected him profoundly. In the lyrics of "Where Is It Written?" Mark heard the question he so often asked himself:

Where is it written what it is
I'm meant to be, that I can't dare
To have the chance to pick the fruit of every tree,
Or have my share of every sweet-imagined possibility?

"No Matter What Happens" gave voice to his desire for authenticity. "I've wanted the shadows," Streisand sang, "I don't anymore." What followed seemed to Mark almost an anthem for gay-lib:

> I need him to touch me
> To know the love that's in my heart
> The same heart that tells me
> To see myself
> To free myself
> To be myself at last!

Back in Lawton for Christmas, Mark returned for a second viewing, this time with his mother. *Yentl* offered them the chance to spend a little time together, to share a wonderful film with beautiful music both would both enjoy. Was it also, he wonders now, an attempt to send a coded message that the Christmas gift he wanted most was to be himself at last?

In the fall of 1985, the year Mark graduated from law school, Rock Hudson died in Paris, the first celebrity casualty of the HIV/AIDS epidemic. As the number of dead and dying rose, shock waves rippled across the country and the general public fell prey to an epidemic of fear. If homophobia had been a problem before, it rose in the late eighties and the nineties to new heights. Coming out seemed impossible, and when the possibility he would be discovered came too close, Mark panicked. On a visit to New Orleans that summer, Neal Chadwick, a straight friend, took a seat on the terrace of a gay bar and ordered a beer. When Mark followed his lead, Neal tried to dance with him. To his friend, it was all a joke; to Mark it was a sure sign that the secret he most wanted to keep close had slipped out. "I ran out of that bar," he laughs now, "quicker than you can say 'beer.'"[15]

And if coming out after the start of the AIDS epidemic seemed hard, for a young man hoping to prosper as an attorney it seemed harder still. When the Supreme Court decided *Bowers v. Hardwick* in June 1986—incorrectly as it would turn out—Mark was a young associate at the San Antonio firm where he had clerked two years earlier. He was disappointed that the Court's 5–4 vote upheld Georgia's statute restricting the private sexual behavior of consenting adults. "Disappointed, dismayed, but not surprised," he wrote to a friend.[16] Still more hurtful was Chief Justice Warren Burger's concurring opinion stressing the "very ancient roots" of what he clearly felt to be justifiable bias against homosexuals. Citing Sir William Blackstone, the most prominent jurist in eighteenth-century England, Chief Justice Burger condemned sodomy as "the infamous crime against nature . . . an offense of 'deeper malignity' than rape, a heinous act 'the very mention of which is a disgrace to human nature,' and 'a crime not fit to be named.'" Wagging a metaphorical finger in the face of the LGBT community, Justice Burger concluded that "To hold that the act of homosexual sodomy is somehow protected as a fundamental right would be to cast aside millennia of moral teaching."[17] More than ever, Mark felt excluded: "It is hard now," he remembers, "to appreciate how hurtful the Chief Justice's words were to a twenty-six-year-old, closeted, gay attorney."

Reading the decision in 1986, Mark was not convinced *Bowers* had been correctly decided—and judicial history would in time prove him right. Justice Lewis Powell, Jr., the swing vote in the case, admitted on retiring that he had erred: "When I had the opportunity to reread the opinions a few months later," he opined, "I thought the dissent had the better of the argument."[18] In Justice Blackmun's strongly worded dissent—largely written by one of his clerks, Pamela Karlan, now a professor of law at Stanford where she cofounded the Stanford Supreme Court Litigation Clinic, celebrated most recently as the outside expert Roberta Kaplan brought in to consult on *Windsor*—Mark found some small comfort. Going head to head with Justice Burger, Justice Blackmun wrote that "It is revolting to have no better reason for a rule of law than that so it was laid down in the time of Henry IV." What *Bowers* was really about, he argued, was "'the most comprehensive of rights and the right most valued by civilized men,' namely, 'the right to be let alone.'"[19]

Justice Blackmun—and Mark—would ultimately be vindicated in 2003 when the Court took up the same question in *Lawrence v. Texas*. In her concurring opinion Justice O'Connor delivered the death blow to Justice Burger's appeal to "moral teaching" as a valid basis for law: "The State cannot single out one identifiable class of citizens for punishment that does not apply to everyone else, with moral disapproval as the only asserted state interest for the law."[20] Justice Kennedy's now famous reference to the impact of doctrinal changes—"times can blind us to certain truths and later generations can see that laws once thought necessary and proper in fact serve only to oppress"—was in some ways more conciliatory. But in the end, *Bowers* was set aside as bad law, "not correct when it was decided . . . not correct today."[21]

Discussing *Bowers* with other attorneys at the firm in the summer of 1986, Mark saw clearly what for others was still beyond the horizon. Few agreed with him. And as a young man hoping to rise in the law, he concluded regretfully that being openly gay would dead-end his career.

For a while after law school he rented a room in the house of a straight friend. From there he moved in with an aunt, Almareeta Billington, who had recently been widowed, hoping to save money for a down payment on his own house. As a young associate at Matthews & Branscomb, he worked impossibly long hours that left little time for socializing. When the workload eased, he sought the ultimate cover. For three years he dated Robin Lane, a beautiful young woman, a Vanna White look-alike he describes still as "one of the sweetest and kindest people I have ever known." He knew he couldn't be gay, felt at the time it would dishonor his parents—but he couldn't handle being as alone, as desperately alone, as he had come to feel.

When his mother died in her sleep in November 1986—a heart attack, perhaps brought on by grief over his father's death of emphysema just two months earlier—the sense of loss and aloneness that strikes so many in the LGBT community was overwhelming. His parents had been together for forty-six years; he was frighteningly alone. "I had lost the only person," he wrote in those dark days, "who I thought would still love me if she knew I was gay." Mark tried self-help books, he tried drinking—straight bars only—but nothing worked. Just a few years later he pitched downward yet again as another hole opened in his life. In January 1990, a week before his thirtieth birthday, Mark and Robin broke off their long relationship. She wanted—Mark would say deserved—unequivocal love and marriage, a home and a family, things Mark knew he could never give her. But most of all he was tired of pretending to be what he was not. Though he knew he was doing the right thing, he fell into a funk. "I was more depressed," he admits, "than I have ever been on any birthday before or since."[22] But for the subterfuge, life with Robin had been an enjoyable whirl of parties, political rallies, tennis matches, dinners, weekends away. She was a wonderful hostess whose "Breakfast at Wimbledon" the morning of the men's championship was legendary and for several years she had prepared a magnificent dinner for Mark and a close circle of friends to celebrate his birthday. Facing a birthday alone, hoping to cheer himself up, Mark decided to treat himself to a movie. But the film he chose, *Driving Miss Daisy*, the story of a woman growing old alone, worsened his depression. Only Winston, the newly adopted beagle pup whose nighttime whimpering nine months before had elevated him from the kennel to Mark's comfortable bed, could cheer him up.

Afraid he would be alone forever, Mark cried occasionally on Winston's steady shoulder, waiting for the world, his world, to turn. Eventually, it did. At least a half turn. Visiting in Copenhagen in August of 1991, he slipped away from the friends with whom he was staying, David and Caroline Sovell, who didn't know at the time that he was gay. Free to be himself far from Texas, he found a gay bar and spent the night with a man he met there—a first step away from the shame and self-loathing, from the wrenching fear of discovery that had been his private hell for almost two decades. But only a first step. Returning to the house the Sovells had rented—they had been worried, but not "too worried" at his sudden disappearance—Mark confessed that he had spent the night with "a gorgeous blond." But he couldn't bring himself, not yet, to confess that the "gorgeous blond" had been a man.

Home again, looking to recreate the good feeling brought on by his tryst in Denmark, he ventured for the first time ever into a gay bar in the United States. But that first visit turned out to be so traumatic that Mark still remembers the date—November 7, 1991. Settling onto a barstool, beer in hand, he glanced at the television over the bar—just in time to hear a newscaster report that Magic Johnson had announced he was HIV positive. "I promptly put my beer down and left the bar," Mark remembers; "I did not want to get AIDS."[23]

Months would pass, a new year would begin, before he summoned up the courage to venture again into a gay bar. Part of what kept him away was the fear of AIDS. Part was the fear of discovery, the possible loss of friends and even of his job. Perhaps the biggest part was that in spite of all that had happened he was still wrestling with the idea of being gay. Ultimately, driven by the need to talk with someone who would understand what he was going through, Mark walked in the dark of night into the Bonham Exchange, that lumbering, Romanesque hulk of a building Hap Veltman turned into San Antonio's gay bar of choice in 1980. Sitting alone at the bar, nursing a beer, Mark got lucky. Someone willing to help was sitting just a few seats away.

"I remember seeing Mark," Dean Carter recalls of that first meeting; "I remember that he was so incredibly nervous you couldn't help but notice him. Clearly, he was looking for someone to talk to." Offered the opportunity to open up, Mark held nothing back. He had not been to many gay bars. That was obvious. He wasn't really gay; he wasn't really sure. Dean had been down that road before. "He had a bunch of questions and we wound up talking until late at night about being gay and not being gay. It's something that's definite and not definite. We talked about coming out. It's so hard to come out; *so* hard. And at the time the consequences were substantial. You could lose your family; you could lose your job. You could lose everything. It was 1991. Sleep with the wrong person and you could die. The consequences were big and scary."[24]

For several months before Dean left San Antonio to take a job in California, he and Mark met from time to time for dinner. And talked. "Mark was," in Dean's memory, "incredibly smart and kind—and naïve." Both men were about the same age, but Dean had begun dating men in college. Though not yet out to his parents, he had traveled further and come to terms with who he was. "Mark sticks out as my gay Sherpa moment," Dean jokes now. "My message to him was simple enough. 'It's all going to be okay. A life lived truthfully is better than one lived in the dark. It's all okay if you can live with yourself in truth.'"[25]

Over time, Dean's message sunk in. Driving back to his aunt's house after a night with a man he met at the Bonham, Mark found himself talking aloud in the car. "I'm gay! I'm gay and that's wonderful!" he kept repeating. For the first time he was joyously okay with that. When in July 1992 he bought his first house and was free at last to date men, Mark had accepted who he was. He was ready, too, at least to begin what would be the long process of coming out.

That fall, largely as a result of the gift bestowed on him by Dean Carter, Mark summoned the courage to call Neal Chadwick, his law school roommate and one of his most trusted friends. Hoping Neal would understand, but at the same time desperately afraid he would lose a friend, Mark confessed he was gay, that from time to time he had fallen so low that he had considered suicide. Opening up for the first time to a straight friend, every part of Mark's body shook and he struggled to hold back the tears. Neal's response was pitch-perfect. That you're gay doesn't matter to me; that you've thought of suicide does. For the suicidal impulses he urged Mark to seek help, but in fact he had already provided the help Mark needed most—acceptance, validation, permission to know and to be who he was.

Settling into his newly purchased home—a milestone for any young adult, an important *rite-de-passage* on the road to autonomy—Mark celebrated the joy of his new independence and his growing acceptance of his sexual orientation by filling the bookshelves with rows of books on the gay experience. For a brief, shining moment, it seemed, he was an adult able to chart his own course. But the limits of his freedom quickly became apparent. One limit was the family to whom he was not yet ready to come out. He gave a key to friends, a key and strict instructions to pull the tell-tale books should anything happen to him. Another was the prying eyes of his new neighbors who missed nothing. Returning one night from a gay bar, Mark found a message waiting on his answering machine, a theological warning of damnation he understood as the prologue to the threat of physical harm: "Mark, there is a heaven and a hell," an unidentified voice told him, "Don't go there. Don't be gay. Choose life."[26] Lurking always in the background was the very real danger of being beaten, perhaps even beaten to death, for being gay—straight culture's ultimate warning to the LGBT community to keep a low profile.

"Choose life," Mark thought, "or else." He had been eighteen when Harvey Milk, the first openly gay man to hold public office in California, was murdered. If a gay man can't be safe in San Francisco, he thought at the time, is it possible for a gay man to be safe anywhere? Reflecting in the 1990s on what was happening closer to home—to Paul Broussard, for example, beaten to death in the summer of 1991 outside a gay bar in Houston by twelve thrill-seeking teenagers who attacked him with fists and boots, nail-studded two-by-fours and even a knife, breaking his ribs, bruising his testicles, stabbing him three times—Mark resolved to take no chances. Driving home from gay bars after that, he checked his rear-view mirror compulsively—and his caution may well have saved his life. Over the next few years several San Antonio friends were attacked as they made their way home from gay bars. In January 1994 Michael Benishik was murdered, his head smashed with a blunt instrument, his throat slit. In January 1997 the LGBT community, frightened that over a seven-week period as many gay men had been attacked by groups of three or more, complained to the city that the police had been unresponsive.

As the instances of gay-bashing mounted, Mark couldn't get out of his head a study done by the New York City Gay and Lesbian Anti-Violence Project in 1994. "Bias-related slayings of homosexuals are often gratuitously violent," David Dunlap reported in the *New York Times*. "[A]lmost 60 percent of the homicides in the survey . . . involved what the report called 'overkill': victims had four or more gunshot or stab wounds or were beaten, or assailants used more than one killing method."[27]

* * *

Vic's path to that first meeting with Mark was in some ways very much the same and in other ways very different. As he came of age, he heard the same message about being gay, learned the same lessons as Mark. But his rough and tumble youth was very different from the ordered suburban life Mark knew as a boy. Born in St. Louis in February 1970, Vic was the second child of Mary and Floyd Rednour. Not long after his birth, Floyd fled with his young family to Cairo, Illinois, dodging impatient creditors, hoping to borrow enough money from his parents to begin again. But there was no money, and what little Floyd earned through part-time work he often squandered on alcohol. Even the arrival of a younger sister, Tanya, was not enough to change Floyd's ways, and as the financial situation grew worse he became physically abusive. Vic's mother had been willing to suffer through economic hardship; the possibility of physical harm to herself or the children was too much. She filed for divorce. When Vic speaks now of Floyd Rednour, and he does so only when pressed, he recognizes him only as his "biological father," distancing himself from the man who abandoned his family, drifted away.

In desperation, Vic's mother moved her children—Vic, his older brother, Nicky Joe, and their younger sister, Tanya—into the projects of Cairo, Illinois, where rent subsidies and food stamps made a hardscrabble life at least possible and stories of her part-Cherokee heritage and the hardships of the Trail of Tears brought a sense of pride. Determined that her family's future would be better than their past, Mary applied for help through the Comprehensive Education and Training Act (CETA) and studied pre-nursing at Shawnee Community College, five miles from the family's subsidized apartment. Since the family had no car, Mary's CETA grant covered transportation, and soon a new man, Billy Joe ("Bill") Holmes, the cab driver who picked her up daily, came into her life—and into Vic's as well. By the time Mary graduated in 1974 her divorce from Floyd Rednour was final and she began dating Bill; they married in 1977. Bill Holmes quickly stepped in as Vic's father, so much so that at eighteen, as soon as he was legally able, Vic changed his surname to honor the only father he now acknowledges. Reassured by the love Mary and Bill so obviously shared, Vic was happy. But Bill wanted more, a better life for his new family. In 1979 he moved them west to Apache Junction and took a job with the Arizona Department of Corrections.

A late bloomer, Vic didn't figure out the whole sex/gay thing until he was fifteen. But by the age of thirteen he had realized he was somehow different. Part of what separated him from others his age was money. Even in rural Arizona his parents were less well-off than most, and with the cruelty all too common among the young, other children let him know he was not one of them. In Apache Junction Bill and Mary bought a small plot of land—"They had to build a road to where our lot was," Vic remembers, "so it was pretty far out there"—and brought in a single-wide trailer that made the 1100-square-foot ranch in which Mark spent his first years seem palatial. But the air was clean, the desert landscape beautiful, and the projects of Cairo a distant memory. "That was the first place I ever felt we were really at home," Vic says now, and when his mother gave birth to Bobbi, a baby sister, his happiness seemed complete. To stay cool in the brutal heat of the Arizona summers, he and his siblings sought out the shade and wore as little clothing as decency allowed. But money was still tight. Temperatures inside the trailer were controlled with a condensation cooler; later, when Vic and his father built-on a bedroom, they added an air-conditioner. But both were strictly monitored to save money, turned off each night as soon as the desert air cooled.

What really made Vic different, even before he understood he was gay, was a deep-set sense of independence. Living in Apache Junction, surrounded by Mormons and evangelical Christians, Moral Majority types unwilling to tolerate difference—*Stepford Wives* territory as he likes to say—Vic looked about at the sameness of middle-America and turned away. With all the seriousness, and perhaps no small touch of the moral superiority that marks newly minted teenagers, he decided consciously on December 12, 1983, that would not change his self to fit in. "I wanted to be me," he remembers, "not another one of them."[28] Branded as "weird and odd and a lot of other things," bullied on occasion, he learned early on to celebrate his sense of difference.

Confidence born of independence and its upshot, a sense of self well beyond his years, made Vic's early life easier in some ways. Unlike Mark, he didn't grow up in a home where religion played a central role and shaped his way of seeing the world. Though an aunt often took him and his siblings to church on Sunday, he was unimpressed. "I tried them all," he quips, a smile spreading from his eyes. Mormon services, Catholic services, Southern Baptist services, but nothing stuck. "I dodged the religious bullet," he says, "I decided to have faith in myself."[29]

As a result, when at fifteen he figured out that he was gay, he didn't pray to be different, didn't fear the fires of hell, didn't think about committing suicide to escape an overweening sense of guilt. But if he didn't pray to be different, he didn't at all like being gay. And he did worry. In the fall of 1985, changing for a P. E. class, Vic realized just *how* different he was. "It came as a double whammy," he remembers. "I realized I was gay and, the next moment, realized I was surrounded by guys who made it a point to come down on gay people. I knew I was in trouble." He remembers, too, "this incredible sense of shame that suddenly I was one of 'them' and that the guys around me were no longer my friends."[30] Terrified, he threw on his clothes and ran out of the locker room, past the cross-country trails, out and out, away and away, until he collapsed under a tree and cried. From that day forward, he never again changed his clothes in the locker room, never again showered at school.

Vic never for a moment worried how his mother would react were she to discover he was gay. She was a nurse; she was open-minded; she was his mother. "She went out of her way," he remembers, "to accept who I was. I knew the depths of her love." About his father, a guard at the Arizona State Prison, he was less sure. Not that he doubted his father's love. But he had heard stories about the prison from his father, stories that revealed a troubling homophobia. "He would come home in the morning," Vic recalls, "with all these grisly stories of things that happened to the inmates, things they would do to themselves and to each other. And a lot of it had to do with the terrible indignities heaped on 'queers.'" Recognizing in one moment that he was gay, Vic recognized in the next that the things he was feeling were the very things his father had so often reviled in those early morning conversations, the things he had condemned as unnatural. For a boy who revered his father—"He taught me how to build. How to measure a board, how to saw. Wiring. Plumbing. Concrete. But what he really taught me was that you have to do the right thing, even when nobody else is looking."—the dilemma was gut-wrenching. "I wasn't afraid of my dad," Vic laments; "I was afraid of disappointing my dad."[31]

Watching as his friends began to date, Vic concocted a boyish plan to hide from the world. No dates, no expressions of romantic interest in anyone. Not in men. Not in women. But being alone, he discovered, is hard. "I'd see all these people walking the streets, boy-girl couples holding hands, kissing in parking lots, doing things together in the mall," he recalls, his voice sad with the memory. Like the couples he watched so closely, he wanted to be bound by emotional ties, close connections, strings that pulled him toward other human beings. But every cultural sign, everyone he knew, told him the connections he wanted were taboo. "I thought when I first realized I was gay that there just wouldn't be any attachments in my life. I wouldn't be able to do the things everybody else did. I wouldn't *be* like everybody else."[32]

Driven by loneliness, recognizing how much his parents wanted him to be like other girl-crazy, teenage boys and struggling to be the good son, Vic tried getting closer to Brandi Chivette, a close friend for years, so close that their classmates assumed they were a couple long before that happened. Vic's father was delighted to come home one day and find them together in the back bedroom. He and Mary had already begun to suspect their son was gay, fretted about Vic's relationship with Toby, his best friend and go-everywhere companion, and were relieved to have evidence to the contrary. Vic was less happy: "When we tried to make the romantic part work," he recalls, "it just didn't." To please his parents, Vic had gone through the motions, but he knew in his heart, knew from the start, that his efforts would be futile. Though barely into his mid-teens, he understood better than many adults the value of authenticity; he knew how difficult it would be, faced with a culture that insisted he deny his real self, to maintain his integrity. For a young man more self-aware than most, what he calls his "experiment" came at a cost. "I knew from that point forward," he remembers," the sadness audible in his voice, "that I wasn't going to be me anymore."[33]

When Vic enlisted in the Air Force in 1988, he was just eighteen, just out of high school—very young, very uninformed, and very, very naïve. At the Military Enlistment Processing Station in Phoenix, no one ever asked, "Are you gay?" What the interviewer did ask allowed for a bit of wiggle room: "Have you ever had gay sex?" At the time, the answer was no. He had never had sex with anyone, male or female. Still, the question knocked him on his heels. "Why the hell," he thought, "are you asking me this question? Are you crazy?"[34] The best he could muster by way of an audible response was an enraged "What!" And that was enough to forestall further questions. The interviewer moved on—and Vic moved into the Air Force. Not until he had finished training and reported to his first duty station, McClellan Air Force Base in Sacramento, did he fully understand how the Uniform Code of Military Justice (UMCJ) could cut short his military career. The American Psychological Association had declared in 1975, more than a decade earlier, that homosexuality was not a mental disease, but the armed forces had refused to bow to science. According to provisions in the UCMJ, sexual misconduct would result in a Bad Conduct Discharge, perhaps even a Dishonorable Discharge—and in 1988 homosexuality was still defined as sexual misconduct. Terrified at the potential consequences, Vic resolved to have no gay contacts whatsoever.

Vic loved the military, loved his work as an optometry tech. "The problem was," he remembers, "that I was so incredibly lonely." By August 1992 when he was transferred to Wright-Patterson Air Force Base near Dayton, Vic had regained his footing, had started dating men. It simply wasn't possible for a twenty-two-year old man, or at least Vic at twenty-two, to remain on the sidelines. He managed a few trysts, brief relationships, but nobody he met seemed a possibility for the kind of all-consuming, permanent relationship he so much wanted. Still afraid of being found out, he tried again, this time with Brenda O'Connor, for the kind of relationship of which society—and the United States Air Force—would approve. For six months they grew closer and closer until both realized that they would have to move to the next stage or move on. Vic saw it coming, bobbed and weaved to avoid the pain he knew was inevitable, and finally broke off the relationship. "We were headed for places she wanted and I didn't," Vic remembers. "I didn't want to hurt her for the rest of her life, didn't want years later to betray her with a man. And so I hurt her just a bit now so the rest of her life would be saved."

Two years later Vic was again seeing men, was in a relationship with Warren, a bisexual man, when he enrolled in a human anatomy course and was paired with Sherri Martingale as his lab and study partner. At first he and Sherri were content to study the text; as they grew closer, a more physical approach to anatomy seemed natural. "I remember thinking, 'Why not?" Vic recalled. "We were at her place and I just decided to do it, to see if maybe I was bisexual too." For a while, things went well with Sherri. Until, that is, one evening a few days before Christmas when Vic had settled in his apartment to watch television with Warren and someone knocked on the door. Expecting no one—he was scheduled to fly the next morning to Phoenix to spend the holidays with his parents—Vic opened the door to find Sherri waiting. She had come by to offer a "send-off" that would carry him through the holidays. Vic's friend left them alone. The next day as Warren drove him to the airport, Vic asked why. "I just couldn't watch you fake it anymore," came the response."[35] Just a few words from a friend, but in those few words the life lesson Vic was struggling to learn.

"Yeah," Vic realized as his time dating women was coming to an end, "I could do this. I could make it look like it was working. I could go through all the motions. But on the inside there's nothing there."[36]

Of course, the problem of concealing who he was continued. A gay man in the Air Force where witch hunts made possible by Don't Ask, Don't Tell demanded, day after day, that he not be himself, Vic reeled at the indignity. But he loved what he was doing. What at eighteen began as a combination of adventure and escape had become a calling. "I genuinely wanted to give back," he says echoing so many servicemen and women. "Once I joined that Air Force family there was a job to do, and I felt important for doing it." And so, he struggled to pass, though once or twice some small behavior gave him away. "Unless I could figure out how to behave around women," he remembers, "I was going to be screwed." A problem-solver by nature, he went to work. He watched how other men interacted with women. From a friend in the Air Force, and again later from a Navy Seal, he learned what he could about "masculinity":

> I watched what he did. I watched how he interacted with people. I watched how he interacted with women. I watched how he carried himself in "that way," what he did and how he did it. From him I tried to learn how to be a straight guy.[37]

For the most part he succeeded, but there were still moments of sheer terror. Being found out, he insists, wasn't the worst thing. Finding out that one of your friends had been discovered was far more terrible. When that happened, Vic remembers, you worried, day and night, that they'd betray you to avoid a dishonorable discharge that would haunt them for the rest of their lives.

And then, one day in the spring of 1994, it happened, the nightmare scenario; on that day Vic's worse imagining played out in real time as the Air Force Office of Special Investigations (AFOSI, commonly shortened to OSI) swung into action. Over the years the moment loomed so large in his life that he wrote his own account—and nothing catches the terror better:

> It was just a phone. I could see it on the end table, hear it across the apartment. It had rung twice already; in just a second it would ring again. And I was afraid. I knew it was Rick. He had left a message earlier, a message I'd destroyed as soon as the voice stopped speaking.

Another voice had warned me earlier not to take Rick's call. "For your own good," the voice whispered, "don't even be seen talking to him." And then the words I dreaded most: "OSI." Everyone knew the acronym for the Office of Special Investigations, the unit that investigated crimes—and "special issues" like being gay.

Once begun, OSI investigations spread like an infectious plague. First, they pried into the most intimate details of the victim's life. Next, the investigators turned to the victim's friends and co-workers, reaching out to wreak havoc on every relationship, past and present.

A third ring. One more would trigger the answering machine. I reached for the phone but shied away. Touching that phone would, I feared, set my own future ablaze. In my mind's eye the film was already rolling, an old B-movie, black and white, with the suspect slumped over a bare table in a darkened room, a single high-key light swaying above, investigators leaning in to threaten him. "Are you gay?" they keep asking.

Rick's earlier message contained only a few broken phrases: "Look, I know you don't want to . . . I just need . . . I don't know what to do . . .." Then, silence. I pulled the cartridge from the machine, pulled the tape from the cartridge, ran a magnet along its length. In the physical world I made the words go away, but I couldn't erase the tape playing in my head, couldn't make the desperation, the raw hurt in Rick's voice go away.

Nor could I make the other voices go away. A year earlier a young airman in the supply department had been caught in an undercover OSI operation. Before the investigation was closed, four others had been identified and discharged. When their lives had been ruined, I overheard two airmen in the dining hall, their voices no more than harsh whispers, talking about what had happened.

"The faggot got what he deserved," one of them said.[38]

Turning away as the OSI tore at Rick tore as well at Vic. He had never thought of suicide as a way of not being gay, but understanding the impulse was all too easy: "People feel that since they can't be themselves they are just not going to be at all."[39] Watching Rick's solitary ordeal he did, briefly, wonder if he was worthy of being around.

Vic was distraught. "Don't Ask, Don't Tell was killing me slowly," he says thinking back to that dark night of the soul in Ohio. "That was the only time I ever considered suicide. I was lonely beyond belief, knew beyond a doubt that I would never be able to find someone and be happy." To make matters worse, the psychological terrors of being outed were compounded by the threat of physical violence. In the Air Force Vic faced the same dangers Mark saw in the rear-view mirror as he drove home from gay bars—though raised to the nth-degree by swarms of young men brought together in a testosterone-fueled environment. The high-profile cases of servicemen killed because they were gay—Allen Schindler, brutally murdered in October 1992 by a shipmate in Nagasaki who stomped on him repeatedly, singing while blood poured from his victim's mouth; Barry Winchell, murdered in his sleep in 1999 by a soldier who smashed his head with a baseball bat—were, Vic suggests, barely the tip of the iceberg. "There was a lot of violence," he says, "that never made the papers . . . I was genuinely afraid." The problem was never the kind of top-down, Code Red beatings dramatized by Tom Cruise and Jack Nicholson in *A Few Good Men*. The problem was lone wolves, individuals determined to weed out anyone not like them—"You're gay?" he imagined them asking. "That's OK. I can fix that because I can beat it out of you. And if not, I'll just keep going until you're not there anymore."[40]

Two years after he listened to his phone ring, knowing his terrified friend was reaching out, Vic came frighteningly close to being beaten in San Antonio—though whether by another serviceman or a civilian he could never be sure. Knowing that friends on blind dates had been set-up and attacked, he learned early on to arrange first meetings in public places. Sitting one afternoon in the bleachers as friends played tennis, he watched as his "date" climbed out of a pickup and walked toward him, his hands behind his back. Not until the man rounded a corner did Vic see the blackjack he was trying to hide—and by then he could see as well the angry look in his eyes. Moving to the tennis court where friends circled around him, Vic escaped harm, but the incident changed his behavior forever. "That scared the hell out of me," he remembers, "that was the last time I ever met anybody as a blind date."[41]

What got Vic through the hard times was the memory of a brief encounter in high school, a chance meeting at another time when despair had crept close. Resigned to a lifetime without close connections—"that was just the way it was going to be," he thought, "and I should get used to it"—Vic met a man who helped him change directions. "It was just an hour of my life. Just an hour. Nothing happened, nothing sexual at least."[42] And yet somehow that hour of conversation brought Vic to believe that he would in time find love, the life-saving connection he wanted and needed—though not the love others wanted him to find. It was enough. Vic's next transfer—October 1995—would take him to San Antonio where Mark was waiting to meet him.

* * *

When Mark first called, Vic thought he had laid out the ground rules with the friend who asked to pass his number along. Already in a relationship, he didn't want to complicate his life, wasn't looking to connect romantically with anyone else. "I can only do one relationship at a time," he had suggested. He'd be happy to meet new people and join in group activities—bowling, movies, dinners—that fell short of "dating." But the friend from whom Mark got Vic's phone number didn't convey any of that. One evening after a dinner with Vic and two other friends, Mark grew amorous. "I had a really good time tonight," he said, slipping his hand onto Vic's knee as they pulled away from the restaurant.

"That's great," Vic replied as he moved Mark's hand away. "I'm glad you had a good time. But remember, I'm seeing someone."[43] From the look on Mark's face, Vic recalls, "you would have thought that I'd just kicked his puppy."[44] He pretty much had. By the spring of 1997 Mark had been dating men off and on for five years, but no encounter in all that time had grown into the kind of all-in, loving relationship he so much wanted, the kind of all-consuming relationship that had bound his parents together for forty-six years. Nothing had come even close, and the months before meeting Vic had taken shape more and more as the winter of Mark's discontent. Ironically, Vic's proviso, intended to create space, spoke to Mark of integrity and drew him closer. Seeing Vic as a friend was better than not seeing him, but being so near and yet so far was exasperating.

Though Mark couldn't have known it yet—perhaps he sensed as much—Vic had for years been looking for the same thing. "What I really wanted," Vic would reveal later, "really, really wanted, was what my parents had. They love each other. They care about each other. They have a really strong sense of commitment."[45] For months things between Mark and Vic continued as they had been. They hung out with friends, went to the movies, had an occasional dinner. Vic continued dating his boyfriend. Until, that is, he realized that with the man he was seeing—a man who in time revealed himself as so dangerously dependent, possessive, and obsessive that Vic feared his commanding officer would learn too much—he could never have the kind of relationship he so much wanted. They parted ways.

"That's how it began," Mark says looking back with a smile and remembering the beginnings of their life together. "I hung out with Vic as a friend until he was single. And then I pounced."[46]

Newly elected to the Board of Governors of the Human Rights Campaign (HRC), Mark had already made plans for the weekend before Vic told him that he and his boyfriend were going their separate ways. Mark had organized an HRC Federal Club fundraiser for Saturday, August 9, 1997, at the luxurious Olmos Park home of Guillermo Nicolas, had invited his cousins, Rita and Jerry Polen, to the event, was scheduled to speak briefly about work being done for the LGBT community by the HRC. Making the event their first date seemed only natural.

Set well back from the street behind neatly trimmed hedges, its grassy front yard shaded by mature magnolias whose branches stretch skyward to form a canopy, the Nicolas home at which they arrived that night is an impressive sight, the kind of carefully crafted space most people encounter only in the pages of *Architectural Digest*. Inside, the understated, modern feel is no less impressive. From the oval shaped foyer, a gallery leads visitors to a stunning great room at the back of the house where the sunken bar is bathed in natural light. Nicolas no longer lives there, but at the time of the event, the white walls were covered with art from his extensive collection. The kitchen, a chef's delight, features a huge central island surrounded by the kind of cabinet and counter space that is the stuff of dreams. Off the master bedroom is a sumptuous bath and a super-sized dressing room with marble walls, a built-in dresser, even a couch. Quite a site for a first date, Mark and Vic joked; even the island in the kitchen could sleep six!

But on the day of the HRC fundraiser, what was most impressive in Olmos Park was not the house but the people who had gathered to listen—Guillermo Nicolas, determined to give back to the community; City Councilpersons Jose Menendez and Debra Guerrero, whom Mark had been lobbying about the need for a non-discrimination ordinance in San Antonio; Cehlia Menendez, Jose's wife who, after listening through the evening, put an HRC bumper-sticker on her car—and to speak, Worth Ross, a member of the national Board of Directors of the HRC; Elizabeth Birch, then Executive Director of the Human Rights Campaign; Betty DeGeneres, Ellen's mother and the first non-gay spokesperson for the HRC's National Coming Out Project.

Though Mark had invited his cousins, Rita and Jerry, he had never told them he was gay—but that would change as soon as he began to speak. To illustrate why the LGBT community needed job protection, why everyone needed to support the HRC, hard at work trying to move the federal Employment Non-Discrimination Act (ENDA) through Congress, Mark told a story about his own experience with another attorney. Betty DeGeneres was so impressed she included it in *Love, Ellen: A Mother/Daughter Journey*, changing Mark's name since he was not out of the closet at work. "I recently heard an inspiring example," she begins, "from a young man in the South whom I'll call Joe":

Joe came out to a straight friend who was also a co-worker. "I thought he knew," Joe told me. "He seemed to be dropping hints, you know." But the friend looked down and after a moment said, "My coach was right—you should all be put in a stadium and an atom bomb dropped on you." The friend said he no longer wanted Joe to see his wife or children, and warned Joe not to tell the wife—who was pregnant—why, or "She might have a miscarriage." The inspiring part of the story is that over time the friend went from complete rejection to complete acceptance. The friendship has grown even closer and, yes, Joe is also close to the friend's wife and children—proving absolutely that love is always more powerful than hate, ignorance, and fear.[47]

"It's such a powerful story," Betty told Mark in a letter she sent after *Love, Ellen* was published. "I'm so glad I know about it."[48] Mark's story was in fact more powerful—and more revealing of public attitudes toward homosexuality—than the version Betty included in her book. Realizing he had left his child with a gay babysitter, Mark's friend made the usual illogical, insulting leap. "Are you," he had asked, "a pedophile?" offering to help Mark find treatment.

Mark told "Joe's" story because he saw it as a powerful representation of the dangers and the indignities people in the LGBT community face every working day, a perfect illustration of why federal protections against discrimination were needed. But on this day he was concerned how that power—coupled with the admission that he was gay—would affect Rita and Jerry. Gay men determined to make their way in a world that had often proved hostile, even dangerous, Mark and Vic had long since learned to scan the horizon in search of cultural signs. What would be tolerated? What would be punished?

Several years earlier Mark had felt the too familiar sting of rejection when he revealed to a friend that he was gay. For years he had played racquetball regularly with a student from Trinity University. By the time the young man was about to graduate, they had become good friends, so much so that he invited Mark to join his family for the graduation ceremony. Flattered, wanting to reciprocate, Mark invited his friend to dinner, told him he wanted to stay in touch as the young man moved from San Antonio to Dallas where his first job awaited—and, wanting to be entirely honest before he met his friend's family, told him he was gay. During dinner the young man acted as though he wasn't bothered by Mark's revelation; as the evening came to a close, he promised to send details of the graduation ceremony. And then, silence. Mark never heard from him again. Presumed to be straight, Mark had been a good friend, a kind of older brother whose advice on getting started in the world had been a valuable help. As a gay man—the kind of rejection Mark so much feared—he was sent quietly away.

Cultural warning signs seemed at times to appear everywhere. Just a year before their first date, Mark had watched, saddened, as Texas and the nation bid good-bye to Barbara Jordan, one of his heroes. He watched as Jordan's partner of thirty years, Nancy Earl, was relegated to the second row of pews at the funeral where she would draw less notice.

Jordan's life had been a succession of firsts: the first black woman elected to the Senate in Texas, the first southern black woman elected to the United States House of Representatives, the first black woman to deliver a keynote address at the Democratic National Convention. A member of the House Judiciary Committee when it considered articles of impeachment against President Nixon in July 1974, she spoke with heart-rending honesty about her experience of racism in the United States. "I felt somehow for many years that George Washington and Alexander Hamilton just left me out by mistake," she said in speaking of the Preamble to the Constitution of the United States. "But through the process of amendment, interpretation and court decision I have finally been included in 'We, the people.'"[49]

That same year she challenged the graduates of Howard University to take up the banner she and others had already carried so far. "Reaffirm what ought to be," she told them; "Get back to the truth; that's old, but get back to it. Get back to what's honest; tell government to do that. Affirm the civil liberties of the people of this country. Do that." No one understood Barbara Jordan's pioneering ways better than President Lyndon Johnson: "She proved that black is beautiful," he proclaimed, "before we knew what it meant."[50] Unless that someone was Mark. When Barbara Jordan spoke, Mark listened as though she were speaking only to him. If she had endured, triumphed over discrimination, could he not do the same? If she had shown America that "black is beautiful," could he not show them that gay is beautiful as well? What she had wanted—to live the truth, to get back to what is honest, to affirm the civil rights of a repressed minority—was exactly what he wanted.

But on January 20, 1996, when family and friends gathered for Barbara Jordan's funeral at the Good Hope Missionary Baptist Church in Houston, where the sanctuary is as plain-spoken as Barbara Jordan herself, no amendments, interpretations, or Supreme Court decisions had yet moved the public to respect the rights of the LGBT community. For all of her firsts, in spite of her unstinting advocacy of civil rights for African Americans, Barbara Jordan never —perhaps understandably given the risks involved, particularly for people in the public eye—acknowledged publicly that she was a lesbian, never proclaimed to the world that to be a member of the LGBT community is beautiful. Would Rita and Jerry prefer that Mark and Vic be equally discreet?

Nine months after the sadness of Barbara Jordan's funeral, Mark and Vic found new hope in another pioneering woman determined to take that next step. Though not yet dating, they sat together in Mark's house on the last day of April 1997 as Ellen Morgan came out in the now-famous "Puppy Episode" of *The Ellen Show*. Morgan's real-life counterpart, Ellen DeGeneres, had come out two weeks earlier on the cover of *Time Magazine*. The full-page photo of Ellen that dominated the cover—dressed in trendy black, looking up and smiling reassuringly—was accompanied by a cover-line calculated to draw attention. "Yep," she shouted in bold red print, "I'm gay." "I didn't do it to make a political statement," Ellen maintained in the interview inside; "I did it for my own truth."[51]

For months no show had passed without hinting at Ellen's sexual orientation. At one point the fictional Ellen blundered into a closet so she could literally "come out." Waiting as she prepped for a rare and much-anticipated date with a man, her unsuspecting friends spoke in *double-entendres*: "Ellen, are you coming out or not?" and "Yeah, quit jerking us around and come out already!" Until finally, on April 30, propelled by her attraction to another woman, Ellen shouted the truth into an airport microphone, "I'm gay!"

"We were thrilled when she came out," Mark recalled; "we thought she handled it humorously and diplomatically. We felt it was a huge milestone."[52]

As what was happening on *The Ellen Show* became clear, viewers chose sides. The American Family Association—recognized in 2010 as a hate group by the Southern Poverty Law Center—pressured ABC to keep Ellen in the closet and advertisers to drop their support. Two sponsors, J. C. Penney and Chrysler, chose not to buy time during "The Puppy Episode"; Wendy's never again advertised on *Ellen*. Worried about public reaction, most ABC affiliates refused to air advertisements from the Human Rights Campaign and a lesbian travel company, Olivia Cruises, during the broadcast. Jerry Falwell, who in 1977 lent his support to Anita Bryant's notorious "Save Our Children" campaign and whose next anti-LGBT initiative would pit him against the Teletubbies as agents of "gay recruitment," railed against "Ellen DeGenerate."[53] The Media Research Center ran a full-page ad in *Variety*—an open letter signed by Pat Robertson, Charles Colson, Phyllis Schafly, and Jerry Falwell—claiming that the Ellen was "a slap in the face to America's families . . . [a] blatant attempt to promote homosexuality to America's families."[54] In San Antonio, Linda Nelson of the Bexar County Christian Coalition complained that the show "will send the wrong message to people that are more susceptible, like children . . . We as Christians," she proclaimed, "think homosexuality is immoral and for the media to pay so much attention to this, sort of makes it acceptable."[55]

Determined to generate positive publicity, GLAAD lobbied to "Let Ellen Out" and urged supporters to organize "Come Out with Ellen" house parties. HRC went a step further. They offered "Ellen Coming Out House Party" kits with posters, invitations, even an *Ellen* trivia game—and shipped 3,000 as demand rose beyond all expectations. When an ABC affiliate in Alabama refused to air the show, Pride Birmingham rented—and sold out—a 5,000-seat theater for a viewing party. In the end forty-two million people across the country—the show's largest audience ever—joined with Mark and Vic, sitting in living and family rooms across the country to watch as Ellen DeGeneres did what no one had done before. Critical reaction was overwhelmingly positive: a GLAAD Media Award, a Peabody Award, and a Primetime Emmy Award for Outstanding Writing for a Comedy Series.

But the religious right, chagrined that the LGBT community had suddenly become visible and that most Americas were just fine with what they saw, struck back—and Mark and Vic were amazed by the severity of the backlash. The studio received a bomb threat. Mike Driscoll, executive producer and co-author of the script, received an anonymous phone call threatening him with the fires of hell. A suspicious man followed Ellen to the studio. Laura Dern—Susan in "The Puppy Episode," the woman to whom Ellen was attracted—found herself out of work for a year and a half. Yielding to public pressure, ABC began each show in the next season with the TV-14 icon and a blunt message that had been used before only to signal violence or nudity: "Due to adult content, parental discretion is advised." The year after that *Ellen* was cancelled. "It destroyed me," Ellen admitted years later.

"For somebody who makes a living trying to make people happy and trying to please everybody and wanting so desperately to be loved . . . to all of a sudden feel like you're not only not loved — you're hated?"[56]

Mark and Vic shared Ellen's question. If a woman as powerful on the national scene as Barbara Jordan had to hide the person she loved from the world, if a woman as powerful in the entertainment industry as Ellen could find herself out of work when she admitted she was gay, what would the world do to them? Telling at the HRC fundraiser of the colleague who, on learning he was gay, rejected him, insulted him with talk of pedophiles, thinking about the young man who disappeared into the night when he learned over dinner that the friend with whom he had played racquetball for years was gay, Mark wondered. Would his cousins be counted among the millions ready to celebrate Ellen's—and his—coming out? Or would he feel the sting that drove Ellen from show business for three years?

* * *

In fact, Mark needn't have worried. His coming out to Rita and Jerry went well. They hugged him; told him they loved him. Even more important, his and Vic's first date went well. From Guillermo Nicolas's house they drove to Mark's where they spent the night cuddling. And the next night. And the next. By October 1997 when Mark began lobbying the city council in earnest to enact a non-discrimination ordinance that would protect the LGBT community in San Antonio, they were living together—and as the fight wore on Mark would be glad for Vic's reassuring presence. Knowing he would face an uphill battle, the ordinance Mark drafted was limited in scope. It provided protection only for municipal employees; employees in the private sector were not included. Working methodically, he put together a notebook that included editorials from newspapers around the country supporting similar ordinances, a list of local companies that already banned discrimination on the basis of sexual orientation and gender identity, and ready answers to frequently asked questions. To promote the idea, he met individually with members of the City Council and their staffs.

Councilman Roger Flores agreed to sponsor the measure. After the city attorney struck protection for gender identity and added language indicating that the city would not be obligated to provide benefits to the partners of same-sex couples—hardly a surprise given that in 1997 only one state, Minnesota, provided protections for gender identity and versions of the Employment Non-Discrimination Act introduced in Congress did not yet include such protections—ten of the twelve council members agreed to support the ordinance and it was placed on the Council's agenda.

Then, in the week before the January 29 meeting at which the Council was to vote, Adam McManus, a talk show host on a religious radio station in San Antonio, rallied the Christian right. "Are we going to protect pedophiles and bestiality?" he asked. The Rev. Lewis Lee, director of the San Antonio Baptist Association, told the *San Antonio Express News* that "homosexuality is a threat to society. When you give approval to this kind of aberrant, illegal, irrational and immoral lifestyle," he asked, "where do you stop?"[57] More than 350 angry people showed up at the meeting; 70 signed up to speak. Rick Casey, a columnist for the *San Antonio Express News*, wrote of "the mood in the council chamber as teetering between a prayer service and a lynching." Faced with overwhelming opposition, fearing that a loss would set the movement back years, not just in San Antonio but in Texas and around the country, Mark agreed on the advice of two sympathetic members of the Council to pull the ordinance. Not satisfied with that, four councilmen—Robert Marbut, Jr., Raul Prado, Mario Salas, and Rick Vasquez—pushed for a vote, even after the city attorney reminded them that voting after the ordinance had been withdrawn would be a violation of the Texas Open Meetings Act. The audience— more and more unruly, moving quickly from "crowd" to "mob"—began to chant, "Vote! Vote! Vote!" To assuage their anger, the City Council allowed those who wished to speak against the ordinance even though it would not be voted on—and the bilious, anti-gay rhetoric flowed. "What they were doing," Casey suggested, "was a clear case of trying to rub the faces of the defeated into the dirt."[58] Listening in shock, Councilwoman Debra Guerrero told Mark she was more convinced than ever that gays' and lesbians' fear of discrimination was real and protections were necessary.

That night, Mark returned to Vic stunned. Devastated. He had seen hatred. He had seen mob rule. He had seen what "Christians" were willing to do to human beings who did not share their beliefs. Frightened by what he had seen, he watched the rear-view mirror obsessively. For the first time since he and Vic became a couple, Mark cried that night in bed, cradled in Vic's arms. Any doubts he might have had that people were waiting beyond the door to do harm to him and others in the LGBT community had been dispelled.

When in March of 1998 the lease on Vic's apartment came up for renewal, he and Mark made official what had for months been their day-to-day reality. They moved in together. But as the neatnik and the free spirit came together—to the amusement of friends who helped move Vic's things from his less-than-organized apartment and carried his decrepit couch to the Goodwill Store—they were painfully aware of the risks they faced. For most of Vic's nearly twenty-three years on active duty with the Air Force—ironically, he retired in December 2010, the month legislation to repeal Don't Ask, Don't Tell was signed into law and less than a year before the Obama administration finally consigned it to the dustbin of history—the threat of exposure embodied in President Bill Clinton's 1994 compromise allowing gays and lesbians to serve in the armed forces as long as they remained in the closet hung constantly over him and Mark, a kind of latter-day Sword of Damocles that could fall and destroy them at any moment.

Were anyone to discover "credible evidence" of a homosexual relationship, Vic would face a career-ending discharge, and both men knew there was reason to worry. Mark had been present in 1996 when the guest speaker at the San Antonio Black Tie Dinner, Colonel Margarethe Cammermeyer, the highest-ranking officer discharged from the Army for being a lesbian, had lamented that under Don't Ask, Don't Tell a crippling paranoia had descended on gays and lesbians in the armed services. And for good reason. Between 1993 and 1995 discharges for "conduct unbecoming" rose 124 percent, peaking in 2001 when 1,273 gays and lesbians had their military careers cut short.[59] Worse yet for Mark and Vic, a disproportionate number of those discharges occurred in Texas, the bulk in San Antonio where they lived.

To protect themselves from the prying eyes of the government that Vic had sworn to support and defend—and wrenchingly aware of the irony—they signed a lease agreement that spelled out Vic's rights and obligations as a tenant in Mark's home. According to the terms of the elaborate ruse, in return for a monthly payment Vic was to occupy the second bedroom in Mark's modest, two-bedroom ranch. He was to use the second bathroom and would be free to use the public areas of the home as well. For the sake of appearances, Vic set up a bedroom—full-sized bed, shelves for his stuffed animals and the science fiction books he loves, a desk as a computer station where he could work. On the one hand, the contract meant nothing. Not wanting to defraud the Air Force, Vic did pay rent so there would be a string of cancelled checks should anyone raise questions about his living arrangements, but Mark found ways to return the money by picking up more than his share of other expenses. On the other hand, the contract meant everything: it served as a humiliating reminder of the place to which society had relegated the LGBT community, of the fact that gays and lesbians would be allowed to make their way in the land of the free only if they maintained a low profile. Only if they remained invisible.

By the time Vic met Mark he had served in the Air Force for eight years, moving regularly from base to base as his orders dictated. From Phoenix where he was inducted, he was sent to Lackland Air Force Base in San Antonio for basic training, then to Sheppard in Wichita Falls for training as an optometry specialist. From there he was posted to McClellan Air Force Base in Sacramento, to Wright Patterson near Dayton, and finally to Brooks in San Antonio where Mark was unknowingly waiting to meet him—and where he would enter the Physician Assistant Program at Fort Sam Houston. "A serviceman arriving at a new post," Vic suggests, "knows he'll be there for only a few years. You begin planning for your departure the day after you arrive. There's no sense of permanency." The result is a culture of "permanent leavers," people trained to leave things, and even people, behind.[60]

But when in August 1999 the first year of Vic's Physician Assistant course in San Antonio came to an end and he was ordered to report to the Naval Medical Center in San Diego for his clinical rotations, the easy leaving of the past gave way to a much more difficult present. Mark threw a going-away party and spent the not-so-festive occasion on the edge of tears. On the way to the airport, both men cried. Saying their reluctant good-byes at the gate, they had no way of knowing that for the next eleven years they'd live apart, their love tested as they flew around the country to spend what time they could together. When his duties with the Air Force permitted, Vic returned to San Antonio, later to Addison, still later to Plano. Over the years Mark and Vic all but memorized the schedules of airlines that would take them between home and San Diego, Biloxi, Panama City Beach, Little Rock, and Wichita Falls. Whenever possible, they traveled as a couple to visit family and friends for birthdays, weddings, funerals, reunions, opportunities to forge and renew the bonds that tied them to larger communities. Traveling together for vacations, they favored far-away destinations where no one was likely to report "credible evidence" of homosexuality—the seacoast and mountains of New England, Banff National Park in Calgary, Yellowstone National Park in Wyoming, and a host of foreign countries: Italy, Spain, Ecuador, China, Australia, even the Arctic and Antarctica—having concluded reluctantly that they could truly be themselves only when far from home.

Like most Americans, averse to risk and to conflict, Mark and Vic wanted only to live their lives quietly and enjoy the love they had found. Coming out at work seemed perilous to Mark; coming out in the Air Force was impossible for Vic. Telling their families was hard. Looking to put off as long as possible the drama they feared would play out in ways everyone would regret, they kept their counsel as long as reasonably possible—perhaps longer. Ultimately, Mark's brother's ex-wife took the decision out of his hands. But when his brother Greg called in the summer of 1997 to recount his ex-wife's taunts—"Your brother's gay. You *know* your brother's gay."—he realized in the moment that he was ready to share the truth of who he was.

"Well," Mark said, "she's right."

Greg's response was everything Mark had hoped for. "I don't care," he said. "I don't understand, but I don't care." Pretty good, Mark thought at the time, for a wrestling and football coach from Oklahoma! His twin sister Marsha, born again as an evangelical Christian, was less accepting. Mark doesn't remember, has perhaps suppressed, her half of their coming-out conversation, but the thousand sermons by fundamentalist preachers to which she had been exposed took their toll.

When Mark and Vic first visited as a couple—Christmas Eve, 1998—the familial drama they had wanted so much to avoid swirled around them. Worn out from a ten-hour drive through ice and snow, the car laden with the long list of presents his sister had requested, Mark began soon after their arrival to make up a bed for himself and Vic on the floor of the den. Two pillows and a blanket.

"What are you doing?" his sister demanded. "You know you and Vic can't sleep in the same room."

"Why not?" Mark asked.

"Because you're not married."

"But Marsha, we can't get married!" Mark countered. "I won't spend Christmas apart from Vic!"

"It doesn't matter," she shot back, "my house, my rules."

Tired as they were, late as it was, as cold as the night had become, Mark and Vic shuffled their luggage and Winston, their beagle, back into the car and drove to a motel fifteen miles away. On Christmas day they returned, anxious for the sake of Marsha's children to keep the peace—but the drama continued behind their backs and they slipped away early the next morning, anxious to return to the calm of their home in San Antonio. Years later, still pontificating, Marsha tried to persuade her daughter, Kristen, from letting Mark and Vic stay at her home. Though she insisted that she loved her brother and his partner, she feared their corrupting influence. "It will bring a curse on your house and your family," she claimed.[61] Mark and Vic never again stayed the night at Marsha's house; though invited on numerous occasions, Marsha has never visited their home and they speak only on rare occasions—a story all too familiar in the LGBT community.

Vic came out to his mother in August 2000 when she visited in San Diego to celebrate his graduation as a physician assistant and commissioning as an officer. Though he left before Mary arrived, Mark had come too, unable to stay away despite the risk—considerable since it was Mark who pinned the badge of Vic's new rank to his uniform during the commissioning ceremony. He had met Mary, Vic's mother, three years earlier in Phoenix when he was invited to Christmas Eve dinner with the family. Vic introduced him then as a friend. In San Diego things must have begun to look a little different to Mary. Talking with Vic one day during their week together, Mary suggested that he had a lot in common with her brother Leroy. That seemed unusual to Vic; he knew little of his Uncle Leroy beyond the fact he was gay and had parted ways with the family. Was his mother's seemingly casual comment an invitation? For a while, nothing more was said, but at the end of the week, Vic seized the moment as he walked his mother to her departure gate.

"You know, Mom," he said, "that I've been dating Mark now for about three years. Right?" It was the moment his mother had been expecting for years.

"Yeah," she replied without missing a beat, "we kind of knew. Don't worry about it. Nothing changes our love for you."[62] And that was that.

* * *

In the years Vic moved about the country, Mark moved from San Antonio to Addison, and in February 2003 to Plano—and with each return to their home Vic found himself standing with Mark, shoulder to shoulder, as they faced dangers that reached almost to their doorstep.

Less than two miles from the street on which they lived, Jack Graham, president of the Southern Baptist Convention and the evangelical pastor of the Prestonwood Baptist Church, had built a congregation of 30,000 and more, in part by preaching a virulently anti-LGBT message the men feared would find its way to their front door. Understanding the ever-present threat was important to Mark. He traced the Southern Baptist Convention's anti-gay stance back to 1976 when a resolution "urge[d] churches and agencies not to afford the practice of homosexuality any degree of approval through ordination, employment, or other designations of normal life-style."[63] He discovered that the following year they commended his Oklahoma-born nemesis, Anita Bryant, "for her firm stand on the issue of homosexuality."[64] Mark came to see how, year after year, his new neighbor, the Prestonwood Baptist Church, as part of the Southern Baptist Convention, had hammered away at the LGBT community. As early as 1985 they opposed anti-discrimination ordinances that would give "public approval to the homosexual lifestyle," had "deplored the proliferation of all homosexual practices," and had "oppose[d] the identification of homosexuality as a minority with attendant benefits or advantages."[65]

Not content to govern its congregants' private lives, the Prestonwood Baptist Church and the Southern Baptist Convention made clear their intention to govern more generally, to set aside the Establishment Clause of the First Amendment and to merge church and state. Members were directed to "oppose all efforts to provide government endorsement, sanction, recognition, acceptance, or civil rights advantage on the basis of homosexuality."[66] Meeting at the Plano facility in October 2004, delegates to the Southern Baptists of Texas Convention—"messengers" in the local parlance—affirmed that "we believe Texas to be our Jerusalem and Judea" and in various "Resolutions" declared their intention to establish a statewide theocracy.

Resolution #3 reminded believers that the "Convention has historically encouraged Christian citizenship" and emphasized that 2004 would be "an important election year." Eager to draw the church and the state together, the "messengers" celebrated the Convention for its political activism, particularly the "great and noble effort" of creating the "I VOTE VALUES" campaign.[67] Citing "ten landmark decisions handed down since 1962"—with particular censure for the 2003 *Goodridge* decision in Massachusetts they vilified for opening the door to marriage equality—Resolution #4 asserted that "these decisions result in sinful laws bringing God's condemnation on our Republic for institutionalizing sin" and affirmed that "our nation was founded and predicated on a fundamental commitment to individual religious liberty as stated in the First Amendment of the Constitution."[68]

"Messengers" to the Southern Baptists of Texas Convention in 2004 stubbornly refused to acknowledge that civil law contrary to their beliefs bound them in any way—that the First Amendment to the Constitution prohibits the adherents of one religion from forcing their beliefs on others, or that the Supreme Court's decision in *Lawrence v. Texas* (2003) found in the Constitution justification for the principle that "moral disapproval as the only asserted state interest" is not by itself sufficient justification to uphold a law. According to "The Baptist Faith and Message," included as part of the Prestonwood Baptist's *Internship Manual*, marriage can be only one thing—"the uniting of one man and one woman." Section XV: The Christian and the Social Order insultingly groups homosexuality with adultery and pornography as a form of "sexual immorality."[69]

Not long after Mark and Vic moved to Plano, they watched in alarm as their new neighbor brought the fight against gay rights to their doorstep, linking arms with others in the Texas Restoration Project, a network of conservative Christian pastors, to pass Proposition 2, Texas's constitutional ban on same-sex marriage. Though statutory law in Texas had on several occasions in the past defined marriage as being between one man and one woman, after Mary Bonauto's successful arguments in *Goodridge v. Department of Public Health* brought marriage equality to Massachusetts, conservatives across Texas wanted the added protection of a constitutional amendment as a bulwark against "judicial activists." Encouraged by a coalition of churches, legislators moved the proposed amendment quickly through the Texas Legislature where it passed by large majorities in the House (101 to 29) and the Senate (21 to 8).

On November 8, 2005, after a public campaign that raised again many of the anti-gay slurs Mark and Vic had found so hurtful in the past—ironically, Mark picked up his phone one evening to listen to a robo-call from then-attorney general Greg Abbott, his law-school friend, urging him to vote for Proposition 2 in order to protect children—it passed with more than 76 percent of the vote. "The victory was won," State Representative Warren Chisum proclaimed, "from the pulpits of the state of Texas."[70] Saddened, Mark and Vic looked toward the Prestonwood Baptist Church and worried about potential dangers the climate of animosity its teachings had generated might bring.

Their worry turned to anger when in early June Governor Rick Perry, hoping to rally conservatives in response to a serious challenge from Comptroller Carole Strayhorn in the upcoming primary election, appeared with the Reverend Rod Parsley, one of the country's most virulent anti-LGBT ministers. Flanked by the governor on a dais raised in the gymnasium of the school sponsored by the Calvary Cathedral International, a conservative mega-church in Fort Worth, Parsley unleashed a stinging attack on the LGBT community. "Everyone knows the effects of the homosexual agenda are substantial," he told the thousands who had gathered to celebrate a victory over "the gays." "Homosexuals are anything but carefree. Most of them suffer from low self-esteem and depression. Gay sex is a veritable breeding ground for disease."[71] With the crowd at a fever pitch, the governor signed Proposition 2. Though his signature was purely ceremonial—under Texas law proposed constitutional amendments in Texas go directly to the people and do not require the governor's signature—Mark and Vic recoiled at the symbolic gesture of disrespect.

Every sign from then on added further cause for alarm. When in December 2014 the Plano City Council passed an anti-discrimination ordinance extending legal protections to members of the LGBT community, Dr. Jack Graham, Senior Pastor at Prestonwood Baptist, spoke first as a coalition of eighty anti-gay pastors called together by the Houston-based Texas Pastor Council gathered in an emergency meeting at the church to work toward repealing the ordinance. Anticipating that in *Obergefell v. Hodges* the Supreme Court would rule in favor of same-sex marriage, Graham all but called for mass civil disobedience:

> We want to stay in the system. We want to work in the system. We want to support our government. We want to obey its laws. But there's coming a day, I believe, that many Christians personally and churches corporately will need to practice civil disobedience on this issue.[72]

When the decision was handed down on June 26, he spoke in open contempt of the Court: "We will not accept, nor adhere to, any legal redefinition of marriage issued by any political or judicial body"; mixing the legal and moral issues, a confusion that seemed to many purposeful, he added that "we cannot and will not affirm the moral acceptability of homosexual behavior."[73]

Looking for a church to host a forum for the most conservative of the Republican hopefuls in the 2016 presidential race, Ralph Reed, founder of the Faith and Freedom Coalition, turned predictably to Prestonwood Baptist. Welcoming the speakers who appeared on Sunday, October 18, Pastor Jack Graham noted that all of the candidates had been invited—and that "the right ones" showed up. The six who came—Jeb Bush, Ben Carson, Ted Cruz, Carly Fiorina, Mike Huckabee, and Rick Santorum—were not just "the right ones," but the far right ones; more than a few skeptics felt that the Prestonwood Baptist Church had once again lived up to its derisive, megachurch nick-name, "Six Flags over Jesus." Preaching to the choir in the coded language the radical right uses to signal animus toward the LGBT community, Ted Cruz told the 7,000 who had come—and the 12,000 watching online—that "Religious liberty is under threat today like it never has been in this nation.

As these threats grow darker and darker," he asserted, "they are waking up people in Texas and all across the country."[74]

Mark and Vic didn't need waking up. Since moving to Plano they had been aware of Ralph Reed's professed goal, the fulfillment of God's supposed promise in Deuteronomy that his chosen people would dominate all others: "And the Lord shall make you the head, and not the tail, and you only shall be above, and you shall not be underneath." Or, in the more accessible language of Ralph Reed's twenty-first-century rephrasing, adapted to the times and colored with the language of power politics, the promise that Christians would be "the head, and not the tail of our political system."[75] That Jack Graham and his flock at the Prestonwood Baptist Church shared Reed's political ambitions was no secret.

Living in Plano where evangelicals wield so much power and are forever angling for more, Mark and Vic worried about their house being damaged, about their dogs being hurt, about bodily harm to themselves. With 40,000 members of the Prestonwood Baptist Church hovering about, they learned early on to refrain from the public displays of affection that come naturally to people in love. "If Vic and I are holding hands in the car," Mark admits, "I'll pull my hand away if a truck goes by and I know the driver can see in."

"Unless we're in a part of the city where we feel safe," Vic adds, "we never hold hands while walking down the street."[76]

* * *

The lessons taught by the treatment of Nancy Earl at Barbara Jordan's funeral, by the backlash at Ellen's coming out, by the military's refusal to allow members of the LGBT community to serve openly, by the virulently anti-LGBT politics of the Prestonwood Baptist Church, perhaps most of all by the vicious hate crimes to which LGBT Americans were subjected—none of it was new to Mark or Vic. Growing up in a hyper-masculine military town in Oklahoma (where Anita Bryant, who first entered the public eye as Miss Oklahoma, would soon become a culture-hero for Christian conservatives), Mark learned that being gay is not an option. Vic, raised primarily in Arizona by a seemingly homophobic father who worked as a prison guard and regularly brought home stories of what happens to "queers," quietly absorbed the same lesson. Years of schooling, experiences spread across their whole lives, had taught them to keep a low profile.

Looking back in the fall of 2010 as Vic prepared to separate from the Air Force and find work as a civilian—a watershed moment that prompted them to take stock of where they had been, where they were going—Mark and Vic began to realize how many of the things they had done over the years to keep their secret close, how many of the things they continued to do even now, had carried them to the edge of absurdity—and perhaps beyond.

Racists, whose lives are guided by an indefensible idea that denies the full humanity of others, descend inevitably into absurdity because their behaviors can't be justified. But their racism generates absurdity as well in its victims who, over time, internalize the ideas of their oppressors and are driven to behave in odd ways. The same is true of homophobia. The irrationality of homophobia, denying as it does the full and complete humanity of other human beings, prompts behaviors that are irrational. And over time, the victims of homophobia, forced to cope with a culture that habitually denies the fullness of their humanity, that denies to them the significance and authenticity human beings instinctively crave, are pushed into similarly odd behaviors.

Reflecting on the course of their lives, Mark and Vic realized that so much of what they had or hadn't done had been controlled by the nagging fear of discovery. Much of it seemed at the time—and continues to seem—funny. But just below the comedic surface they had, more and more, begun to recognize how dark the comedy had become. More and more, they recognized that in reacting to the irrationality of homophobia, struggling to cope with a culture that denied their authenticity, their integrity, they had behaved at times in ways that seemed now to be strange and foreign. Examples were too easy to come by.

When Mark's brother's bachelor party ended at a strip joint in 1988, Mark played a leading role, the older brother knowledgeable in the ways of the world and of woman. "I showed some of Greg's friends how to tip," he jokes, "by leaning back on the bar and letting the stripper get the dollar bill out of my mouth. Of course," he adds, "it was all for show." When friends urged him to go with them for the Gay March on Washington, D. C. in the spring of 1993, Mark stayed home, much against his inclinations, out of fear that someone at his law firm would connect the dots were he out of town on the weekend of the march. Heading to his first Black Tie Dinner the next fall, Mark was terrified he would meet someone he knew—and he did though they agreed on mutual silence. For five years Mark helped to organize the San Antonio Black Tie Dinner, but he consistently refused to chair the event, afraid that if his name appeared in the press, he would be discovered and his successful legal career would turn to dust. After he and Vic became a couple, they worked together in the shadows to support the Human Rights Campaign. Moving into the light would, they felt, involve too much risk. Ten years after Mark skipped the March on Washington for fear of his employer, he threw a party for the legal department of the company of his new employer, Safety-Kleen, and found himself once again denying who he was. He felt compelled to "straighten up"—the term he uses to describe stashing anything that signals his sexual orientation into a drawer or closet. "I hid all the photos of Vic," he remembers, "including the painting over the fireplace of Vic and me with Winston and Churchill."[77]

Hiding their relationship from the Air Force brought out some of the strangest behaviors. If Mark was visiting and they spent the night in a motel, they would always insist on a room with two beds—and carefully rumple the unused bed before the maid arrived lest the long arm of the Office of Special Investigations reach out to them. Because Vic's co-workers were often within earshot, able to hear not only his end of the conversation but the male voice on the other end, even a gesture as natural as saying "I love you" became complicated. One solution was to speak in code. Mark might say, "Oh, the password to the computer is **141," to which Vic would reply, "Ah, I thought it was **141!" Another way of hiding was to slip into a foreign language. Spanish was out of the question, and anyone who has seen two old films knows enough French to recognize "*Je t'aime*." But after a trip to China they learned enough to get along in Mandarin: "*Wo ài ni*." When nosey colleagues checked Vic's phone and wondered why he talked so often with "Mark Phariss," Vic replaced Mark's name and photo with the name and photo of a married woman friend, Torri Cruz. A similar trick worked when several of the women in Vic's physician assistant course made a play for him. Mark arranged for a friend, an especially good-looking young woman, to pick Vic up for lunch. She sailed into the classroom, planted a big kiss on his lips, and drove him away in her shiny new Porsche. Vic's fellow students got the message.

The most painful, the most outrageous occasion on which the men had to hide their relationship from the Air Force began early one September morning in 2001. Vic was stationed at the time in Biloxi, Mississippi; Mark, who had taken a job in Addison, Texas, was preparing for work in the tiny, one-bedroom apartment he had rented there.

"Mark was talking to me on the phone," Vic remembers, "when suddenly his voice changed."

"It was like a special effect for a movie," Mark told him, "but then I realized I was still watching the news." The date was 9-11 and what Mark had just seen was the fireball that erupted as a second plane smashed into the World Trade Center. Seconds later, Vic's second line clicked. It was the base ordering him to report immediately.

Realizing that the roads were jammed, Vic slipped his arms through the straps of his mobility bag, hopped on his mountain bike, and raced to the base. Bypassing the stream of cars stalled by security at the gate, he was the first in his chalk to report to the readiness officer, the first ready to deploy as needed. As others filtered in, Vic made an excuse to duck out for a moment, told the officer in charge that he wanted to retrieve his stethoscope from his office. What he really wanted was to call Mark—and to do that he had to move a hundred or so feet away from the building to be sure that no one would overhear their conversation.

"I wanted to tell him that I loved him," Vic remembers, "that even though I couldn't share what was happening, I'd see him again soon. This was the first time the possibility of losing him crossed my mind and, unlike the others, I couldn't tell him how much he meant to me without checking that no one was listening over my shoulder. We didn't know what we were facing, but whatever the outcome, I wanted him to know that no matter where he is or where I am, I will always love him."[78] For his part, Mark was caught between the present and the morning of another September 11, fifteen years in the past when his father had died. He didn't want to lose the two most important men in his life on the same day.

Rejoining the others, many still on their phones talking with loved ones, Vic felt again the familiar pain of hiding. Ready to go where the Air Force needed him, perhaps into danger, he had to run away to say good-bye to the man he loved—and it seemed to him, well, just crazy.

Sometimes it was amusing, sometimes grating—and always the bag of tricks they used to hide their relationship from the Air Force seemed an existential insult. In the era of Don't Ask, Don't Tell, gay people weren't supposed to exist publicly, at least in the armed services. But they did. The solution, the right response to living in a world that denies one's meaning, is defiance: authenticity and integrity. Face to face with nothingness, be honest, be yourself—and create meaning where none exists. That's no easy task for a young person struggling to carve out a place in the world, harder still for a young person who happens to be gay. But as the years wore on Mark and Vic were determined to find a way.

* * *

Neither Mark nor Vic needed rigorous training in existential philosophy to understand the human need for integrity and authenticity. Surrendering their selves, first as teenagers, later as adults, brought home the lessons they needed to learn better than any book. And yet, Vic's final assessment of Don't Ask, Don't Tell, the *bête noire* that drove his life for most of his twenty-three years in the Air Force, might have come from the mouth of an existential philosopher commenting on what a culture of repression does to the people held down. "At some point it didn't matter to me," he claims, exaggerating for emphasis, "if Don't Ask, Don't Tell got repealed. The policy wasn't the real problem. The real problem was that Don't Ask, Don't Tell existed in the first place because we weren't real people. If we had been real people from the start, Don't Ask, Don't Tell would never have been."[79]

Fixing that "real people" problem meant seeking a fresh start—and in real terms that meant separating from the service that had tried so hard for so long to deny personhood to himself and so many others. Beginning that process in August 2010, applying for a position as an Instructor and Staff Physician Assistant at the University of North Texas Health Science Center,

Vic found bringing together the separate lives he had lived for so long harder than he had expected. What he wanted was simple. No secrets, no lies, acceptance and respect for who he was. But he was still on active duty, didn't want to jeopardize his retirement—and opted one more time not to tell the whole truth. Asked if he was married, he said no and offered no explanation. When the "girlfriend question" arose, he intimated that he'd been so busy planning his retirement, seeking a new job, even looking at houses, he'd had no time for romantic attachments. Not completely honest, perhaps, but at least he hadn't felt it necessary to spin a whole other "life" as he had done so often during most of his almost twenty-three years in the Air Force.

Five months later, filling out medical forms that would introduce him to his new primary care physician, his first as a civilian, Vic took that first giant step back into his own skin. Question after tedious question, he made his way through the pages. Until he came to the block that read "In case of emergency call." Though he and Mark had been a couple since 1997, Vic had never before responded to that question with anything other than his mother's contact information. Next to that was another potentially threatening query: "Relationship." And finally, the greatest challenge of all, the block that caused his pulse to quicken. "Sexual Preference: __ Heterosexual __ Bisexual __ Homosexual."

For fifteen minutes, maybe more, Vic sat in the waiting room, hesitating, debating how to answer. "Should I leave it blank?" he wondered. "Should I tell the truth?"[80] The offices of the doctor he had chosen were directly across the street from the Prestonwood Baptist Church. Stepping from his car, Vic had looked up to see the soccer fields. Staring at the form, he could feel members of the church he and Mark so much dreaded looking over his shoulder. And he was afraid. After what seemed an eternity, he filled in Mark's name and contact information, wrote "Partner," and checked the box for "Homosexual." Turning the page to fill out the rest of the form, he realized that he had turned an important page in his own life.

Two years later he and Mark would take the next step toward authenticity and integrity, toward dignity, together, ready at last to turn to a new page in the history of their own lives—and in the history of Texas.

Chapter 2

Should We?
Or Shouldn't We?

Human progress is neither automatic nor inevitable . . . Every step toward the goal of justice requires sacrifice, suffering and struggle; the tireless exertions and passionate concern of dedicated individuals.

—Martin Luther King

Talking of the future as their love deepened, Mark and Vic knew in their hearts that only marriage would do. Holding a commitment ceremony, even entering into a legally recognized civil union, was never a real option—neither was being willing to accept what Justice Ruth Bader Ginsburg would later belittle as "skim milk marriage." "I saw civil unions as too much in the vein of separate but equal," Vic suggested; "Not so much a compromise as a way of getting people to shut up without giving them what they want."[1] Arguing *Goodridge et al. v. Department of Public Health*, Mary Bonauto had spurned any such half-steps. "One of the most important protections of marriage," she wrote, "is the word because the word is what conveys the stature that everyone understands is the ultimate expression of love and commitment."[2] Mark and Vic could not have agreed more wholeheartedly. Romantics at heart, what they wanted for themselves was nothing more—and certainly nothing less—than what their parents had.

Like tens of thousands of same-sex couples in the Lone Star State, they never dreamed while growing up that marriage would one day be open to them. On those dark days when clouds settled over their heads and their patience wore thin, they sometimes talked of traveling to marry in a state where same-sex marriage was allowed. They knew, however, that though marrying out-of-state would be emotionally satisfying, it would not change their lives at home. On returning to Texas their marriage would not be recognized. Article 1, Section 32 of the Texas Constitution specifically prohibited them from sharing in the legal rights and protections bestowed on heterosexual couples. Then too, they were Texans to the core; they wanted desperately to be married in the state where they had chosen to make their lives.

And yet, as more and more states embraced marriage equality, Mark and Vic began to hope that Texas would one day come to its senses, change its discriminatory laws, and allow them to marry in their home state. Neither harbored any illusions about how difficult, how impossibly long the road to marriage would be. But in the summer of 2013 after the Supreme Court decided *United States v. Windsor,* compelling the federal government to recognize same-sex marriages contracted in states where such unions were legal, everything seemed to have changed. "We knew," Mark remembers of that summer, "that when you applied *Windsor* to amendments banning same-sex couples from marrying, you can reach only one conclusion: that the bans are unconstitutional."[3] Like tens of thousands of same-sex couples in Texas and across the country, he and Vic stood inches from the door Edith Windsor and her attorney, Roberta Kaplan, had pried halfway open, peering through it into the brave new world of equality that beckoned. Like the others, however, they knew full well the perils of crossing the threshold.

As is so often the case when people and events converge, the call to action was not long in coming. Talking a day or two after the June 26 *Windsor* decision, Mark and Frank Stenger-Castro, deputy general counsel in the San Antonio office of Akin Gump Strauss Hauer & Feld, agreed that Texas's ban on same-sex marriages could not be constitutional. When Stenger-Castro suggested they needed to find someone to challenge Texas, Mark offered a quick response: "We need a law firm first!" Days later, Frank made his way to the office of Barry Chasnoff, general counsel at Akin Gump. "Barry," he told him, "we need a lawsuit." Quick to see the possibilities—"I wanted an opportunity to do something on a civil rights issue that I view as important"— Chasnoff set out in early July for Washington, D. C. where he presented the idea to the Management Committee of Akin Gump.[4]

Good fortune had brought Mark and Vic to the right place at the right time. Akin Gump handles as many as 800 *pro bono* cases each year, referred to the Management Committee from legal aid partners across the country. Steven Schulman, head of *pro bono* practice at Akin Gump and president of the Association of *Pro Bono* Counsel, has pointed out with justifiable pride that "There are many social justice issues that require dedicated, qualified litigation and many clients whose rights are not being looked out for if not for the type of *pro bono* work that is part of Akin Gump's DNA."[5] In 2013 and 2014 Akin Gump was honored as one of *Law360*'s *Pro Bono* firms of the year, an award given to law firms that "went above and beyond for their *pro bono* clients." Moreover, Akin Gump's track record with regard to LGBT causes was unmatched. Two attorneys at the firm submitted an amicus brief in the *Windsor* case. For the past six years Akin Gump has received a perfect 100 score on the Human Rights Campaign's Corporate Equality Index. Predictably, the Management Committee agreed to take the lawsuit in Texas as part of their *pro bono* work. And they set a handsome budget—$100,000 in fees for expert witnesses to bolster the case, a million dollars in billable hours.

No sooner had the Management Committee approved than Neel Lane, one of Akin Gump's top litigators, approached Barry Chasnoff. He wanted in. As he would later tell Pamela Colloff of *Texas Monthly*, "How could the case have been more compelling? There were laws on the books aimed at depriving gays and lesbians of their rights. And there was a group of people— our friends, people we love—for whom Texas was still a Jim Crow State." A Texan whose roots go back to Sam Maverick, one of Texas's founders, Lane didn't want hotshot lawyers from the coast rushing in to make things right in Texas. "I thought that we needed to vindicate the rights of our fellow citizens and neighbors ourselves," he said. "I thought it was important that this case be argued with a Texas accent."[6]

Akin Gump had no sooner agreed to take the case than Frank Stenger-Castro turned his considerable energies to finding a set of plaintiffs who would represent in the most positive way possible the six-hundred thousand gays and lesbians in Texas whose right to marry hung in the balance. The "laundry list" of needs and wants was formidable. The legal team knew their best chance of success lay in having at least two couples: one that sought the right to marry in Texas, and a second that had married outside of Texas and wanted the state to recognize their marriage. Finding a couple raising a child or children would be a boon, as would finding one or more plaintiffs who had served in the armed forces. They didn't want to build a case around plaintiffs who were all male or all female. And, of course, the plaintiffs had to check out as "squeaky clean"—Stenger-Castro's own phrase—well-spoken, model citizens with whom the public could empathize.

Beginning his search for plaintiffs willing to commit to a case that would likely be years making its way through the courts and that involved a certain element of personal danger as well, Stenger-Castro got back to Mark. Barely two weeks had passed since their first conversation a few days after the *Windsor* decision. First, he trotted out the good news. Akin Gump had agreed to take a same-sex marriage case in Texas *pro bono*. Then came the request for help. He sketched the profile of the "perfect" plaintiffs, dwelling just a little longer than necessary on the legal team's desire for a veteran, and asked—perhaps a bit disingenuously—if Mark or Vic knew of any possibilities.

Mark's first thought—"Well, there's Vic and me"—was exactly what Stenger-Castro wanted. But he was at work, and busy, and wanted to talk with Vic—and to think more himself about what saying yes would mean—before taking even that first step. "Let me think about it," he replied knowing full well what was afoot; "I'll get back to you tomorrow with some names."

At about the same time as Stenger-Castro was recruiting Mark and Vic, others at Akin Gump reached out to Nicole Dimetman, once an associate with the firm in its San Antonio office, living now in Austin with her wife, Cleopatra DeLeon, but still in touch with her former colleagues. Together for twelve years when they talked with Akin Gump about the possibility of a lawsuit, they had married in Massachusetts in 2009 and wanted their marriage recognized in Texas. "We knew we were going to start a family soon," Nicole told the *San Antonio Express-News*; "When you're bringing a kid into the world, you want to be able to say you're as married as you can be."[7] Like Vic, Cleo had served in the Air Force; like Mark, Nicole was an attorney. Together, the two couples seemed the "perfect plaintiffs" Akin Gump needed to represent the cause of marriage equality in Texas.

The night of Frank Stenger-Castro's second phone call, darkness settling around their home in Plano, Mark and Vic talked about couples they knew who fit "the profile." They talked, too, about what had not been spoken in Frank's phone call, that he had clearly identified them as one of Akin Gump's ideal couples, that he was quietly offering them a chance to make a difference, to play a role in changing Texas's vengeful laws on same-sex marriage. And as they talked, they wondered. If they went ahead, would another kind of darkness settle on them? Neither felt comfortable with the kind of open conflict likely to follow; neither relished the idea of moving from the half-light of the wings to center stage and the limelight.

Realists, they knew in the summer of 2013 where they stood—and the hard road they had traveled to arrive at what seemed a new starting point. They knew as well how much they owed to the people who had worked and sacrificed for generations to advance the cause of gay rights in general and marriage equality in particular. Politically aware from his early teens—a member of the high school debate team, Mark subscribed not just to general interest magazines like *Newsweek* but, thanks to his congressman, to the *Congressional Record* as well—and he had watched obsessively over three decades for stories about oppression and the legal status of the LGBT community. Though by nature less of a political junkie, forced later by his commitment to the Air Force to maintain a careful distance, Vic picked up Mark's activist strain when they began dating. The history was clear in their minds.

* * *

In their first six years as a couple Mark and Vic lived in the demeaning shadow of *Bowers v. Hardwick*, a Georgia case testing the constitutionality of anti-sodomy laws decided in 1986 by the Supreme Court of the United States. Writing for the majority, Justice Byron White had upheld the criminalization of sex between homosexuals—and did so in language so dismissive as to seem vindictive. "To claim that a right to engage in such conduct is 'deeply rooted in this Nation's history and tradition' or 'implicit in the concept of ordered liberty' is," he asserted, "at best, facetious."[8] Drawing a questionable line between heterosexual and homosexual couples, the decision refused to extend the privacy rights granted by *Griswold v. Connecticut* (1965) to the LGBT community and upheld Georgia's anti-sodomy laws only as they applied to homosexuals.

For Chief Justice Warren Burger, the majority opinion did not go far enough in excoriating homosexuality and undermining gay rights. His concurring opinion, an emotional appeal to the "ancient roots" of proscriptions against homosexuality, was still more hurtful—and potentially more dangerous. "Decisions of individuals relating to homosexual conduct have been subject to state intervention throughout the history of Western civilization," he wrote. "Condemnation of those practices is firmly rooted in Judeo-Christian moral and ethical standards," so much so that in ancient Rome homosexuality was a capital crime. Working himself—and presumably his readers— into a high dudgeon, Justice Burger cited Blackstone's inflammatory description of sodomy as " 'the infamous crime against nature' as an offense of 'deeper malignity' than rape, a heinous act 'the very mention of which is a disgrace to human nature,' and 'a crime not fit to be named.'" Accepting the premise that the business of civil law should be to uphold "millennia of moral teaching," he rejected in a voice edging toward hysteria any suggestion that "the act of homosexual sodomy is somehow protected as a fundamental right" by the Constitution of the United States.[9]

For ten years the darkness of *Bowers v. Hardwick* held sway as the last word on gay rights. Not until the summer of 1996, a year before Mark and Vic were to meet and fall in love in San Antonio, did the first signs of a new day begin to appear. As laws banning discrimination on the basis of sexual orientation popped up in cities and counties across Colorado, conservatives had fought back with Amendment 2, "which precludes all legislative, executive, or judicial action at any level of state or local government designed to protect the status of persons based on their 'homosexual, lesbian or bisexual orientation.'"[10] When the matter appeared before the Supreme Court as *Romer v. Evans*, Justice Anthony Kennedy, appointed to the Court by President Reagan, made it clear in the first of his landmark opinions on gay rights that the days when members of the LGBT community could be treated differently under the law were drawing to an end.

Justice Kennedy began by finding "implausible" the state's contention that it was not so much denying rights to homosexuals as refusing to grant them "special rights." In cases that do not involve a fundamental liberty interest or a suspect classification, courts most often apply the rational basis test, the most deferential form of judicial scrutiny. The law or classification being challenged must be rationally related to a legitimate government interest. The burden of proof falls on the challengers, and even a loose fit between the law and the governmental interest it is supposed to serve is sufficient reason to uphold the law. Applying the rational basis test to Amendment 2, Justice Kennedy concluded that it "identifies persons by a single trait and then denies them protection across the board. The resulting disqualification of a class of persons from the right to seek specific protection from the law," he wrote in what seems an impatient reprimand, "is unprecedented in our jurisprudence . . . It is a status-based enactment divorced from any factual context from which we could discern a relationship to legitimate state interests."

Twice he suggests that the lawmakers who framed Amendment 2 were driven by *animus*. The gap between the breadth of the law and the rationale for the law put forth by the state, he argues "seems inexplicable by anything but animus toward the class it affects." And again, "laws of the kind now before us raise the inevitable inference that the disadvantage imposed is born of animosity toward the class of persons affected." Had the decision in *Romer* upheld Amendment 2, it would have been an enormous setback for gay rights. Justice Kennedy's often-quoted last sentence sent a clear and reassuring message that would in time move the needle in the opposite direction. The Constitution demands, he concluded, that the government protect minorities from the tyranny of the majority: "A State cannot deem a class of persons a stranger to its laws."[11]

But if the holding of the Court in *Romer* made the night seem a little less dark, Justice Antonin Scalia's ill-tempered and intemperate dissent—joined by Chief Justice William Rehnquist and Justice Clarence Thomas—made it all too clear to the LGBT community that the hour of full light was yet a way off. Lashing out at "the elite class" from which Supreme Court justices are selected ("elite class" defined here as people who had concluded "'animosity' toward homosexuality is evil"), Justice Scalia railed against the "terminal silliness" of the Court's opinion. He mocked the "eminent reasonableness" of the majority opinion that dared to include "grim, disapproving hints that Coloradans have been guilty of 'animus' or 'animosity' toward homosexuality, as though that has been established as un-American."[12]

Not content with mocking his colleagues on the Bench, Justice Scalia wrote into his dissent comparisons belittling the LGBT community. Unable or unwilling to recognize that the love gay men and lesbians feel for one another is no different from the love heterosexual couples share, his defense of the inequality sanctioned by Colorado's Amendment 2 was nothing less than insulting. "It would prevent the State or any municipality from making death-benefit payments to the 'life partner' of a homosexual," he wrote with dismissive quotation marks, "when it does not make such payment to the long-time roommate of a non-homosexual employee." At his lowest point, Justice Scalia compared "homosexual conduct" to "murder . . . or polygamy, or cruelty to animals"—all behaviors so "reprehensible" that people should be allowed "to exhibit animus toward such conduct."[13]

In the second paragraph of his dissent Justice Scalia introduced *Bowers v. Hardwick*. Though the legal landscape had changed—by 1996 most states had decriminalized sodomy—the Court had affirmed in *Bowers* "that the Constitution does not prohibit . . . making homosexual conduct a crime," a prohibition supported in the eyes of many by the beliefs advanced in Chief Justice Burger's concurring opinion arguing that homosexuality was immoral, that the state could and should impose the moral code sanctioned by the majority. With those ideas as his premises, Justice Scalia took the argument a step further along the road to intolerance: "If it is constitutionally permissible to make homosexual conduct criminal, surely it is constitutionally permissible for a State to enact other laws merely *disfavoring* homosexual conduct" (italics in original). Moreover, he claimed, "it is rational to deny special favor and protection to those with a self-avowed tendency or desire to engage in the conduct." Unable to stop there, he argued that "the only sort of 'animus' at issue" in *Romer* stems from the "moral disapproval of homosexual conduct" and justified that moral condemnation with a predictable reference to "centuries old criminal laws." The people of Colorado are, he concluded, "*entitled to be hostile toward homosexual conduct.*"[14]

As a member of the HRC Board of Governors lobbying in Washington, D. C. for the Employment Non-Discrimination Act in 1997, Mark found himself face to face with the animus of which Justice Kennedy had spoken and the hostility Justice Scalia sought to justify. In the office of Texas Senator Kay Bailey Hutchison he tangled with a young staffer. Arguing for the senator's refusal to add her vote, the young man parroted at first the standard Republican objection. Passing a non-discrimination bill would, he asserted, result in "frivolous lawsuits." But as the conversation wore on, he made all too clear the real basis for his objections. Comparing homosexuality to bestiality, he played his trump card. "Isn't it still a felony in Texas to engage in homosexual conduct? Given that, why shouldn't an employer be allowed to discriminate?" The hint of a smile playing around the corners of his mouth signaled to Mark his antagonist's sense of moral superiority.

Two years after *Romer* the hostility to which Justice Scalia claimed people morally opposed to homosexuality were "entitled" found a brutal outlet on a remote road outside of Laramie, Wyoming. On October 6, 1998, a cyclist found Matthew Shepard lashed to a fencepost where he had been left to die, his skull broken, his clothing soaked in blood. Discovering he was gay, Aaron McKinney and Russell Henderson had offered him a ride home from the Fireside Lounge, driving him instead to remote spot where they delivered a horrific beating, pistol-whipping Matthew with a .352-Magnum, so badly that his brain was no longer able to regulate his heartbeat and body temperature. Six days later, Matthew Shepard died. McKinney and Henderson were tried and convicted of murder, each sentenced to two consecutive life sentences.

As word of what had happened in Laramie spread, flowers poured into the hospital in Ft. Collins, Colorado, where Matthew lay dying—so many that the staff was overwhelmed. Shocked, grieving, angry strangers from every corner of the country sent messages of condolence to the family: 65,000 e-mails, 10,000 cards and letters. Protests broke out around the country; in New York alone 4,000 people marched. In San Antonio Mark and Vic, now living together, shared in the general grief and horror, one more frightening confirmation of what they knew could happen without warning to one of them or to a friend. The same feelings returned in the spring of 1999 when Mark listened at a meeting of the Human Rights Campaign Board of Directors and Governors as Matthew's mother, Judy Shepard, spoke movingly of her son's death. "But for the occasional sniffling," Mark remembers, "you could have heard a pin drop. There wasn't a dry eye in the room."[15]

"Something positive must come out of something so horrible," she told the HRC Board of Directors and Governors, desperate to ensure that no more would die as her son had died after suffering for hours alone in a field, his only company the cold wind whistling around him. "I will not let this window of opportunity pass."[16] Representative John Conyers of Michigan set out to help in 2001 when he introduced the Matthew Shepard and James Byrd Hate Crimes Prevention Act into the 107th Congress. When it failed to pass, he reintroduced the bill four more times—in 2004, 2005, 2007, and, finally, in 2009. Time after time opposition from Republicans kept hate crimes legislation from becoming law. In 2007 it passed both houses of Congress, but the Democratic leadership was forced to drop it when President George W. Bush threatened to veto the Defense Reauthorization Bill to which it had been attached. Finally, eleven years after her son's death, Judy Shephard got what she wanted and the country needed. Over the steep objections of many Republicans, President Barack Obama signed the Matthew Shepard and James Byrd Hate Crime Prevention Act into law on October 28, 2009.

Matthew Shepard's brutal death brought the lesson home one more time. Despite the win in *Romer*, as long as moral disapproval of homosexuality was enshrined in laws that banned even consensual sex between homosexuals in the privacy of their homes—and in the opinion of at least three Supreme Court justices "entitled" people to hostility—the law had not moved far enough. And yet, though they felt federal hate crimes legislation had been a long time coming, with its passage in 2009 Mark and Vic had no doubt that the tide was turning, however slowly. Mark was old enough to remember how, well before the turn signaled by *Romer* and the passage of hate crimes legislation, a few visionaries had looked beyond impossibly harsh laws that vilified gays and lesbians to imagine a better tomorrow. He remembered how in August 1989 Andrew Sullivan had stirred controversy when his cover story in the *New Republic*, "Here Comes the Groom: A (Conservative) Case for Gay Marriage," proclaimed that "the gay movement has ducked the issue [of same-sex marriage] primarily out of fear of division." Though they were grateful for what the rebellious Stonewall generation had done for gay rights, Sullivan suggested that among younger gays and lesbians "the need to rebel has quietly ceded to a desire to belong."

Turning the usual arguments from the New Right on their head, he argued that legalizing same-sex marriage would promote the same "family values" conservatives trumpeted. "It would foster social cohesion, emotional security, and economic prudence," he wrote; and since gay couples would be allowed to adopt, "it could also help nurture children."[17] "Offer homosexuals the *same* deal society now offers heterosexuals," Sullivan argued, make marriage equality the law of the land and allow them to understand that "gay relationships are not better or worse than straight relationships . . . that the *same* is expected of them" (italics added).[18]

The language he used was revolutionary, but not unprecedented. Though neither Mark nor Vic would learn of it for years to come, six years before Sullivan's manifesto, Evan Wolfson had built his thesis at Harvard Law School—"Same-Sex Marriage and Morality: The Human Rights View of the Constitution"—on the same premise. Love is "the great leveler," Wolfson argued with Shakespearean insight, "which comes to each of us not entirely by design." Caught in its web, we are all the same:

> The interests of gay lovers in getting married are the same as any others seeking marriage: an occasion to express their sense of self and their commitment to another human; a chance to establish and plan a life together, partaking of the security, benefits, and reinforcement society provides; and an opportunity to deepen themselves and touch immortality through sexuality, transcendence, and love.

Focusing on likeness rather than difference would, Wolfson hoped, allow the LGBT community access to "the resonant vocabulary of marriage—love, commitment, connectedness, and freedom," previously the sole property of heterosexual couples. In time, he hoped, allowing same-sex couples to marry would "transform non-gay people's understanding of who gay people are and why exclusion and discrimination are wrong."[19]

* * *

Even before Evan Wolfson dreamed of legal paths to marriage equality or Andrew Sullivan drew attention to a younger generation ready to move from sexual freedom to marriage, gays and lesbians had on occasion found ways to defy the system and marry. Taking advantage of the way Minnesota's marriage law was phrased—it did not in 1970 expressly forbid marriage between same-sex couples—Jack Baker and Mike McConnell went before a clerk in Hennepin County to demand a marriage license. Refused, they sued the state, lost, and ultimately took their case to the Supreme Court of the United States where in 1972 *Baker v. Nelson* was "dismissed for want of a substantial federal question." But though they lost in court, they won in love. Moving south to nearby Blue Earth County, Baker and McConnell obtained a license to marry in 1971 and married on September 3—the first same-sex couple to be legally married in the United States.

Inspired by Baker and McConnell, same-sex couples across the country sought licenses to marry. Most failed, but in October 1972 Antonio Molina and William "Billie" Ert found their way to the altar in Texas with a bit of subterfuge. When the Department of Motor Vehicles mistakenly sent a driver's license identifying Ert as "female," he and Molina seized the opportunity. Appearing before the Wharton County Clerk, they looked like any happy couple on the verge of marriage. Molina dressed for the day in a suit and tie. Ert, who worked as a female impersonator, wore a white beaded dress, gloves that reached to his elbows, and a curly blond wig. His deep voice, he explained, was the result of laryngitis. "We wouldn't have issued any license if we'd known he wasn't a female," the County Clerk said at the time.[20] But they did issue a license and Texas's first same-sex marriage took place the next day at the Dallas Metropolitan Community Church. "It is really hard for most of us now to realize how brave they really were," Mark told the *Houston Chronicle* decades later, "but they were undoubtedly brave."[21] After a moment of happiness, Texas's same-sex marriage pioneers paid a heavy price. The County Clerk refused to record the marriage certificate.

The Houston Police threatened to charge Molina and Ert with fraud. The Attorney General ruled that marriage was open only to opposite-sex couples. The stress of a lawsuit and trial took a tragic toll on the men. A year after they married, Molina left his partner; Ert, disconsolate, attempted suicide. The gay community paid a price as well. A year after Antonio Molina and Billie Ert exchanged rings at the altar, the Texas Legislature passed 63R HB 103 which defined marriage as between "a man and a woman"—the first of many anti-gay marriage laws in Texas.

Seizing on language similar to what Jack Baker and Michael McConnell discovered in Minnesota—the Colorado statute governing marriage used the phrase "any two persons"—Clela Rorex, the clerk of Boulder County and an ardent feminist who saw discrimination against gays and lesbians as equivalent to discrimination against women, began issuing licenses to same-sex couples in 1975. Richard Adams and Anthony Sullivan, famous now because the United States Immigration and Naturalization Service refused to recognize Sullivan, a native of Australia, as Adams's husband and as a citizen, were among those who took advantage of the short-lived opportunity. But they too had their victory snatched away. "You have failed to establish that a bona fide marital relationship can exist between two faggots," the letter from the INS contended in humiliating language all too indicative of societal attitudes at the time.[22]

In the 1990s occasional end runs around laws restricting marriage to heterosexual couples gave way to serious attempts to change the law. In December 1990, three same-sex couples applied for and were refused marriage licenses in Hawaii. *Baehr v. Miike* (originally *Baehr v. Lewin*), the lawsuit they filed the following May, took years to make its way through the state courts. By 1993 when the case reached Hawaii's Supreme Court, Evan Wolfson, who would later found Freedom to Marry, had joined straight attorney Dan Foley as co-counsel. Together they persuaded the court to rule that denying licenses to same-sex couples potentially violated the equal protection clause of Hawaii's constitution. Sending the case back to the trial court, Chief Justice Ronald Moon ordered the judges there to apply the more demanding standard of strict scrutiny. "The burden will rest on Lewin," he wrote, "to overcome the presumption that HRS § 572-1 [Hawaii's marriage statute] is unconstitutional by demonstrating that it furthers compelling state interests and is narrowly drawn to avoid unnecessary abridgments of constitutional rights."[23] Three years later, Judge Kevin Chang found that the state had failed to meet its evidentiary burden and ordered that licenses be issued to otherwise qualified same-sex couples. For the moment it seemed as though Hawaii would be the first state to legalize same-sex marriage.

What followed the victory for marriage equality in Hawaii was unsettling for gay and lesbian couples: a nationwide wave of hatred and ill-will that seemed at the time as tall as the monstrous walls of water that break against the north shore of Oahu in winter. Crashing against the shores of Hawaii, the wave first ground hopes for marriage equality there against the sand. In 1994, the year after *Baehr v. Lewin* was decided, the legislature passed a statute defining marriage as a relationship "only between a man and a woman." Amendment 2 appeared on the ballot in November 1998: "Shall the Constitution of the state of Hawaii be amended to specify that the Legislature shall have the power to reserve marriage to opposite sex couples?" That fall voters in Hawaii approved the first state constitutional amendment designed specifically to keep gays and lesbians from marrying. The Legislature moved quickly to exercise its new power, and in 1999 the State Supreme Court reversed its decision in *Baehr v. Lewin*. When the same wave crashed on the shores of the mainland, it carried with it the Defense of Marriage Act.

Looking ahead early in 1996 to the September trial date set to hear new arguments in *Baehr*, conservatives knew that the state would not be able to meet the burden of proof imposed by Hawaii's Supreme Court. Acting on their fears—and as Representative Barney Frank pointed out in a May 23 appearance on the PBS *Newshour*, seizing the opportunity to divert attention "from Medicare and the environment and Medicaid and education"—they rushed the so-called Defense of Marriage Act (DOMA) through Congress.[24] Introduced in the House on May 7 by Georgia Congressman Bob Barr, who was, ironically, in his third marriage at the time, it passed on July 12 with a veto-proof majority; on September 10 it cleared the Senate, again with veto-proof majority. President Bill Clinton reluctantly signed the bill into law on September 21—no signing ceremony, no photos allowed. Opponents of marriage equality had delivered a significant blow. Section 2 of DOMA insured that the states would not be required to recognize same-sex marriages legally contracted elsewhere. Section 3 defined marriage as "only a legal union between one man and one woman as husband and wife" and spouse as "only a person of the opposite sex who is a husband or a wife," punishing same-sex couples, even those living in states that recognized their marriages, by denying them the relief promised in 1,049 federal statutes related to marital status: Social Security, housing, taxes (income and estate), healthcare, bankruptcy, criminal sanctions, copyright, and veterans' benefits.[25]

The Report of the House Judiciary Committee revealed with frightening clarity the extent of the animus that lay behind the Defense of Marriage Act:

> Civil laws that permit only heterosexual marriage reflect and honor a collective moral judgment about human sexuality. This judgment entails both moral disapproval of homosexuality, and a moral conviction that heterosexuality better comports with traditional (especially Judeo-Christian) morality.

Allowing same-sex marriage to be "sanctified by the law," Representative Henry Hyde, the Chairman of the Committee suggested, "legitimates . . . a legal status that most people . . . feel ought to be illegitimate . . . it trivializes the legitimate status of marriage and demeans it by putting a stamp of approval . . . on a union that many people think is immoral."

Reflecting twenty years later on what happened in Hawaii, Marc Solomon, the national campaign director for Freedom to Marry, remembered with just a touch of poetic wonder that after *Baehr* in 1994 "marriage for gay couples was a real possibility shimmering on the horizon."[26] Worried conservatives warned in the 1996 report of the House Judiciary Committee that for a sinister cabal of "gay activists" Hawaii was but "the first step in a national effort to win by judicial fiat the right to same-sex marriage." In language calculated to inflame a volatile segment of the electorate, they packed the report with ominous passages that evoked images of war and destruction:

• The prospect of permitting same-sex couples to "marry" in Hawaii *threatens* to have very real consequences . . .

- It is critical to understand the nature of the orchestrated legal *assault* being *waged* against traditional heterosexual marriage . . .
- The legal *assault* against traditional heterosexual marriage laws achieved its greatest *breakthrough* in the State of Hawaii in 1993 (italics added).

Sensing "an impending *attack* on their marriage laws," the report noted that no fewer than fourteen states had already enacted laws to prohibit gay couples from marrying and to prevent having to recognize same-sex marriages legally performed elsewhere. But, the report warned ominously, "The threat posed by the Hawaii situation is enough to persuade the Committee that federal legislation is warranted."[27]

A decade later a similar scenario played out in Massachusetts. Undeterred by action at the federal level, encouraged by a 1999 ruling from the Vermont Supreme Court in *Baker v. State of Vermont* recognizing that same-sex couples were entitled to the same benefits and protections of marriage as heterosexual couples, seven couples denied licenses to marry came together in Massachusetts in 2001 to file *Goodridge v. Department of Public Health*, asserting their right to marry under state, not federal law. After an initial loss in Suffolk County Superior Court, they appealed directly to the Supreme Judicial Court of Massachusetts where on March 4, 2003, Mary Bonauto argued for the plaintiffs—and won. The decision, announced in November 2003, put Massachusetts on the leading edge of the debate swirling around same-sex marriage.

Writing for the Court, Chief Justice Margaret H. Marshall established at the outset the premise that "The Massachusetts Constitution affirms the dignity and equality of all individuals." After a careful review of "the nature of civil marriage itself," she established a second premise—that "civil marriage is an evolving paradigm." Systematically reviewing and rejecting the State's arguments against same-sex marriage—the State has failed to demonstrate "any reasonable relationship" between the ban on same-sex marriage and the "protection of public health, safety, or general welfare"—she suggests that "the marriage restriction is rooted in persistent prejudices against persons who are (or who are believed to be) homosexual." Because arguments advanced by the State failed to meet even the modest demands of rational basis analysis—"The marriage ban works a deep and scarring hardship on a very real segment of the community for no rational reason"—the Court declared "that barring an individual from the protections, benefits, and obligations of civil marriage solely because that person would marry a person of the same sex violates the Massachusetts Constitution."[28]

Reaction in Massachusetts to Mary Bonauto's victory in *Goodridge v. Department of Public Health* was mixed. Members of the LGBT community and straight allies were ecstatic. Former Governor William Weld, a Republican often in trouble with his party because of his support of gay rights, greeted the decision with an enthusiastic thumbs-up. "It is a thunderbolt, but a thunderbolt correctly heard," he told the *Boston Globe*. "It's all over."[29] But it wasn't. Within days another kind of thunder began to roll across Massachusetts. President George W. Bush, faced with stiff competition from Senator John Kerry in the 2004 presidential race, called for a constitutional amendment prohibiting gays and lesbians from marrying; Governor Mitt Romney, seconded by the Catholic Church and the religious right, called for an amendment to the state Constitution. Jerry Falwell's Liberty Counsel filed a lawsuit, one of four designed to keep same-sex marriage from Massachusetts. Political and legal challenges dragged on for over four years and through four Constitutional Conventions before in 2007 conservatives in Massachusetts would admit the battle had been lost.

* * *

The legalization of same-sex marriage in Massachusetts wasn't the only—or even the first—good news for the LGBT community in 2003. In March the Supreme Court heard oral arguments in *Lawrence v Texas*, the first case bearing directly on the constitutional rights of gays and lesbians since *Romer*. On September 17, 1998, John Lawrence and Tyron Garner were arrested in Houston and charged with having "deviate sex." Understanding that, as Dale Carpenter wrote in *Flagrant Conduct*, the definitive book on *Lawrence v. Texas*, anti-sodomy laws "served no public purpose other than to justify discrimination and to dignify animus in every realm against a tiny minority," lawyers for Lawrence and Garner appealed to the Equal Protection Clause of the Fourteenth Amendment. Living in the shadow of laws criminalizing gay sex, Carpenter continued, "Generations of homosexuals learned silence and shame. Heterosexuals learned privilege and power. The laws conditioned gay men and lesbians," he suggests, "to pay their fines and move on."[30]

When *Lawrence* came before the Court, only thirteen states still criminalized sodomy—though as Mark and Vic were painfully aware, Texas was one of the holdouts. *Bowers v. Hardwick* was still law, and the conventional connection between morality and law that led to the Defense of Marriage Act—"It is inevitable and entirely appropriate that the law should reflect such moral judgments," the Judiciary Committee had argued—posed a substantial barrier to same-sex marriage.[31] If states could criminalize homosexual sex between two consenting adults, even in the privacy of their own homes, they could certainly ban same-sex marriage. To maintain momentum in the struggle for marriage equality, Mark and Vic knew that *Lawrence* was a must win. They had no illusions, however, that it would be an easy win.

But when the majority opinion in *Lawrence v. Texas* was handed down on June 26, 2003, Justice Kennedy challenged the dangerous connection between laws that criminalized homosexual sex and the practice of marginalizing the LGBT community. "When homosexual conduct is made criminal by the law of the State, that declaration in and of itself is an invitation to subject homosexual persons to discrimination both in the public and in the private spheres," he wrote in a passage that seemed to many a quiet tribute to Matthew Shepard.[32] "The foundations of *Bowers* have sustained serious erosion from our recent decisions in *Casey* and *Romer*," Justice Kennedy observed—an observation with which Justice Scalia sadly and reluctantly agreed in his dissent. Finding fault with *Bowers* was an easy thing. The "historical premises" set forth to justify criminalizing homosexual sex are, he wrote, "not without doubt and, at the very least, overstated." Similarly, Chief Justice Burger's "sweeping references . . . to the history of Western civilization and ethical standards did not take account of other authorities pointing in an opposite direction."[33]

What matters most in *Lawrence*, however, grows less from the fact that it overturned *Bowers* than from Justice Kennedy's growing understanding and compassionate vision of people in the LGBT community whose lives depend on the law. *Bowers* was never just about criminalizing gay sex. It was about humiliating a despised minority, about legitimizing animus and justifying discrimination. In Justice Kennedy's hands, *Lawrence* emerged as a decision about more than just decriminalizing gay sex. His praise of the men "who drew and ratified the Due Process Clause of the Fifth Amendment or the Fourteenth Amendment" has become justly famous:

> They knew times can blind us to certain truths and later generations can see that laws once thought necessary and proper in fact serve only to oppress. As the Constitution endures, persons in every generation can invoke its principles in their own search for greater freedom.[34]

Seventeen years after *Bowers,* recognizing the essential humanity of gays and lesbians as one of those late-emerging "certain truths," Justice Kennedy and those who joined with him in the majority (Justices Stevens, Souter, Ginsburg, and Breyer) lifted the stigma of moral disapproval by changing the law and so reshaped the conversation about homosexuality in America.

As framed by Justice Kennedy, *Lawrence* is a liberty case in which Texas's anti-sodomy laws "seek to control a personal relationship that . . . is within the liberty of persons to choose without being punished as criminals." Central to his argument is the idea that sex between consenting adults is more about creating the intense emotional bonds that tie us to others, bonds that shape us as human beings, than it is about the physical act of sex. "When sexuality finds overt expression in intimate conduct with another person," he writes, "the conduct can be but one element in a personal bond that is more enduring." In the famous "sweet mystery of life" passage derided by Justice Scalia, Kennedy borrowed from *Planned Parenthood of Southeastern Pa v. Casey* (1992) to expand on the importance of "personal decisions relating to marriage":

> These matters, involving the most intimate and personal choices a person may make in a lifetime, choices central to personal dignity and autonomy, are central to the liberty protected by the Fourteenth Amendment. At the heart of liberty is the right to define one's own concept of existence, of meaning, of the universe, and of the mystery of human life. Beliefs about these matters could not define the attributes of personhood were they formed under compulsion of the State.

Where *Bowers* harped on "difference," *Lawrence* focused on "likeness," humanizing the LGBT community. To deny an individual—heterosexual or homosexual—the autonomy required to develop the kind of intense relationship necessary to fully realize his or her humanity strips that person of dignity, Justice Kennedy argues, demeans him or her in a way that runs counter to the liberty promised by the Due Process Clause of the Fourteenth Amendment.[35]

Justice Scalia's scathing dissent in *Romer*, yet another manifestation of his unrelenting opposition to constitutional protections for gays and lesbians, had berated members of the LGBT community for seeking to be treated with the same respect due any human being. "They devote [their] political power," he complained with an insensitivity Mark and Vic found incomprehensible, "not merely to achieving a grudging social toleration, but full social acceptance, of homosexuality."[36] Aware of how Justice Scalia and other conservatives would react to reversing *Bowers*, aware that the Court and the public prefer to move by slow, incremental steps, Justice Kennedy twice pointed out that *Lawrence* did not reach the issue of marriage equality.

Toward the end of the majority opinion he spoke definitively. "The present case," he wrote, "does not involve whether the government must give formal recognition to any relationship that homosexual persons seek to enter." But the wording of an earlier passage seemed to leave the question open. Statutes restricting "the right to engage in certain sexual conduct," he argued, "seek to control a personal relationship that, *whether or not entitled to formal recognition in the law*, is within the liberty of persons to choose without being punished as criminals" (italics added).[37] The mere suggestion that the Court might one day find in favor of same-sex marriage was enough to provoke another vitriolic attack from Justice Scalia.

Justice Scalia's dissent—every bit as splenetic as his dissent in *Romer*, but touched now with something between resignation and desperation, the rear-guard action of a man not ready for the new day he saw dawning—is perhaps the best measure of how much winning *Lawrence* meant to the LGBT community. As in *Romer*, Justice Scalia seized the moment to demean the LGBT community and to ridicule Justice Kennedy's reasoning. "Distinguishing homosexuality from other traditional 'morals' offenses" is, he declared, an "impossibility," inviting comparisons to "bigamy, same-sex marriage, adult incest, prostitution, masturbation, adultery, fornication, bestiality, and obscenity." He excoriates Justice Kennedy because he has "signed-on to the so-called homosexual agenda" and because he has "laid waste the foundations of our rational-basis jurisprudence."[38]

What truly startles, however, is the self-defeating nature of his argument—the destructive admission that if the link between moral judgment and valid legislation established in *Bowers* is broken, the high-road to same-sex marriage will lie open. The premise of Justice Scalia's argument grows from his position as an originalist; the Fourteenth Amendment, he contends, protects only "those privileges long recognized at common law." What the Court has done in *Lawrence*, he argues, ignores or negates the limitations placed on the Fourteenth Amendment by originalists and ushers us into a world turned upside-down:

> "societal reliance" on the principles confirmed in *Bowers* and discarded today has been overwhelming. Countless judicial decisions and legislative enactments have relied on the ancient proposition that a governing majority's belief that certain sexual behavior is "immoral and unacceptable" constitutes a rational basis for regulation.

If the Texas law behind *Lawrence "furthers no legitimate state interest,"* and if "the fact that the governing majority in a State has traditionally viewed a particular practice as immoral is not a sufficient reason for upholding a law prohibiting the practice," then we have, Justice Scalia proclaims, come to the edge of a very slippery slope:

> This effectively decrees the end of all morals legislation. If, as the Court asserts, the promotion of majoritarian sexual morality is not even a legitimate state interest, none of the above-mentioned laws can survive rational-basis review.

"This reasoning," he concludes, "leaves on pretty shaky grounds state laws limiting marriage to opposite-sex couples."[39]

For Justice Scalia the implications of what had happened were lamentable: "Today's opinion dismantles the structure of constitutional law that has permitted a distinction to be made between heterosexual and homosexual unions, insofar as formal marriage is concerned." If "moral disapprobation" was no longer enough to proscribe certain conduct, he added, and if the open expression of one's sexuality is an important element in forming "a personal bond that is more enduring," then "what justification could there possibly be for denying the benefits of marriage to homosexual couples exercising the liberty protected by the Constitution?" Setting aside the most often cited argument against same-sex marriage, the need to encourage procreation, Justice Scalia answered his own question—and pointed the way to the future.[40]

If the quick movement of the Defense of Marriage Act through Congress had been a setback, overturning *Bowers v. Hardwick* was a resounding victory. Remembering the pain he felt on first reading *Bowers*, remembering his encounter in 1997 with the dismissive aide in Senator Kay Bailey Hutchison's office, remembering the silence and the shame, the thousands of small indignities he had suffered across the years, Mark couldn't help but smile. He and Vic understood that with *Lawrence* the cultural landscape had shifted. That the victory had come against Texas, which had for years done everything in its power to remind him and Vic of their second-class status, was all the more satisfying. The Court's decision would, they realized, have immediate practical significance. After *Lawrence* it would be more difficult to discriminate against gays and lesbians. But there was more. In years past when sexual intimacy between gay couples was a criminal act, marriage was beyond hope. After *Lawrence*, that barrier had been lifted.

Predictably, Mark and Vic weren't the only ones to understand that decriminalizing sex for gay men and lesbians had changed everything. The combined impact of *Lawrence* and *Goodridge* set off a cultural storm that would soon become a political storm. Frightened at how much ground they had lost, America's right wing sprang into action. Realizing that same-sex marriage could be used as a wedge issue to motivate conservative voters, they rushed to draft a series of state constitutional amendments prohibiting gay marriage. At the beginning of 2003 only three states had such amendments: Alaska, Nebraska, and Nevada. By March when the Court heard oral arguments in *Lawrence*, eleven more states were readying constitutional amendments prohibiting same-sex marriage for the November ballot. Three more would be added before November—and all would pass.

And yet, despite the backlash, Evan Wolfson and Mary Bonauto saw marriage on the near horizon. In May 2005 they brought together a "working group" of gay activists in Jersey City, New Jersey, to chart a route into the future. The result was "Winning Marriage: What We Need to Do" which laid out the 10/10/10/20 plan they hoped would make same-sex marriage a reality in fifteen to twenty-five years. The goal was simple enough: over the next fifteen to twenty years, target "the movable middle." Show them that "LGBT people have the same aspirations for a good life, the same dreams, hopes, and fears that other Americans have," change the way they felt about homosexuality. The strategy was equally simple:

- Win the right to marry in 10 states,
- Win civil marriage or its equivalent in 10 more states,
- Win limited protections/rights for LGBT people in another 10 states,
- Grow support for LGBT rights in the remaining 20 states.

Win first in the states; when a critical mass has come into line, work for change through Congress and the Supreme Court. The last paragraph of the report left no doubt about priorities:

> Efforts to get the federal government to end discrimination against same-sex relationships that have been sanctioned by the states . . . will likely go forward in courts and Congress before any attempt to get the federal government to bring "hold out" states into line.[41]

In 2005 not even the visionaries who penned "Winning Marriage" could put a name to the case that would overturn DOMA and open the road to samesex marriage. Leaving Jersey City, Mary Bonauto was painfully aware that the current state of affairs—couples legally married in Massachusetts could legally be denied benefits at the federal level—made no sense. But she knew as well that the first order of business had to be turning back legislative challenges to marriage in Massachusetts. That done, in March 2009 GLAD filed the first lawsuit challenging the Defense of Marriage Act, *Gill v. Office of Personnel Management*, and began a string of victories. In July 2010 the

Federal District Court for Massachusetts issued the first-ever district court opinion striking down DOMA. In May 2012 the First Circuit Court of Appeals unanimously affirmed the lower court's decision—the first appeals court to rule against DOMA.

Four months after Gill won at the district court level, Edith Windsor stepped forward, angry at the injustice of having to pay more than $360,000 in estate taxes after the death of her spouse, Thea Spyer. They had been legally married in Canada; the state of New York recognized their marriage. But none of that made any difference. Under Section 3 of the Defense of Marriage Act, which for the purpose of determining eligibility for federal benefits defined marriage, even marriages contracted in states where same-sex marriage was legal, as only between a man and a woman, in the eyes of the law, Edith Windsor and the woman she had loved for more than fifty years were strangers. Represented by Roberta Kaplan of Paul Weiss LLP, she threw down the gauntlet.

A consummate professional, Roberta Kaplan recognized that in *United States v. Windsor* her first duty was to her client and the tax case at hand. "This was a lawsuit in a federal court under the U. S. Constitution," Kaplan writes in *Then Comes Marriage*, "not a political campaign to win marriage equality nationwide."[42] But the road to victory in Edith Windsor's tax case ran through the federal definition of marriage at the core of DOMA, the last federal barrier to marriage equality. Having recognized that same-sex marriage would remain out of reach until federal law ceased to divide marriages into classes, GLAD had launched a two-pronged attack on DOMA, *Gill v. Office of Personnel Management* in the First Circuit, *Pedersen v. Office of Personnel Management* in the Second Circuit.

When *Windsor* was filed in the District Court for the Southern District of New York, Justice Ginsburg's observation that the Court had moved "too far, too fast" in deciding *Roe v. Wade* (1973), a comment often seen as a caution to advocates of same-sex marriage, had not yet been repeated a hundred times in newspapers across the country.[43] Nonetheless, Kaplan knew that the Court prefers to move by slow, incremental steps; she was determined not to press the Justices into taking up the question of marriage equality before a majority had grown comfortable with the idea. Like the twin strands of a DNA molecule, a double-helix whose parallel ribbons twist in unison, always close but never touching, yet bound together at crucial points, arguments for *Windsor* and for marriage equality would have to be kept discrete.

As in *Romer* and *Lawrence,* Justice Kennedy wrote the majority decision in *Windsor*—and as in *Romer* and *Lawrence* the decision was immediately heralded as a victory for LGBT rights. "DOMA writes inequality into the entire United States Code," Justice Kennedy concluded; it constitutes "a deprivation of liberty of the person protected by the Fifth Amendment of the Constitution." Fittingly, the argument begins by recalling a key element in *Lawrence*, his much-quoted observation that "times can blind." Though some may have recoiled at the idea of same-sex marriage, others found there "the beginnings of a new perspective, a new insight," ultimately the opportunity to make right "an injustice that they had not earlier known or understood."[44]

Shortly thereafter, Justice Kennedy's writing recalls a second key passage in *Lawrence*. Because sexual intimacy between consenting adults can be "but one element in a personal bond that is more enduring"—in effect, a means of realizing one's self-identity, a means of defining oneself as a person—it is protected behavior and cannot be punished by the State. Understanding that, it follows that states would allow "same-sex couples who wish *to define themselves* by their commitment to each other" to marry. In recognizing same-sex marriage, New York "sought *to give further protection and dignity to that bond*" between two loving, committed adults, to extend "a far reaching *legal acknowledgment of the intimate relationship* between two people" that allows them to realize their full humanity (emphasis added).

Reviewing "the history of DOMA's enactment and its own text," Justice Kennedy observes that "interference with the equal dignity of same-sex marriages . . . was more than an incidental effect of the federal statute," adding just a few paragraphs later that "The principal purpose is to impose inequality." In what is perhaps the most famous passage in the *Windsor* decision— it is certainly the most moving—he examines what the resulting inequality looks like for the very real, vulnerable human beings affected:

> This places same-sex couples in an unstable position of being in a second-tier marriage. The differentiation demeans the couple, whose moral and sexual choices the Constitution protects and whose relationship the State

has sought to dignify. And it humiliates tens of thousands of children now being raised by same-sex couples. The law in question makes it even more difficult for the children to understand the integrity and closeness of their own family and its concord with other families in their community and in their daily lives.

Justice Kennedy's ability to empathize with human beings harmed by an unjust law, a manifestation of his own humanity, pervades the *Windsor* decision. Time after time—ten times in twenty-six pages, never more forcefully than in his concluding paragraph—he speaks of the "dignity" owed to gays and lesbians seeking to marry:

> DOMA singles out a class of persons deemed by a State entitled to recognition and protection to enhance their own liberty. It imposes a disability on the class by refusing to acknowledge a status the State finds to be dignified and proper. . . . The federal statute is invalid, for no legitimate purpose overcomes the purpose and effect to disparage and to injure those who the State, by its marriage laws, sought to protect in personhood and dignity.[45]

Edith Windsor had won her tax case. DOMA was dead and the community had taken yet another step toward marriage equality. Small, incremental, but critical.

Predictably, Justice Scalia's dissent was, as Ryan Grim wrote in *The Huffington Post*, "choked with rage."[46] Giving way as usual to rhetorical excess, he declared the majority opinion "overcooked," "rootless and shifting in its justifications," filled with "scatter-shot rationales," a "high-handed invalidation of DOMA," and—perhaps the most amusing phrase from any of his dissents, certainly the best known— "a disappearing trail of . . . legalistic argle-bargle." Though Justice Kennedy had confined the reach of *Windsor*—"This opinion and its holdings are confined to those lawful marriages" recognized by the States—Justice Scalia correctly understood that the legalization of same-sex marriage was but one small step away. "It takes real cheek for today's majority to reassure us," he wrote, "that a constitutional requirement to give formal recognition to same-sex marriage is not an issue here." And again: "How easy it is, indeed how inevitable, to reach the same conclusion with regard to state laws denying same-sex couples marital status."

Unable to comprehend Justice Kennedy's humanity in recognizing the need of gays and lesbians to be acknowledged as full and equal human beings, Justice Scalia rails in parts of two paragraphs against "personhood and dignity," repeating Justice Kennedy's phrase no fewer than three times, surrounded always by sarcasm that seems nothing less than hateful:

> that Court which finds it so horrific that Congress irrationally and hate-fully robbed same-sex couples of the "personhood and dignity" which state legislatures conferred upon them, will of a certitude be similarly appalled by state legislatures irrational and hateful failure to acknowl-edge that "personhood and dignity" in the first place . . . challengers will lead with this Court's declaration that there is "no legitimate purpose" served by such a law, and will claim that the traditional definition has "the purpose and effect to disparage and to injure" the "personhood and dignity" of same-sex couples.

Working on her brief for *United States v. Windsor*, Roberta Kaplan stuck a Post-it note on the screen of her laptop. "It's all about Edie, stupid," the note reminded her. And for her, it was. But for Mark and Vic, and for hundreds of their friends, it was much, much more. "Now we had a base, something to build on," Vic said; "The fact that this huge, groundbreaking thing had occurred . . . it covered up everything else on the planet!" Mark agreed completely. "There was an incredible sense of accomplishment. The cause was advancing; after *Windsor* we had a sense of inevitability."[47]

* * *

Though in San Antonio and Dallas Mark had played an active role in advocating for gay rights, he had been careful to keep a low profile. Having learned that his career as a corporate lawyer would be jeopardized if his employers discovered he was gay, in the summer of 2013 Mark was out to only one person at Expert Global Solutions, Inc. where he worked as assistant general counsel. Vic's situation at work was much more positive;

his colleagues knew he was gay. He and Mark had invited them to their lake house for a housewarming party and, as Vic put it, "there was absolutely no '*straight*-ening up.'" As a teacher and health care worker—professions in which, he points out with considerable satisfaction, "there is no stigma attached to being gay"—he had no concerns about how administrators or colleagues would react barring pressure from the governor's office.[48] But nearly twenty-three years in the Air Force, including eighteen perilous years while "Don't Ask, Don't Tell" was the law of the land, had taught him about the job-related dangers of being gay. He understood Mark's "business community" predicament.

Potential problems at work were barely the tip of the "should we, or shouldn't we?" iceberg Mark and Vic confronted as they steered their way that summer night through unseasonably cold waters. "Politics in Texas . . . it's a full contact sport," Mark thought with no little trepidation; "it's a blood sport!" Granted, filing a lawsuit would not under normal circumstances be construed as a political act. But this was Texas and these were hardly "normal" times. Attorney General Greg Abbott—ironically, he and Mark had become friends as law students at Vanderbilt, a friendship that later prompted Mark to rush to Abbott's bedside when a falling tree paralyzed him—was running for governor. Karl Rove, the Republican operative, notorious for his bare-knuckled style, had advised Abbott during his first campaign. What if Rove returned for an encore performance? "Are they going to come after us?" Mark wondered. "They'll just make stuff up!"[49]

Most of all, Mark and Vic talked that night about safety. They worried about damage to their house in Plano and their lake house in Gun Barrel City, about attacks on their dogs, about physical harm to themselves. "We weren't worried that there would be this massive uprising," Vic said, "that suddenly a horde of people with pitchforks and torches would come tap dancing in our direction. What we worried about was that one extremist, that one hard-core nut case, who had decided he was going to 'fix' all this with his long-shot rifle."[50] Given their natures, they worried about others as well, particularly their neighbors. Would teams of newsmen descend on their neighborhood with satellite trucks, trampling lawns, disrupting traffic, and generally upsetting the quiet equilibrium of their street? Would children accustomed to playing on what were usually lightly trafficked streets be endangered?

In the end, of course, though Mark and Vic had imagined a hundred, a thousand reasons to say no, they said yes. Others had been asked to join the suit, some by the plaintiffs, some by attorneys at Akin Gump. All but Cleo and Nicole had turned away at the possible consequences. For Mark and Vic participation was a matter of conscience. The prospect of what might happen if they took the lead was scary, nerve-wracking. But so was the prospect of what would happen if they did not. They thought of couples they knew when one partner had died, some legally married out of state, some married in informal ceremonies in Texas, some unable to marry despite decades together: Roberto Flores, whose partner of thirty-six years, husband of one year, Dan Graney, was heartbroken at not being listed as "spouse" on Roberto's death certificate; Don Taylor, married informally for fifteen years when his husband, Bruce Jarstfer, died and the State refused to recognize the most important relationship in their lives; Kathy Safford, distraught when her partner of thirty-six years, Barb Melzer, died. Mark and Vic thought it a shame that they had never been able to marry legally in Texas. When one of them died, Mark and Vic wanted more.

Like gay men and women everywhere, subjected too long to slings and arrows cast by unfeeling strangers, they had had enough. "We chose to step forward, to force the change we wanted," Vic said, "because of all the little indignities, all the little pieces that had come together in the kaleidoscope of our lives, all the little horrors, really. They aren't things that people should do to other people, they aren't things that people should have to live through. They aren't things that should go on. They need to stop. What we saw was the opportunity to make it stop."[51]

As he had promised, Mark returned the call from Frank Stenger-Castro the next day. "Well," he asked, "what about us, Vic and me?" By September the attorneys at Akin Gump had begun gathering information to prepare the petition; Frank asked Mark and Vic in an e-mail to send their CV's and a brief summary of the facts of their lives. What Frank saw when he looked at the materials Mark and Vic sent made him more enthusiastic than ever. "It reads," he told them, "like a telenovela!"[52]

In Austin, Nicole and Cleo had wrestled with the same questions and arrived at the same conclusion. As Nicole would later tell a reporter from the *San Antonio Express News*, "Nobody does this because they want to, because it's fun. It's just a fundamental feeling that I think every American shares—that I should be treated like everybody else."[53] In a conference call that brought Nicole and Cleo together with the legal team at Akin Gump, the women spoke of the indignities, small and not so small, they suffered every day—and in particular of the pain and fear they had endured when Cleo gave birth to their first child and Nicole's parental rights were nil until she was able to adopt their son legally. It was the kind of conversation about rights Mark and Vic and Frank had had many times. But for some on the legal team it was an awakening. "You think, looking from the outside into their lives," Barry Chasnoff would remember after the complaint was filed, "that you have some feel for the difficulties being gay creates, but hearing their stories of unequal treatment . . . it's pretty overwhelming."[54] When in mid-August Nicole and Cleo signed on, Akin Gump had the squeaky-clean, ideal plaintiffs they needed to bring marriage equality to Texas.

By way of encouraging the plaintiffs to take that last fateful step, to sign letters of intent authorizing Akin Gump to file suit on their behalf against the State of Texas, Frank wanted a meeting between the plaintiffs and the attorneys who would represent them: Barry Chasnoff, Neel Lane, Matt Pepping, and himself. They needed to be sure that Mark and Vic, Nicole and Cleo understood the difficulties that lay before them, that despite the obvious stresses involved they were committed for the long term; perhaps most of all they wanted to reassure the plaintiffs that Akin Gump was committed for the long term, that they believed passionately in the rightness of the cause and were willing to devote whatever time, talent, and treasure would be necessary to bring marriage equality to Texas. The principals agreed to come together for the first time on Sunday, September 15, a low-key meeting in the living room of Barry Chasnoff's home in San Antonio.

Before that first meeting Matt Pepping e-mailed Akin Gump's draft of the Plaintiffs' Original Complaint to each of the plaintiffs, their first indication of how the case would be argued. Chasnoff's first step in the Complaint was to establish the "unique and central social, legal, and economic role" marriage plays in our culture. It has been recognized, he observed, as "one of the vital personal rights essential to the orderly pursuit of happiness by free men" (*Loving v. Virginia*), as the "most important relation in life" (*Zablocki v. Redhail*). That being the case, Texas's prohibition of same-sex marriage, its refusal to recognize valid same-sex marriages performed out-of-state, its refusal to allow "any legal status identical or similar to marriage"—punitive actions taken with "no rational basis, much less a compelling government purpose"—constitute "a grave deprivation of constitutional rights that directly harms a discrete but substantial minority." Homosexuals in Texas and beyond have, the Complaint asserts, been subjected to "a long and painful history of societal and government sponsored discrimination" that is rooted in nothing less than "animus against a politically unpopular group."

Echoing the language of Justice Kennedy's decision in *Windsor*, the Complaint argues that "Texas 'places same-sex couples in an unstable position,' 'demeans' same-sex couples, 'humiliates tens of thousands of children now being raised by same-sex couples,' and 'instructs all [State] officials, and indeed all persons with whom same-sex couples interact, including their own children, that their [relationship] is less worthy than the [relationship] of others.'" Denied fundamental liberties guaranteed to all Americans—the right to marry, the right to have out-of-state marriages recognized in Texas—denied "the same dignity, respect, and stature afforded officially recognized heterosexual family relationships," the Complaint concludes that same-sex couples in Texas can invoke the Due Process Clause of the Fourteenth Amendment. Further, since constitutional and statutory law in Texas allows marriage for heterosexuals but prohibits marriage for homosexuals, same-sex couples are "unequal in the eyes of the law" and can invoke as well the Equal Protection Clause.[55]

Though they liked very much what they read, Mark and Vic were growing more and more nervous, so much so that they considered changing their minds. Mark in particular, the attorney trained to look in microscopic detail at every side of every question, tilted first one way, then the other. Time after time Mark would ask, "Do you want to do this?" "But I knew," Vic recalls, "What he was really saying was 'I'm not sure I want to do this.'" The dilemma they faced was serious, life-changing serious, but true to form Vic's memory of the days leading to the gathering in San Antonio highlights the comedy. "The week of the meeting at Barry Chasnoff's house," he remembers, "and especially the night before, Mark was a mess. A chocolate-covered-Easter-Bunny-left-in-the sun mess. At night, he'd toss and turn, or just lie there awake and staring, clearly contemplating the action we were considering."

Vic knew all too well the kind of pain his partner was feeling. Mark's anxiety reminded him of his transition to civilian life, of the difficult moment in a doctor's office when, completing a medical history, he checked the box that said "homosexual" and admitted for the first time in print that he was gay. He knew from their years together exactly how to comfort the man he loved. His response, a latter-day take on the love and loyalty the biblical Ruth shows for Naomi—"Wither thou goest; I will go"—could not have been more perfect. "If you want to do this," he told Mark, "that's fine. If you don't want to do it, that's fine too. Whatever you do, I will do it with you and there's absolutely no negative consequence to us, to our relationship. If you decide you never want to think about this again, it's not a big deal. I won't hold it against you. How you feel is how I'll go."[56]

Despite Vic's reassuring calm, Mark's reservations were so strong that they almost canceled the trip to San Antonio. But they had made a promise—and they made the trip. Welcoming the newcomers to his home, Barry was in top form and working hard to keep the atmosphere low key. Introductions went around: the lawyers they would come to know so well and, most important, Nicole and Cleo, their prospective co-plaintiffs. Writing later in his journal, Mark would note, "We loved them immediately." Later, Barry would lead them on a tour of the house and yard, introduce them to his wife and children, but for the moment everyone found a comfortable spot in the living room and settled in for "the talk."

Though they looked at what lay before them from different perspectives, plaintiffs and lawyers wondered about many of the same questions, shared many of the same concerns. Would the case go to a full trial on merits? Would there be depositions? Would both the plaintiffs and their attorneys stay with it for the duration? If the case grew too expensive, if Akin Gump were to get backlash from important clients, would they leave the plaintiffs out on a limb? Vic remembers that Barry did a lot of relaxed leaning forward. "I just want to make this clear," he said; "we have to make sure and talk about this. The thing we need to understand is that this is something that could go on for a year, two years, five years. We don't know how long this case is going to take; it could be a very, very long time. You're making a big commitment, and we're going to see this thing all the way through."[57]

What mattered most to Mark and Vic was the "feel" of the afternoon, the kind of emotional shift that comes from hearing, really hearing, the sound of human voices rising from the heart. Listening to Barry Chasnoff and Neal Lane, to Matt Pepping and Frank Stenger-Castro, they came to see that Akin Gump hadn't rallied to their side because they craved publicity. They were "all in" because they thought Texas marriage law was wrong, that it needed to be fixed. They believed. "I got there and they were so passionate," Mark said, "so moving. It was a lot like—to shift to a football analogy—like a coach pumping up the team. They were so convincing that all my concerns, all my worries, just melted away." As the afternoon came to an end, the plaintiffs agreed that their names would appear alphabetically on the lawsuit. Their case would enter Texas history as *DeLeon v. Perry*.

On September 18, three days after the meeting at Barry Chasnoff's home, Mark and Vic mailed letters of engagement to Akin Gump. Nicole and Cleo followed soon after. Signing the letter that outlined Akin Gump's responsibilities to the plaintiffs, the plaintiffs' responsibilities to Akin Gump—a vital step empowering the law firm to represent them—Mark and Vic heaved a sigh of relief. They had crossed the Rubicon, but they had no sooner crossed one river than the next came into view. To establish their complaint, they had to be refused a marriage license, and on October 3 they traveled to the Bexar County Courthouse in San Antonio where they were politely but firmly turned away. Back on the job that afternoon, Vic got a first taste of his new "celebrity status" from Chris Cooper, the Assistant Director of the Physician Assistant Program and one of the few people who knew why he had not been in the office that morning. "I cannot believe," his friend told him, "that I'm standing in front of someone who is going to go into the history books. What you're doing is just incredible."[58]

With the defining moment in San Antonio behind them, Mark e-mailed Elizabeth Birch, formerly the Executive Director of the Human Rights Campaign and an old friend from his early days as an LGBT activist in San Antonio. Years earlier when she and her then-partner adopted two children in San Antonio, there had been "issues." Mark had written to her earlier as he and Vic contemplated joining the lawsuit, wanting to know how hard it had been, seeking her advice on getting involved. Her reply had made him more nervous still: "The whole right wing came after us before the kids' adoption was final." Now he wanted to bring her up to date. "Vic and I decided to proceed," he told her. "The lawsuit should be filed this week or next. A little nervous. Actually, a lot nervous."[59] Her enthusiastic reply arrived the next day. "SO VERY PROUD OF YOU!!!!!"[60] But a week passed, and then another. The lawyers at Akin Gump had hoped to file the Complaint and the Motion for a Preliminary Injunction simultaneously and assembling the pages and pages of expert testimony they wanted to include was taking longer than expected. Mark found the delay excruciating. "It's one of my strengths and weaknesses that I can see both sides of any question," he admits. "I was changing my mind on a daily, no, an hourly basis. It was unnerving."[61] Almost three weeks later, utterly at his wits' end, he called Frank Stenger-Castro. "Please file or I'm going to change my mind!" he pleaded.

Throughout the weekend before the Complaint was at last filed, Mark and Vic sought what distractions they could: a Fireside Chat at the Texas Lyceum's State of Philanthropy conference on Friday evening, an OU football game Saturday afternoon in Norman, a musical performance featuring a friend's daughter in Dallas on Sunday.[62] But they were never able to put the lawsuit out of their minds. Friends who joined them for the game offered their home as a safe haven if their lives suddenly spun out of control. On the way to see their friend's daughter perform, Mark contacted another old friend, Worth Ross, a former HRC governor and director, to tell him about the lawsuit that would be filed the next morning. At the Texas Lyceum conference Mark quietly confronted the speaker, Margaret Spellings, during the social hour that followed her formal talk. It was not their first encounter.

In April 2004 while Director of the Domestic Policy Council for President George W. Bush—not quite a year before she became Secretary of Education and struck out at the LGBT community through the "Postcards from Buster" controversy, what Mark Stern called "perhaps the decade's most galling act of homophobic censorship"—Spellings had addressed a gathering of the Texas Lyceum at the Eisenhower Executive Office Building in Washington, D. C.[63] When the Lyceum moved to the Indian Treaty Room for cocktails, Mark and Vic sought her out. Realizing how important it was to put a human face on gay rights, Mark told her that he was gay—and watched as the two women flanking Spellings backed away. "You would have thought," Mark said later, "that I was going to spit at her."[64] With Vic standing firmly at his side, he told Spellings that he had been in a committed relationship for seven years—and that the administration's support for a ban on same-sex marriage was hurtful. Politically astute, Spellings danced around the issue but refused to give an inch. After Senator John Cornyn addressed the Lyceum the next day, Mark approached him with the same argument. He found Cornyn's response—that because of couples like Mark and Vic those pushing a marriage ban were doing so "respectfully"—less than convincing.

Now, days before the lawsuit was to be filed, Mark confronted Spellings again. He reminded her of their earlier meeting and asked the key question. "Do you still support the ban or have you, like Ken Mehlman, changed your views?" To Mark and Vic's delight, Spellings told him she had changed her views, that she would not do the same thing again—a convincing sign that minds were changing, an important boost to their confidence.

That same week both men told family and close friends that in just a few days they would be caught in a maelstrom. Vic's parents reacted as expected—proud that Vic and Mark were determined to challenge the State, consumed with worry at what might happen. "Please, please, please," they asked, "do what you can to stay safe." Mark's brother, Greg, seemed not to bat an eyelash. But his niece, Kristen Johnson, was frantic with worry. "Mark, that's Texas . . . you're going against! Texas! You're taking on Texas!" She just kept repeating herself, her voice shaking with emotion. Tom Arnst, Mark's boss and the only one at work to whom Mark had confided that he was gay, was concerned as well. "One crazy. It only takes one crazy," he reminded Mark as he urged caution and wished him well. Vic's boss was similarly concerned. "Have you thought about where you live?" he asked. "We can always call down and take care of security here, but something is going to come up. Try and take as many measures as you can to be safe."[65] Two days before the Complaint was at last filed, Peter Myers, a friend from Mark's undergraduate days who lived now in Texas, sent a text—half a warning, half a joke. "How's the lawsuit going?," he wondered; "Hey, I mean you do know you lose control when you become a public figure? Imagine Cornyn making you a campaign issue?"[66]

As those around them grew more excited, Mark and Vic had at last settled down. "If they come after us, they come after us," Mark replied. "If they want to invite a comparison to George Wallace, I am happy to make it." And then—three weeks to the day after he had e-mailed Elizabeth Birch—it happened.

Recognizing that the quiet life to which he and Vic had been long accustomed would in the course of the day almost certainly slip into the past, on the morning of October 28, 2013, Mark posted on his Facebook page an inspirational passage he attributed to Mark Twain:

> Life is short, break the rules, forgive quickly, kiss slowly, love truly, laugh uncontrollably, and never regret anything that made you smile. Twenty years from now you will be more disappointed by the things you didn't do than by the ones you did. So throw off the bowlines. Sail away from the safe harbor. Catch the trade winds in your sails. Explore. Dream. Discover.[67]

A year earlier while they were on vacation in Antarctica, Twain's words had given Mark the courage to take the Polar Bear Plunge into water six degrees below freezing. Hours after Mark's post, *DeLeon v. Perry* was filed in the Federal District Court for the Western District of Texas. He and Vic feared that when the Complaint was filed they would be subjected to shocks beyond what they had felt in the freezing waters of the South Pole.

The first call came within an hour from Elayne Ayala of the *San Antonio Express News*. Not long after, the phone rang again; this time Ryan Poppe of Texas Public Radio was on the line. Though they had known their lives would change, Mark and Vic had to some extent deluded themselves. Akin Gump had agreed to handle public relations and the plaintiffs had imagined they could maintain a low profile. By evening, with requests for interviews coming thick and fast, Mark and Vic realized that they, together with Nicole and Cleo, had suddenly been thrust to the center of the stage where the spotlight was focused on them—and they didn't feel at all prepared. Mark, who in his lawyerly way had turned their resolution to file suit against Texas this way and that, looking at it from every possible angle, fretting over the enormity of the challenge they had issued, left his office that evening literally sick to his stomach—something that never happened to him. The last call that evening came from Neel Lane, soon to emerge as Akin Gump's lead attorney for

DeLeon v. Perry. He had heard Mark was upset, was calling to reassure him. A touch of humanity on a difficult day—and it worked.

On the morning of October 28 few people knew what was afoot: Mark and Vic, Nicole and Cleo, the legal team at Akin Gump, members of the plaintiffs' families, and a handful of close friends. Mark's "Mark Twain" Facebook post had revealed nothing, appearing to online friends no more than another expression of his usual personality. For those who didn't catch the story on the news, Mark's post the next morning provided a bit of context:

> Yesterday, Vic and I and another gay couple filed a lawsuit in federal court against the State of Texas challenging the constitutionality of its ban on gay marriages. We have no idea whether we will prevail or how long this will take (it's likely to be years), but we are hopeful and optimistic. We are represented by Akin Gump, a national law firm with a great reputation. We are in good hands.[68]

"It's so cool," a friend wrote in the comments section, "to be friends with the folks who just might drag the red state of Texas into the current millennium." Two days later, Mark posted again, this time to express his and Vic's gratitude:

> Thanks to Akin Gump and all of its attorneys, including Barry Chasnoff, Frank Stenger-Castro, Matthew Pepping and Neel Lane, for representing Vic Holmes, Nicole Dimetman, Cleopatra DeLeon and me in challenging the constitutionality of Texas' ban on gay marriage. It will require a lot of hard work and is not without the risk of some negative backlash.[69]

Neel Lane, attentive as ever, had the perfect response. "It is an honor and a privilege to have you as my clients in the pursuit of justice."

Chapter 3

The First Blast
of the Trumpet

Under our constitutional system, courts stand, against any winds that
blow, as havens of refuge for those who might otherwise suffer because
they are helpless, weak, outnumbered, or because they are nonconform-
ing victims of prejudice and public excitement . . . No higher duty, no
more solemn responsibility, rests upon this Court, than that of translating
into living law and maintaining this constitutional shield deliberately
planned and inscribed for the benefit of every human being subject to
our Constitution—of whatever race, creed, or persuasion.

—Justice Hugo Black, *Chambers v. Florida* (1940)

"I just want it to be remembered that it's about more than the four
plaintiffs," Mark told the *Dallas Voice* just after the Complaint was
filed; "It's about enabling all gays and lesbians in Texas to be able to marry."[1]

As they moved from "someone should file a lawsuit" to "we'll file a
lawsuit," Mark and Vic somehow convinced themselves that they would be
able to stay out of the public eye. Akin Gump had, after all, agreed to handle
whatever publicity arose because of *DeLeon v. Perry*. Hoping to maintain a
low profile, they tightened their internet security settings when Akin Gump

informed them they were about to file and removed their faces from social networking sites like LinkedIn and Facebook. Their families would know what was afoot. Close friends would know. They would share progress in their case with a wider, but still contained circle on Facebook. Beyond that, they hoped not to be noticed, to move quietly through each day as they had moved through the last. That the public would insist on seeing faces, would fully understand and empathize with the story of same-sex marriage in Texas only after they came to know the human beings behind the headlines, was a lesson they learned early on. It was also a lesson in which they would need periodic refresher courses.

Mark and Vic were caught off-guard when the media caught up with them so quickly on the day the lawsuit was filed. They were surprised again at the end of their first interviews with the *San Antonio Express* and Texas Public Radio when they were asked for photographs. They had scrubbed images of themselves from the internet; didn't want people to recognize them on the street. And now they were being asked for pictures? The *San Antonio Express* and Texas Public Radio got the photographs they requested—the men didn't want to hurt the case by declining—but after that first day they did decline interviews with MSNBC and *Texas Lawyer*. "Have no problem with you giving an interview," Mark wrote in an e-mail to Barry Chasnoff who had relayed the requests; "in some ways it's preferable because it keeps the press focused on the issues and not on us."[2] Directing the public gaze away from themselves and onto the social and legal arguments for same-sex marriage was, however, only part of the problem. Both men had limited experience dealing with the press. Knowing how much was at stake—the future of marriage equality in Texas— neither wanted to be responsible for a misstep that would hurt their cause.

Though requests from the press had thus far been few, Mark and Vic realized that others would follow as surely as night follows day. *DeLeon v. Perry* was at its core about "enabling all gays and lesbians in Texas," but it would out of human necessity also be about the plaintiffs, about who they were and why they deserved the same protections granted to other Americans. Though Akin Gump might coordinate the interviews, Mark and Vic, Cleo and Nicole, would become the public face of same-sex marriage in Texas—and perhaps beyond.

In order to prepare for the interviews they knew would come, Mark drafted a set of likely questions and suggested answers that borrowed heavily on information posted on the website of Human Rights Campaign which had poll-tested language known to move hearts and minds. Still attuned to the way things were done in the Air Force, Vic suggested another approach. "I'm fine with a television interview," he wrote in an e-mail to his co-plaintiffs and the legal team at Akin Gump about MSNBC's request for a live appearance, "but I've never done one before. It would be nice to talk to someone for a heads-up on how the process works and maybe do a mock session. We practiced everything in the military."[3] Within hours Barry Chasnoff wrote back to announce that Akin Gump had hired Angela Hale and Susan Risdon, managing partners at the Red Media Group in Austin, to handle public relations.

That evening, Angela and Susan arrived at Mark and Vic's house for the first of many coaching sessions, the beginning of a relationship that would stretch across the years to Mark and Vic's wedding. Mark and Vic liked the women from the start, knew they could work with them, but the more the four talked, the more the men realized how much they had to learn about successful interactions with the press. A few weeks later, Angela and Susan returned with a cameraman for more intense media training, first in settings where Mark and Vic could focus on an interviewer sitting a few feet away in the direction of the camera, then in more difficult settings in which a remote interviewer left them face to face with the camera's impersonal lens. "I was terrible looking at the camera and answering questions asked remotely," Mark remembered later. "I was petrified when we finally did our MSNBC interview remotely. I still remember how badly I did in our practice sessions."[4]

The initial burst of publicity was short-lived. No new requests for interviews arrived on Thursday and Friday, and by the weekend Mark and Vic had settled, tentatively, back into the usual quiet of their lives. Both were ecstatic. Vic was gloating. "See," he reminded Mark at the week's end, "I told you there'd be a brief spurt and then it would all die away." For a few brief weeks that would prove true. Eventually, though they would never become as comfortable in front of cameras and microphones as they would have liked, the skills learned from Angela and Susan would be called into use on an almost daily basis.

* * *

With Mark and Vic busy learning what it meant to be plaintiffs in a controversial, high-visibility case, the legal team at Akin Gump began jockeying for legal position with lawyers from the office of the Attorney General. Though for a moment *DeLeon v. Perry* seemed the only light in the Texas sky, within days the plaintiffs discovered that they had become part of a three-star system, an Orion's Belt of marriage equality cases hovering above the Lone Star State. On October 31 Shannon and Catherine Zahrn, joined by Alexius Augustine and Andrew Simpson, filed *Zahrn v. Perry* with the Austin division of the U. S. District Court for the Western District of Texas. A few days later the Attorney General's Office informed Akin Gump of another same-sex marriage case, *McNosky v. Perry*, filed by Chris McNosky and Sven Stricker on July 29, also in Austin. A fourth star, *Nuckols v. Perry*, filed in mid-July, had already fallen from the sky, withdrawn on the advice of the ACLU and Lambda Legal days after it was filed.

Though pleased at the way independent stars had aligned to fight the same injustices, lawyers and plaintiffs in *DeLeon v. Perry* recognized that the coming together of a sudden constellation of cases challenging Texas's ban on same-sex marriage created procedural problems. The attorneys in *Zahrn* had filed and were determined to pursue a class action suit; the plaintiffs in *McNosky*, more than a bit naïve about the difficulties they faced, intended to appear in court *pro se* (acting on their own behalf without counsel) and were already overwhelmed by procedural complexities. For a while the parties in *DeLeon* considered asking McNosky and Stricker to join their suit, but the latter wanted to retain complete control of their case. Moreover, adding plaintiffs adds complexity and costs. Fearing complications that would slow the progress of their own case, the attorneys at Akin Gump wanted neither a class action suit nor additional plaintiffs.

Then too, from the outset the plaintiffs and lawyers in *DeLeon v. Perry* detected something odd about the couple planning to represent themselves. Mark shared his concerns with the others and discovered that they shared his reservations. McNosky and Stricker had built their case on sex discrimination only, not on the more common grounds of sexual orientation. In their pleadings they never claimed to be gay or to be a couple and gave separate addresses in their pleadings. Stranger still, no one in the gay community had ever heard of them. Ultimately, concluding that their case had been more carefully prepared than the others, the attorneys at Akin Gump preferred to move forward alone—though attorneys for Texas had other ideas.

Where and by whom *DeLeon v. Perry* would be heard quickly became a bone of contention between Akin Gump and the State of Texas. In San Antonio *DeLeon v. Perry* was assigned to Judge Orlando Garcia, appointed to the bench by President Bill Clinton; in Austin both *McNosky* and *Zahrn* were assigned to Judge Sam Sparks, appointed by President George H. W. Bush. Thinking that their chance of success would be greater with a more conservative judge, lawyers in the Attorney General's office filed a motion in November 2013 to consolidate all three cases in Judge Sparks's Austin courtroom, and at the consolidation hearing on January 9, 2014, their supposition was confirmed. Judge Sparks made no secret of his skepticism about the legal arguments supporting same-sex marriage, openly wondering whether any court had the power to overturn 200 years of jurisprudence.

"I'm concerned," he told the lawyers and plaintiffs gathered before him, "that one judge, a district judge, or two circuit judges, or five Supreme Court judges, will tell the majority of people that live in this state that the legal institution of marriage, which was formed by the state in the powers given them by the Constitution because they're reserve powers, can be changed by two people. I'm not so sure that's going to be correct." Minutes later, Judge Sparks extended his version of the "men in black robes" argument. "The truth of the matter," he continued, is that "these cases are asking for a change in the law that has been there for centuries . . . I know of no referendum in any state that supports the contentions of these lawsuits."[5] About voters and ballot boxes—and by implication the discovery that public opinion on marriage equality was shifting rapidly—he was, of course, wrong. In November 2012 voters in Maine, Maryland, and Washington had passed referenda approving same-sex marriage by significant margins. On that same night in November, Minnesota voters convincingly rejected a proposed amendment to the state constitution, placed on the ballot by the Republican-dominated legislature, that would have banned same-sex marriage. But in the moment, the lawyers for *Zahrn* and *DeLeon* and the *pro se* plaintiffs in *McNosky*, thinking of little beyond the most effective way to oppose the state's motion to consolidate, let the judge's error pass unchallenged.

Though Mark and Vic believed that the principals in all three cases were struggling to right the same wrongs, they were particularly dismayed by Texas's motion to consolidate. First, they wanted to win, and emerging from Judge Sparks's court with a victory seemed unlikely. "We need the ruling to come out of Judge Garcia's court," Mark wrote in an e-mail to Neel Lane and Matt Pepping, "for our case, but also for the cause nationally."[6] More important, they wanted to finish what they had begun. If they had hesitated before getting in, hoped on first getting in to remain anonymous, the alchemy of engagement had catapulted them to "all in." Having risked so much— future employment opportunities, emotional and physical harm, even friend- ships and ties to family— they discovered to their surprise that their ability to tolerate risk had grown by leaps and then by bounds. They didn't want to see their case, buttressed by a wealth of expert testimony and positioned to win, disappear or stall while another case advanced.

Describing the moment when he shared a news article about filing the Complaint with a colleague at the University of North Texas Health Center, Vic incidentally gave voice to the new mood that had come over both men. "He was amazed and visibly proud," Vic wrote, "that someone was standing up to this situation. He told me he honestly thought no one would ever do it because 'Texas is too big.'" The importance of the moment lies in Vic's reac- tion to his friend's endorsement. "Texas is a place. A place with people who have minds and hearts," he continued. "The place will always be big; that will never change. But the hearts and minds can change if someone shows them how."[7] Seeing what was possible, Mark and Vic wanted nothing more than to stand with Cleo and Nicole to show Texans how. Perhaps to stand with LGBT couples across the nation to show all Americans how.

From the beginning of the hearing Judge Sparks made it clear that because of procedural problems—in particular, his respect for the docket set by another judge—he did not see any way to consolidate cases filed in differ- ent divisions of a district court. "Do I just ride up there," he asked lawyers for the state, "and twist Judge Garcia's arm and say: I'm bigger than you are, I'm older than you are, give me a transfer? Do I do that?"[8] Given Judge Sparks's reluctance, Neel Lane had little difficulty turning back the state's motion. Judge Sparks's order, issued the afternoon of the hearing, consolidated *Zahrn* and *McNosky,* the two lawsuits filed in Austin; it left *DeLeon v. Perry* to stand alone in San Antonio. But as Mark and Vic read and re-read the transcript of the hearing, they realized that the state was not done venue shopping. Attorneys for Texas had queried a non-committal Judge Sparks about the possibility of a transfer. In a last-ditch effort to try their case before a sympathetic judge, Texas filed a motion the next day to transfer *DeLeon v. Perry* to Judge Sparks. Not until three weeks later when Judge Garcia denied the motion were Mark and Vic able to take a deep breath.

For a moment, all seemed well. Until, that is, they realized that other dangers might keep *DeLeon v. Perry* from the courtroom. In the consolidation hearing Judge Sparks made it clear that the caseload in the U. S. District Court for the Western District of Texas was almost unimaginable. "We have more cases," he declared, "than any other district in the United States." He and Judge Garcia had agreed that trying the marriage equality issue twice would be a waste of the court's time. Moreover, whatever the outcome in district court, both judges knew the decision would be appealed to the Fifth Circuit and neither wanted to cloud the issue with potentially conflicting opinions. For Mark and Vic the uncertainty about which case would go to trial was emotionally overwhelming—and the legal team at Akin Gump shared their concerns. "All of us agree that the state defendants are trying to obtain a ruling from Sparks before Garcia," Matt Pepping wrote in an e-mail to the plaintiffs. But Mark and Vic knew that they had an edge. Judge Sparks's proposed timetable for *Zahrn* and *McNosky* in Austin stretched into the late summer or early fall; by the time of the consolidation hearing Judge Garcia had already set a date for oral arguments in San Antonio. Unless other factors derailed *DeLeon v. Perry*, theirs would be the first case to be heard and, most likely, the first same-sex marriage decision to be decided in Texas.

True to form, Mark grabbed with both hands at dangling threads and worried them—and himself, and the legal team at Akin Gump—half to pieces thinking about the ways *DeLeon v. Perry* might fall behind the cases in Judge Sparks's court. In a series of e-mails, he peppered the lawyers at Akin Gump with a series of "What if's?" At the consolidation hearing the state had argued that the appropriate level of scrutiny for same-sex marriage cases was the rational basis test. Given that premise, Michael Murphy, speaking for the Attorney General, suggested there would be no need for discovery. Akin Gump, armed with an impressive portfolio of expert testimony and prepared for a trial on the merits, was reluctant to dispense with discovery, at least not until a session with Judge Garcia in the courtroom allowed them to assess his thinking. Mark worried that the time required for discovery would allow the Austin cases access to the inside lane, the shortest and fastest route to the finish. What if, he wondered, we moved to speed things up by asking Judge Garcia to convert the hearing on the preliminary injunction to a hearing on the merits?

Reassuring e-mails from Matt Pepping at Akin Gump had little effect; ten days and several e-mails later Mark wrote even more openly of his fear that *DeLeon v. Perry* would be eclipsed:

> Even if we win the preliminary injunction, won't we need to go to a hearing on the substance and won't it be well after the timetable set by Sparks? I'm concerned.[9]

What if we win the Motion for Preliminary Injunction? Mark wondered, taking up another set of hypotheticals. What is our game plan then?

Because he kept a weather-eye on legal developments in marriage cases across the country, some of the "what if's" with which Mark besieged the legal team at Akin Gump came from beyond the borders of Texas. When the Supreme Court issued a stay in *Herbert v. Kitchen*, the case that had allowed same-sex marriages to begin in Utah—both the U. S. District Court for the District of Utah and the Tenth Circuit Court of Appeals had refused to stay the decision—Mark felt the shock waves in far-away Texas. What if Texas uses the stay to argue against our motion for a preliminary injunction? he asked. Should we ask to proceed immediately to a hearing on the merits? When Judge Michael Urbanski of the U. S. District Court for the Western District of Virginia certified *Harris v. Rainey* as class action lawsuit representing all same-sex couples in Virginia, Mark worried again. What if Texas seizes on the Virginia precedent to argue that *DeLeon v. Perry* should be swept up into the class action proposed in *Zahrn v. Perry*? Should we, Mark wondered, "seek permission to file an opposition brief in Sparks' court on the basis [that] those plaintiffs are not well-positioned to represent the class because they have offered no evidence and seek no discovery?"[10]

"We never mind your questions," Matt Pepping wrote when at the end of a difficult week Mark became concerned that the lawyers who had generously offered *pro bono* representation to the plaintiffs in *DeLeon v. Perry* would tire of the unending questions that Mark, an in-house lawyer who managed litigation, couldn't help asking. They too were concerned that Judge Sparks would rule before their case came to trial, but they refused to let that risk dictate how they tried their own case. And in the end their caution was rewarded. *DeLeon v. Perry* would be the first of Texas's three marriage cases to have a hearing and in time the first to be decided. As it moved from the United States District Court for the Western District of Texas to the Fifth Circuit Court of Appeals, the State of Texas would ask Judge Sparks to stay proceedings in *Zahrn v. Perry* and *McNosky v. Perry* pending a decision from the Fifth Circuit. Like Alnilam, the middle star in Orion's Belt, a blue supergiant that shines as one of the brightest stars in the night sky, *DeLeon v. Perry* would separate itself from the other stars in its constellation to light the way in Texas.

* * *

Had events unfolded according to plan, the two documents Akin Gump wanted to submit to set *DeLeon v. Perry* on the road to trial—the Plaintiffs Original Complaint for Declaratory and Injunctive Relief (required) and the Motion for Preliminary Injunction Enjoining Defendants from Enforcing Texas' Same-Sex Marriage Ban (which they hoped would bring quick relief)—would have been filed simultaneously. But the attorneys were thinking ahead, determined to prepare methodically for a trial on the merits and possible appeals all the way to the Supreme Court; they wanted to include with the motion for a preliminary injunction fifty-eight exhibits, a wealth of expert testimony that would buttress their case—and on October 28 when the Complaint was filed Frank Stenger-Castro's team was still struggling to impose order on the mountain of data they had assembled. At the time, Barry Chasnoff thought the motion would follow within a week, perhaps two.

By November 22 when the Motion for Preliminary Injunction was at last submitted to the court, three weeks and more had passed. But Mark and Vic found the results well worth waiting for.

They had no sooner been notified that the Motion for Preliminary Injunction had been submitted to the court than Mark turned to Facebook to update their friends. "Today, the law firm of Akin Gump filed a motion for a preliminary injunction to enjoin the State of Texas from enforcing its ban on same-gender marriages," he wrote. "It is incredibly well-written."

Substantial portions of the motion were drafted in workmanlike, lawyerly prose—though no less effective for their plainspoken language and logic. Marriage is a fundamental right protected by the Due Process and Equal Protection Clauses of the Fourteenth Amendment, the legal team argued; consequently, Article I, Section 32 of the Texas Constitution, springing as it does from nothing more substantial than "unfounded fear and irrational beliefs," should be "declared unenforceable." They traced Texas's long and unfortunate history of discriminating against gays and lesbians and catalogued evidence that the state's anti-LGBT legislation was driven by *animus* deriving in this instance from the moral disapproval of gays and lesbians. They cited an impressive array of precedents in gay rights cases and more widely ranging marriage rights cases: *Loving, Zablocki, Lawrence, Romer,* and *Windsor.* Perhaps in the hope that what began in Texas could be brought to an end in Texas, that the state could be set once again front-and-center in the national debate over gay rights, no case was referenced more often than the Supreme Court's landmark 2003 decision in *Lawrence v Texas.* Twice they flat-out accused politicians in Texas of manipulating the public to gain political advantage. "Public policy in Texas," Akin Gump declared, "is nothing more than a discriminatory animus that targets an unpopular minority."[11]

When the motion turned to the harm inflicted on members of the LGBT community in Texas—"irreparable harm—not in some theoretical sense, but in real human terms"—the language soared to heights infinitely above the yeoman-like, workaday language of most legal documents

This morning, plaintiffs woke up in a world unimaginable to the majority of citizens, a world in which Plaintiffs are denied equal rights, and thus deemed inferior, because of their sexual orientation—a characteristic as immutable as their sex, their skin color, or their nationality. Today children of same-sex parents attended school and suffered the stigma that their parents are not permitted to wed, that they are the product of relationships between citizens the state deems unworthy and inferior, and they will wear that badge of inferiority to bed tonight. Today, or perhaps tomorrow, someone in a long-term committed same-sex relationship will die without ever having been married to the person he or she loves, or without having their marriage recognized by the State of Texas.

Too much time had passed already, the lawyers argued, without redress. Nothing the court could do would "heal the wounds inflicted today, or restore the status deprived today, or repair the harm already incurred today," but immediate relief would "forestall the harm that is certain to occur tomorrow, the next day, and the day after that."[12]

Mark had no trouble choosing his favorite passage: "If morality is to be our guide, let it be that fine quality of morality enshrined in the Constitution, which requires that we treat all citizens with equal dignity and respect under the law."[13] One sentence, one perfectly crafted short sentence, lyrical prose that lingered in the mind and embodied the ideals he and Vic and Cleo and Nicole were struggling to bring to Texas: the beacon of civil morality, the rule of law, the hope for dignity. But to the vulnerable men and women at the heart of *DeLeon v. Perry* that one sentence meant everything.

Responding to Mark's comment on the quality of the writing, Barry Chasnoff had nothing but praise for his colleagues. The motion was, he asserted, "a strong effort by a large team," but he offered "special kudos to Neel Lane, who drafted . . . a poetic introduction." Frank Stenger-Castro couldn't resist extending Barry's "poetic." "Neel may be," he suggested in a follow-up e-mail, "the Walt Whitman of our time." Remembering his years in San Antonio, Mark knew in his heart that Frank—though joking—had gotten it right. A vague memory told him that in the late 1800s Walt Whitman gave a reading at the Bonham Exchange where the rooms are named for the heroes of the Alamo, perhaps passages from *Leaves of Grass*, perhaps Section 34 of

"Song of Myself" which begins by recalling the fall of the Alamo and goes on to tell of the battle at Goliad. Within a few months the plaintiffs in *DeLeon v. Perry*, newly christened Texas heroes leading the fight for a new liberty, would be headed for their own battle in San Antonio. That Barry Chasnoff and Neel Lane, Walt Whitman's silver tongue, reborn in a new era and a new profession, would lead the charge on their behalf—that brought comfort in a time of uncertainty.

Three weeks after Akin Gump filed its Motion for a Preliminary Injunction, Judge Garcia issued an order setting February 12, 2014, as the date for oral arguments—and events that seemed already tumbling out of control, new developments forever nipping at the heels of the last, suddenly accelerated to warp speed. When on December 19, 2013, the New Mexico Supreme Court voted unanimously in favor of same-sex marriage, Mark and Vic felt a surge of confidence. Marriage equality was now the law in seventeen states and the District of Columbia; better yet, the court explicitly rejected the argument that the state's interest in promoting responsible procreation and insuring that children were raised in optimal families outweighed any harms done to same-sex couples—the argument they expected Texas to use in their case. Their spirits rose again when in early January 2014 Judge Garcia denied Texas Values' Motion for Leave to File Amicus Brief in *DeLeon v. Perry*, rose high enough that they and their attorneys were able to joke about an organization dedicated to suppressing gay rights. Jonathan Saenz, president of Texas Values, had angered Mark and Vic and Cleo and Nicole the previous December when he asked rhetorically, "Do laws mean anything to the homosexual advocates? It's gotten to the point where the only way they win is people don't enforce the laws. That kind of mob rule," he charged, "will not work."[14]

Identifying Texas Values by reference to an earlier struggle he remembered, Mark spoke of them in an e-mail written at the end of a long day as "the sane organization that opposed San Antonio's nondiscrimination ordinance." Rereading the e-mail chain the next morning, he recoiled in horror at his typo. "'Same' group, not 'sane' group," the correction he sent read. "I definitely think they are crazy." Michael Cooley at Akin Gump didn't want to let Mark's mistake go without extending the fun. "Talk about a Freudian slip," he wrote. To which Vic, stretching the game still further, replied, "I had one of those once but I gave it to Goodwill since it always showed no matter which dress I wore it with." Playful laughter—a constant in communications between plaintiffs and clients in *DeLeon v. Perry* helped to keep the darkness at bay.[15]

A few nights later Mark and Vic settled on the couch in their living room to watch a film, beagles beside them, beagles draped across their laps and despite the comforts of home and of the dogs, they felt the darkness creep closer once again. *Bridegroom*, the award-winning film they streamed that night—when it premiered at the Tribeca Film Festival former president Bill Clinton provided an introduction and it won the Audience Award for Best Documentary—tells the story of Shane Crone and Tom Bridegroom, six years into a loving, committed relationship when in 2011 Tom slipped at the edge of a roof and fell to his death. What happened to Shane after Tom's death—without marriage he had no legal rights and was ostracized by Tom's family, was threatened with physical harm if he so much as attempted to attend Tom's funeral—was Mark and Vic's worst nightmare. "If it does not bring tears to your eyes," he told lawyers and plaintiffs the next morning, "nothing will." As he had done so often before, Mark thanked the legal team at Akin Gump for all they had done. "If in the heat of the battle and all the hard work and late nights you begin to wonder why you're doing this," he added, "*Bridegroom* will remind you."[16]

The skies darkened again on January 8, 2014, when, as Mark had expected, the Attorney General's Office filed an advisory to Judge Garcia's court contending that the Supreme Court's stay in *Herbert v. Kitchen* supported Texas's argument against granting a preliminary injunction in *DeLeon v. Perry*. Judge Robert J. Shelby's district court decision the previous December made same-sex marriage legal in Utah. Both the district court and the Tenth Circuit of Appeals had refused Utah's request for a stay, and for seventeen days same-sex couples were allowed to marry. More than a thousand did. And then, on January 6, the Supreme Court granted the stay the district court and circuit courts had refused until the Tenth Circuit acted on the state's appeal. That the Court stayed Judge Shelby's decision so long after it had been implemented, plunging the two thousand people who had married into uncertainty as to the validity of their marriages, was particularly worrisome to Mark. "It pulls the rug out from under our motion," he wrote to the others involved. With oral arguments barely a month away, every sign seemed more portentous.

* * *

When at the end of the week in which the Complaint was filed the first wave of publicity disappeared again, Mark relaxed enough to joke with a friend. "It could have been worse," he concluded, "our filing the lawsuit didn't make it into *The Huffington Post* or the *Dallas Morning News*."[17] Susan Risdon had no sooner sent out a press release that Akin Gump had filed its motion for preliminary injunction than requests for information and interviews picked up again. Within five days *The Huffington Post* published what would become the first of their many articles about *DeLeon v. Perry*. Barry Chasnoff, Neel Lane, and Mark did interviews at various radio stations. Writers for the *Dallas Morning News*, *Texas Monthly*, *San Antonio Current*, and the *San Antonio Express* stopped by Mark and Vic's home or called to do interviews. As word of what was afoot spread in Texas and beyond, Billy Ross, a friend from Mark's days at Safety-Kleen, familiar with Mark's desire to stay out of the limelight, sent a note of joking reassurance that seemed an acknowledgment of the new normal. "I'm afraid that your quiet home-body life has changed my friend," he wrote. "But if you can win in Texas you will win nationally, so good luck in your upcoming battle! This definitely took a lot of guts and will certainly change some things for you and Vic by now being formally 'out' in the big state of 'Don't Mess with Texas.' Take care, buddy."

As the holiday season approached, Mark and Vic clung stubbornly to the "normal" they sensed was slipping away and to the families they loved. For Thanksgiving they drove to Walters, Oklahoma, to spend the weekend with Mark's brother, Greg, and his family, riding four-wheelers and pitching horseshoes when they weren't laughing with nieces and great-nephews or Mark's last surviving uncle, Mitch Free. For Christmas they drove to Cape Giradeau, a Missouri river town, to spend time with Vic's mother and father. And there was, of course, holidays or not, lawsuit or not, the ever-present need to earn a living. Just before Christmas the University of North Texas Health Science Center posted an article about Vic's bi-weekly trips to treat disabled adults at a Home Community-Based Services (HCS) camp in Mansfield where goats, horses, and mules grazed just outside the window of his clinic. "It's basically a house call," Vic suggested explaining the program he began a year earlier. "The familiar setting makes it much more comfortable for patients and much easier for me to meet their basic medical needs and keep them healthy."[18] As the year drew to a close, Mark found himself working non-stop to finish one major transaction for his company and to close another into escrow. On Christmas Eve at Vic's parents' house, the press continued. On Christmas day he was still working out the details, reading and answering work-related e-mails.

Still, amid all the hubbub both men found time for reflection and for thanks. The day before Thanksgiving Mark posted Jesse Wills's "I Would Give Thanks" on Facebook, an expression of his and Vic's love of family and of the home-based values they shared. "I offer thanks of course for major things," Wills's poem begins, "For daily bread, my home's sequestered hours,/For those who share these, love that ever rings." Reeling from stress long endured, they recognized that the love of family and friends had become a sustaining constant in their lives, all the more important as the possibility of "sequestered hours" slipped through their fingers. "I'm thankful too, for things ephemeral," Wills's poem continued, "For casual scenes remembered from the past . . . a scene at breakfast, Mother laughing, Dad/Intent upon his paper." Jesse Wills's poem, pressing the boundaries of sentimentality, could have come from Mark or Vic, particularly his elegiac salute to loved ones lost to death. "Give thanks for memories; men and women gone," Wills wrote, "Who were once good and kind and winsome in their ways." The last stanza, a look to the future, caught perfectly at Mark and Vic's hopes for the coming year:

And also I give thanks for books not read,
Places not seen, for friends I barely knew,
For work not done, for all the words unsaid,
Hopes unfulfilled in days that are too few.[19]

Most who read Mark's Thanksgiving post knew full well what "hopes unfulfilled" he and Vic were carrying into the new year. When Mark returned to

Facebook on New Year's Eve, he resolved any doubts. "Happy New Year, everyone!" he began. "May 2014 be your best yet!! My wish," he continued, "is to be allowed to legally marry the one I love in 2014."[20]

In the weeks between the beginning of the year and the mid-February hearing scheduled in San Antonio, Mark and Vic strove to find the point of balance between the two elements struggling to become the story of their lives. Facebook posts about their hopes for and concerns about *DeLeon v. Perry* are interspersed with reflections on and photos of their travels together, photos of the dogs they love, curled up on a couch or a chair or on Mark's or Vic's lap, photos of their house in Plano that might have been lifted from a Currier & Ives lithograph—a lit fireplace glowing softly with the promise of warmth, a festive Christmas tree loaded with ornaments that remind them of their lives together, lights shining through windows on a snowy winter's night, beating back the darkness—photos taken from the deck of their vacation home in Gun Barrel City, the lake bathed in the soft light of dawn, or a bird in flight, frozen for all time in the moment before it settles once again to earth.

At times keeping the legal and the personal apart proved impossible. Betsy, the chubby beagle Mark and Vic adopted from the Collin County Humane Society in 2011, the much-loved beagle who snored so loudly that Mark found it impossible to sleep until (for that night only!) she was banished to the far corners of the room, was diagnosed with Stage IV mast cell cancer early in 2014. When Andrew Dial, the veterinary oncologist who treated and ultimately stopped Betsy's cancer discovered that Mark and Vic were one of the couples suing for the right to marry in *DeLeon v. Perry*, he sent a letter of appreciation. "Thank you," he began, "for taking a stand for what you believe, and we know, is right. We deeply admire your passion and your strength." Like Vic, he was a veteran. Unlike Vic, he was found out and his military career ended abruptly when in 2006 he refused to lie about how he lived his personal life. "I can't tell you enough," he wrote to Mark and Vic, "how I felt for the two of you, putting your lives, careers, potentially all on the line for what you know is right."[21]

Just how much they were putting on the line was still very much on their minds, perhaps more so than ever as the February 12 court date for

DeLeon v. Perry drew closer. Chris Kelly's feature in the February issue of *Texas Monthly* appeared on the newsstands on January 22, the first in a new round of stories published in the weeks just before the hearing that thrust Mark and Vic more than ever into the public eye. An unsmiling photo of Ted Cruz dominated the cover, an irony that amused and horrified both men and many of their friends, but Chris Kelly's story about "the men who want to marry" was set FOB, magazine slang for "front of the book," the placement most likely to attract readers.

For the half-page photo that dominates the first page the men had donned formal wear, black-tie tuxedos that made them look as though they had just stepped away from a dinner scene in *Downton Abbey*. Mark is seated with two dogs snuggled on his lap, a third curled up beside him. Vic sits behind him on the arm of the couch, his chin resting on the top of Mark's head, his arms encircling the man he loves. Behind Vic are shelves of matched-set books, their spines embossed in gold, and rows of pictures of their life together. But for the gender of the subjects everything about the photograph suggests a steady, conservative world where change comes slowly if at all, an idea Chris Kelly toyed with in his text. "They may not look like rabble-rousers," he wrote, "but these men are engaged in a dramatic, possibly revolutionary act, suing the State of Texas for the right to marry each other."[22]

Though the dramatic, low-key lighting the photographer employed for the illustration cast shadows Mark didn't like—"Who is that old man?" he quipped to a friend—he and Vic liked everything about the article except for the added exposure it brought. The same issues—Mark's comic hyper-sensitivity about his age and the potential dangers of publicity—resurfaced a few days later when the *Dallas Morning News* previewed *DeLeon v. Perry* for its readers. After acknowledging the danger—"Even in 2014, when a Super Bowl Coca-Cola ad features a gay family, there's a certain risk to being the plaintiff or law firm filing such a suit"—the reporter cited Mark's reflection on filing the lawsuit. " 'It's not done happily,' said Mark Phariss, 58, of Plano. 'It's far more publicity and being out there than I'd ever wanted.' "

Waking early on a Saturday morning, Vic sleeping contentedly by his side, Mark rolled over to go back to sleep when he remembered the story was due to appear. Still abed, reading on his iPad, he shuddered when he came to his age. "No!" he screeched. Though not at first quite sure what he had heard, Vic sensed the alarm in Mark's voice and bolted upright. "What's the matter? he asked, to which Mark replied, "*The Dallas Morning News* wrote that I'm 58! I'm only 54!" Vic looked at him quizzically, rolled his eyes, and went back to sleep. "I'm going to sue," Mark muttered jokingly as Vic began to snore again.

Though both men laugh when one of them tells the story, they realized even as Vic settled once again into sleep how much on edge they were. Looking at reader comments later that morning drove home once again the dangers they faced. Most were positive, but they couldn't drive the hateful taunts from their minds. "Plano residents should drive these two degenerates to the Texas border," one bigot wrote. The worst threatened physical harm. "Heck, this is Texas—there could be *personal* costs," one reader intimated, encouraging the violence he seemed to condemn; "I just hope some wingnut doesn't take a shot at them."[23]

As the day wore on, the men talked about the ever-increasing need to be cautious, even about adding weapons to the shotgun already safely tucked away, but near at hand. The nightmares from which Mark suffered when the Complaint was first filed had already returned, dreams now of a shadowy figure breaking into the house intent on murdering him and Vic. Napping the afternoon after the *Dallas Morning News* article appeared, he woke to the sound of the doorbell ringing and Vic's steps moving toward the front of the house. "Check who it is before you open the door!" he shouted. Vic checked—and then opened the door to a smiling Girl Scout delivering the cookies they had ordered. Face to face with innocence, they gave way yet again to the nervous laughter of those marked by too much experience.

* * *

"It's clear that the wind is at our backs," Mark had told the *Dallas Morning News*. "Not just in Texas, but nationally."[24] He was speaking, of course, of momentum in the marriage equality movement, but on the drive from Plano to San Antonio for the February 12 hearing in Judge Orlando Garcia's court, Mark and Vic could feel the wind from the north blowing gently at their backs, literally as well as metaphorically. Despite the ever-present construction on I-35, despite the inevitable congestion, for the moment, all seemed well as they rolled by the seemingly endless succession of small towns and farms in their winter-brown colors, and looped around Austin. Over the years they had grown accustomed to the five-hour drive, but the desire to be in San Antonio, to get the hearing under way made the trip feel longer than usual. Their primary concern of recent days, security, had been allayed. Neel Lane had checked with officials at the court and discovered, reassuringly, that extra federal marshals would be on duty to insure the safety of all involved. They were in a good place—and headed, they felt, for a better one.

Talking quietly as miles slipped by, Mark and Vic thought of friends and family. Most had been supportive, but not all. And the failure of a few to understand had been more painful by far than they had anticipated. For the second time, perhaps the third, they mulled over a text Mark had received from Paul Lee, an old friend he had not seen in a year. "Just saw your picture in the *Dallas Morning News,*" the friend wrote. "#1 You're famous. #2 I didn't know you were gay. #3 You never mentioned your partner. #4 Congrats. #5 I think I'm still a little shocked I didn't know. I think you're my only gay friend, but I'm not sure."[25] For Mark and Vic the friend's sudden confusion was familiar. The man had worked with Mark for almost seven years, liked and respected him, never suspected he was gay and even felt a bit sorry that he embarked—or so Paul thought— on all those exotic trips alone.

Did he have other gay friends, still closeted? Probably, they thought. Most people do. Mark's friend and thousands like him were, in fact, the reason they were headed for a courtroom in San Antonio, the reason Mark had decided to come out fully—to "shock" the world, to demonstrate that gay men and women are no different, that they are as likely to lead happy, productive lives as their heterosexual friends. Prompted by the text, Mark had picked up the phone to reconnect. What he discovered about his deeply religious friend didn't surprise or faze him. Though he was delighted that Mark was happy, glad that Mark had found someone with whom to share his life, he didn't support gay marriage. "I could have gotten angry about that," Mark wrote in his journal, "but it would have done no good. And I think over time he'll come around."[26] It was the same position Mark had taken so often before—with his twin sister, for example, and with Greg Abbott, his erstwhile friend from their days at Vanderbilt Law School who had been elected Attorney General of Texas and was even now dispatching lawyers to argue in the Federal Court for the Western District of Texas against the plea for equality at the heart of *DeLeon v. Perry.*

In San Antonio there was much to be done the night before the hearing, a purposefully full schedule intended to keep them from fretting about the possibilities of the next day: two television interviews filmed in front of an historic American flag at the home of Curtis Johnson, a meet-and-greet fundraiser with Judge Nelson Wolf, a late dinner with Frank Stenger-Castro at EZ's Brick Oven and Grill, a comfortable place Mark and Vic frequented in their early years as a couple. To keep the tension at bay, Mark and Vic had turned throughout the day to humor. In an interview with MSNBC on the trip to San Antonio, Mark had quipped, "I'm an Oklahoma football fan, and I think more Texans would have a problem with that than with my being gay." Introducing Mark and Vic to the thirty-or-so supporters who had gathered for the evening, Judge Wolf mentioned Mark's profession. "Judge Wolf," Mark cracked when asked to speak, "I don't have a problem with people knowing I'm gay, but you've just told people I'm a lawyer. I do try to keep that a secret."

"Same-sex marriage is an issue whose time has come," Pam Massey, a paralegal who worked with Mark at Safety-Kleen, had written the day before the men left Plano. "It's high time Texas stepped into the 21st century. Of course," she added," with its present leadership it will be more of a monumental leap out of the Stone Age." Waking at Frank's house the next morning, Mark and Vic knew that Texas would leap from the Stone Age only after they stepped into the John H. Wood, Jr. Federal Courthouse, the space-age drum at the center of the Federal Complex in downtown San Antonio. Built originally as the Confluence Theatre for HemisFair '68, reconfigured in 1979 as a courthouse and named to honor the first federal judge assassinated in the twentieth century, the building would, they knew, see more drama today.

Arriving downtown, Mark and Vic had no sooner stepped from Frank's car than a reporter from Fox News approached them for an interview. Crossing the street, heading up the walk to the courthouse, one sound rang in their ears—click, click, click, click, click, click. Overnight temperatures had dropped into the mid-thirties and had risen only a few degrees when the photographers zeroed in on Mark and Vic making their way up the hill. Over the dark suit he had chosen for the day Mark wore an overcoat, open and flapping in the slight breeze. Vic, his dark suit a match for Mark's, had decided to brave the cold without a coat, but he had worn earmuffs. Conscious of the images likely to appear on the news, Mark asked Vic to remove his earmuffs.

"No," Vic replied. "It's cold!"

"Take them off!" Mark repeated, laughing. "They'll be in the photographs."

"I don't care. It is really cold." And that ended it.

News photographs from that morning show Mark and Vic laughing and joking as they make their way into court, seemingly unconcerned at the start of a tense day. Few knew they were laughing over earmuffs, and why they were laughing didn't matter to them. They were together, heading into court, and enjoying each other's company. That was enough. That the photographers flocked to the windows and continued snapping pictures as the men made their way through security—no photographs are allowed inside as the plaintiffs discovered when they posed in the travertine-paneled lobby for a friend—seemed less amusing, yet another reminder of the extent to which they lived now in the public eye. "Inside," Mark would remember two years later, "we were all nerves."[27]

As the hour approached, Mark and Vic joined Cleo and Nicole in the front row of Judge Garcia's courtroom, just behind the barrier that separates officers of the court from the public. Two women sitting behind them produced copies of Akin Gump's Motion for a Preliminary Injunction and asked the plaintiffs and lawyers to autograph them. And then, seven months after the plaintiffs' first tentative thoughts of suing Texas for the right to marry, the hearing that had once seemed so far off began. Judge Orlando Garcia took his seat and announced the start of proceedings in "Cause Number 13 Civil 982. DeLeon, Dimetman, Holmes, Phariss v. the Honorable Rick Perry, Governor of Texas. The Honorable Greg Abbott, Attorney General of Texas. The Honorable Gerard Rickhoff, County Clerk for the

County of Bexar and David Lakey, the Honorable David Lakey, Commissioner of the Texas Department of State Health Services."[28]

* * *

In his opening statement Judge Garcia made it clear that he wanted to hear the best arguments each side could muster. Take whatever time you need, he counseled the attorneys; time should not be a factor. Barry Chasnoff, arguing for the plaintiffs, opened with an emotional appeal. Marriage law in Texas, he contended, "helps to perpetuate the myth of the impropriety of homosexual love." In a strongly worded attack he argued that denying same-sex couples the right to marry "is abhorrent . . . and a violation of the Constitution . . . It places an unfair financial and emotional burden on all homosexuals and forces these plaintiffs to live their lives with a stigma that they do not deserve." When Chasnoff began to speak of the burden placed on Cleo and Nicole by the need to adopt each other's biological child, Judge Garcia interrupted to ask for additional information. Is the adoption problem, he asked, parallel to the problem in the Ohio case in which the state official creating a death certificate was prohibited from listing the man's spouse? Well prepared, when Chasnoff indicated that same-sex marriage was allowed now in seventeen states, Judge Garcia corrected him. "Seventeen states and the District of Columbia." Minutes later, another question from the bench—"Is the right to marry and the right to marriage recognition the same right or are those two different rights?"—allowed Barry Chasnoff to argue against the relevance of a Utah case in which the judge had addressed only one half of the question before the Court.[29]

Judge Garcia's questions and interjections in the opening minutes of the hearing would continue until the last word was spoken. As he listened to lawyers for the plaintiffs and the State, the Judge shaped and guided the discussion. "He was exploring areas in which he was interested," Matt Pepping, one of the Akin Gump lawyers present that day suggested later. "More important, perhaps, he was educating the audience in the courtroom on a topic he knew was important for Texas and Texans—and he did an exceptionally good job."[30]

A significant portion of Chasnoff's argument was necessarily devoted to laying the legal groundwork for the plaintiffs' argument. He talked the Court carefully through the four-factor test for a preliminary injunction and the four factors to be considered in determining whether to apply heightened scrutiny. But before he turned to legal technicalities, he introduced a ringing quotation from Justice Hugo Black. "Under our constitutional system, courts stand against any winds that blow as havens of refuge for those who might otherwise suffer because they are helpless, weak, outnumbered, or because they are non-conforming victims of prejudice and public excitement." The case before the Court today, he contended, offered a clear opportunity to secure the constitutional rights the plaintiffs in *DeLeon v. Perry* had been denied, to offer shelter from the storm.[31]

Anticipating that Texas would propose that *DeLeon v. Perry* be decided using the most deferential level of scrutiny, the rational basis test, the legal team at Akin Gump had identified the three most likely arguments for the State's constitutional ban on same-sex marriage: the weight of tradition, the desire to encourage rational procreation, and the need to provide a stable environment for children. Working methodically to rebut each argument, Barry Chasnoff had finished with the argument from tradition and was moving to "rational procreation" when Judge Garcia broke in. "Let's go back to tradition," he insisted. Would it not be better, the judge asked, to free gays and lesbians to marry by means of a constitutional amendment— the same means our country once employed to free African Americans from slavery? When Chasnoff argued that a law's constitutionality is not subject to the will of the voter, Judge Garcia probed further. "In other words, as has been argued and stated by the Supreme Court, I believe in *West Virginia v. Barnette*, a fundamental right or a constitutional right is not subject to the outcome of an election." Moments later, the judge suggested an additional citation, "the District of Utah case."[32]

Rounding the corner and heading down the home stretch in his presentation, Chasnoff personalized his arguments by referencing his own marriage. "The suggestion that same-sex marriage will undermine heterosexual marriage and procreation [is]," he asserted, "absurd." Turning with a smile to his wife who was sitting in the courtroom, he continued. "I've been married for 43 years to my lovely wife . . . I can assure the Court that if Vic and Mark are married, I'm not going to rush to a divorce lawyer"—a clever and effective way of suggesting that love is love, marriage is marriage, that all people, regardless of their sexual orientation, are equal and deserve equal protection under the law.[33]

As Akin Gump's opening argument drew to a close, Chasnoff argued against the precedential value of *Baker v. Nelson*—the marriage case dismissed by the Supreme Court in 1971 "for want of a substantial federal question"—and introduced a new problem. "The second argument I suspect you will hear from the state is that *Windsor* affirmed the State's right to define marriage," he began. "But if you read the whole sentence or the several sentences where they say that, they say: But only to the extent that a definition given by the State is constitutionally permitted." By way of an ending, Chasnoff brought to the Court's attention a series of civil rights cases that dealt with education and interracial marriage, reminding Judge Garcia and all present one more time that "The Courts are a bastion for citizens who suffer any violation of their civil rights."[34]

Mark and Vic found it difficult to listen as Michael Murphy, the Assistant Solicitor General for Texas, argued the State's case. Listening to Barry Chasnoff talk about the personal histories of the plaintiffs, Mark had teared up. Their lives were on the line, and listening as the most intimate details of their lives were put on public display was no easy thing. And yet, as he brushed the tears away, he worried about who might be watching. He had always been taught not to cry, let alone not to cry in public. As Murphy began to speak, tears turned quickly to anger. Ignoring all that had been said about the legal relationship between constitutional rights and the will of the voters, Murphy began with a populist rhetorical flourish. "This country is engaged in a robust democratic and social debate about the merits of same-sex marriage," he insisted. "Plaintiffs in this case ask this Court at the preliminary injunction stage to remove this inherently political issue and this divisive issue from the democratic process and make it a constitutional question." The Court, he argued, should not do that.[35]

If Mark and Vic found Murphy's opening difficult, their difficulties only increased as he continued. "What plaintiffs don't recognize," he contended, "is that factual support is irrelevant and the State is not required to supply any evidentiary basis for the rational basis of State law." That, Mark thought, legal quibbles aside, is a silly position to take, understandable only when one realizes that the State really lacked any justification beyond anti-gay *animus* and the conservative religious beliefs driving the opposition. He and Vic listened in pain as Murphy reiterated his point—"Texas marriage law must be upheld if there's *any* theoretical rational justification for the law." When the Assistant Solicitor General admitted that DOMA was struck down "because [the Court] concluded the only reason for the law was *animus* against gay men and lesbians," and moments later asserted that claims of *animus* in Texas were "baseless," both men felt their blood begin to boil. When Murphy contended that the plaintiffs had "failed to show an irreparable harm," Mark and Vic had trouble remaining in their seats.[36]

The Assistant Solicitor General ended as he had begun—with a rhetorical flourish Mark and Vic saw as calculated to draw attention from substantive problems in the State's argument. Tradition: "Plaintiffs have not clearly shown," he contended, "that temporarily rewriting 150 years of Texas law would serve the public interest." Populism and the democratic process: "The public interest is well established—is not served when democratically enacted law is suspended because democratically enacted law is itself a declaration of public interest."[37]

Their ordeal almost over, Mark and Vic heaved a sigh of relief when Neel Lane rose to deliver Akin Gump's responsive argument. His message to the Court was simple: enforce the Constitution of the United States. Tradition? The State had introduced a definition of marriage from a dictionary published in 1700, Lane pointed out, a time when many Americans owned slaves, when theft was punishable by death, drawing and quartering were public spectacles, and women could not vote. Democratic process? The American people, including the citizens of Texas, had voted on protections for minorities when they ratified the Fourteenth Amendment. As a result, "A citizen in the United States does not have to go to the ballot box to secure equal protection of the laws."[38]

Hoping to avoid or at least postpone an adverse decision, the State had dragged the summary dismissal of *Baker v. Nelson* once again before the Court. Lane cited case after case—*Romer v. Evans, Lawrence v. Texas, United States v. Windsor* to demonstrate how thoroughly the doctrinal landscape had changed since 1972. "Summary dismissals are not binding," he told the Court, "if doctrinal developments indicate that the Supreme Court would no longer brand the question as unsubstantial." The State's contention that "marriage to a person of the same sex is wholly different in character from a marriage to a person of the opposite sex" seemed almost to anger Neel Lane. "Same-sex and opposite-sex marriage are simply," he argued, "the manifestations of one right applied to people with different sexual identities."[39]

Perhaps the most entertaining, the most convincing thrusts in Lane's argument were delivered in folksy analogies that encouraged everyone present to cut through the convoluted language the State had conjured up to obscure simple truths. Texas had contended that gays and lesbians had the same marriage rights as anyone else; they were free to marry a person of the opposite sex. "Saying someone is free in this context," he maintained, "is of course a little perverse. It's like holding someone's head under water and saying you're free to breathe." Responding to the State's rational basis arguments on tradition, rational procreation, and the rearing of children, Lane struck out in a similar way. "It's as if the State in making these arguments has simply picked a common characteristic of married couples and tried to use it as their rational basis for prohibiting same-sex marriage," he suggested. The punch line the second time around made the absurdity of the State's position evident. "We could just as well say," Lane told the Court, "the State has a vital interest in promoting marriage because it has an interest in promoting joint checking accounts."[40]

After Neel Lane put the State's best arguments in perspective and the hearing concluded, Mark and Vic found themselves wreathed in smiles for the first time since the proceedings had begun. Still, Mark had a bit of business he wanted to take up with Michael Murphy. For the first time in decades, the past year he had received no Christmas card from Greg Abbott. Worried that filing the lawsuit had soured their friendship, he approached Michael Murphy, introduced himself, and asked him to convey his greetings to the attorney general. Mark wanted his old friend to know that while the State's position was deeply hurtful to him and so many others, he assumed that the governor didn't intend his opposition personally and didn't take it that way. As Mark was finishing his conversation with Murphy, Gerry Rickhoff, the clerk of Bexar County whose office had refused to issue him and Vic a marriage license in October 2013, approached him to apologize. "I have no problem with same-sex marriage," Rickhoff told him, "but I had to behave in accordance with the laws of Texas."[41] Mark assured Rickhoff that he knew of his support for marriage equality and bore him no ill-will.

At the press conference that followed, speaking carefully into a bank of microphones, Mark called on the attorney general to drop the appeal. He spoke honestly of his frustration, his and Vic's irritation with the State's oft-repeated argument that federal judges should not override decisions made at the state level by voters and legislators. In 1868 voters ratified the Fourteenth Amendment, he pointed out, insuring that all citizens would receive equal protection under the laws. "The U. S. Constitution trumps anything that Texas does," he told a reporter for the *Dallas Morning News*.[42] After a bite to eat with Nicole and Cleo and the legal team from Akin Gump at the appropriately named Liberty Bar, perhaps a half-conscious attempt to influence the course of *DeLeon v. Perry*, he and Vic headed to Plano.

* * *

If the trip to San Antonio was emotionally difficult, the return to Plano and the indefinite wait for Judge Garcia's decision was more difficult still. Mark and Vic didn't for a minute doubt that what could be done had been done. But would anything, they wondered, be enough to turn the tide in Texas? Granted, a rapid-fire series of victories since the start of the year made the "big picture" comforting. In January Judge Terrence C. Kern of the United States District Court for the Northern District of Oklahoma declared Question 711, which banned both the recognition and performance of same-sex marriage, unconstitutional; later that month, Mark Herring, the Attorney General of Virginia, refused to defend his state's ban in court.

Two days before oral arguments in *DeLeon v. Perry*, Catherine Cortez Masto, the Attorney General of Nevada, having concluded that in the rapidly changing legal landscape "arguments [against same-sex marriage] grounded upon equal protection and due process are no longer sustainable," withdrew her brief opposing same-sex marriage; oral arguments in San Antonio had no sooner come to an end than Judge John G. Hayburn II of the United States District Court for the Western District of Kentucky struck down statutory and constitutional prohibitions against same-sex marriage in Kentucky. And in the week before Judge Garcia issued his decision, Ellen Rosenblum, the Attorney General of Oregon, admitted that the state's ban against same-sex marriage "cannot withstand a federal constitutional challenge under any standard of review" and the United States District Court for the Northern District of Illinois held that the state's same-sex marriage ban violated the Equal Protection Clause. Three times the lawyers at Akin Gump filed Notices of Recent Authority with the court, legal cautions designed to insure that Judge Garcia took into consideration the "changing legal landscape" to which Attorney General Masto had deferred.

On the morning of oral arguments in *DeLeon v. Perry*, *The San Antonio Express News* had published an op-ed piece by Julian Castro, then mayor of San Antonio, and Evan Wolfson, founder and president of Freedom to Marry. Arguing that Texas's ban on same-sex marriage was "a blot on the state Constitution that is both unconstitutional on equal protection grounds and morally wrong," they pointed to growing support for marriage in Texas, to ever increasing corporate support, to the hollowness of fear-mongering arguments against the freedom to marry that had not come true. Citing the *Texas Tribune's* observation that while the rest of the country seemed to be sprinting toward the freedom to marry, "Texas appears to have been moseying along in the same direction," they concluded that as a result of the suit filed by Mark and Vic, Cleo and Nicole, "Moseying may be turning into a dash here soon."[43] Though they recognized marriage as a consummation devoutly to be wished, longed for the day they could share their love before the world, Mark and Vic hardly dared to hope for a favorable decision.

For the two weeks before Judge Garcia ruled, Mark and Vic rode the emotional roller-coaster they had come to know all too well, an exhausting thrill-ride that seemed to stop only long enough to allow time for yet another interview. Three days after the hearing they returned to San Antonio for a live interview with KENS 5 where Mark grew irritated when a less than sensitive interviewer asked if he and Vic had pursued their lawsuit only for financial reasons, a suggestion both men found insulting. Thinking that the decision would come quickly, hoping to bring plaintiffs and lawyers together for a press conference in San Antonio soon after it was announced, Neel Lane contacted the court the day after Presidents' Day to ask for advance notice. What he learned wound Mark and Vic—if possible—into a tighter-than-ever emotional coil. Judge Garcia, the clerk told Neel, would rule before the end of the week. But the clerk followed his information with what seemed a revealing question. Why did the plaintiffs need to know in advance? They had, after all, agreed to a stay and the decision would not immediately bring same-sex marriage to Texas. Though afraid to read too much into the clerk's slip, afraid that even the tiniest, most private celebration would jinx their chances, Mark and Vic relaxed enough to let their spirits soar—only to have them plunge again at the end of the week when a second phone call to the court revealed the decision had been postponed.

Fortunately, the plaintiffs and their no less anxious lawyers would not have to wait much longer. Just before the close of business on Tuesday, February 25—Mark had only minutes earlier finished the paperwork for a multi-million-dollar deal set to close the next day; Vic was nearing the end of a long day treating patients at the University of North Texas Health Sciences Center—Neel Lane sent the e-mail for which everyone had been waiting: "I have just received word that the decision will be released tomorrow (Wednesday). Please do not share this information with anyone."[44] Hours that had passed so slowly since the hearing began to fly by. Sprint home to pack, carve out a minute to call the dog sitter, dash to the airport for two bites of barbecue and the last flight to San Antonio, taxi in the dark and cold to the Marriott Rivercenter—everything governed by the need for secrecy. They turned away the dog sitter's questions about where they were going; told her only that they were all right. They chose a hotel over a friend's house to lessen the chance of a leak. Too tired even to look from their eighth story window at the view of San Antonio by night, they slipped into a fitful sleep.

Thinking the decision would come as soon as the court opened, Mark and Vic rose at six, showered, shaved, and ate a hasty, room-service breakfast. By eight o'clock they were dressed and ready to head out the door. And then it began—the hours of waiting, tense, nail-biting waiting where the heart beats too quickly, the breath comes in shallow gulps. For hours they paced the floor of their hotel room, checked their screens for e-mails, listened for the phone that refused to ring. At eleven Mark broke the tedium by checking-in with the dog sitter. Telling her where they were, swearing her to secrecy, he urged her to keep the doors locked, the dogs inside, the security system on. Then, at 12:37 p.m., an e-mail from Barry Chasnoff. "I just got a call from the NYT reporter on this," he wrote, "seeking to confirm what he had heard: Judge Garcia is issuing the ruling at 1:00 o'clock today; he granted our motion; he issued a stay."[45] Was the reporter fishing? Did she have a reliable source inside the court? For another half hour they lived in hope. Until at last Neel Lane sent the shortest, most meaningful text possible under the circumstances: "We Won!"

More fleet of finger, Nicole managed the first response—"Yay yay yay yay!!!"—the usual commas giving way to a surfeit of exclamation points. Mark added a "Yay" of his own and shouted the news to Vic. And then, bedlam. "We won," they shouted over and over, echoing the simple eloquence of Neel's text, roaring so loudly that they feared the receptionist eight floors below would hear. They hugged, they cried, each told the other, over and over, how much he loved him. Only later would Vic settle down enough to make sense of all he felt in the moment of that first victory in court. "It was," he said in retrospect, "a kind of validation of myself as a person, of my love for Mark as a real thing, a sign that we weren't a sideshow that could be ignored at will. Suddenly, we were real people and our lives and emotions were no less real than those of everyone around us."[46] Wanting to share the joy, they texted the news to friends and family; his fingers still shaking, Mark sent the news into the world via Facebook:

We—Vic Holmes, Cleopatra DeLeon, Nicole Dimetman, and I—won. Judge Orlando Garcia found Texas' ban unconstitutional and granted our motion for a preliminary injunction. As expected, he stayed his injunction pending the state's appeal. Thanks to our lawyers at Akin Gump!!!

An hour later, heading out the door for a hastily arranged press conference at the nearby Westin on the Riverwalk—where Cleo and Nicole, happy beyond words, would jump into Neel Lane's arms—they were still fielding calls and texts from reporters in Dallas, anxious to arrange interviews when the men returned to Love Field in the evening.

Flying again through the dark, back now to Dallas, Mark and Vic used their few minutes in the air to read Judge Garcia's decision and to scan the hundreds of e-mails, texts, and Facebook comments that had poured in throughout the day. They were pleased to see that Judge Garcia had recognized and condemned the "far-reaching legal and social consequences" of Section 32, beginning with "the pain of humiliation, stigma, and emotional distress" it inflicted on the LGBT community and continuing with an extensive list of economic penalties, harms that together qualified as "state sanctioned discrimination." They were pleased as well to read the judge's conclusion that the State's arguments regarding childbearing, procreation, and tradition had done no more than to echo "the same rationale that has been uniformly rejected by district courts in the most recent same-sex marriage cases." The State had failed, he concluded, to demonstrate "some rational relationship between Section 32 and a legitimate governmental purpose"; their defense failed even the most cursory rational basis review. As other jurists had found before him, and others would after, Judge Garcia concluded that "While Texas has the 'unquestioned authority' to regulate and define marriage, the State must nevertheless do so in a way that does not infringe on an individual's constitutional rights." "Equal treatment of all individuals under the law," he reasoned in granting the request for a preliminary injunction, "is not merely an aspiration—it is a constitutional mandate."[47]

Messages from friends were no less gratifying. Among the first was a message from Matt Pepping, an attorney at Akin Gump who had logged hundreds of hours on *DeLeon v. Perry*. "Thank you," he wrote. "You guys took significant personal risks and subjected yourselves to attention you did not seek. You did a great thing and should be proud."[48] Elizabeth Birch, an old friend and the former Executive Director of the Human Rights Campaign, needed only two words to convey her sentiments: "My heroes!" Chad Griffin, the current president of the Human Rights Campaign, needed just a few more: "Huge!!! Thank you for leading."[49] Evan Wolfson's press release, they discovered, summed up perfectly their own feelings about the way forward:

> Today the 6th federal judge in a row has ruled—in Texas—that there is simply no legitimate justification for denying marriage to loving gay and lesbian couples. The court's holding is solid and serious, and follows the language and logic of the Supreme Court's marriage ruling last year and the Constitution's clear command. With 47 marriage cases in 25 states now moving forward, and the possibility that a freedom to marry case will again reach the Supreme Court as soon as 2015, we must continue the conversations and progress—Texan to Texan, American to American—that show that all of America is ready for the freedom to marry.

The same themes, the same metaphors appeared repeatedly: Mark and Vic and Cleo and Nicole had gone into battle, not for themselves alone but for the entire LGBT community; they had shown great courage in the face of danger; they deserved thanks beyond what words could express. "This effort obviously required incredible guts," Andy Caine, an attorney with whom Mark had worked in the past, wrote from Los Angeles, adding for good measure, "great article about you today in the *LA Times*."[50] Lauren Mutti, a friend with whom Mark worked on the board of The Family Place, was astounded at the great leap forward for gays and lesbians. "Hard to believe that only 10 years ago Texas passed that amendment," she wrote; "I admire your willingness to be the brave ones to put your name in the lawsuit."[51] Debbie Jo Hauppert, a friend from Mark's Oklahoma childhood, wondered if he remembered days they spent on the playground at Hoover Elementary School talking about changing the world. "I think you're off to a pretty good start," she added. "Tears of joy! Well done my brave friends!"[52]

Glen Maxey, elected in 2001 as the first openly gay member of the Texas legislature, penned a lengthy tribute on Facebook:

> Today I was so honored to stand before an Austin press confer- ence and call out four Texans as heroes. Margaret Meade, the noted

anthropologist, said, "Never doubt that a small group of thoughtful, committed citizens can change the world; indeed, it's the only thing that ever has." Today, four thoughtful, committed Texans did just that. Thank you Mark and Vic![53]

By 7:00 p.m. when they stepped from the plane at Love Field, tired but elated, Mark and Vic were ready to relax—or ready, at least, for the next round of interviews.

Stepping onto the escalator that would take them to the luggage carousels, Mark and Vic spotted the gaggle of reporters and photographers waiting at the bottom.

"Oh, my gosh," one of them muttered. They had expected two or three reporters, perhaps a lonely photographer, maybe even two. But a swarm of ten? Knowing the drill, they walked to the media cluster, greeted the cameras with smiles, put down their coats and books, and began answering questions that for two emotionally exhausted men seemed to go on forever. Passers-by, curious, stopped to stare, to listen, to snap photos of their own. When the last reporter's question had at last been asked and answered, they stooped to pick up their books and coats and set off in search of their luggage, surprised that several camera crews continued tracking their movements. But as they moved toward the few suitcases still circling the carrousel, their strange day grew stranger still.

A middle-aged couple and their teenaged son looked at Mark, turned with a question in their eyes to look at each other, turned back to look again at Mark, then turned to look again at each other, more befuddled than ever. Finally, the father spoke.

"Are you," he asked hesitantly, "the Olympian?" Mark laughed.

"No," he replied, still smiling, and pointed to Johnny Quinn, the six foot, 220 pound Texas football player turned bobsledder who had made the news a few days earlier when he battered his way through a stuck bathroom door at the Sochi Olympics. Vic, laughing, thought the couple's mistake a wonderfully comic end to a long day.

"What?" Mark joked as he turned to Vic. "I couldn't be an Olympian?" As they left the terminal, camera crews still tracking their every step,

Mark realized that, though Johnny Quinn was younger and more athletic, they did in fact have something in common. Both had, each in his own way, broken down doors, overcome obstacles that stood between where they were and where they wanted to be. Tired, happier than they had been since the lawsuit began, the men finally gave way to the hunger they had carried from San Antonio. Neither had found time for so much as a bite since their slim breakfast at the hotel. Their quest for justice over, at least until the same arguments played out again in a court of appeals, they set off on a new quest, this time to The Corner Bakery near their home in Plano. What they wanted most was an Olympic-sized meal.

* * *

Hoping to rebound from their stinging loss in Judge Garcia's District Court, attorneys for Texas appealed *DeLeon v. Perry* to the Fifth Circuit Court the next day. Matt Pepping's e-mail informing the plaintiffs raised everyone's hopes for quick action. "Assuming there are no extensions and the record is filed in relatively expeditious fashion," he told the plaintiffs, "we expect the State's brief to be filed around the end of May."[54] For the moment at least there was more than enough to keep Mark and Vic busy. Back at work the next morning, a teaching day at the University of North Texas Health Science Center, Vic realized that word of his good news had spread quickly. Recognizing the courage he had shown, how much he had risked to lead a reluctant Texas into a brighter future, his students rose when he entered the classroom, greeting him with a standing ovation. Mark's experience at Expert Global Solutions was no less encouraging. All day co-workers dropped by his office, closed the door, and thanked him for what he had done. I have a gay child one offered, others had gay friends, still another admitted to being gay. Susan Kay, a much-loved, much-respected professor from Mark's days at Vanderbilt Law, sent a warm note. "Just wanted you to know," she began, "how proud I was to see your name as one of the plaintiffs in the Texas marriage equality case. It takes a huge amount of grit, determination and especially courage to serve as a named plaintiff, and I am truly humbled to know you."[55]

Setting up for a lunch-time interview the next day, Shelly Kofler of KERA warned Mark that she was going to ask about his friendship with Greg Abbott. As the story behind *DeLeon v. Perry* began to draw more and more national attention, Mark had carefully avoided any mention of his connection with the Attorney General, now a candidate for governor. The focus, he thought, should be on his and Vic's relationship, not the personalities contesting the issues. Molly Hennessy-Fiske of the *Los Angeles Times* had talked with Mark about his friendship with Abbott almost two weeks earlier, but at Mark's request agreed to keep what she learned off-the-record. Realizing that there was no longer any way of holding the story back, Mark agreed to talk with Kofler—and out of fairness green-lighted other stories. But he made it clear that he would speak no evil of the man with whom he had once been close.

In a matter of hours accounts of the long-standing friendship between the men who stood now on opposite sides of the marriage equality issue, a social and political continental divide that had risen to separate them, appeared on KERA, in the *Los Angeles Times*, the *Huffington Post*, and elsewhere. They had first met in the early 1980s as classmates at Vanderbilt University Law School where Abbott was a year ahead of Mark. Both had grown up in conservative territory—Mark in Lawton, Oklahoma, Abbott barely fifty miles away in Wichita Falls, Texas—but by his law school days Mark had become an outspoken liberal. "Greg and I, frequently with his wife, would have dinner," Mark told Kofer, "and would talk as law students are inclined to do, talk law and politics." They didn't agree on much, but political differences never seemed to affect their friendship.[56] Even Abbott's ambition to be governor of Texas, confided to Mark while they were still students, didn't alter their friendship despite Mark's awareness of his friend's conservative views.

After law school—always cautious, Mark was still very much in the closet—they continued to be friends. When a falling tree limb sent Abbott to a Houston hospital, Mark, clerking that summer in Tulsa after his second year of law school, flew to his bedside to offer what comfort he could. He brought books, consolation, and encouragement, glad he had made the trip since his friend had just moved to a new town and had met few people. Most of the time, Mark remembers, the only ones in the room were Abbott's wife, Cecilia, his mother, and himself, with occasional visits from the managing partner at Butter & Binion where Abbott had begun working. Mark also remembers his friend's grit and determination. Lying in bed, knowing he would never walk again, he managed to smile, even to laugh at times, far more accepting, Mark felt, than he would have been. "We remain grateful that Mark visited the hospital during the trying time after my injury," Abbott told KERA, commenting on the early days of his friendship with Mark in a prepared statement.[57] Out of the hospital, wheelchair bound but back at work, he showed how grateful he was. When Mark graduated from law school, he received a job offer from Abbott's firm.

Despite their political differences, when Abbott ran for a judgeship, his initial foray into Texas politics, Mark was full of good will. He contributed to the campaign, picked his old friend up at the San Antonio airport and drove him to a campaign stop, introduced him to other lawyers at his firm, Matthews & Branscomb, and encouraged them to donate to his campaign, even attended a fundraiser. Though they had not spoken in the decade before the lawsuit was filed, they kept in touch as so many old friends do with annual Christmas cards—a tradition Abbott dropped after *DeLeon v. Perry* was filed but which Mark continued. "He was a very good friend then and I consider him a very good friend now," Mark told Kofler. "I disagree with his decision in this lawsuit. I disagree with his decision to pursue the appeal. And I disagree with his take on what the status of the law is. But I don't take it personally."[58] When the story of Mark's long enduring friendship with Greg Abbott broke at last, it was a far cry from the story many were expecting. Even-tempered almost to a fault, Mark wanted to leave the door open, imagining in his mind's eye the day when he would sit once again over dinner to talk of law and politics with his old friend, Vic and Cecilia joining in the conversation.

* * *

At the end of the week, anxious to get away, Mark and Vic loaded the beagles into the car and headed to their house on Cedar Creek Lake for a little much-needed downtime—only to discover that getting away was no longer possible. They had no sooner unpacked the car in Gun Barrel City than two of the neighbors—parents of a gay daughter—stopped by to offer thanks and congratulations. Other couples appeared in short order, a virtual flash mob in Vic's eyes. Dinner that night at the home of Jeff Thomas and Richard Garcia brought more of the same, even from straight Republicans whose sympathy for marriage equality surprised them—congratulations on the win in Judge Garcia's court, compliments on the interview with KERA, good wishes for the eventual hearing before the Fifth Circuit. Invited by other neighbors to a celebratory breakfast at the Huddle House, they were surprised when waitresses they had come to know over the years, thrilled to be serving "celebrities" who had been in the news, greeted them with squeals of delight. "Everyone turned to look," Mark wrote in his journal; "it was embarrassing." Embarrassing, yes, but at the same time he and Vic realized that something fundamental had changed. For the first time being uncomfortable had a paradoxical up-side. The positive attention was, they knew, a sign of how far everyday Texans had come in accepting marriage equality.

Through March and April and into May, Mark and Vic, Cleo and Nicole, and the legal team at Akin Gump waited impatiently for the Fifth Circuit to set the briefing schedule for *DeLeon v. Perry*, hoping the court would make good Matt Pepping's prediction that the state's brief would be required "around the end of May." In the interim the men did what they could to stay busy as a means of keeping worry at bay. Their appearance on KLRN's *This Week with Rick Casey* caught the attention of Barbara Nellermoe, a state district judge in San Antonio. "Watching Mark and Vic on KLRN as they explain the most deeply human needs and benefits," she wrote. Turning to address Mark and Vic directly, she added, "you are such an inspiration to all of us, straight or gay."[59] On March 16, 2014, they appeared live on MSNBC's *Melissa Harris-Perry Show*, interviewed by Jonathan Capehart. Setting the context for the interview, Capehart reminded listeners of *Lawrence v. Texas*, the 2003 landmark case that overturned Texas's sodomy law. "That case," he asserted, "changed our nation and now it is again two men in Texas who are challenging the law and hoping to advance rights for gay individuals."[60] The national, Sunday morning spot grouping Mark and Vic with John Lawrence and Tyron Garner— online the segment was titled "The Champions for Justice in Texas"—drew respectful attention even from their teenage great nephews, Austin and Daylin Mcanulla. Days later Adam Polaski of Freedom to Marry talked with them for an article on the website. "We're very optimistic—and we're very hopeful," Mark told Freedom to Marry. "We were happy with Round 1—now we're looking toward Round 2." Challenging Texas, Vic admitted, was "scary and nerve-wracking . . . Now that everything is rolling," he added with just a touch of impatience, "this process can't move fast enough."[61]

Jeanne Rubin, President of the Gay and Lesbian Alliance of North Texas, invited them to appear as "special guests" at a Happy Hour in late March. About the same time, Dan Rafter, Director of Communications for the HRC, flew them to Washington, D. C. to help with the launch of HRC's Marriage Communications War Room. Speaking after a panel of attorneys involved in marriage cases up soon for federal appellate review, Mark and Vic realized that as the only plaintiffs present, they had to speak for more than six-hundred people who had filed lawsuits over the years. Mark thanked the attorneys for their long days and longer nights of careful work. "Success builds upon success," he told them, adding the refrain he repeated at every opportunity—"Everyone deserves credit and no one deserves all the credit."

At the Texas Lyceum conference in Fredericksburg in late April, Mark and Vic were greeted with applause when the crowd learned they were the men who had successfully challenged Texas's ban on same-sex marriage at the district court level. Chuck Smith, Chief Executive Officer of Equality Texas, recruited them as guest speakers for the Capitol Club reception in Dallas in late May. Just over a week later they were back again with Equality Texas, this time in San Antonio as guests of honor at the Spirit of Texas Brunch. Mark and Vic and their co-plaintiffs, Nicole and Cleo, shared the 2014 Anchor Award given annually to "individuals who steadfastly support the goals of Equality Texas through years of dedication that advance the lives of LGBT people." The legal team from Akin Gump was honored with the Vanguard Award given annually to "an exemplary business who has demonstrated a commitment to LGBT equality in the state of Texas through fair employee policy and community advocacy."[62]

But in the busy spring after the win in Judge Garcia's court, no event in which Mark and Vic participated drew more attention than their appearance on *Watch What Happens Live with Andy Cohen* on March 11. Andy Lella, Talent Associate Producer for *Watch What Happens Live* had sent an invitation the day after Judge Garcia's decision. "Andy asked me to reach out to see if you both would be interested in being our bartenders one night," he wrote. "Our staff was moved by your courage to fight against the same-sex marriage ban in Texas and we want to show our support." Though they didn't know much about the show and weren't quite sure what being a "bartender" entailed, they accepted. Vic, who does not drink, joked nervously about the time he bought a book on mixing drinks and tried his hand at it, only to have friends who tried the results throw the book into a fire pit. Mark channeled his nervousness into his usual self-deprecating humor when in the greenroom an attendant told him they were going to do his hair and make-up. "Is lipo-suction also doable?" he asked.

When the show began, the audience reaction to Andy Cohen's introduction made it clear they had nothing to fear. "You know," Cohen began, "we like to have fun with the folks behind the bar." This night, he explained, would be different. "Tonight's guest bartenders," he told the audience, "are also personal heroes of mine . . . a couple who are two of the four plaintiffs who fought Texas' ban on gay marriage and won." Raising his voice in order to be heard over the screaming crowd, he finished up. "They're changing lives—it's Mark and Vic, everybody!" As the camera panned to the right and closed in on Mark and Vic, the audience, still cheering wildly, rose to their feet. More nervous than ever, surprised by the standing ovation, Mark and Vic kissed, some-thing they rarely do in public. Looking just a bit bewildered by the crowd's reac-tion, Mark waved a bit sheepishly. Both men smiled, and within a few seconds Vic began his own tentative wave. Nicole and Cleo, sitting in front row seats, smiled along. Later in the show Andy Cohen would celebrate them as well.

Appearing on *Watch What Happens Live* provided a bit of comic relief in a stressful time, but from the point of view of plaintiffs looking for a speedy end to the harms inflicted by Texas's ban on same-sex marriage the show's name seemed a less than subtle irony. In *DeLeon v. Perry*, they thought, too little was happening. Hoping to make good on Matt Pepping's prediction that the briefing schedule would call for the State's brief by the end of May, Akin Gump filed a motion to expedite the appeal on April 14. But the Fifth Circuit Court of Appeals seemed determined to move at a snail's pace. Not only did the Court fail to issue a briefing order in a timely manner, they waited five agonizingly long weeks before even denying Akin Gump's motion to expedite. On the ninth of May, two-and-a-half months after Judge Garcia had declared Texas's statutory and constitutional bans on same-sex marriage unconstitutional, Judge Chris Piazza struck down similar prohibitions against same-sex marriage in Arkansas—and cited *DeLeon v. Perry* as a precedent. In a flurry of e-mails—Mark and Vic were angry that though their case had become a precedent, the Fifth Circuit insisted on dragging its feet—Neel Lane spoke of "swimming in the stream of justice." To Mark and Vic the swim felt more like a dog-paddle.

Not until May 30, the last day of the month for business, did the Fifth Circuit Court of Appeals issue the much-awaited briefing order that would in Mark and Vic's eyes restart their stalled case: July 9 for the State's brief, August 8 for the plaintiff's reply, August 22 for the State's response. Through the long, hot Texas summer and into the fall, Mark waited to hear about a date for oral arguments. Hoping to move *DeLeon v. Perry* back into the courtroom before the end of 2014, on October 6 Akin Gump asked the Court "to resolve this issue at the earliest possible time," specifically requesting a date for oral argument in November.[63] For once the Court acted expeditiously, granting the motion only three days later—but the November date was not to be. By the end of October, the hearing before the Fifth Circuit Court in New Orleans was tentatively set for the week of January 5, 2015. On November 20, the Court set the exact date for oral arguments in cases from Louisiana, Mississippi, and Texas, January 9.

After months of waiting, agonizing months, plaintiffs and attorneys involved in *DeLeon v. Perry* were thrilled to learn that in less than two months they would be back in court, arguing once again the case for marriage equality for Mark and Vic, Cleo and Nicole, and the 629,000 LGBT Texans whose dignity depended on the outcome. But as Mark and Vic had come to realize early on, never a blue sky without a cloud. Within hours of the announcement, they learned that attorneys for Lambda Legal who were handling the Louisiana case, *Robicheaux v. George*, had filed for Cert before Judgment with the Supreme Court, essentially a request to skip the Fifth Circuit and proceed directly to the Supreme Court. The sudden turn precipitated a good deal of nervous hand-wringing.

Though the legal team at Akin Gump thought it unlikely that Lambda Legal's motion would be granted, they were concerned. In a conference call that afternoon, attorneys and plaintiffs speculated about how the Fifth Circuit would react and about their own best course of action. Would the Court put the January 9 hearing on hold, reluctant to spend time on a case that might go to the Supreme Court whatever their decision? Should they join Louisiana in petitioning for Cert before Judgment? Should they more actively pursue efforts to lift Judge Garcia's stay? Should they ask that the hearing be moved to December? E-mails and phone calls flew back and forth, continuing into the night as Mark and Vic drove to and returned from a Human Rights Campaign fundraiser, repeatedly on and off their phones. Sick of waiting for a hearing before the Fifth Circuit, Mark's neck tightened, his blood pressure rose at the prospect of further delays. Despite the conservative reputation of the Fifth Circuit Court of Appeals, Mark was convinced they would win, convinced by recent precedent that the Supreme Court would not uphold any stay imposed—and that marriage equality would come sooner to Texas. Thirteen months had passed since he and Vic had traveled to San Antonio and been refused a license to marry. Too long for Mark and Vic. Too long for Cleo and Nicole. Too long for more than six-hundred thousand LGBT Texans.

In the end the Supreme Court rejected Louisiana's filing. But it was increasingly clear that the long months of waiting had taken their toll. On the first weekend in November Mark, an accomplished amateur photographer, snapped an artful photo of a snowy white egret against a bluish, out-of-focus background, its wings spread wide to slow its descent, its feet poised to catch the edge of the deck at their house on Cedar Creek Lake. He posted it to Facebook with a short caption: "Another egret at the lake, exhibiting grace and style."[64] To friends who had followed Mark and Vic's struggle with Texas from the beginning, the caption seemed a coded wish for the grace and style that seemed to be slipping from their lives. When Fred Phelps, head of the notoriously anti-gay Westboro Baptist Church, died in March of 2014, Mark, whose ability to tolerate intolerance is famous among his friends, refused to celebrate. "As much as I might want," he told friends, "I refuse to dance on his grave. I am reminded that I am called to do unto others as I would have them do unto me, not to do unto others as they have done unto me."[65]

But by September when at a friend's birthday party he was reminded just how intolerant and unaccepting Texans can be—"a cute, petite, mid-thirties woman, nicely dressed with her blond hair pulled back into a pony-tail" broke off a conversation when she learned Mark and Vic were plaintiffs in Texas's same-sex marriage case—the anger Mark had kept so long under control bubbled to the surface. "She seemed sweet and had a beautiful smile," Mark told his host the next day. The incarnation of Red State Texas—she had previously made it clear to others at the party that she didn't like it when people who didn't look like her visited the neighborhood park and didn't approve of inter-racial marriage—Mark saw in her "a reminder that gays and lesbians may ultimately win the right to marry, but the fight for full equality will continue after we are all long gone."

Though he refused to be brought low by the cold stare of her disapproval, chose instead to focus on "the majority of good people who now believe in equality for the LGBT community," the confrontation rattled Mark in a way that would not have been possible a year earlier, a sign of the long-term stress he and Vic had endured since signing on to *DeLeon v. Perry*.[66] The same quiet anger surfaced again the next day when Greg Abbott, now a candidate for governor, told the press that he opposed same-sex marriage because he has been married for over thirty-three years. "I have many gay and lesbian friends," Mark retorted on Facebook, "who have been in committed relationships for more than 33 years. Why do their relationships deserve less respect and support from the state than your relationship? What happened to the Golden Rule? Please," he asked his old friend in a rhetorical outburst, "remember you're running to be Governor of the entire State of Texas, not just the straight State of Texas."[67]

* * *

For a brief, shining moment after Judge Garcia's decision, Mark and Vic celebrated the coming of new light with Cleo and Nicole, with the legal team from Akin Gump, with gay and lesbian Texans, with straight allies. Unfortunately, their euphoria was short-lived. Frustrated, disheartened, they found themselves relegated to the sidelines as Texas repeatedly applied for extensions to file briefs. For nearly a year, the Fifth Circuit sat on its hands, quashing any hope that their case would settle the question of same-sex marriage in Texas, perhaps even across the United States. As more months of legal maneuvering slipped by, Mark and Vic came, step by care-full step, to realize that *DeLeon v. Perry* had been cast into a legal limbo.

Elsewhere around the country the cause of marriage equality was moving ahead by leaps and bounds. The day after their hearing in San Antonio, Judge Wright Allen of Virginia ruled that his state's statutory and constitutional bans against same-sex marriage were unconstitutional. On February 20 Attorney General Ellen Rosenblum announced that her office would not defend Oregon's ban on gay marriage, admitting in her brief that "the ban cannot withstand a federal constitutional challenge under any standard of review."[68] As March began the Attorney General of Kentucky, Jack Conway, so overcome with emotion he had difficulty speaking, announced that he could not in conscience defend his state's ban on same-sex marriage, approved by 75 percent of the voters ten years earlier—numbers that reminded Mark and Vic of the overwhelming majority of Texas voters who had approved the 2004 amendment prohibiting same-sex marriage. Before the month had ended, Judge Bernard A. Friedman, who had surprised April DeBoer and Jayne Rowse when he suggested they amend their suit challenging the state's laws against joint adoption by gay and lesbian couples to challenge the state's ban on same-sex marriage, ruled in their favor.

Week by week, Mark and Vic kept a careful count as new victories rolled in. Together with Cleo and Nicole they were still waiting for a briefing order from the Fifth Circuit Court when Judge Chris Piazza struck down the same-sex marriage ban in the Arkansas Constitution. On the thirteenth of May U. S. Chief Magistrate Candy W. Dale declared Idaho's statutory and constitutional prohibitions against same-sex marriage unconstitutional. By late May when Judge Michael J. McShane struck down Oregon's laws prohibiting same-sex marriage the state had already conceded that they were unconstitutional and legally indefensible. That did not, however, prevent Mark's cousin, an Oregon resident, from lashing out on Facebook with an attack that seemed almost personal. "Did we not have a vote on that and it passed?" she asked. "If a judge can strike it down, why did we have a vote?"

When Mark responded, pointing out that the judge had relied on the Equal Protection Clause of the Fourteenth Amendment—ironically, he wrote specifically of "a foundational belief that certain rights should be shielded from barking crowds"—his cousin did not reply. Mark and Vic were pleased that Judge McShane cited *DeLeon v. Perry* in justifying his decision—the second judge to do so. But for two men who had endured too much, the greatest pleasure grew from the humanity evident in Judge McShane's conclusion:

> My decision will not be the final word on this subject, but on this issue of marriage I am more struck by our similarities than our differences. I believe that if we can look for a moment past gender and sexuality, we can see in these plaintiffs nothing more or less than our own families. Families who we would expect our Constitution to protect, if not exalt, in equal measure. With discernment we see not shadows lurking in closets or the stereotypes of what was once believed; rather, we see families committed to the common purpose of love, devotion, and service to the greater community.
>
> Where will all this lead? I know that many suggest we are going down a slippery slope that will have no moral boundaries. To those who truly harbor such fears, I can only say this: Let us look less to the sky to see what might fall; rather, let us look to each other . . . and rise.[69]

After months and months of struggle, his words were a soothing ointment spread across skin stretched too tight for too long.

The next day Judge John E. Jones declared same-sex marriage legal in Pennsylvania, and on June first the state legislature brought same-sex marriage to Illinois. As summer of 2014 began, Mark and Vic, Cleo and Nicole, took stock of their position. Marriage equality was "suddenly" guaranteed by law in nineteen states and the District of Columbia. That lawsuits in many of those states had begun long after *DeLeon v. Perry* was filed was a continuing source of pain for the plaintiffs who had hoped for a quicker resolution of their case in Texas.

Then, a year after the October in which *DeLeon v. Perry* had been filed, the floodgates burst. On October 6, 2014, the day Akin Gump petitioned the Fifth Circuit Court of Appeals for the second time to expedite *DeLeon v. Perry*, the United States Supreme Court sprung its "October Surprise." By refusing to review lower-court rulings from the Fourth, Seventh, and Tenth Circuits, seven cases from five states in which appellate courts had struck down bans on same-sex marriage—Indiana, Oklahoma, Utah, Virginia, and Wisconsin—the

Court boosted the number of states allowing same-sex marriage to twenty-four in a single day. For the first time ever a majority of Americans lived in a state where gay couples could wed and the ripples continued to spread outward. Other states in the jurisdiction of the three Circuit Courts where bans against same-sex marriage were still in effect—Colorado, Kansas, North Carolina, South Carolina, West Virginia, and Wyoming—followed quickly, bringing the total to thirty.

From February and into the summer and fall of 2014, Mark and Vic celebrated as court decisions and legislative action brought marriage equality to state after state. More and more, they believed that when *DeLeon v. Perry* was argued in New Orleans they would win. When the Sixth Circuit Court of Appeals overturned favorable rulings from Michigan, Kentucky, Ohio, and Tennessee, the first judicial setback for marriage equality after a stunning string of victories, they were saddened for the LGBT communities in those states, but encouraged that with a split in the circuit courts the Supreme Court was more likely to take up the question. More than anything they were saddened that their case had lost momentum, that they had not yet been able to bring marriage equality to Texas. In October and November Mark and Vic attended a series of Black Tie Dinners—first, the national dinner in Washington, D. C., then a second in San Antonio, and finally one on their home turf in Dallas where they met the plaintiffs from California's Prop 8 case—Kris Perry, Sandy Belzer Stier, Paul Katami, and Jeff Zarrillo—and the lawyers who had taken their case to the nation's top court, Ted Olsen and David Boies. Mark was beside himself with excitement.

"Vic and I are in hog-heaven!" he told friends on Facebook, asking with his usual self-deprecating humor, "How's that for an Okie-ism?" As he had done before and would do again, he recognized the sacrifices they had made with an appreciative note:

> Thanks to all of them for what they did! Their efforts and successes, as well as the efforts and successes of Edith Windsor, Robbie Kaplan, Evan Wolfson, Chad Griffin, the ACLU, Lambda Legal, GLAD and many, many others have made nationwide marriage a pending reality.[70]

But the same encounter brought a tinge of sadness as well. Though same-sex marriage was legal in thirty-five states and the District of Columbia, their wait in Texas was not over. So much of Mark's and Vic's lives had involved waiting. Too much. For years after recognizing that he was gay, each had waited uncertainly, hoping to meet "the one." In their early years as a couple they had waited to settle down together as the Air Force moved Vic from post to post across the country. For years they had waited for a time when their love would not be criminalized. For most of Vic's years in the Air Force they had waited for the repeal of Don't Ask, Don't Tell so they could appear in public as a couple. More recently, they had waited for the day when they would sit together in court while attorneys explained why their love should be treated no differently from the love of any other couple.

On January 9 in New Orleans, they hoped, the waiting would come at last to an end.

Chapter 4

The Battle
of New Orleans,
Part I Opening Salvos:
Louisiana and Mississippi

The freedom secured by the Constitution consists, in one of its essential dimensions, of the right of the individual not to be injured by the unlawful exercise of governmental power. The mandate for segregated schools, *Brown v. Board of Education*; a wrongful invasion of the home, *Silverman v. United States*; or punishing a protestor whose views offend others, *Texas v. Johnson*; and scores of other examples teach that individual liberty has constitutional protection, and that liberty's full extent and meaning may remain yet to be discovered and affirmed . . . History demands that we continue to learn, to listen, and to remain open to new approaches if we are to aspire always to a constitutional order in which all persons are treated with fairness and dignity.

—Justice Kennedy, *Schuette v. Bamn* (2014)

On the morning of January 9, 2015, Steve Rudner, then chairman of the board of directors of the Equality Texas Foundation, arrived with Zach, one of his fifteen-year-old twin sons, on the steps of the John Minor Wisdom Courthouse in New Orleans at 4:30 a.m. Only one couple, two women from Houston, had arrived earlier. Steve and his son were determined to get seats in the West Courtroom of the courthouse where oral arguments in the Texas case, *DeLeon v. Perry*, would begin at 11:00 a.m., the third set of oral arguments in three same-sex marriage cases before the Fifth Circuit Court. Arguments were set to begin with Louisiana at nine o'clock. Not far behind the Rudners were Angela Hale and Susan Risdon, the media team handling public relations for the Texas plaintiffs, Mark and Vic, Cleo and Nicole. Further back were Jonathan Saenz, president of the ultra-conservative Texas Values, and more than two hundred others, overwhelmingly supporters of same-sex marriage looking forward to following oral arguments they hoped would change their lives. Before the doors opened to the public, the line would stretch far down the block toward Canal Street and the edge of the French Quarter.

Knowing that interest was high and that seating would be at a premium, the Clerk's Office had done everything possible to accommodate an overflow crowd. Forty or so temporary seats had been set up inside the bar for court staff and lawyers; in the area reserved for the public—usually four rows of eight-person benches on either side of the aisle—folding chairs had gone up wherever space allowed. But with twenty seats in the public section reserved for "credentialed members of the press," and still more seats set aside, hour by hour, for the couples whose futures lay in the balance, only fifty-or-so places remained. To ensure that the few seats available would be distributed fairly and without incident, the Clerk's Office had three days earlier issued a media advisory outlining their plan. At 8:00 a.m. court staff would begin passing out seating numbers to people in line outside the main entrance to the courthouse. No "place holders" allowed. Spectators would be allowed to attend only one set of oral arguments, but they could choose which set they wanted to attend. Those not lucky enough to get a place in the West Court-room, or those who wanted to attend more than one set of oral arguments, would be able to listen to a live audio feed in the other two courtrooms. For those who were shut out entirely, or who wanted the opportunity to listen a second time, the Court promised to make recordings of the arguments avail-able online within an hour after the last case was submitted.

For the long wait in the dark and the cold—pre-dawn temperatures that morning in New Orleans hovered in the low-forties, but wind blowing from the northeast, coupled with a misty rain, had dropped the "feels like" temperature well into the thirties—most of those in line had bundled up in heavy coats, hats and mufflers, even the occasional ski mask. Shuffling from foot to foot, shoulders hunched against the cold and damp, sipping coffee, they watched in the half-light as media trucks across the street raised their antennae. Until, that is, reporters arrived, microphones in hand, looking for "the story" and the camera lights drove back the darkness.

"We know that in states like Texas, Mississippi, and Louisiana . . . millions of people were part of the process before," Jonathan Saenz told WDSU News, choosing his words carefully to downplay the real state of public opinion in Texas and to appeal to his conservative base. "And as a matter of fact, those people settled that issue and said that marriage is between one man and one woman. So we just want to make sure that we're in the courtroom today."[1]

But for Steve Rudner of Equality Texas, the father of twin sons, one gay, one straight, the matter was not settled at all. Josh, his gay son, had come out at the age of eleven and Rudner had become an outspoken advocate for gay rights. Standing next to his straight son, Zach—a teenager already thinking of law school and eager to see an appellate court in action—he countered with up to date information that provided exactly the context Saenz had avoided. "The tide has really turned," he pointed out; "Recent polls show that a majority of Texans support marriage equality, and we're going to get there, it's just a question of when and how."[2]

Saenz had more to say. "Redefining marriage equals that private business owners are going to be forced or punished to participate in homosexual weddings even though they disagree with it," he insisted, struggling again to shape the argument in terms that would frighten conservatives into opposition. "We know that redefining marriage has equaled taxpayers being forced to use their funds for same-sex couples' benefits," he added for good measure.[3]

Rudner's response, raising at once the constitutional guarantee of "equal protection" and the very real, very human problems marriage inequality forces families to confront, was masterful: "It's difficult to me to be able to explain to my twins why one of them should have a different set of rights than his brother in the same country," he pointed out. "That's inexplicable. I don't think anybody has a good answer for that question. I'm looking to have that solved for my family today. I'm here with my son to make sure that our close friends and family members throughout the state of Texas have the same rights my wife and I have."[4]

The chill of the early morning made a stark contrast with the warmth of the previous evening when the eleven couples involved in the Fifth Circuit hearings, representatives of their legal teams, and nearly a hundred supporters gathered in a more intimate space, the Cathedral Creative Studios just a few blocks from the magisterial John Minor Wisdom Courthouse. Angry, defiant, and tearful by turns, for an hour the plaintiffs from Louisiana, Mississippi, and Texas shared the stories that had brought them to New Orleans. Time and time again, they spoke of love and family, of dignity and equality. Derek Penton-Robicheaux, one of the plaintiffs from Louisiana, set the theme: "These aren't rights that people are asking for that are special," he reminded the tightly pressed crowd; "these are rights that are guaranteed. These are families." Havard Scott, also of Louisiana, spoke through tears of his hope that the court would grant same-sex couples "the same equality, dignity, and respect that all marriages are accorded." Many of the couples had brought their children to the rally—Cade Blanchard, a vision of two-year-old, tow-headed cuteness whose mothers, Nadine and Courtney, were plaintiffs in the Louisiana suit, seemed here, there, and everywhere—and as speaker followed speaker, cries from children underfoot occasionally rose above the voice at the lectern. No one paused, not even for a moment, in the celebration of love and family.

Next to speak was Joce Pritchett of Mississippi, who began by recounting an interview with a reporter from *USA Today*. He made a big deal about family values in Mississippi, she said, and expressed surprise that gay people had turned the tables on conservatives, that they were now the ones using family values as their argument. Joce, the mother of two young children she shares with her partner of eleven years, Carla Webb, laughed, her eyes already brimming with tears as she told of her surprise at his surprise. "It's not so much an 'argument' as it is . . . well, it's what's important to us. It just comes down to taking care of families. We have children and we want them to be safe, and the only way to do that is to have legal protections." Afraid she would forget something important as she continued, Joce unfolded a sheet of paper and apologized for speaking from notes. No need. She didn't miss a note; she was, in fact, pitch perfect.

What followed was an old-fashioned civics lesson, a first-hand account of the harms done to the children of same-sex couples prohibited from marrying that explained why she and Carla had joined the fight for change in Mississippi. "Our little girl—six years old—came home from school one day last year," Joce began, "and asked why we weren't married like her friends' parents." That day, she revealed, she and Carla began planning a trip to Maine where they were married—though they knew Mississippi would not honor their out-of-state ceremony. "We had to explain to Grace," Joce continued, "that there are some bad laws in Mississippi that didn't allow us to get married." They taught their daughter about Ruby Bridges, the six-year-old who in 1960 stood up to racial prejudice; surrounded by federal marshals, she walked bravely into the William Frantz Elementary School in New Orleans, a moment immortalized by Norman Rockwell in a painting that appeared four years later on the cover of *Life* Magazine. They taught their daughter the hard truth that though "most laws are good and are made to protect us, some are bad and can hurt us." Most of all, they taught their daughter that "When we find bad laws, it's up to us as good citizens to work to change them into good laws." Tears running freely down her face, Joce brought the lesson home. "It seemed so simple to Grace," she said, "that laws that hurt people should be changed. And it seemed simple to us too."

Before the applause subsided, Nicole Dimetman of Texas, visibly pregnant, stepped to the lectern, eager to add her voice to the growing chorus. "I'm especially honored to be here," she began, "beside the person I love most in this world." Turning with a smile toward her wife, Cleopatra DeLeon, who had given birth to the couple's first child four years earlier, she added, "I knew I wanted to spend the rest of my life with Cleo the moment I saw her." Though Nicole and Cleo had traveled to Massachusetts to marry before the birth of their son, Texas had stubbornly refused to recognize their union and both women were angry at the indignity. When their first child was born four years earlier, they had discovered that no legal step they could take would guarantee them the same protections Texas grants to heterosexual couples.

Had Cleo died before the birth certificate was amended, their son would have legally been an orphan. Now, Nicole's voice rang with defiance as she spoke out against the injustice. "Our marriage," she insisted, "is a message that we provide to ourselves and to our children that we are going to be a family. The fact that Texas doesn't recognize our marriage is demeaning and humiliating, not only to us, but to our children."

Mark was the last to speak for the plaintiffs, and on this evening he spoke as another Texan whose frustration with the State's attempts to deny the dignity of marriage to same-sex couples had long ago reached the boiling point. He began by recalling the story of Mildred and Richard Loving whose landmark civil rights case in 1967 made interracial marriage possible. "The night before the Supreme Court was to hear the case," Mark remembered, "the lawyers asked Richard Loving what he most wanted them to tell the Court." The reply was simple. "I want you to tell them that I love my wife and it's unfair that Virginia will not recognize our marriage." The edge in his voice increasingly evident, Mark continued. "I love Vic more than anything else in the world. I've loved him since the first minute I met him and for the entire past seventeen years. And it is unfair that Texas will not allow us to marry." As the crowd began to applaud, Mark made it clear that he was ready with more, a double-barreled argument. "The other thing I want our lawyers to tell the Fifth Circuit tomorrow is that Vic served in the military for almost twenty-three years. And when he was serving our country, he was serving for everyone's freedoms, not just one set, but everyone's including gay and lesbian Texans."

Emotions were running high. The room crackled with energy. A long minute passed before the cheers and applause dropped away and the crowd was ready to move on. John Denison, Chairman of the Board at the Forum for Equality and master of ceremonies for the evening, waited patiently, knowing how eager the plaintiffs were to celebrate what they hoped would be the end of the struggle that had brought them together. Earlier, Joce Pritchett had laughed as she remembered the number of times she had watched *Finding Nemo* with her children, Grace and Ethan. On this night at the Cathedral Creative Studios, the night before the eleven couples would stand before the Fifth Circuit Court, Joce's fertile imagination turned the film into a parable of solidarity. "Toward the end of the movie," she told the crowd, "Nemo's friend, Dory, gets trapped in a net full of fish. The fishermen are reeling the net in and the fish are panicking, afraid they're all going to die. But Dory convinces the fish to swim in the same direction, downward and away from the boat. And they do. They break the boom holding the net, the net sinks to the bottom, and all the fish are freed."

"This is what I'm trying to say to you tonight," Joce concluded. "You're an important part of this; we are all part of the movement." An overconfident attorney for the State of Mississippi had boasted to the plaintiffs there that it would be a cold day in hell before his state tried a gay marriage case. "But then," Joce continued, "Judge Carlton Reeves said 'It's cold outside.' And it's going to be even colder tomorrow here in New Orleans. We are going to say to the Fifth Circuit, 'Get out your gloves and your parkas because if New Orleans can freeze over, so can hell!'" When the moment was right, John Denison stepped to the microphone with a smile on his face and a final word on his lips. "In Louisiana we had a district court ruling that . . . well, they gave us a lemon. But you know what? We're making lemonade."

The organizations involved in the cases from Louisiana, Mississippi, and Texas that sponsored the rally—the Campaign for Southern Equality, Equality Texas, the Forum for Equality, Lambda Legal— had done what needed to be done. Eleven couples, eleven families from three states had arrived one by one in New Orleans, but in the course of a single evening they had come together as one extended family, hands joined, hearts beating as one, to look toward the dawn of a new day. Ready to experience the fulfillment of the psalmist's words, ancient wisdom offered to believers and non-believers alike, that "weeping may endure for a night, but joy cometh in the morning."

* * *

After the emotional intensity of the rally, Mark and Vic slipped away with Nicole and Cleo, members of the legal team from Akin Gump, and a handful of friends and supporters for dinner at Galatoire's, courtesy of Steve Rudner. A drink to relax, great food, even better conversation, a moment of calm before the storm they knew would sweep them through the next day. When at last the men settled in for the night—as a concession to Mark's perpetual fear of being late, of missing something, anything—they set two alarms. True to form, Vic slept peacefully through the darkness; Mark woke, fretted, read e-mail and checked Facebook before sleeping again. And when the alarms sounded at 5:45 the next morning, they answered the call. Not much talk, no television. Just the quiet business of getting ready for what both knew would be an emotional day. But when their room-service breakfast arrived—an egg-white frittata, orange juice, and hot tea for Mark, raisin bread toast and water for Vic—they managed only to pick and nibble, eating barely enough to get them through the morning. And yet, somehow, they found themselves as Mark had feared, behind the schedule set the previous night, late for a meeting in the lobby with a friend. Worse, the cabbie taking them to the John Minor Wisdom Courthouse did, as Mark had feared, wander, eventually dropping them blocks from their destination. And yet, somehow, by 7:10 a.m., twenty minutes before the Clerk of the Court had told them they would be admitted, they were greeting friends on the steps of the Fifth Circuit Court. Knowing they had been standing in the cold for hours, looking for a way to honor their dedication, Mark offered a bit of wry humor to ease the tension everyone felt.

"Gosh," he quipped, a twinkle in his eye; "I'm cold."

"Don't even go there!" Angela Hale replied, a different kind of twinkle in her eye.

Security at the Fifth Circuit was on full alert for the day, higher by far than it had been the previous week when the Court heard arguments in a potentially controversial abortion case. In most appellate court cases, only the attorneys and, perhaps, a handful of interested parties show up. Everyone knew that would not be the case today. To ease confusion, people entering the courthouse had been divided into three groups. The general public was to enter through the main door on Camp Street, through the long row of arches and beneath the dramatic colonnade where the gravitas of the building's Italian Renaissance Revival style is most evident; members of the press through a handicapped accessible door on Capedeville Street, hidden away in a dark hollow that leads as well to an underground parking garage; litigants and their attorneys through a door off Lafayette Street, at this point a pedestrian mall complete with a bricked walkway, tables and benches, trees and bushes, all protected from the bustling traffic on Camp Street by *les bittes,* a row of slender metal posts that rise from the pavement as a reminder of New Orleans's French heritage. At 7:30 a court official swung open the door and began calling lists of names. First, Louisiana, lawyers in the lead, then the plaintiffs. Then Mississippi, then Texas, always in the same order, lawyers first, plaintiffs following. Passing through the doors and into the warmth of the courthouse, they left in the cold outside a substantial police presence ready to restore order should trouble arise.

Inside, an officer of the court, polite but stern, issued instructions: they were to walk in single-file along the L-shaped great hall toward the Camp Street entrance where metal detectors waited. Looking about, Cleo succumbed quickly to the majesty of the space. The marble columns, the succession of arches that seemed to disappear in the distance, the vaulted ceiling with its dizzying array of flowers, allegorical figures, and geometric designs, bas reliefs cast in plaster—on any other day she'd have wanted to stop for an architectural tour. On any other day, Mark might have been equally dazzled. But not today.

Making his way through the metal detectors, beltless and shoeless, Mark found himself next to Michael Murphy, the attorney who had argued the case for Texas in San Antonio. "I should wish you well," Mark said, that characteristic gleam back in his eye, "but I don't." The attorney smiled back, not at all offended by the humor. When at last Mark and Vic arrived at the East Courtroom, reserved for the Texas contingent, the instructions from the court were no less stern. "Sit down and stay seated." For a brief minute they obeyed, settling onto one of the hard wooden benches, using the time to look around at the thirty or so others who had gathered around them. Realizing that they were surrounded almost entirely by friends, old and new, Mark and Vic, Nicole and Cleo, rose to greet the crowd. Hugs went round. Two faculty members from a college in Texas asked them to sign their admittance card, promising to put it into a scrapbook for the students back home to see. They posed for a dozen or fifteen selfies, most of which were posted within hours on Facebook.

As the Louisiana case was about to begin, Mark leaned toward Frank Stenger-Castro and Barry Chasnoff, two of the attorneys from Akin Gump. Two people in the room, he pointed out, were there as representatives of

Texas Values, the conservative group that had fought, often in hurtful and hateful ways, to keep same-sex marriage from Texas. But the rest, more than thirty others, were there to support marriage equality. "It's about the same ratio," Mark suggested, grinning at the obvious irony, "as the ratio of wins to losses for same-sex marriage in courts across the country." For the moment, everyone within earshot chuckled. As the laughter faded, Mark thought about two of his great-great-great uncles: William Priestly, a neighbor to Andrew Jackson in Tennessee, who with his brother Thomas had traveled south as an aide-de-camp to General Jackson to drive the British into the sea at the Battle of New Orleans.

A new Battle of New Orleans was about to begin, one in which he and Vic would play a role, but a positive outcome seemed even less certain than in 1814 when a rag-tag band of Americans confronted a numerically superior British force. After their win in San Antonio, Mark and Vic and Cleo and Nicole were at first skeptical about their chances at the next level. Though in the late 1950s landmark civil rights decisions by the "Fifth Circuit Four"—Chief Judge Elbert Tuttle, Judge John Brown, Judge Richard Rives, and the man for whom the current courthouse is named, Judge John Minor Wisdom—pushed the South to desegregate and to register African-American voters, by late November 2013 when the Court set the date for *DeLeon v. Perry* the Fifth Circuit had long since established its reputation as a bastion of conservatism. Writing in the *ABA Journal* less than a year before Mark and Vic journeyed to New Orleans, Mark Curriden branded it "the nation's most divisive, controversial and conservative appeals court."[5] Diana Wray, a staff writer for the *Houston Press*, put it more colorfully. "Calling the Fifth Circuit conservative," she wrote, "is like calling a unicorn a pony: it's kind of accurate but it couldn't possibly cover the horned grandeur of the Fifth."[6]

But when on December 30 the Court announced the panel of judges who would hear their case, Mark and Vic saw a break in the clouds. The youngest member of the panel, Judge James E. Graves, an African American appointed to the Fifth Circuit Court of Appeals by President Obama in 2010, seemed more likely than not to come down on the side of marriage equality. Mark and Vic knew, however, that Judge Jerry E. Smith, a Reagan appointee who rose to power speaking against the LGBT community, would undoubtedly vote against them. As far back as November 1977 when the National Women's Conference met in Houston—Smith, recently elected chair of the Republican Party in Harris County, Texas, was at the time an ambitious young man looking to shore up his credentials as a staunch conservative—he had railed in his acceptance speech against the 2,000 delegates gathered under the direction of Congresswoman Bella Abzug to advocate for women's issues. Though three current or former First Ladies had added legitimacy by speaking at the opening ceremony, Smith told the *Houston Chronicle* that the conference was a "lesbian-abortionist gathering" and "an illegal use of taxpayer money." The "gaggle of outcasts, misfits, and rejects," he added, would do well to "get out of town."[7]

The swing vote, Judge Patrick E. Higginbotham, was, like Judge Smith, a conservative appointed by President Reagan, but he seemed to Mark and Vic a conservative cut from very different cloth. "When I joined the 5th Circuit, I may have been the court's most conservative judge," Higginbotham said in a fall 2014 interview. "Now, I'm probably left of center, even though I don't think I've changed my views at all."[8] Many of his decisions—an order to redraw congressional district maps in ways more respectful of minorities, another upholding federal laws limiting the sale of firearms, still another holding that Texas judicial elections are governed by the federal Voting Rights Act and, most recently, his vote to uphold affirmative action in admissions at the University of Texas—led Mark and Vic to hope that he would follow in the footsteps of another Republican appointee, Judge Jerome Holmes of the Tenth Circuit, who had defied expectations in June 2014 when he voted to strike down Utah's ban on same-sex marriage.[9] Charles Matthews, formerly general counsel of Exxon Mobil Corporation and a friend of Judge Higginbotham, claimed for his friend a kind of "cowboy common sense about life."[10] Sitting in the East Courtroom, waiting for the day's work to begin, Mark and Vic pinned their hopes on that "cowboy common sense."

* * *

By 7:30 a.m. members of the press began to filter into the West Courtroom, relieved to be out of the cold. Plaintiffs in the Louisiana case and lawyers for both sides followed soon after. For a long while, the plaintiffs sat talking among themselves in hushed tones, heads leaning close with each exchange, visibly nervous; lawyers from the two sides, accustomed to courtrooms and to the work that lay before them, shook hands and made small talk. With an hour and a half before the proceedings were to begin there was ample time for those lucky enough to be admitted to fall under the spell of the room itself. Restored in 1971–2, the West Courtroom inspires respect. Designed as a double-cube, twice as long as it is high and wide (or close enough to those dimensions to fool the eye), the West Courtroom's mathematical proportions call to mind Palladian harmonics (the acoustics of such rooms are supposedly excellent though that would not prove the case today) and the belief that such perfectly proportioned rooms could lift the spirits and elevate the mind. The room fits well with the building's Italian Renaissance Revival style. The walls, paneled in dark gumwood, the ceiling with its elaborate plasterwork, and the high windows, draped with velvet curtains, call to mind double-cube rooms in English country houses, an age-old model of stability fitting for a courtroom. Four wall sconces on each side of the room, cast in brass to look like intertwined snakes (Lady Justice is often represented with her foot crushing a snake, the symbol of evil), hold globes that, in conjunction with globes on two large chandeliers that hang from the ceiling, light the room softly. The West Courtroom is a serious space deliberately constructed to encourage the thoughtful pursuit of truth—and everyone seemed to know that instinctively.

As nine o'clock drew near, the hour when arguments were scheduled to begin, the air in the West Courtroom seemed suddenly to change. After a final flurry of activity as the last seats in the spectators' section were filled, the low-buzz of conversation in the room suddenly dropped away, only to rise again when nothing happened. The Louisiana plaintiffs shifted nervously in their seats, worried but hopeful, cautiously optimistic that in the next hour the legal battle would swing their way. Finally, the door to the left of the dais swung open, Judges Smith, Higginbotham, and Graves stepped quickly to their seats, and the voice of the clerk rang out. The first of the day's three sets of oral arguments had begun.

Tensions among supporters eased quickly as Camilla Taylor, Senior Counsel at Lambda Legal, began to present the case for the Louisiana plaintiffs, her carefully modulated tone and measured pace signaling the confidence that comes with careful preparation and the conviction that one is right. The State's case, she argued, had been built on "two false premises," which she systematically undercut in the first three minutes of her carefully crafted argument. To the surprise of many—surprise that grew exponentially as she continued—the judges allowed Taylor to speak almost without interruption. The first two questions came from Judge Graves. The first came three and a half long minutes into Taylor's argument, a request for clarification that diverted Taylor for barely five seconds. When Judge Graves broke in a third time, seventeen-and-a-half minutes into Taylor's presentation, he complimented her on "a very compelling argument as to why Louisiana should recognize a same-sex marriage from another jurisdiction" and asked if it would be "legally inconsistent to conclude that Louisiana should recognize same-sex marriages from other states, but at the same time conclude that the state of Louisiana had a right to ban same-sex marriages"—a friendly question that invited Taylor to note that the two had to be linked since "the reasons the State has offered for both situations are the same."

Because the judges remained largely silent, allowing Taylor to move methodically from point to point in her argument, she was able to highlight the logic and coherence of the plaintiffs' case and build to an emotional conclusion: "Liberty's full extent and meaning may remain yet to be discovered and affirmed," she asserted, pointing to the future with a citation from Justice Kennedy's decision in *Schuette v. Coalition to Defend Affirmative Action*. For good measure she added an even more famous passage from Justice Kennedy's decision in *Lawrence*: "later generations can see that laws once thought necessary and proper in fact serve only to oppress," a conclusion that left heads nodding in agreement.

Kyle Duncan, Special Counsel to the State of Louisiana, did not fare so well with the judges. He asserted in his opening that *Windsor* admitted same-sex marriage was a new and challenging idea, an idea so new that in refusing to accept it the people of Louisiana were "not banning anything . . . [only] deciding not to go the way of other states who are engaged in a novel social experiment." But Duncan had been allowed to speak for barely fifteen seconds when Judge Graves interrupted, and the interruptions kept coming, so many that he was never able to speak for more than a minute or two before being challenged. "There is more in *Windsor* that you have to deal with," Judge Graves warned. And when Duncan raised the familiar "rational procreation" argument, Judge Graves beat him down—to the delight of those in the courtroom — with reference to a decision from the Seventh Circuit Court: "Judge Posner says that's ridiculous. That's his characterization of it." When Duncan pressed the argument, Judge Smith, the most sympathetic of the three-judge panel, cautioned that "the inference of animus jumps at you."

What emerged as Duncan pressed ahead was a reading of *Windsor* so out of the ordinary that it raised eyebrows across the courtroom. Kennedy's decision contains, he argued, seven pages on the matter of state authority over marriage, demonstrating that "The Constitution allows the state citizens to make up their minds about difficult issues of social policy, especially where the predictive consequences [of change] are unknown and unknowable." The Defense of Marriage Act was overturned, he maintained, because Section 3 ran afoul of New York's decision to allow same-sex marriage. "And now," he concluded, "you have the plaintiffs in so many cases saying 'Now we want the Federal judiciary to override the State determination that the citizens made on marriage.' That's just as much an interference with State sovereignty as DOMA Section 3 was.'" Judge Graves's reaction to Duncan's reading was incredulity. "*Windsor?*" he asked as if he found it necessary to confirm that he and Duncan were speaking of the same Supreme Court decision. Camilla Taylor's rebuttal, unchallenged by the Court, set the record straight. According to *Windsor*, she pointed out, "State laws defining and regulating marriage must respect the constitutional rights of persons." Moreover, she asserted, the Court had "found it unnecessary to decide whether DOMA's federal intrusion on state power was a violation of the Constitution."

When the first session of the day had come to an end, Emma Margolin of MSNBC summed up perfectly the reasons behind the optimism growing among supporters of marriage equality. "Judge Higginbotham, the swing, seemed not only skeptical of Louisiana's defense of same-sex marriage ban, but amused by it."[11] Buzzfeed's Chris Geidner sent a tweet no one was expecting: "Breaking: MS and TX arguments remain, but after LA args, the 5th Circuit appears poised to strike down state same-sex marriages bans. Court seems likely to overturn same-sex marriage bans" and Buzzfeed immediately put up a story to that effect on its web page.[12] Listening from the East Courtroom, Mark and Nicole, lawyers both, had at one point during the Louisiana arguments begun to hope for what had seemed completely out of reach only an hour earlier, a three-zero decision in favor of same-sex marriage. But questions and comments from Judge Smith had tempered their hopes. By the break when Mark talked with Shannon Minter, a fellow Texan he had come to know from encounters at HRC meetings and nationally known for his work on LGBT rights, they agreed that the decision would be two to one. Nonetheless, in the short recess between sessions, feelings in the courtroom were running high—good feelings.

Twenty minutes later the Court reconvened to hear arguments in the Mississippi case and the good news for supporters of same-sex marriage continued. Justin Methany, who had argued the case for Mississippi the previous November before Judge Carlton Reeves in the Southern District of Mississippi, appeared to be reeling still from the drubbing delivered there by Roberta Kaplan, the hero of *Windsor* and a formidable presence in the courtroom. Squaring off against Kaplan for a second time, Methany was visibly uncomfortable. He spoke unnaturally slowly. His responses were marked by long periods of silence as he struggled to respond to the judges' questions, painfully afraid that a wrong word would lead to another loss. At the end of the rebuttal period, Judge Smith asked an easy question that required only agreement. Unable to follow, Methany stammered and stuttered, completely baffled, until Judge Higginbotham, a Reagan appointee, reached out with still more help. "That's a friendly question," he quipped, to which Judge Graves, chuckling, added, "Just say yes." Methany did, glad at last to be off the hook, and a wave of laughter swept across the courtroom. Some court watchers felt Justin Methany was out of his depth; others suggested that he was unconvincing not just because his arguments were specious, but because he didn't believe them himself.

Not all of Methany's half-hour before the Court was quite so comical as the final moments, but persistent questions from Judges Higginbotham and

Graves kept him consistently on the defensive and unable to gain traction. Mississippi should prevail, Methany argued in his opening statement, for three reasons: 1) the question before the court was foreclosed by a binding precedent, 2) Mississippi's laws banning same-sex marriage meet the standard for rational basis review and, 3) the Court would find no reason to employ a higher standard of review.

Judges Higginbotham and Graves were lying in wait with challenges to all three assertions. When Methany argued that *Baker* should control, Judge Graves demanded to know why the precedential value of *Baker* had not been negated by "doctrinal developments." Responding to Judge Smith's contention that *Baker* had been briefed in *Windsor*, but was not mentioned in Justice Kennedy's decision (and was therefore still precedential), Judge Higgenbothan had a ready reply. Perhaps, he suggested, "the Supreme Court gave such short shrift to it they didn't even deem it worthy of talking about." With the state's attorney relegated to the sidelines as the judges sparred with one another, Judge Higginbotham went on to cite Justice Ginsburg's observation that "there's been a sea-change in the whole area of human rights and equal protection in particular since 1975."

Nor did Methany's fortunes improve as he moved to the second and third parts of his argument. Like other states' attorneys arguing same-sex marriage cases, he wanted the Court to embrace an expansive understanding of fit in rational basis review. "Judges don't substitute their policy judgments for those of legislators," he informed the Court peremptorily; "what you're looking for [is] any conceivable rationale for legislative choices." But when Methany laid out the details of the familiar procreation argument—they hoped "to incentivize [procreation] through subsidies and benefits"—Judge Higginbotham undercut the argument with humor: "You don't need any incentive to have sex," he joked to the delight of the gallery. Judge Graves couldn't resist piling on. "You're not going to disagree with that are you?"

The same judges were equally dismissive of Methany's assertion that there was no need for the Court to move to a higher level of scrutiny. When he mistakenly claimed that "The level of scrutiny applied in *Windsor* was rational basis review," Judge Graves moved quickly to correct him. "Is that your interpretation of *Windsor*," he asked skeptically, "or is that what the

Court said in *Windsor*?" While Methany adjusted to the reality of Justice Kennedy's "careful review," Judge Higginbotham referenced a nursing school case in which gender had determined a suspect class and added his voice in favor of an intermediate level of scrutiny.

By contrast, from the moment she stepped forward to address the Court Roberta Kaplan took charge of the room—though in the most agreeable way possible. Modeling her description on the web page of her law firm, Paul Weiss, as "a litigation superstar" and a "pressure junkie," she lost no time demonstrating why in 2013 *The American Lawyer* named her to their list of "The 100 Most Influential Lawyers" and singled her out as "Litigator of the Year," or why in 2014 *Above the Law* chose her as the "Most Innovative Lawyer of the Year."[13] Her opening gambit set the context for the day's hearings, inviting the judges to consider their place in history. "I am delighted to be down here in New Orleans," she told the judges, adding a touch of humor as she apologized for bringing New York's cold weather with her. "It's an honor to be arguing this case in the John Minor Wisdom Courthouse," she continued, intentionally linking the same-sex marriage cases before the court to the African-American struggle for civil rights in the 1960s in which the Fifth Circuit Court played a key role.

To the surprise of none, Kaplan set the language of Justice Kennedy's decision in *Windsor*, which she had argued and won, at the center of her argument. Again and again, she returned to the idea of "dignity" which was foundational in Justice Kennedy's thinking, the word itself having appeared no fewer than ten times in his twenty-six-page opinion. "Marriage," Kaplan reminded the Court, "affects practically every sphere of everyday life, from death to taxes, to children and benefits, to status and dignity . . . Once you accept the fact that gay people have equal dignity, then any purported justification for the government to treat them differently in marriage is unconstitutional no matter what level of scrutiny applies." She also echoed Justice Kennedy's reminder in *Lawrence* that the men who framed the Constitution knew that "times can blind us to certain truths and later generations can see that laws once thought necessary and proper in fact serve only to oppress." In her own voice she brought Kennedy's observation into the present: "Times have blinded this country about African Americans, times have blinded this country about women, and times have blinded this country about gay people," once again placing the same-sex marriage cases before the Court in the context of the broader struggle for civil rights.

Most in the courtroom knew from long experience the issues with which she would have to deal: the question of "fit" in rational basis review, the responsible procreation argument, the presence of *animus*, the precedential value of *Baker*, the federalism controversy, the alleged need for caution as the idea of marriage enters a new era. And yet, Kaplan had a surprise or two tucked away. Predictably, she argued for the presence of *animus*, not in the obvious form of overt hatred or open bigotry, but as a defensiveness that grows from difference and distrust and imposes "broad and undifferentiated liabilities on a class of people." She argued as well against the need for caution, pointing out that before imposing a ban Mississippi had sought no testimony about the possible impact of same-sex marriage, had held no hearings, had conducted no studies—had in effect done nothing that signaled the need for caution. She dismissed the federalism issue, politely taking to the woodshed Kyle Duncan, the Louisiana attorney who had claimed that Kennedy's decision in *Windsor* confirmed the states' right to control marriage, reminding the judges that Kennedy "made it clear that he was not reaching the federalism issue in DOMA." But Kaplan's predictability ended there.

Even veteran court watchers like Buzzfeed's Chris Geidner were caught off-guard when she addressed the matter of fit in the light of *St. Joseph Abbey v. Castile*, a little-known case decided in 2013 by the Fifth Circuit Court with an opinion from the senior member of the current panel, Judge Higginbotham. From a case that revolved around a monastery's right to make and sell caskets, Kaplan plucked key lines that narrowed the range of fit in rational basis review. "The Court's analysis" in *St. Joseph Abbey*, she asserted, " 'does not demand judicial blindness to the history of a challenged rule or the context of its adoption, nor does it require courts to accept nonsensical explanations. For this reason, a hypothetical rationale, even *post hoc*, cannot be fantasy.' " And on that basis, she concluded, the state's responsible procreation argument must fail. Her energy rising with every word, Kaplan told the Court, "There is no rational reason to believe that the exclusion of gay couples from marriage somehow incentivizes straight couples to do anything at all. In the words of *St. Joseph Abbey*, it's a fantasy to assume that any young woman who gets pregnant will decide to marry the father of her child because my clients cannot." When Judge Smith cited *Heller* in an attempt to check her momentum—"courts are compelled under rational basis review to accept a legislature's generalizations even when there is an imperfect fit between means and ends"—Kaplan refused even to slow down. "I believe that it's not the fact that it's imperfect fit, your Honor; I believe that there's no connection, there's no fit."

Kaplan was equally dismissive—and in her language no less surprising—when Judge Smith raised the red flag of *Baker*. She recalled Judge Higginbotham's observation in the Louisiana case that since 1972 there had been a "sea-change" affecting the way gay men and lesbians live their lives and in our understanding of civil rights. In that long-ago era, she contended, her enthusiasm pushing her momentarily beyond the usually restrained language of the courtroom, "that kind of rationale makes a hell of a lot more sense . . . and there's a lot more connection than there would be in today's world."

But the biggest surprise in her argument may well have been her distinction between the holding and the logic of the *Windsor* decision. Prodded by Judge Smith, who recalled the last sentence of *Windsor* in an attempt to limit its reach ("This opinion and its holdings are confined to those lawful marriages," meaning, he said, "those marriages the Federal government had tried to define or constrict"), Kaplan turned a potential negative into a positive. "While the holding of *Windsor* clearly does not apply to the right of couples to marry under the state law under the Fourteenth Amendment," she countered, "the logic of *Windsor* does." She took advantage of the moment to circle back to "dignity," sounding again the trumpet that had drawn so much attention in her opening remarks: "Because the logic of *Windsor* says that gay people have a dignity that's equal to everyone else . . . when you look at the logic and language of *Windsor*, it's hard to imagine treating gay people in such a discriminatory manner if you accept the fact that they are the same as anyone."

By the time Justin Methany rose for rebuttal, Judge Smith, largely silent during the Louisiana proceedings, had made his position more clear. In the East Courtroom, Mark and Vic, Cleo and Nicole, realized that their early hope for a unanimous decision in their favor would not be realized. Nonetheless, in the closing minutes of the Mississippi case they found cause for celebration. Realizing that the day had gone against him, Methany tried to shift the focus of his argument to stress the need for caution. "There is," he admitted, "a trajectory that the law is moving in a certain direction, but it's not there yet." The court should respect the democratic process, he argued. "We're talking about a social policy issue, not a constitutional rights issue . . . That's what makes it important for the state to be able to decide for itself on a policy issue like this. Perhaps if given time the people of Mississippi will change their minds." Judge Higginbotham's response made it clear that he was not convinced. "Those words—'Will Mississippi change its mind?'—have resonated in these halls before." The all-important swing vote had clearly swung toward the acceptance of same-sex marriage.

Chapter 5

The Battle
of New Orleans,
Part II Texas Engages

Those human beings, our friends who died so horribly, have dignity
now. It doesn't matter what unknowledgeable people have stooped to
say, our friends will have respect because they are forever in our hearts.
I can almost feel their presence. If they could speak, they would tell us
to hold our heads up high.

—The Reverend Troy Perry speaking at the funeral for the thirty gay men
who died in a tragic fire at the UpStairs Bar in New Orleans (1973)

Flying to New Orleans for oral arguments before the Fifth Circuit Court of
Appeals, Mark and Vic heaved a well-earned sigh of relief. In the nearly
sixteen months since they joined with Cleo and Nicole to file suit against Texas,
they had been busy beyond anything they had expected—busy getting through
the otherwise ordinary days, busy preparing for the tomorrows that rushed relent-
lessly toward them. Settling into their seats, they found a few minutes to relax,
time to look back and reflect on all that had happened. Part of what had happened,
however, was unsettling. New Orleans has a dark past in gay culture.

When on Sunday, June 23, 1973, the UpStairs Bar in the French Quarter
was ravaged by fire, the handful of newspapers that bothered to report the

story at all failed to report the *whole* story. Not one saw fit to mention that the bar destroyed had been a gay bar, that it was often used for services of the Metropolitan Community Church, founded by the Reverend Troy Perry to minister to the LGBT community, or that in the twelve months before the fire two other MCC churches—the motherhouse in Los Angeles and a branch in San Francisco—had been targeted by arsonists and burned to the ground. Forty years later, more people know what happened that evening when fire roared through the bar; more people have learned how badly the men who died that night were treated. Staying at a hotel that reached to the corner of Chartres and Iberville Streets where the UpStairs Bar was located, Mark and Vic realized that on stepping through the door they would be reminded of the horrors of that night, the flesh charred beyond recognition or burned entirely away, of the affronts to the dignity, to the very humanity of the victims in the days that followed.

Religious services Troy Perry held in the back room of the UpStairs Bar encouraged the men who came to think of themselves as a community, to think of the bar as their community center. On the afternoon of the fire, more than 125 had gathered to pass the time among friends—and to take advantage of the free beer and all you can eat dollar-a-head special. By 7:00 p.m. when the special ended—about the time someone poured Ronsonol lighter fluid on the stairs leading from the bar's steel entrance door to the street and set them ablaze—only forty or so remained. For a few fateful minutes the fire grew undiscovered—until a buzzer rang and Buddy Rasmussen, the bartender, asked Luther Boggs to open the door. Pulled by a draft toward the windows, a fireball exploded across the room fed by old rugs, heavy draperies, wallpaper, even the plywood behind the bar. Within seconds the lights failed, darkness descended, and confusion reigned. Led by the bartender, a few men escaped through the back door to a nearby roof. But most were drawn to the glow of the windows.

As the fire raged behind them, some jumped to their deaths, six on Chartres, four more on Iberville. Most were held back by wrought-iron grilles that covered the windows. Bodies piled up at the openings, arms and legs reaching desperately through the ironwork toward safety; the screams of the dying echoed on the streets below as the flames consumed them. Though firemen arrived in minutes and the inferno was quickly contained, twenty-nine men died that night. Fifteen more were rushed to the burn center at nearby Charity Hospital, three of whom died within a few days. Though no one was ever arrested, police made it clear that the fire had been the work of an arsonist. They also made it clear that the dead were undesirables: "Some thieves hung out there," the New Orleans Police Department's chief of detectives told a newspaper, "and you know this was a queer bar." Talk-radio hosts the next day mocked the men who died in agony. "What do we bury them in?" one joked. "Fruit jars" came the sneering reply.[1]

The next day Troy Perry organized a prayer service for the victims at St. George's Episcopal Church on St. Charles Avenue, just a couple of blocks the other side of Canal Street. And within hours the Episcopal Bishop of New Orleans rebuked the rector, forbade him to repeat his offer of a place to grieve. The governor ignored a direct appeal to declare a day of mourning for what had emerged as the worst tragedy in New Orleans in 200 years. Not a single public official sent a message of condolence. A week later Troy Perry held a second service, this time at St. Mark's United Methodist Church, the only church in the French Quarter willing to offer its sanctuary to homosexuals. Encouraged by the presence of Finis Crutchfield, the Methodist Bishop of Louisiana and a closeted gay man, Perry proclaimed in his sermon that day, "Those human beings, our friends who died so horribly, have dignity now."[2]

Flying to New Orleans, Mark and Vic hoped for a win in court that would redouble that dignity.

* * *

When the Texas plaintiffs filed into the courtroom, those already there, mostly members of the press, noticed two things: Nicole Dimetman's gentle baby bump and Vic Holmes's uniform. Nicole, of course, had no choice; her baby was due in March and there was no denying that she and Cleo were expecting their second child. Vic had made a careful choice. Nicole's pregnancy was a visible reminder to everyone present that arguments the State would make about couples in same-sex marriages not bearing and raising children were patently untrue. Vic wanted to make a second positive statement, wanted to remind the court that he had served his country honorably for almost twenty-three years and contributed as much to civil life in America, perhaps more, as anyone in the courtroom.

But neither he nor Mark was quite sure about military protocol. When is it permissible—or prohibited— for retired officers to appear in uniform? The last thing Vic wanted was to create a disturbance that would detract attention from the substance of the day's proceedings. For answers, Mark contacted Gordon Tanner, a friend-in-the-know whose title—General Counsel of the U. S. Department of the Air Force and Chief Legal Officer and Chief Ethics Official for the Air Force—stretches nearly as far as the wingspan of a C-47 Galaxy. Like Mark, Tanner is a graduate of the Vanderbilt University School of Law. Like Vic, he is a retired Air Force officer who served during the "Don't Ask, Don't Tell" era. And like Mark and Vic, Tanner is an openly gay man. His reply came back within hours:

> There is no prohibition on a retiree wearing a uniform in this situation and no specific approval required. Uniform must be properly worn. No specific JAG opinion on this issue, but need to be careful that wearing of uniform doesn't represent official AF endorsement (their concern, not mine). In other words, if you'd like to wear your uniform, go ahead – and wear it proudly.[3]

And so, when Vic entered the courtroom, smiling and shaking the hands of well-wishers, ready to listen to oral arguments he hoped would change not only his life and Mark's, Cleo's and Nicole's, but the lives of tens of thousands of men and women in Texas waiting for marriage equality, he stood tall and proud in his Air Force Dress Blues, the insignia on his collar signaling his rank as a major in the armed forces of the United States of America.

The battle for marriage equality in Texas, on hold since Judge Garcia's favorable ruling in the Western District of Texas eleven long months earlier, was about to begin again.

* * *

When at last Judges Smith, Higginbotham, and Graves entered, took their seats, and signaled their readiness to begin, the courtroom came quickly to order, most of those present hoping for more of what they had seen and heard in the two earlier hearings. Jonathan Mitchell, Solicitor General of Texas, stepped to the lectern and braced himself. For two hours he had watched and listened as attorneys from Louisiana and Mississippi presented many of the arguments he was about to make. He knew how the judges were lining up: Smith as the conservative voice inclined to listen sympathetically to arguments in favor of upholding bans against same-sex marriage, Higginbotham and Graves more and more skeptical as case succeeded case and fresh arguments failed to appear. He knew how badly and how often attorneys for Louisiana and Mississippi had stumbled before the onslaught of skeptical questions and barbed humor from Higginbotham and Graves. He knew—he had to know—that the ground beneath his feet was shaky at best.

After the obligatory "May it please the Court," Mitchell opened with an attempt to answer one of the fundamental questions weighing against Texas's case. If having children was to be considered an essential part of marriage, on what basis could the state allow infertile couples to marry but refuse to marry same-sex couples? He began by calling to the Court's attention an observation Judge Smith had made during oral arguments from Louisiana and Mississippi about the level of "fit" between means and ends necessary in rational basis review. The match-up, Mitchell asserted in an argument he hoped would prove crucial to his case, does not have to be "perfect," and an imperfect match is not necessarily irrational.

With refinements so subtle that many in the courtroom, unable to understand Mitchell's line of argument, turned to each other in confusion, Texas chose to double-down on the "responsible procreation" argument the State made unsuccessfully before the Federal Court for the Western District of Texas in San Antonio. "There are two different interests in procreation," Mitchell explained. The first was the State's interest "in encouraging couples to produce new offspring." Working his way carefully around more blanket statements he would make later about "the biological reality that only oppo-site-sex couples are capable of producing children," he spoke carefully, in an attempt to turn the Court's attention from the thousands of children being raised by same-sex couples. "Everyone knows," he continued, "that same sex couples are biologically incapable of producing children."[4]

Before Mitchell had even finished his sentence, Mark and Vic and Cleo looked first at each other, then at Nicole's protruding belly. Dumbfounded, the three rolled their eyes as Mark drew the attention of those surrounding them to Nicole's obvious pregnancy. Sitting next to physical evidence that refuted Mitchell's assertion, they simply couldn't believe their ears. Nor could they believe what they heard when Mitchell moved to the State's second interest, "discouraging unplanned out-of-wedlock births that impose negative externalities on society and burden taxpayers." Prohibiting same-sex marriage would, Mitchell asserted in concert with his predecessors from Louisiana and Mississippi, advance both interests. Everyone knew, of course, that Judges Higginbotham and Graves had in the course of the morning peppered attorneys for Louisiana and Mississippi with questions about the discredited, shop-worn argument for responsible procreation.

Mitchell's next move suggested that in his mind there was a fourth judge in the courtroom, a kind of bogeyman whose long shadow cast a pall over the argument he hoped to make. "Judge Higginbotham noted in the earlier case," Mitchell admitted, "that Judge Posner was unimpressed with this argument"—an allusion to Posner's decision in *Baskin V. Bogan*. But Posner had not, he pointed out, challenged the State's "empirical claim that same-sex marriage will do nothing to advance the State's interest in reducing unplanned, out-of-wedlock births. He simply thought that that was not a valid justification" for withholding the benefits of marriage from same-sex couples. And that, Mitchell contended as he brought together the two strands of his introduction—his two justifications for Texas's ban on same-sex marriage—was the problem. Judge Posner "was not applying rational basis review" correctly. He had in fact "crossed the line from applying rational basis review into second guessing the Legislature's policy judgment."[5]

Mitchell had good reason to fear the influence of Judge Richard A. Posner, a champion of legal conservatism (though by his own admission "less conservative since the Republican Party started becoming goofy") much respected by his peers on the circuit court bench.[6] In August 2014 when the U. S. Court of Appeals for the Seventh Circuit heard oral arguments in same-sex marriage cases from Indiana and Wisconsin, Posner made no attempt to hide his contempt for procreation arguments from the states he called "pathetic" and "absurd." To the amusement of the spectators—and the horror of the attorneys subjected to his withering blasts—he sighed and muttered, groaned, and on one occasion even laughed aloud as he presided over what quickly became a judicial bloodbath.

The opinion the Seventh Circuit Court of Appeals issued just nine days later gutted the responsible procreation arguments both states had offered. In the opening pages Posner announced quickly that though the cases at hand were "rich in detail" they were "ultimately straightforward to decide." As if he wanted to discredit Mitchell's procreation argument in advance, Judge Posner wrote in *Baskin v. Bogan* that "the only rationale that the states put forth with any conviction—that same-sex couples and their children don't *need* marriage because same-sex couples can't *produce* children, intended or unintended—is so full of holes that it cannot be taken seriously" (emphasis in the original). His language toward the end of the forty-page decision was even more dismissive. "The grounds advanced by Indiana and Wisconsin for their discriminatory policies are not only conjectural; they are totally implausible."[7]

In the body of Judge Posner's decision, the stinging bench slaps he had directed at Thomas Fisher, Solicitor General of Indiana, and Timothy Samuelson, Deputy Director of Special Litigation & Appeals for Wisconsin, found equivalent expression in the bitterly sarcastic tone of his prose. "Heterosexuals get drunk and pregnant, producing unwanted children; their reward is to be allowed to marry," he wrote in a passage criticizing the responsible procreation argument; "Homosexual couples do not produce unwanted children; their reward is to be denied the right to marry. Go figure." Later, countering Wisconsin's assertion that the courts should wait until the people have come around and are willing to change policy in the voting booth, Posner quips, "Minorities trampled on by the democratic process have recourse to the courts; the recourse is called constitutional law." The impatient voice rising from the page could not speak more clearly. Nor could Posner's voice—angry now—be more clear when he laments "The harm to homosexuals (and, we'll emphasize, to their adopted children) . . . [who are] among the most stigmatized, misunderstood, and discriminated-against minorities in the history of the world." Being denied the right to marry, he asserts "is a continuing source of pain to the homosexual community." Citing one of the most poignant passages in *Windsor*, Posner calls to mind once again the emotional impact of denying human beings a fundamental right: "The differentiation demeans the couple . . . [and] humiliates tens of thousands of children now being raised by same-sex couples."[8]

For those in the courtroom familiar with Judge Posner's reasoning in *Baskin v. Bogan*—and there were many—Mitchell's challenge to Posner's understanding of rational basis plus review seemed a daring reach. Desperate to find his way across the minefield left by Posner's decision and by objections Judges Higginbotham and Graves had repeatedly raised to arguments from Louisiana and Mississippi, Mitchell set out to demonstrate that "the Plaintiffs . . . throughout this litigation, have mischaracterized the nature of rational basis review." Nine times in the course of the thirty minutes allotted him—most of those listening interpreted the repetition as signaling both insecurity and the scarcity of believable arguments available—Mitchell insisted that in order to win Texas did not have to prove that same-sex marriage is harmful, only that it does not advance the interests of the State to the same degree as heterosexual marriage. He backpedaled so far as to assert repeatedly that Texas did not have to prove that allowing same-sex marriages would undermine the State's interest in procreation, would increase the number of out-of-wedlock births, would reduce the number of heterosexual marriages, or even "that recognition of same sex marriage will be harmful." It was enough, he asserted, for Texas to claim that those harms would result from allowing same-sex marriage.

Mitchell next contended that the plaintiffs had not only misrepresented the nature of rational basis review, but had also misrepresented the nature of marriage. "They view the institution of marriage as existing only to celebrate the mutual love and commitment of two people," he claimed. Looks of surprised delight spread around the courtroom as same-sex couples who had assembled to support Mark and Vic and Cleo and Nicole realized that for once they had been cast as hopeless romantics rather than villainous rebels determined to undermine the social order. In the eyes of the State, he asserted, marriage is at its core little more than a legal construct. Sounding like a first-year graduate student in the social sciences enamored with important-sounding jargon, Mitchell told the Court that though "the celebration of love" in marriage might be important, "it's secondary to the [State's] interests in generating positive externalities and positive benefits for society in the form of encouraging the creation of new offspring and in reducing the incidence of unplanned, out-of-wedlock births."[9]

More and more taken aback as Texas's argument unfolded, Mark and Vic, Cleo and Nicole held on as the Lone Star State pitched over the edge. "What marriage means from the State's perspective is that there will be a package of benefits conferred on the married couple," he asserted. "What we're saying is that marriage is a subsidy and that the State is entitled to reserve that subsidy for the relationships that are more likely to advance the State's interests." Recognizing certain marriages and not others, Mitchell argued, was analogous to a school district choosing to provide subsidized lunches only to poor children. "It would probably advance the State's interests in nutrition to subsidize school lunches for everyone, but the State is deciding to reserve the subsidy to the group of people who will most likely benefit from the subsidy, and for whom the State's interest in nutrition is more likely to be advanced, and advanced to a greater extent. It's the same type of rational distinction that's being made here with the State's marriage laws." And that, Mitchell concluded, is "all we have to show to prevail on a rational basis . . . that conferring these benefits on opposite sex couples will advance some State interest to a greater degree than conferring these rights on same sex couples."[10]

Mark and Vic, Cleo and Nicole were flabbergasted, aghast that Texas had reduced marriage to a mere subsidy, a financial transaction. They knew they didn't see marriage in terms of "positive externalities" and "subsidies"; they were confident no honest-to-goodness, flesh-and-blood Texan viewed marriage that way, devoid of love and commitment, the very emotions that compelled them to sue Texas in the first place. "That's monstrous," Vic thought, struggling to contain his rage. Listening as the Solicitor General of Texas listed all the things he could not do, all the things he could not have because he was a gay man, Vic felt the tears welling in his eyes. "I don't remember exactly when the tears came," he would tell friends later; "I don't remember feeling them until they were dropping onto my hands, clenched in my lap. I looked to my left and my right and the wetness that must have shone in the fluorescent lights of the courtroom was reflected in the faces of my fellows. What I do remember is the moment Mark and I clasped hands and I felt the strength of our shared bond." [11]

Judge Smith, a Reagan appointee and the staunch conservative on the panel, listened for the most part in silence as Mitchell laid out his case. On the few occasions when he did interrupt, it was to help Mitchell frame a question in a way less likely to generate resistance or to help him steer clear of vulnerable positions the other judges might use to reject his arguments. By contrast, barely three minutes had passed before Judge Graves broke the flow of Mitchell's argument. Justice Higginbotham reacted to the State's analogy in the same way as the plaintiffs. "I'm trying to follow your analogy," he told Mitchell, "because the lunch analogy sounds like I'm not denying you the right to eat lunch, I'm just telling you I'm not going to pay for it." Mitchell began a response—"The State is not denying the right to live together, it's not denying the right to choose their names or hold a wedding ceremony, it's simply"—but Higginbotham was having none of it. More skeptical by the moment, he interrupted Mitchell with the obvious question: "You can't just get married?" Mark, infuriated, thought back to Neel Lane's response to the State's arguments at the district court level a year before: "That's like holding someone's head under water and saying the person is free to breathe, just not air."[12]

Thereafter, barely a minute passed without an interruption as Higginbotham and Graves grew more and more skeptical of and impatient with Mitchell's reasoning. When on several occasions the Solicitor General pressed for a broad understanding of fit in rational basis review, Judges Higginbotham and Graves made it clear they were not at all ready to go along. "All one has to ask," Mitchell asserted as the discussion began in earnest, "is whether it's possible *to imagine* a rational reason for the State to proceed with caution when changing the definition of the institution of marriage." Minutes later, he returned to the same theme: "To declare [Texas's ban on same-sex marriage] unconstitutional on rational basis review would mean that there's *no conceivable rationale* that could be imagined that could support the Legislature's decision" (emphasis added).

Graves argued for a less stringent standard, that "rational basis review just says you've got to show some rational relationship between the law and the purposes articulated for the passage of that law." Even Judge Smith felt it necessary to point out that "There are limits . . . [the fit] can't be fantasy," an admission necessitated by the Fifth Circuit Court's decision in *St. Joseph Abbey v. Castille* which Roberta Kaplan brought to the court's attention in the previous hour. Mitchell had in fact been sent earlier signs that his hopeful reach was in trouble. At one of the many points where Mitchell argued the "greater degree" argument, he had claimed, "That's enough to pass rational basis review." Higginbotham's reply had sucked the wind from his sails: "I'm not too sure," he replied in a deadpan voice that spelled trouble for Texas.[13]

Yet another sign that Texas's case was in trouble appeared in the difficulty the judges had in following Mitchell's arguments, convoluted at best, sophistical at worst. Judge Graves was the first to throw up his hands. "I'm not following what you're saying," he told Mitchell at one point with more than a touch of impatience. Later, puzzled yet again by Mitchell's fuzzy presentation, Judge Graves grew just a bit snippy—"I *guess* it's your assertion that . . ." (emphasis added). But it was Judge Higginbotham who interrupted most often in the hope of understanding arguments that furrowed brows across the courtroom and left both judges and spectators looking quizzically at one another. "I'm trying to follow your analogy," he told Mitchell at one point, only to reject the analogy when Mitchell at last made himself clear. Two minutes later, confused once again at where the Solicitor General was going, Higginbotham stopped the forward rush with a question that sprung from his confusion: "Then what are you arguing?" Later, when Mitchell tried yet again to press his "greater degree" argument, Higginbotham's attempt to paraphrase the State's position went awry. "That's not our argument," Mitchell insisted. In response, Higginbotham turned Mitchell's words into a question. "That's not your argument?" Told again that he had gotten it wrong, Higginbotham seemed to grow just a bit angry. "It sure sounded like it," he growled.[14]

Confusion turned to consternation as Texas surprised judges and spectators alike with its next move. "We should be clear," Mitchell told the Court, "we are not conceding that sexual orientation is immutable . . . There is a dispute in the scientific literature." For those in the courtroom it was hard not to call to mind "disputes" in the scientific literature about evolution and global warming—the 1 or 2 percent, the fringe studies so popular in Texas. Calling to mind statements by "every medical association," Judge Higginbotham gave voice to the wave of incredulity that swept across the courtroom: "There is?"[15] Again, Judge Posner seemed a shadow presence in the courtroom as Mark remembered the language in the Seventh Circuit's same-sex marriage decision: "And there is little doubt that sexual orientation, the ground of the discrimination, is an immutable (and probably an innate, in the sense of in-born) characteristic rather than a choice."[16] Mark, Vic, Nicole, and Cleo looked at each other again, wondering if they had misheard, wondering how their State could be so wrong and misguided. Under questioning, Mitchell contended that his goal was "to distinguish race and sex" adding that he hoped to use the distinction to argue against the application of strict scrutiny.

Ironically, Texas's immutability gambit—perhaps intended to forestall comparisons with *Loving v. Virginia*, used by Judge Vaughn Walker in California's Proposition 8 case to conclude that "the [constitutional] right to marry protects an individual's choice of marital partners regardless of gender"—pitched Mitchell into a world of unexpected trouble. "The question here is," Higginbotham mused aloud, "why is Texas doing what it's doing?" Minutes later, his question had become more pointed—and more threatening to the Texas case. "The question is," he suggested, "whether there is— [whether] it's really a product of animus."[17] If animus was a factor, the Court would subject Texas's ban to heightened scrutiny rather than the more lenient standard of rational basis review, a hurdle Mitchell knew would be almost impossible to overcome.

Hoping to avoid a charge he knew would be fatal, Mitchell argued that "the reason it can't be animus is because sexual orientation is relevant to the State's interests in procreation"—and he dove one more time into the "greater degree" argument he had made so many times before with regard to the State's right to grant benefits and subsidies. In response to Judge Higginbotham's follow-up question—"There's no consequence, then, other than the fact that you save State resources?"—Mitchell introduced the "Go Slow" and "Democratic Process" arguments. "Same sex marriage," he suggested, "hasn't been around long enough for anyone to know with any certainty what the ultimate effects will be." And moments later, "The people of Texas have every right to proceed with caution, and they can decide to wait and see how this social experiment plays out."[18] Once again, however, Mitchell's arguments plunged him into unexpected trouble.

Judge Smith, who in the course of the morning had shown himself most inclined to accept arguments from Louisiana, Mississippi, and now Texas, seemed suddenly to grow skeptical. "What is the concern or the fear," he asked, "that we're waiting to . . . that we should wait to see if it's real?" Mitchell's response was that Texans were troubled by "a theoretical fear . . . a hypothetical concern. [If] the notion that marriage exists not only primarily, but perhaps almost exclusively, as an institution to celebrate the love and commitment of two people" took hold, he argued, "it could undermine the idea that marriage is existing [*sic*] to encourage procreation"—a complete about-face from his earlier claim that Texas was not arguing same-sex marriage undermined procreation.[19]

Unconvinced at what seemed a weak argument, and perhaps recalling Mitchell's earlier claims, Smith raised the specter once again: "My question to you," he told Mitchell, "is at what point does this hypothesis fade into animus?" Judges Higginbotham and Graves were quick to leap into the breach Smith's skepticism had opened. Mitchell argued—once again—that Texas law was rooted in biological realities and, therefore, not a product of animus. But Graves pressed hard, pushing Mitchell toward a more inclusive definition of animus dangerous to the State's case: "Fear of the unknown or lack of understanding of people who are different, and insensitivity to the preferences of people who are different, those are not things you equate with animus?" Higginbotham was equally insistent: "It's not confined to the malignant animus of things like racism of a sort . . . it is the uncertainty that is the fear of this strange animal that's new to them." Higginbotham's final words as Mitchell prepared to step away from the lectern were unsettling. "You were," he warned by way of parting, "characterizing [animus] in other ways I would not agree with on the law."[20]

* * *

When Neel Lane stepped to the lectern to speak for the Texas plaintiffs, the sociological and legalistic arguments on which the State of Texas had based its case gave way to a comforting touch of humanity. For the most part, Mark and Vic, Nicole and Cleo sat quietly through the hearing, eyes straight ahead and betraying no emotion. They had listened in pained silence as Texas stubbornly refused to acknowledge that gays and lesbians are often parents, that in their home state 11,000 same-sex households were happily raising 19,000 children. Part of who they were, part of their humanity, was being ignored. Eventually the burden proved too much. As Mitchell gabbled on and on about "benefits," "subsidies," and "positive externalities," even the assertion that same-sex marriage was no more than a "social experiment," Cleo sought refuge from ideas they found insulting in an old children's rhyme: "First comes love, then comes marriage, then comes Cleo with a baby carriage." Everyone knows, she thought, that it all begins with love. She and Nicole had in fact become so upset that they penned a note to their attorneys, handing it to Mark, who handed it to Roberta Kaplan, who passed it across the bar to Jessica Weisel, a lawyer on the Akin Gump team. They needed to be sure Neel Lane would remind the Court that they had traveled to Massachusetts to marry because they hoped for children they would raise together, the outward expression of their love.

That hope became Lane's opening. He chided Texas for having "created a caste system abhorrent to the core values of the Fourteenth Amendment" and offered Nicole's pregnancy as his first example of unequal, discriminatory treatment. "When that child is born," Lane warned, "on that birth certificate there will be Nicole's name. But where Cleo's name should appear, there will be a blank, as it was with their first child." No one in the courtroom, including some who had brought babies in carriers, needed to be reminded of the troubles that would follow should anything happen to Nicole before she and Cleo could jump through the requisite legal hoops—an enormous expense and a frightening delay—to amend the birth certificate of the daughter they were expecting. No one needed to be reminded that each dollar spent—and they knew from hard experience that costs would run into the thousands—would mean one less dollar available for their daughter's health, education, and welfare. No one needed to be reminded of the pain even the faint possibility of that had caused Nicole and Cleo and so many others in their circumstances.[21]

Lane turned his attention next to the men and the fear that troubled their sleep. "If Mark, one of my other clients, dies tomorrow, when he dies, where there should be a surviving spouse named, Vic, his partner of seventeen years, there will be a blank space." Mark, who has heard too many real-life stories of long-term partners separated by death before they could marry, teared up. Though in the remainder of his thirty minutes Lane would round the diamond, touching carefully on all the necessary legal bases, he made it clear from the outset that his case would be about the harms done to vulnerable human beings by "stigmatizing differentiations," an approach his clients very much appreciated.[22] For the sympathetic audience in the courtroom, the argument that followed seemed a metaphorical home run.

For Texas's cold and clinical description of marriage, Lane had the perfect rejoinder. "What you heard from this lectern," he asserted, "is an incredibly narrow, blinkered view of marriage that would be unrecognizable, really, to anyone who has experienced it, witnessed it, or aspires to it." The emotional temperature of the room rose moment by moment as he eased the Court back into the consideration of the real lives human beings lead. "It's amazing," he continued; "Really, it's quite amazing because one of the consistent accusations has been . . . that we are attempting to redefine marriage. And I have never seen as radical a redefinition of marriage as I heard at this lectern [from] the State of Texas." Turning the focus away from ideas most in the courtroom found cryptic, almost indecipherable and towards people who live and breathe and feel, especially toward children and the harms done to them, Lane alluded to Justice Kennedy's conclusion in *Windsor* that the federal government's failure to recognize same-sex marriage "demeans the couple, whose moral and sexual choices the Constitution protects, and whose relationship the State has sought to dignify . . . [and] humiliates tens of thousands of children now being raised by same-sex couples."[23] For good measure, he alluded as well to Mitchell's *bête noir*, Judge Posner, whose influential decision in *Baskin v. Bogan* concluded that though "Formally these cases are about discrimination against a small, homosexual minority . . . at a deeper level, as we shall see, they are about the welfare of American children."[24]

If the number of questions appellate court judges ask attorneys for one side or the other is an indication of the way they are leaning, and if more questions are a sign of the judges' skepticism, then the Texas match-up spelled trouble for the State. The Solicitor General, interrupted almost sixty times, mostly by Judges Higginbotham and Graves, was rarely allowed to speak for more than a minute before the hammer fell. By comparison, Neel Lane was allowed to speak freely—only twenty-four interruptions, and some of those were "friendly questions" that invited him to make a point favorable to the plaintiffs' case.

The first question came from Judge Graves who wanted to know if splitting the question—deciding, for example, that Texas must recognize same-sex marriages performed elsewhere, but could continue its prohibition against performing same-sex marriage—would be "legally inconsistent." Before Lane could fully explain how *Loving v. Virginia* precluded such a decision, almost as though the details of the argument mattered less than the opportunity to dismiss the possibility, Graves interrupted again. "So as regards your plaintiffs, it's everybody wins or nobody wins?" A wave of laughter swept across the courtroom at Lane's reply. "It's everybody wins, your Honor."[25] Judge Graves laughed along, seemingly pleased to have Lane's response on record.

In the arguments for Louisiana and Mississippi, Judge Smith had been the one to conjure the weary ghost of *Baker v. Nelson*. Now it was Judge Higginbotham, whose questions across the morning had shown him more sympathetic to same-sex marriage than to the State's prohibitions, who moved from *Loving* to *Baker*. "Don't you find it striking," he asked Lane, "that only four or five years after *Loving* the Court took the action it did in *Baker v. Nelson*?" Higginbotham would return later in Lane's presentation to problems raised by *Baker*; his question rose from genuine concerns. But at the same time, it allowed Lane to lay out the now familiar case against the precedential value of the Supreme Court's one-line summary dismissal of *Baker v. Nelson* in 1972. "That was forty-two years ago," Lane began, "forty-three years ago . . . *Baker* was decided at a time [before *Lawrence v. Texas*] when homosexual conduct was actually illegal." We live now, he maintained, in "a different world" where doctrinal developments "expressly recognized in *Windsor*" have taught us that "views do evolve" and have consigned *Baker* to the dustbin of history.[26]

Lane didn't cite Judge Martha Craig Daughtrey's spot-on minority opinion in the Sixth Circuit case with its literary dismissal of *Baker* as vampiric, an undead thing prowling the earth long after its time: "If ever there was a legal 'dead letter' emanating from the Supreme Court, *Baker v. Nelson* is a prime candidate. It lacks only a stake through its heart."[27] But he did allude to Judge Richard A. Posner—yet, again—whose opinion in *Baskin v. Bogan* virtually laughed *Baker* from the courtroom. "*Baker* was decided in 1972—forty-two years ago and the dark ages so far as litigation over discrimination against homosexuals is concerned," Posner wrote; "Subsequent decisions such as *Romer v. Evans*, *Lawrence v. Texas*, and *United States v. Windsor* are distinguishable from the present two cases but make clear that *Baker* is no longer authoritative."[28] Judge Graves, who had listened to three hours of arguments that returned again and again to the precedential value of *Baker*, plunged the courtroom into another wave of laughter with his summary—and dismissal—of the discussion. "I'll just note that all of this talk about *Baker* and the 1970s is making me nostalgic for my Afro and my eight-track tapes."[29]

Free to return to the argument he had laid out in advance, Neel Lane directed the Court's attention once again to the charge of animus left hanging in the air when Mitchell retreated to the lawyer's table. In what was almost certainly the strongest language heard in the course of the day, Lane charged the State with duplicity, shredded the premise on which the State's argument depended, and attacked its logic. The State had argued that restricting marriage to heterosexual couples would encourage responsible procreation, more births to married couples, fewer births to unmarried women. But as Lane pointed out, Mitchell had admitted under questioning "that restriction doesn't promote that end, it doesn't stop births to single parents." Worse yet, the State had been unable to show how "prohibiting same-sex couples from marrying will somehow encourage opposite-sex couples who otherwise wouldn't do so, to procreate within marriage." Lane drew attention as well to the shaky logic of the State's case. "If marriage is good for children," he asked, "why deny marriage to same-sex couples with children?"[30]

After the unanswerable question had hung in the air for a few seconds, he drove home the obvious conclusion. "The reality is that this law depriving same-sex couples of the right to marry is not intended to modify or guide the behavior of opposite sex couples at all. Everyone knows that this law is really about the moral disapproval of homosexuals." Pure animus. And since the Supreme Court in *Lawrence v. Texas* rejected moral disapproval as a legitimate state interest in upholding discriminatory laws, he continued, "counsel for the State has to come up here and attempt to redefine it with *this somewhat half-baked justification* that narrows what actually marriage is and attempts to redefine it, and convince you that this is what the people of Texas believe marriage is." The only conclusion possible, Lane told the Court, is that "the purported justification is *ludicrous*" (emphasis added).[31] Across the courtroom, spectators, whose brows had furrowed repeatedly as they tried to understand Texas's slippery arguments, smiled their agreement. Neel Lane's clients went further, nodding their heads affirmatively.

To advance his claim of animus and to argue for a level of scrutiny higher than rational basis review, Neel Lane turned to the same Fifth Circuit case Roberta Kaplan had introduced earlier, *St. Joseph Abbey v. Castille*. Judge Higginbotham had written that "The great deference due state economic regulation does not demand judicial blindness to the history of a challenged rule or the context of its adoption." The Court was, he declared, free to examine "setting and history."[32] Taking advantage of that opening, Lane brought the history of Texas's attempts to prohibit same-sex marriage—by statute in 1973 and 2003, by a constitutional amendment in 2005—to the attention of the Court. On each occasion, Lane pointed out, Texas was responding to immediate fears that marriage licenses would be granted to same-sex couples. In 1973 several same-sex couples had applied for marriage licenses; Antonio Molina and William "Billie" Ert were mistakenly granted a license by a clerk who did not realize both applicants were male. In 2005 same-sex marriage had become legal in Massachusetts awakening fears that the same-sex marriage question would rise again in Texas. "There is," he maintained, "no evidence that the State passed the measures that are challenged here and that were struck down by Judge Garcia, to channel opposite-sex couples into marriage for the purpose of procreation." More suspicious yet, in a departure from prior law, the State had expressly refused to recognize same-sex marriages legally performed in other states. "The history and background of these measures," Lane concluded, "exposes the State's rationale as *this sort of post-hoc hypothetical fantasy* that the Court rejected in *St. Joseph Abbey*" (emphasis added).[33]

Lane's argument from *St. Joseph Abbey* was, given its origin in the Fifth Circuit Court, more convincing than a similar case from another jurisdiction might have been. "The Court made it clear," he reminded the judges, that it "will not merely rubber stamp just any asserted rational basis for a statutory restriction. A hypothetical rationale, even post-hoc, cannot be a fantasy . . . the Court will actually examine whether the chosen means rationally relate to the State or to interests that it articulates." Echoing the attorneys who had pleaded for the plaintiffs in Louisiana and Mississippi, and even Judge Higginbotham at one point, Lane asserted that in *DeLeon v. Perry*, "It's not a matter of an imperfect fit, but no fit at all."[34]

But in fact Lane hoped to drive the court to a level of scrutiny higher than rational basis review. When an "unpopular minority" is subjected to "a disadvantage imposed or borne of animosity," he argued, "a more searching form of review is required." He urged the Court to consider carefully the factors that might lead to heightened scrutiny and asked, at the very least, that the Court employ the loosely defined "careful review" of which Justice Kennedy spoke in *Windsor*—"rational basis with a bite," he called it. A flurry of questions from Judge Higginbotham—Has discrimination against homosexuals been of an "unusual character"? Is the same-sex marriage movement moving too quickly? Would the same-sex marriage movement be better off without judicial involvement?—gave Lane the opportunity to end where he began with reference to human beings and harms done. "I don't represent a movement," Lane told Judge Higginbotham. "The quickness of the 'movement' does not bear on whether my clients have a present Constitutional right. They are discriminated against. They are not treated the same as their fellow citizens."[35]

* * *

When the Court adjourned, the plaintiffs, their attorneys, and their supporters were smiling, cautiously optimistic that the latter-day Battle of New Orleans had gone their way. Arm in arm, hand in hand, they carried the warmth of their smiles outside onto the steps of the courthouse and into the bright sunlight of an unseasonably cold day—a day with temperatures so low one reporter covering the outdoor press conference joked that her mouth had frozen in place and she could hardly form the words of her question. Confronted by a swarm of media as they came through the main door, plaintiffs from the three states whose cases had been argued stood shivering on the steps as photographers snapped photo after photo. Eventually they walked to the side of the building where microphones had been set up, Mark and Vic so distracted by the crowd and the cameras following their every step that they very nearly walked into a tree. One by one, attorneys and plaintiffs stepped forward to speak, the order determined by the order in which the Court had heard the states' cases: Louisiana, Mississippi, Texas. In each case the attorneys—the first to speak—were professionally cautious and reserved, the plaintiffs less guarded.

Camilla Taylor of Lambda Legal—her success in arguing *Baskin v. Bogan* before the Seventh Circuit Court of Appeals played a role in the morning's proceedings—had argued the Louisiana case. She claimed only that "we got a respectful hearing" and that the judges asked "a lot of great questions." Watching and listening, she had detected among the judges "significant discomfort with the unequal treatment same-sex couples and their children have been experiencing" and pronounced herself "hopeful that the Court will act soon to strike down the marriage bans." Havard Scott, first to speak for the Louisiana plaintiffs, was nothing short of ebullient. Brimming with newfound confidence—the eight couples from Louisiana were the only ones who had not emerged victorious from a federal district court—he told the crowd, "Today we asked the Fifth Circuit to force the State of Louisiana to recognize the dignity and respect and equality of our marriage and the marriages of all same-sex couples in Louisiana. I think we had a wonderful reception from the Fifth Circuit. I'm very optimistic," he added; today was "a great day for equality."

Roberta Kaplan of Paul, Weiss drew the crowd's attention to the oversized letters on the courthouse spelling out "John Minor Wisdom"; she praised him as she had in Court as "one of the greatest defenders of civil rights in our nation's history." "I only hope today," she added, "that the Court and the judges who heard our argument so carefully, and who were so well-prepared, do so in the spirit of Judge Wisdom and grant equal rights under the Constitution to our clients." Kaplan's wife and son, standing nearby, beamed with pride. Asked about the similarity of arguments for the plaintiffs from state to state, Kaplan returned again to the Constitution. "The reason you don't hear any differences in the arguments from the states is that the Constitution is the Constitution, and the Fourteenth Amendment applies just the same way to Texas, and Louisiana, in New York and Mississippi . . . we're here to enforce the Constitution."

Andrea Sanders spoke for the Mississippi plaintiffs, talked in endearingly human terms of her ten-year, committed relationship with Rebecca Bickett. "In the beginning," she remembered, "we had great dreams of getting married and starting a family, but those dreams were quickly overcome by the reality of Mississippi's current laws." They did start a family, she continued, a very ordinary, American family. "We have a home, we have pets; we comfort our kids, we teach them right from wrong and how to love our family dearly." But for years they had dreamed of marrying. "We never let go of our dream," she confided; "we held on to that ember of hope that we would someday see a change in a positive way in Mississippi. We guarded that ember and shared its warmth and happiness with those close to us." And now, she concluded, channeling the feeling of the previous night's rally, "we stand together with others from Louisiana and Texas and Mississippi with the country watching our small flame grow."

Neel Lane of Akin Gump at first echoed Camilla Taylor's caution when he spoke for Texas: "We had a fair hearing today." But when asked about Texas's "subsidies" argument, he opened up. "I have never understood marriage as about lining up for subsidies," he asserted; "I don't see marriage as a food line or a benefit check . . . I think the notion that marriage is merely the provision of economic benefits from the state is ludicrous." What Lane really wanted was to speak directly to "the 600,000 gay and lesbian citizens of the State of Texas who live under a badge of inferiority, the more than 90,000 couples who live together in committed relationships"—and to celebrate the courage Mark and Vic, Cleo and Nicole had shown in fighting "to vindicate your rights. Justice will come," he assured the thousands back home in Texas. "Equality will come; it's going to happen." When he was done, the crowd roared its approval.

Mark stepped forward, Vic by his side, the first to speak for the Texas plaintiffs. It's not about subsidies, he argued, it's about love and the freedom to marry the person you love most in the world. Encouraged by what he had heard in all three arguments, Mark summed up the day with the kind of parallel phrasing so familiar from the speeches of Winston Churchill he studied as an undergraduate. "Vic and I knew when we came here," Mark began, "that we were on the right side of history, and the right side of love and compassion. And after hearing our lawyers, as well as the lawyers for Louisiana and Mississippi make our case, we know now that we are on the right side of the law." In his eyes, and in the eyes of the joyful plaintiffs surrounding him on every side, there was no room for ambiguity. Cleopatra DeLeon stepped next to the microphone, her partner, Nicole Dimetman, by her side. What had caught their attention during the oral arguments was, Cleo revealed, a simple phrase, a few words she feared would pass without notice by those who enjoyed all that they implied. They summed up perfectly what she and Nicole yearned for with all their hearts: "the shelter of marriage . . . Over the course of our relationship we've been denied that shelter of marriage, and that is the reason we are fighting, not only to have our marriage recognized, but also for the rights of other people who want to get married." That shelter, Cleo asserted, would "protect the children that come about because of our marriages," guaranteeing them the rights children born to heterosexual couples enjoyed without question.

***

Days before leaving for New Orleans, Mark had written on his Facebook page that he and Vic had received "a wonderful Christmas gift" from some "dear friends"—a copy of Richard Blanco's masterful poem about inclusiveness,

For All of Us, One Today, autographed and inscribed to him and Vic. Blanco, the gay, Cuban poet who read his poem at President Obama's Second Inauguration, had been told of the struggle to bring same-sex marriage to Texas and had written accordingly on the title page: "For Mark and Vic . . . Here's to *your* amazing journey. *Buena Suerte!*" Good luck! Looking to Blanco's text, Mark zeroed in on two sentences. "Every story begins inside a story that's already begun by others. Long before we take our first breath, there's a plot well under way with characters and a setting we did not choose but which chose us." Blanco's reflection led Mark to a celebration of his and Vic's parents and grandparents and of the values they passed along. "They live on through us," Mark wrote, "as do many others, including our friends who gave us this wonderful present." What made Mark think of family and friends made Michelle Garcia think of Mark and Vic and the ways people who know them embrace them. "What a touching gift," she wrote in the comments; "You are both so thought of in many peoples' lives."[36]

When Michelle Garcia wrote her Facebook comment, she had no way of knowing just how right she was. In the days just before and after oral arguments in New Orleans, everybody, or so it seemed at times, felt compelled to reach out to Mark and Vic and Cleo and Nicole. E-mails, texts, messages sent via Facebook, comments on Facebook, poured in, some from relatives, some from friends, most from complete strangers. Some came from gays and lesbians grateful that Mark and Vic, Cleo and Nicole had stepped forward to lead the fight against discrimination in Texas; some came from straight friends embarrassed that Texas was fighting so hard against equality and the future. Some messages were just a few simple but heartfelt words, like the text from Kristen Johnson, Mark's niece. "I love you guys and am thinking about you this morning!!!" Her message ended with emoticons, two red hearts.[37] Messages from strangers tended to be longer, like the one from Jim and Michael Rainbolt-Baily. "Mark, please know how grateful Michael and I are to you and Vic! We also reside in Plano. We were married in Santa Fe last April. Because of your selfless and brave efforts we are almost 'there' in Texas. A big hug of gratitude to you both! Prayers for strength, endurance, and safety as you guys travel."[38] One of Mark's law school friends, Rich Ehret, had reached out to offer the use of his firm's conference room across the street from the John Minor Wisdom Courthouse. Randall Raison, a certified court reporter, sent a transcript of the oral arguments, his way of thanking Akin Gump and the plaintiffs for what they were doing.

Texas for Marriage gathered notes of thanks and encouragement from well-wishers and posted them on their web site—so many that printing them out, even in a tiny, eight-point font, requires fifteen sheets of paper. Every one tells a story.

—As a conservative 60 year old Baptist woman, I have changed my views of Gay Marriage over the years. I know that God loves you and will bless you in your fight to be married. My prayers are for your strength and resolve. Steel your hearts from those that don't understand and pray for their eyes to be opened. God bless and best of luck. –Cathy Hickman, Arlington, Texas

—Texans love their pioneers! Thank you for being the pioneers in an effort that we didn't think we would see in our lifetimes. –Vicky Hennigan, Round Rock, Texas

—My fiancée, Kim, and I can't thank you enough for your bravery, hard work, and determination to bring marriage equality to Texas. We are raising two boys and dream of the day we will be able to get married and be recognized where we call home. The work you are doing is such an important thing for all couples and families and we just want to send all our gratitude and best wishes to your families. Love will win! —Heather Johnson, Fort Worth, Texas

—As a pastor, I am proud of your efforts to ensure marriage equality and I want you to know that many in the faith community support your efforts! Thanks for leading the way! —John Frey, Spring, Texas

—I just want to thank you for what you are doing. All the sleepless nights and hard work are greatly appreciated. You are not only paving the way for the current generation, but also for younger generations. My son is seventeen and one day he WILL marry a man who makes him happy. This would not be possible without your efforts. —Jenna Guswha, Mineola, Texas

In message after message the same words appear over and over and over again: Mark and Vic, Nicole and Cleo are "heroes" who are "selfless" and "inspirational." They are icons of "strength," "courage," "bravery," "tenacity," "patience," and "perseverance." For the plaintiffs, the deluge of messages from so many supportive hearts was itself "inspirational."[39]

Back in Plano after the excitement of New Orleans, back to the mundane chores that take up so much of our lives, Mark found still more reassurance when he stopped one afternoon at the dry cleaners.

"How did it go?" the woman who works the counter asked. She listened to Mark's estimate of the proceedings, fidgeting all the while. Clearly, she had more to tell.

"My daughter, seven years old, was watching the news when she saw you. 'Mom,' she yelled, 'your customers are on the news.'"

"I know," I said. She wanted to know why you were there so I explained it to her. "Because the man and his partner want to get married."

"Well," the little girl told her mother without skipping a beat, "I think they should be able to."

Mark agreed and left the shop with a smile on his face.[40]

***

Convinced that oral arguments had gone their way, hoping that the Fifth Circuit would rule quickly, one of the attorneys at Akin Gump put together a pool for the plaintiffs and their lawyers—a bit of sympathetic magic intended to "make it happen." Moved, perhaps, by her desire for a decision before Nicole gave birth to their second child, Cleo chose the earliest date that seemed half-reasonable, January 23. "Why not?" she thought. Judge Orlando Garcia's decision in the Federal Court for the Western District of Texas had been handed down in only two weeks. It could happen again. Matt Pepping's choice, March 20, the last date chosen and an impossible two months away, seemed at the time an unlikely contender. "Fingers crossed that Cleo's pick is the right one," Mark wrote in an e-mail to the lawyers and plaintiffs.[41] Great expectations for an early victory in Louisiana, Mississippi, and Texas had become the order of the day.

A week later, the narrative changed. Since the *Windsor* decision in June 2015, advocates of marriage equality had basked in the glow of what an editorial in the *New York Times* called "a remarkable and nearly unanimous string of more than 40 lower-court rulings around the country" in which "arguments against same-sex marriage have been thoroughly dismantled . . . Federal and state judges," they declared, "have found that state bans violate the Constitution's guarantees of due process and equal protection."[42] Victories in four Circuit Courts of Appeals—the Fourth, Seventh, Ninth, and Tenth Circuits—had become keystones in the triumphal arch most imagined would soon be complete. But on November 6, 2014, the Sixth Circuit's split decision in *DeBoer v. Snyder* brought an end to the string of victories. Writing for the majority, Judge Jeffrey S. Sutton found *Baker v. Nelson* precedential; though the legal ground on which opponents of marriage equality had built their hopes was eroding elsewhere, Judge Sutton's decision found the bans against same-sex marriage in Ohio, Michigan, Tennessee, and Kentucky constitutional. Then, January 16, 2015, the Supreme Court announced that it would hear the cases appealed from the Sixth Circuit—cases from four states involving sixteen same-sex couples, a widower, seven children, an adoption agency, even a funeral director—consolidated as *Obergefell v. Hodges*.

Everyone following the struggle for marriage equality knew Jim Obergefell's heart-wrenching story, how his partner of twenty-one years, John Arthur, had died of Lou Gehrig's disease just three months after their wedding on the tarmac at the Baltimore-Washington International Airport in a medivac plane, how the state of Ohio refused to recognize their love on John's death certificate. Fewer people knew the stories of the other plaintiffs in the consolidated cases, or for that matter in the hundreds of same-sex marriage cases filed across America—tales of birth certificates that named only one parent, adoptions denied and adoption forms that named only one parent, medical authorization forms ignored, benefits of every description denied, marriage licenses denied. But their stories, Mark and Vic's and Cleo and Nicole's stories among them, had finally arrived at the highest court in the land.

The Court's order defined two questions: 1) Does the Fourteenth Amendment require a state to license a marriage between two people of the same sex? 2) Does the Fourteenth Amendment require a state to recognize a marriage between two people of the same sex when their marriage was lawfully licensed and performed out-of-state? Quietly recognizing that marriage equality had emerged as the greatest civil rights issue of our time, the Court allowed an extraordinary ninety minutes for arguments on the first question, another sixty minutes on the second.

Some were disappointed by the loss before the Sixth Circuit, but Mark and Vic were not among them. As Evan Wolfson pointed out, every ending is also a beginning. "The Court's decision today," he asserted, "begins what we hope will be the last chapter in our campaign to win marriage nationwide."[43] James Esseks, Director of the ACLU Lesbian Gay Bisexual Transgender & AIDS Project, found another metaphor but gave voice to the same confident idea. "This is it," he claimed in a press release, "the end game in the longstanding campaign to win the freedom to marry for same-sex couples nationwide is upon us."[44] By the time of the Supreme Court's mid-January announcement, same-sex marriage was legal in thirty-six states and the District of Columbia, 70 percent of Americans lived in places where gay couples could marry, and 59 percent of Americans approved of same-sex marriage. Any danger that in deciding for marriage equality the Supreme Court risked getting too far ahead of public opinion had long since passed. As Mary Bonauto pointed out, the issue "is coming to the court at the right time and the right circumstances."[45] Great expectations, this time on a national level, quickly became the new order of the day.

Within days of the Supreme Court's announcement, almost two weeks before the Court declared that oral arguments would take place on April 28, Mark and Vic had begun to think about how much "being there" meant to them. By March 5 they had booked flights and a hotel room. "We may not get into the hearing," Mark wrote on Facebook, "but we want to be there anyway. We can't wait!!!! We must be there for history in the making."[46]

That the Supreme Court would take up same-sex marriage in late April seemed at first good news for the Texas plaintiffs. In a private e-mail, Neel Lane played the cautious lawyer. "The Fifth Circuit will definitely rule," he suggested; "the question is whether it will rule before or after the Supreme Court issues its opinion."[47] Speaking for the record, however, he turned the Supreme Court's action to advantage, calling on the lower court to move quickly to put an end to the harms the plaintiffs had suffered. "We believe that the Fifth Circuit should still answer this question independently—and in the affirmative—because our clients have already waited too long for equality and justice."[48] Mark and Vic were even less ambiguous. "I think it will really encourage the Fifth Circuit to issue its decision quickly and to issue a decision that's in favor of same-sex marriage," Mark told a reporter from a local CBS affiliate.[49] Texas for Marriage, sensing that the long wait for marriage equality in Texas was nearly over, posted invitations on Facebook to rallies in five cities on the day the Fifth Circuit Court ruled. "Join us on Decision Day," they urged, "We're ready to celebrate!"[50]

Swept along by the rising wind, Mark and Vic felt at last ready to let down their guard and to celebrate as well. When his father died in 1986, Mark had inherited and set aside two diamonds from a much-cherished ring given his father by a family friend. The time had come, he felt now, to find a jeweler who could incorporate those diamonds into wedding bands for himself and Vic. For the first time, he and Vic began to talk seriously about honeymoon destinations, researching trips on a scale with their previous travels. Patagonia? Tibet and Nepal? A wildlife safari in India? That once-in-a-lifetime attempt to climb Mt. Kilimanjaro? A trip to east Africa to photograph mountain gorillas? In the new world that promised to open before them, anything seemed possible.

Still, waiting for the Fifth Circuit to bring marriage equality to Texas was difficult—and grew more difficult as days turned into weeks and weeks into months. Fearing he would be away from Texas and the man he loved when the decision was announced, Mark cut short a business trip to New York, flying home the minute his work was done rather than staying an "extra" night for dinner with friends. He put off a business trip to the Philippines for fear of being even farther away when the always-near-but-never-present moment came.

Staying busy seemed the best strategy. Vic threw himself into his work as a physician's assistant and teacher, laboring for hours not just over his teaching and clinical work, but over a portfolio making his case for promotion to assistant professor. At the end of January, both men escaped for a long weekend to Big Bend State Park for a photoshoot with Braden Summers, "A Texas Love Story," which later appeared in *The Advocate*.

Early in February they appeared in El Paso with Steve Rudner of Equality Texas to talk about *DeLeon v. Perry* at the Fifth Circuit Court and to solicit help fighting anti-LGBT bills in the legislature. Later the same month they flew to Austin for an HRC Black Tie Dinner. Early in March they traveled again to Austin to appear with Pamela Colloff and Boyce Cabaniss at a Future Forum event—"Same-sex Marriage: An Idea Whose Time Has Come?"—held at the LBJ Library. The beginning of April found them yet again in Austin for the annual JBR Dinner, a fundraiser for the Travis County Democratic Party, at which—together with co-plaintiffs Nicole and Cleo; Sonemaly Phrasaveth, who on February 17 had convinced Probate Judge Guy Herman to recognize her right to inherit as a result of her eight-year common-law marriage; Sarah Goodfriend and Suzanne Bryant, who on February 19 had convinced District Judge David Wahlberg to issue a marriage license and wed immediately—they were honored for their work on behalf of marriage equality in Texas. And scored a photo with the guest speaker, Senator Bernie Sanders.

But the whirlwind of travel and advocacy, though always exciting and often tiring, was not enough to keep Mark and Vic from dwelling on *the* question: "When? How many days or weeks or months until we are free to marry?" Nor was it enough to keep them from reflecting on the harms and indignities heaped daily on the LGBT community or their mounting frustration with the silence emanating from Fifth Circuit Court. A continual flow of news from near and far broke through their charmed circle of friends and supporters to remind them of another world where people driven by animus waited, eager to do harm. One day might bring a newspaper article about a Colorado funeral stopped in mid-course when the minister learned that the deceased was a lesbian, another day a report that the pediatrician who had promised to care for the daughter of two lesbians had "prayed over it" and refused her services, still another day the sad news that one of their own senators, Ted Cruz, had introduced The State Defense of Marriage Act, legislation intended to strip recognition and benefits from hundreds of thousands of same-sex couples. Even random chance seemed at times to cast shadows. Mark found it hard to drive from his mind the story of Randall Dygert, a Dallas nurse killed in a freak accident by a shuttle bus as he walked to work one January morning, separating him from his long-term partner before they were able to marry. That he and Vic might be separated before they could marry was Mark's worst nightmare, the mere mention of which in Neel Lane's opening remarks before the Fifth Circuit had brought tears to his eyes.

Other threats, closer in time and closer to home, rose up as well. Mark and Vic had no sooner returned from New Orleans than they found themselves caught up in the struggle against the Liberty Institute, working in conjunction with conservative churches and under the guise of "religious liberty" to repeal Plano's recently updated Non-Discrimination Ordinance. In an op-ed for *The Dallas Morning News*, Mark remembered his fear as a seventeen-year-old in Oklahoma when Anita Bryant led a similar crusade in Dade County, Florida. "For the first time it dawned upon me," he wrote, "that there were people in the world who wanted to refuse me a job, an apartment, or a meal, simply because I was gay. This realization scarred and scared me."[51] In the end, history didn't repeat itself, "sexual orientation and gender identity" remained on the list of reasons why one could not discriminate in Plano. Friendly neighbors continued to wave, to bring their children to the door selling Girl Scout cookies and the like, to help round up the dogs when they slipped out the door. Still, they couldn't help but feel that the tide of hatred had risen around them, lapped even at the door of their Plano home.

When the March edition of *Texas Monthly* appeared on newsstands and in the mailboxes of subscribers, more trouble arose. A year and a month earlier as *DeLeon V. Perry* headed for the first time into a Federal courtroom in San Antonio, *Texas Monthly* had run a sympathetic article on Mark and Vic, "The Accidental Activists." Though one of the "sell lines" at the top of the cover tempted readers with a story about "The Men Who Want to Marry," a black-and-white photo of Ted Cruz tucking away a parchment scroll of the Preamble to the Constitution swept all else to the corners. Whatever the reasons—perhaps at the time few readers in Texas saw same-sex marriage as a real possibility— the article stirred little controversy. But in March 2015 the image of Ted Cruz on the cover was replaced by Nicole and Cleo, photographed in vivid color to stand out against a neutral background, toys at their feet, their son in Nicole's arms—and Nicole visibly pregnant. The title of the article, "Modern Family," invited parallels with the sitcom of the same name which features, among other varieties of "married," two gay men who are raising a child together—funny, a bit goofy, always endearing and sympathetic. The "deck"—magazine talk for text under or next to a title that provides more detail about what lies within—read like a question or a challenge depending on one's point of view: "Cleo and Nicole are a devoted couple. They dote on their son. They have a baby girl on the way. So why won't Texas let them get married?"

What the editor in the next issue called "the voluminous inrush of response" was largely negative, often nothing short of hateful—so much so that Pamela Colloff, who wrote "Modern Family," worried about how she would break the news to Nicole and Cleo. "I don't think any of us was prepared for the degree of vitriol," she said. "I was not prepared for the ugliness of the language and the raw bigotry we saw."[52] Some subscribers returned the issue intact; one scribbled across the cover photo "Worst issue ever." Another wrote to cut off all future correspondence: "If this is what I am to expect from *Texas Monthly*, I request a refund for the balance of my subscription and that all mail from *Texas Monthly* to my address cease." One angry subscriber couldn't refrain from outright scatology: "I am return-ing the enclosed cover. Please feel free to use it in lieu of toilet paper."[53] Co-plaintiffs in *DeLeon v. Perry*, Mark and Vic felt the heat for their friends and for themselves as well.

Tensions generated by the hurtful reaction to "Modern Love" were exacerbated by the pain of old harms that threatened to become new again. As February wore on and the one-year anniversary of their victory in Judge Garcia's court drew near, the elation Mark and Vic, Nicole and Cleo had felt on February 26, 2014, gave way to impatience and frustration, even to anger. In a banner year for the marriage equality movement, cases in other states had moved relatively quickly through the courts. In Texas, nothing had changed. "All gay and lesbian Texans," Mark and Vic argued in a statement released early in the month, "those with children and those without, are irreparably harmed every minute of every day that Texas' unconstitutional marriage ban remains in place. No straight couple would want to walk in our shoes—to have to wait over 17 years to marry the one we love."[54] For Nicole and Cleo, whose second child was due in mid-March, every passing day brought them closer to a repetition of the torment to which the state had subjected them when their son was born in 2012.

Though Texas had stacked the legal deck against them, they had done everything in their power to do what was best for themselves and the children they hoped to share. As Nicole told Pamela Colloff, "I wanted to be able to look our kids in the eye one day and tell them, 'We're as married as we can possibly be in the eyes of the law.' I wanted them to know that we went out of our way to make a permanent, lasting, outward legal commitment to each other and that we would always be together." And so, in the fall of 2009, she and Cleo traveled to Massachusetts where in a simple, no-frills ceremony a justice of the peace in Brookline united them in marriage. But in Texas their marriage was legally meaningless, and when Cleo gave birth to their son—forty-two hours of labor followed by an emergency C-section—Nicole had no parental rights despite the heap of paperwork their lawyer had prepared. "He belonged to both of us," Nicole lamented, "But under the law, I was a stranger to my own son." Not until months later—after a second-parent adoption as intrusive as it was expensive—were Nicole and Cleo able to breathe easily once again.[55]

Hoping to spare Nicole and Cleo the terrifying uncertainty that had surrounded the birth of their first child, hoping to put an end to Mark and Vic's long wait to marry, on February 12 Akin Gump filed a motion with the Fifth Circuit Court to lift Judge Garcia's stay. "The District Court expressly found that the denial of the fundamental right to marry causes irreparable harm," the motion read; "Despite this, Plaintiffs continue to suffer irreparable harm—only now the potential consequences are graver . . . Plaintiffs DeLeon and Dimetman are expecting a child any day, and the State's refusal to recognize their marriage risks grave harm both to the Plaintiffs and the child."[56] Unfortunately, when their daughter was born on March 21, the stay was still in place. "Labor is scary and anything can happen," Nicole said after the birth. "I had an infection as a complication of labor that led to an emergency C-section. If I had not made it through childbirth, Cleo would not have been our daughter's legal mother because her name is not allowed on the birth certificate in Texas."[57] The unnerving cycle had begun again.

Neel Lane made no attempt to conceal his frustration. "This otherwise joyous day for Nicole and Cleo is a sad one because, in the eyes of Texas, Nicole is an unwed mother," he said. "Her valid marriage to Cleo is declared void by a Texas law that U.S. District Judge Orlando Garcia declared unconstitutional more than a year ago. Court after court have agreed with him, and no one doubts the U.S. Supreme Court will do the same."[58]

Mark and Vic sent a congratulatory note to Cleo and Nicole who were, they knew, emotionally exhausted by their ordeal. They too were beginning to wear at the edges. "I was never good with Christmas as a child," Mark once joked with friends. "Waiting to open presents, even when I almost always knew I'd get what I had asked Santa for, was torture to me. Waiting for the courts to act tortures me too."[59] Early in March he was still making excuses for the Fifth Circuit. They have, he told friends, other decisions to write; only five weeks have passed since the decision. But by the time Cleo and Nicole's daughter was born, he was fed up. Emotions too long bottled up exploded on Facebook in satire—the last resort of the rational mind forced to deal, day after day, with irrationality.

> This past week a same-sex couple married in Austin.
>
> The consequences of such a marriage were predictable and predicted: Hordes of opposite-sex married couples in Texas promptly headed to their local courthouses to file for divorce and thousands of opposite-sex couples who were engaged called off their nuptials. The wedding industry is in a tailspin; massive layoffs in that industry are expected across Texas. And worse, opposite-sex couples, once incentivized to procreate, are no longer incentivized and sadly have ceased . . . well . . . procreating. In nine months Texas' maternity wards will shutter. What will become now of the great state of Texas if that marriage is not quickly voided? Civilization as we know it will come to an end.[60]

"I must admit," he wrote in a more serious note to a friend the same day, "I get angrier by the day as this drags out. I feel like flying to NOLA and protesting in front of the 5th Circuit."[61]

***

Leaving the Fifth Circuit Court in New Orleans, Mark and Vic, Nicole and Cleo, all eleven of the couples from Louisiana, Mississippi, and Texas who had risked so much when they stood together against wrongs done by the state, believed they had won. They believed that what Joce Pritchett described so simply, so eloquently as "bad laws" prohibiting gays and lesbians from marrying the person they loved most in all the world would in just a few short weeks be found unconstitutional. Standing that afternoon on the steps of the John Minor Wisdom Courthouse, they imagined themselves linked, arm in arm, with the shades of the men who died so horribly at the UpStairs Bar in 1973, ready to take together the final step toward the dignity Troy Perry claimed for them so many years ago. But for months the court held its silence and bitterness rose in the hearts of the defendants.

"The June 24th anniversary of the Upstairs Bar fire will come and go," Mark lamented, "without a word from the Fifth. They played with our lives; they just played with our lives."[62]

Chapter 6

Crossing the Threshold

Let America be America again.
Let it be the dream it used to be.
Let it be the pioneer on the plain
Seeking a home where he himself is free.

                (America never was America to me.)

Let it be that great strong land of love
Where never kings connive nor tyrants scheme
That any man be crushed by one above.

                   (It never was America to me.)

O, let my land be a land where Liberty
Is crowned with no false patriotic wreath,
But opportunity is real, and life is free,
Equality is in the air we breathe.

      —Langston Hughes, "Let America Be America Again"

Shortly before six o'clock on the evening of April 27, 2015, a steady stream of cabs began arriving at 800 17th St. NW, just a block or two from the White House. The men and women stepping onto the curb knew that oral arguments in *Obergefell v. Hodges* the next day would strain their every nerve. But tonight would be different, a time—the invitations suggested—to celebrate the strategy and the stories that had brought their cause to the Supreme Court, a time to give the key players a chance to connect. To mark the historic occasion, Freedom to Marry had organized a reception to bring together plaintiffs from marriage cases—past and present—across the country. Working with colleagues at the ACLU, Lambda Legal, the National Council for Lesbian Rights (NCLR), and GLAD, Freedom to Marry compiled a list of more than 500 couples who had been plaintiffs in same-sex marriage cases since 1970—and recorded every name on a poster created for the occasion, a tribute to those who, year by year, state by state, took up the struggle for marriage equality. Everyone who could be reached was invited.

In the end, more than a hundred plaintiffs representing seventy-five cases from forty-two states, their numbers spanning forty years of court battles, gathered in a space provided by Holland & Knight, one of Washington, D. C.'s premier law firms. Friends, supporters, and a selection of newspeople who had covered the marriage equality movement over the years added to the numbers. Security for the private, invitation-only event was tight. Guests received strict instructions to share nothing in advance with reporters or on social media. Recognizing that publicity could result in trouble, even danger, Mark and Vic complied. But Mark couldn't resist hinting on his Facebook page that something was afoot, an enigmatic post that mentioned only "drinks with some very special people" on Monday night and teased, "More about that on Monday." On the short ride from the Sofitel, Vic spoke little, content to sit still for a few minutes after a whirlwind tour of Washington over the past few days. Mark was plugged into his phone, talking quietly as he set the times for interviews for the next day.

Their moment of relative quiet ended when Mark and Vic stepped into the two-story lobby where staffers checked IDs against the list of those registered, the excited voices of friends reaching out to one another echoing in sharp contrast to the mellow sounds of a decorative water wall in the background. Done with security, they stepped onto a crowded elevator that swept them to the eleventh floor of the PNC Financial Services Headquarters' stunning, glass-walled "trophy building" where spectacular night views of the city spread before them.

Beyond the elevators, drinks and hors d'oeuvres awaited, as did a photographer ready to snap pictures of each group of plaintiffs, each couple. Mark and Vic pulled Evan Wolfson, the man who had done more than anyone in the country to advance marriage equality, into their first shot, stood alone for another. But the real attraction wasn't the photographer; it was the people; smiles came easily as fellow plaintiffs who had followed each others' cases over the years called out greetings from across the room. A handful of reporters who regularly covered the marriage equality movement had been admitted. Mark and Vic had barely left the photo area when one of them, Tony Adams of the *South Florida Gay News*, sought them out. Vic explained the details of *DeLeon v. Perry*; Mark used the moment to talk about how far they had gone in planning a fall wedding. "We can't wait for tomorrow," Mark told Adams; "we are so confident in the outcome that we've put our money where our mouth is. We've booked a site for the wedding, hired a florist, hired a videographer and a photographer—all for a November wedding in the Dallas area."[1]

The reception had been billed as an "historic gathering"—and it lived up to the billing. Tony Sullivan, who with his husband Richard Adams was granted a marriage license and married in Boulder, Colorado, in 1975, was on hand. They became the first couple to sue for recognition in a federal court. Assuming the role of elder statesman, a treasure trove of stories about the movement in uncertain times, he spoke to Chris Johnson, a reporter for the *Washington Blade*, for himself and for Richard, who died in 2010, recalling for younger couples how it all began. "It was our hope; it was our desire," he remembered, speaking of his marriage to Richard, remembering his husband's death with a touch of sadness. Though he and Richard knew their marriage "was valid in every way because we truly loved each other," they knew as well that being denied the rights of a married couple—immigration rights in their case—had brought them face to face with "severe injustice." "We decided to go ahead," Tony asserted of their early case, "because someone's got to correct injustice."[2]

Genora Dancel and Ninia Baehr, one of the three same-sex couples who sued for the right to marry in Hawaii, came to reflect on "changes in the gay community and the world" since their landmark suit was filed in 1991.

"When we started," Baehr remembered, "people thought we were crazy and the national LGBT organizations and civil rights organizations didn't want to take this case." Their initial victory—after years of legal maneuvering a Hawaii court ruled in 1996 that the state had to issue marriage licenses to same-sex couples—was immediately stayed and ultimately reversed by a 1998 constitutional amendment. Marriage equality would not come to Hawaii until 2013 when the legislature passed the Hawaii Marriage Equality Act, but in a very real way their judicial win marked the beginning of the end. Working on their case with Dan Foley, the attorney of record, convinced Evan Wolfson, Marriage Director at Lambda Legal at the time, that a national movement advocating for same-sex marriage, well-organized and well-financed, could in time succeed. In 2003, just a few years later, bankrolled by a grant from the Evelyn & Walter Haas Jr. Fund, Wolfson launched the organization that would guide that movement, Freedom to Marry, and began implementing the "Roadmap to Victory" that had led to this night.

Julie Goodridge came to share her memories of the 2003 struggle in Massachusetts when Mary Bonauto and GLAD led the way to the first-ever enduring victory in a same-sex marriage case. With her were co-plaintiffs Edward Balmelli and Michael Horgan, one of the seven couples involved in that landmark filing. "I'm completely thrilled that Mary is arguing the case," Julie said, "I'm really hopeful." Everyone knew that the arguments Bonauto turned back a decade and more ago in *Goodridge v. Department of Public Health*—the State's much-touted need to encourage procreation, to encourage optimal conditions for child rearing, and to preserve scarce State resources available for subsidies to married couples and their children— would almost certainly be revisited the next day. Julie wasn't the only one happy to see the case back in Bonauto's hands. Kris Perry, one of the four plaintiffs in California's Prop 8 case, was equally enthusiastic. "What I'm feeling right now is just so optimistic and hopeful that the justices will see their way to a majority vote in favor of equality and fairness," she said, "and all of these wonderful, loving couples from all over the country will get to realize their dream of being married."[3]

"We've made our case to the country, and to the courts," Evan Wolfson told the happy crowd; "there aren't going to be any speeches tonight.

We want to keep the focus on being together, meeting each other . . . tonight is for savoring the moment and looking forward in great hope." Like the other plaintiffs, perhaps more so since four months had passed and the Fifth Circuit Court had not yet ruled on their case, Mark and Vic were ready for a night to kick back and enjoy themselves.

Joce Pritchett, a friend from Mississippi and plaintiff in the Fifth Circuit case, was caught between frustration and elation. "We're very disappointed our circuit hasn't come back," she said. "It's disheartening. We have friends who are elderly, and one of them is not well. She's basically trying to stay alive to wait on that hearing. It's not a game; it's peoples' lives!" But on this night, surrounded by so many hopeful and supportive people, she remembered the reception at the Cathedral Creative Studios in New Orleans. "I was very moved by that, that day was impressive," she said, her eyes sparkling as she reveled in the happiness surrounding her.[4] Derek Penton-Robicheaux and his husband, Jon, more friends from the hearings in New Orleans, were less concerned with the delay. "We're very excited for tomorrow because one way or the other—with or without the Fifth—we're going to get this finished," Derek offered. "This part of the job is done," he said. Speaking in his role as director of the Louisiana Equality Foundation, he pointed enthusiastically to the future. "We can move on now to the more humanitarian parts of the job—care for the elderly, for the homeless, suicide prevention."[5]

The brief remarks Evan Wolfson did offer—those who had come wanted, needed to hear from him—returned repeatedly to the governing principles that have guided Freedom to Marry since its founding and brought same-sex marriage before the Supreme Court more quickly than anyone could have imagined. Tonight, he told the excited crowd, is for "celebrating the power of telling our stories, organizing, working, and showing the courage that you all have to stand up for ourselves and believe that others can rise to fairness." Thanking the plaintiffs for their courage—and including a reverential nod to "those who are with us in spirit, those whose memories we cherish," thanking "the advocates, the private attorneys, pro bono counsel, law firms, and fighters" who had devoted themselves to marriage equality, Wolfson sounded the same note yet again. They were the ones who "spoke up, shared stories, touched hearts, and changed minds."

Wolfson's theme surfaced a third time when he turned to the story of President Obama's long evolution on the question of same-sex marriage. Once again, he extolled "the power of speaking out, of stories, of conversations." By speaking in personal terms, Wolfson claimed, the President "gave millions of Americans permission to think anew and to join all of us on this journey toward a more perfect union." Like a jazz pianist weaving his way through and around the melody, half-revealing, half-concealing the chord progressions that will in time reveal all to the cognoscenti, he offered in his own quiet way words of advice born of lessons learned over years and years: Lead good and productive lives, tell your stories, engage the people around you, but do so quietly, in conversational terms. Respect those who stand opposed, give them time and the psychological space they need to grow, to discover their better selves and to become supporters.

To Mark and Vic it seemed almost as if Evan had seized the moment to prepare them for the next stage of the marriage equality battle, a time after the ultimate judicial victory when the inevitable backlash would begin and changing hearts and minds would be no less important. Listening as Evan spoke, Mark and Vic wished aloud that he could have trained plaintiffs nationwide, themselves included, about interactions with the press as they filed their suits and moved through the legal process.

With the crowd already in high spirits, Evan Wolfson called Valerie Jarrett to the lectern, a close friend of both Barack and Michelle Obama since their pre-presidential days in Chicago who served as Assistant to the President for Public Engagement and Intergovernmental Affairs for the eight years of the Obama presidency. Full of praise and gratitude, Wolfson reminded the enthusiastic crowd that Jarrett had been "an exceedingly effective internal voice and champion for our cause, a too-often unsung hero who has helped us to get to where we are today." Most already knew the role she had played. As Jarrett waited for the applause to end, Mark thought to himself that what she would say mattered less than the simple fact that she was here, speaking for a gay-friendly White House, a welcome change from the cold-shoulder the LGBT community had received from George W. Bush. Mark's memories of Bush as governor and president were still raw. In 1995 the organizers of the San Antonio Black Tie Dinner had

asked Governor Ann Richards for a letter of welcome for those attending and she had happily complied. When Mark made the same request of
Governor Bush the next year, he was turned down. Running for president in
1999, Governor Bush courted conservatives by arranging for a hate crimes
bill that would have protected the LGBT community to be killed in the
Texas Senate. Worse, by far, when running for reelection in 2004 Bush had
called for a constitutional amendment to ban same-sex marriage and cyni-
cally used the possibility of marriage equality to play voters, generating
state constitutional amendments in battleground states to increase conservative turnout.

Of course, what Jarrett said did matter a great deal. "Our true north in
the administration," she began, "is that no matter who you are, no matter
what zip code you live in, no matter what your parents did, no matter what
your faith, no matter what your race, no matter what your gender identity,
no matter what you believe in or who you love, you ought to be able to have
equal opportunity in this country." Thanking the plaintiffs for their sacrifice—"I know that you and your families and your community," she said,
"you have to basically put your lives on hold to fight for something that's
not just going to benefit you, but benefit so many other people"—she highlighted four words that summarized the way she felt on the eve of an historic
day at the Supreme Court. For a few minutes she talked about the first three
words—"equality," "freedom," and "justice." A canny speaker, she withheld
the fourth word for several minutes, keeping the crowd in suspense. And
then, the dam broke. "My toast is really going to be to you about the fourth
word . . . the word that really touches me tonight, looking at all of you, is
love. We ought to be able to love anybody we want to, and that's what makes
our country strong. It is a strength. It is not a weakness, and we are the beacon
for the world."

Speaking on behalf of President Obama, Jarrett delivered the perfect end
to the evening of celebration Evan Wolfson had promised. Some of the guests
stayed a while longer to talk, unwilling to let the moment pass. Most made
their way into the night, "love" ringing in their ears, the conviction that love
would win in Court more firmly planted than ever.

* * *

Federal Rule 53, adopted in 1946 and updated in 1972 to include television cameras, dictates that "the court must not permit the taking of photographs in the courtroom during judicial proceedings or the broadcasting of judicial proceedings from the courtroom." Audio recordings are usually made available soon after the conclusion of oral arguments; transcripts usually follow within a week. For those who can't wait, who feel that visceral desire to watch and listen as oral arguments unfold, the only option is a seat in the courtroom and with only 400 or so seats available, snaring a spot can be frustratingly difficult, particularly for high-profile cases. Some seats are set aside for the clerks who serve the justices, others for members of the press. Still others are reserved for guests of the justices and for members of the Supreme Court Bar. By the time seats for *Obergefell v. Hodges* had been carved up this way and that, a mere handful—fifty—remained for the public. And with the thousands of gay men and lesbians who had descended on the nation's capital to celebrate the moment, many of whom had waited decades for the day when same-sex marriage would come to the Supreme Court, everyone knew the competition for seats would be fierce.

Guests of the justices, the clerks who work for them, and members of the press who cover the Court on a day-to-day basis constitute a privileged class. Their seats in the Court are guaranteed. For oral arguments in *Obergefell* other journalists were asked to provide a letter from the news organization they represented—and 117 of the lucky ones were issued seats just a few days before the hearing. For the rest, even for members of the Supreme Court Bar, the only alternative was to wait in line or to pay a surrogate to hold a place. On Thursday, four days before oral arguments were to begin, the line began to form. The first fourteen places were held by paid line-standers. Kathleen Perrin, who in 2010 founded Equality Case Files, an online repository of documents indispensable for anyone following the struggle for marriage equality, was fifteenth, but the first holding a place for herself. As part of her work she had attended all but one of the courts of appeal hearings on same-sex marriage—the Michigan and Texas cases were two of her favorites—and was determined to be in court for the finale of what she called "the civil rights issue of our time."[6] For the most part, the people waiting passed the time amicably, despite the fact that some among them were virulently anti-gay, like Rives Grogan, a Texan who kept his leather-bound bible close at hand, ready at a moment's notice to recite what he interpreted as anti-homosexual verses. Though others in line realized he was clearly an outlier, no one dreamed how much trouble he would cause when oral arguments began.

Through friends, Mark and Vic recruited two students from American University, Michael Cabellero and Caitlin O'Hara, to wait in line and hold seats for them in the courtroom, scheduled them to arrive at noon on Sunday to begin two cool days and two cooler nights on a sidewalk that grew harder with every hour. From far-away Texas the timing seemed safe. With the going rate for line-standers running between thirty-five and fifty dollars an hour, paying surrogates to hold places was an expensive proposition, but Mark and Vic knew how few seats would be available to the general public and wanted desperately to be in the Court.

Even before Friday evening when they arrived in Washington, D. C., Mark and Vic heard that people were already in line for tickets at the Supreme Court, a discovery that amazed and unnerved them. On Saturday morning when they stopped by for a first look, they saw immediately that they had miscalculated. From the steps leading to the plaza, the line stretched along First Street to and around the corner of East Capitol Street—forty-nine people in all, one short of the seats available. Realizing their dream was in jeopardy, they found an agent handling paid line-standers, reached into their wallets for a cash payment, and arranged to have places held until Michael and Caitlin arrived. Later that day, someone ahead of them dropped from the line—and Mark showed his jubilation in a Facebook post. "Good news, all," he wrote, "We are now 49 & 50. Virtually guaranteed admittance." By Monday morning sixty-seven people had joined the line, hoping some miracle would expand the number of seats available.

The danger over—or so they thought—Mark and Vic moved to the plaza for photos that seem in retrospect almost symbolic, the pediment and the pillars of the facade surrounding, protectively, their smiling faces. Chief Justice William Howard Taft's 1929 charge to the architect of the current building, Cass Gilbert, was to design "a building of dignity and importance suitable for its use as the permanent home of the Supreme Court of the United States."[7] Gilbert succeeded. Before the demand for increased security in recent years, visitors approaching the main entrance climbed a set of stairs to the plaza, almost as wide as a football field is long. Crossing the plaza, they climbed another set of stairs, longer and higher, to the massive brass doors, all the while looking up at the sixteen marble columns supporting the pediment. The four-story façade was intended to evoke awe, and it does. But it also inspires reflection. Standing so close to the courtroom where their future would be decided, Mark and Vic couldn't help but think about the power of the law and the daunting task facing the attorneys who would argue for and against their cause.

***

A few days before he and Vic left Texas, Mark posted two photographs and a note of thanks on Facebook: "When full marriage equality arrives, these two, Evan Wolfson and Mary Bonauto, will deserve a huge amount of credit. We cannot thank these two enough for their brilliance and determination!!"[8] With six cases from four states before the Court, the situation complicated further by the fact that the Court had ordered separate arguments on the two legal issues involved in *Obergefell*—the right to marry and recognition of existing marriages—the question of who would argue for the LGBT community had been hotly contested. Because the Department of Justice had submitted an *amicus* brief, most understood that Solicitor General Donald B. Verrilli, Jr. would be granted time before the Court. For Mark and Vic the selection on March 31 of Mary Bonauto of GLAD, "the Thurgood Marshall of the LGBT rights movement" as Mark liked to call her, to argue the case for marriage, and Douglas Hallward-Driemeir of Ropes & Gray to argue the case for recognition had been reassuring. True to form, Mark fired off an e-mail to Mary:

> I just read that you will be one of the two lawyers arguing before SCOTUS for same-sex marriage rights. I am thrilled for you!! You've earned this right and I know you'll do a fantastic job.
>
> Congrats!! And thanks for all you have done and are doing for our community.[9]

That the states had been unable to attract top-flight legal talent from major firms to argue against marriage equality seemed equally reassuring, a sure sign that the tide had turned. John J. Bursch, a former solicitor general of Michigan, now in private practice, had agreed to argue the principal question, the right to marry, but his firm, Warner Norcross & Judd, had refused to stand behind him.

By the time they flew to Washington, D. C. to attend oral arguments in *Obergefell*, Mark and Vic knew the city well. Mark had traveled there first as a Boy Scout and made the usual round of buildings and monuments.[10] In the years he was responsible for governmental affairs at Safety-Kleen, a $1.3 billion-revenue environmental services firm, Mark was in and out of the city three or four times a year, often visiting museums and historic sites to relax after work. Vic had, in the years before he and Mark began dating, been in and out of the city, often on Air Force business, touring the sites in his off-duty hours. Their most memorable visit as a couple took place in January 2009 when, thanks to tickets provided by then-Congressman Charles "Charlie" Gonzalez, they watched history in the making—President Barack Obama's first inauguration—from a space reserved for special guests and, later that night, attended the Human Rights Campaign's Inaugural Ball where Melissa Etheridge, Cyndi Lauper, and Thelma Houston wowed the crowd. Not even the need to get up at 3:00 a.m. or the bone-chilling temperatures—so cold that the power bars they brought to fight off hunger froze, nearly breaking their teeth when they bit into them—were enough to spoil the wonder of that day.

Now, six years later, settling into the city for what Mark called "a humdinger of a weekend" before the main event on Tuesday, the men had big plans that would take them beyond the tourist attractions they had visited and revisited.[11] One friend, Gabe Rozsa, had arranged a visit to the Rose Garden at the White House. Another friend, Gordon Tanner, the General Counsel of the U. S. Department of the Air Force, arranged a private tour of the Pentagon and joined them later for lunch in a dining room reserved for top brass and visiting VIPs. Yet another friend arranged for a visit with Senator Harry Reid and though Senator Reid was called to the floor at the hour scheduled, Mark and Vic were able to sit with key members of the senator's staff on the balcony overlooking the National Mall and the Washington Monument and to watch from the gallery as Senator Reid spoke on the floor of the Senate chamber.

But when in quiet moments they paused long enough to recall times past, work in the District and visits to monuments and museums weren't the first things that came to mind. Even visits in the present to the Rose Garden and the Pentagon, however pleasurable and attractive, or the much welcome chance to meet with Senator Reid were, they realized, diversions, ways of keeping themselves from thinking obsessively about the hearing on Tuesday. Looking ahead to the day the Supreme Court would take up the question of marriage equality, Mark and Vic couldn't help but focus on times when they had come to the city for HRC events advancing the cause. Their most recent visit had been for the 2014 Human Rights Campaign national dinner in October at which President Clinton gave the keynote address, his second for the HRC. They played a more active role, however, at a press breakfast held in March 2014 to launch Americans for Marriage Equality, HRC's marriage equality war room. That visit had begun with an e-mail from Dan Rafter, Associate Director of Communications for HRC. Expressing his thanks "for the work you've done to advance marriage equality in Texas," commending them for their "bravery," adding congratulations on their victory in Judge Orlando Garcia's court in San Antonio, he signaled the importance of *DeLeon v. Perry* by inviting them to speak at the breakfast.[12] When he did, Mark struck what had long since become familiar notes, thanking the press for unbiased stories and the lawyers for intelligent and effective arguments, reminding everyone present that "Success builds upon success—that everyone deserves credit and no one deserves all the credit."[13]

Other, more unsettling memories also came to mind. On an earlier visit to the District of Columbia, the Texas Lyceum conference in April 2004, Mark and Vic, the only gay couple at the conference, had been seated at dinner with Ted and Heidi Cruz. Though neither had met Cruz before, they knew that his was a fast-rising conservative star. He had clerked for Chief Justice William Rehnquist; his work on *Bush v. Gore* (2000) had earned him work as an assistant attorney general in the Justice Department and, later, as director of policy planning at the Federal Trade Commission in President Bush's first term. More important, they knew that in 2003 Greg Abbott, then attorney general of Texas, had lured him back to Texas as Solicitor General. With President Bush already positioning himself for a tight reelection contest in the fall (his margin of victory in the popular vote would be the smallest ever for an incumbent), hoping to draw evangelical votes by painting his likely opponent, Senator John Kerry, as a Massachusetts liberal who represented the only state where same-sex marriage was currently legal, Mark and Vic knew exactly what to expect from a loyalist. For some minutes they listened as Ted Cruz railed against gay marriage and praised the president's call for a no-gay marriage constitutional amendment, seemingly oblivious of the two men across the table—the only male couple at the table for ten.

Increasingly agitated, unable any longer to listen in silence, Mark at last spoke up. He introduced himself and Vic as a couple, pointed out that they had been together for seven years (three years longer than Cruz and his wife), that Vic had served honorably for more than fourteen years in the military, and that bans on same-sex marriage violated the Equal Protection Clause of the Fourteenth Amendment. When Cruz denied any such protection and asserted that requiring the states to accept marriage equality would be a violation of states' rights, Mark counter punched. Cruz had sung a different song, he suggested, when he worked on *Bush v. Gore*, another equal protection case. How ironic, he observed, that the same justices who based their decision there on a broad interpretation of the Equal Protection Clause inevitably narrowed their reading when applying that same clause to civil rights cases. Reddening, Cruz defended the Court's decision in *Bush v. Gore*—at which point Mark pointed out that the justices themselves didn't seem to think much of their decision since they had included a footnote noting that the case would have no precedential value. The debate settled nothing, of course, but the conversation did allow Mark and Vic to take the measure of the man.

Later, they would learn how completely Cruz's insensitivity prohibits him from understanding how human beings interact. When he returned to private practice in 2008, Cruz called Mark with a request that he send appellate work his way, blindly overlooking the possibility that the man whose most important relationship in life he had denigrated might be offended. In 2012 Mark picked up the phone to discover Ted Cruz once again on the line, this time hoping for donations to his campaign for the Senate. "I declined," Mark wrote in his journal, "reminding him politely that we didn't agree on anything politically."[14] Hanging up, Mark remembered Cruz's diatribe eight years earlier, his refusal to grant LGBT Americans full equality. All he could do was shake his head in disbelief.

In the years between that Texas Lyceum dinner and the present, Greg Abbott had left his post as attorney general and moved into the governor's office; Ted Cruz, whose intolerance of the LGBT community seemed to grow as he accumulated power, had become the junior senator from Texas and appeared already to be massing his forces for a run at the presidency. Uber-conservative John Cornyn, elected in November to a third term in the Senate and now Majority Whip, had grown in influence and power, power he was willing to turn against gays and lesbians to rally the conservative base. The Tea Party darlings who had overrun the Texas Legislature, angry that Judge Garcia had found Section 32 of the state constitution in conflict with the United States' Constitution's guarantees of equal protection and due process, were determinedly looking about for any and every opportunity to inflict pain and harm on the LGBT community.

Though oral arguments in January had suggested that the Fifth Circuit Court of Appeals would stand up to Texas, the judges in New Orleans whose words promised so much had failed to act. That Judge Graves had responded to Texas's appeal to "wait and see," to "let the democratic process work itself out," with an impatient question—"What's the magic number? Twenty [years]? Five?"—had meant a great deal to Mark and Vic. And then, nothing. Thinking back to confrontations with Ted Cruz and John Cornyn, Mark and Vic could feel the weight pushing them down, the power wielded by enemies who lived on their doorstep, politicians whose machinations had encouraged Texas to stand against them, one of the dwindling handful of states holding out against marriage equality. Had Greg Abbott, they wondered, now a candidate for governor, directly or indirectly encouraged the Fifth Circuit to sit on their case until the election was over?

But as they paused for photos before the imposing façade of the highest court in the land, a dramatic backdrop so powerful it crowded other thoughts from the viewfinder, they felt even more strongly the presence of a counterweight raising them up: the Supreme Court of the United States, a power greater than even Texas could muster. Though Texas's marriage ban would not come before the Court on Tuesday, the outcome in *Obergefell v. Hodges* would affect Texas. A lawyer and a history buff, Mark couldn't help but remember other occasions when the Supreme Court forced Texas to comply with the Constitution, particularly with regard to the rights of minorities: in 1944 when Thurgood Marshall won an eight-to-one decision in *Smith v. Allright* forbidding the State of Texas from barring blacks from voting in Democratic primaries; in 1950 when Marshall persuaded the Court in *Sweatt v. Painter* that Texas's fumbling and insincere attempt to create a "separate but equal law school" in order to turn a black man away from the University of Texas School of Law did not pass constitutional muster; most recently in 2003 when the Texas statute criminalizing sexual behavior between two consenting adults of the same sex, a statute used to justify discrimination against LGBT Texans, was declared unconstitutional in *Lawrence v. Texas.*

That Barack Obama was president gave them hope as well. Though in Texas his name raised suspicions of foreign birth and Muslim sympathies, Mark and Vic had known from the beginning that he was more compassionate, more in tune with the national mood and with the Constitution of the United States than any politicians who held higher office in their home state. From his days in the Illinois State Senate, President Obama had championed civil rights for gays and lesbians. Repealing Don't Ask, Don't Tell, the policy that made Vic's life difficult from the day it was enacted, was a cornerstone of his first campaign for the presidency—and in December of 2010 he signed into law a bill fulfilling the promise of the party platform. Two years later, with *Gill v. Office of Personnel Management* pending in the First Circuit, *Pedersen v. Office of Personnel Management* and *United States v. Windsor* in the Second Circuit—solid cases likely to overturn the Defense of Marriage Act, that bony finger poked in the eye of the LGBT community, President Obama ultimately prompted the Justice Department not to defend an existing law, an extraordinary step. But though a longtime advocate of civil unions, the president had nonetheless stumbled at the idea of same-sex marriage. For years he had described his attitude as "evolving"—until in an interview with David Gregory on *Meet the Press* a slip of Joe Biden's tongue forced his hand.[15]

On May 9, 2012, three days after Vice-President Biden praised *Will and Grace* for changing hearts and minds across America, recognized the love same-sex couples and their children share, and declared himself "absolutely comfortable with the fact that men marrying men, women marrying women, and heterosexual men and women marrying one another are entitled to the same exact rights," President Obama sat in the White House for a quiet conversation with Robin Roberts, co-anchor of ABC's *Good Morning America*, the number-one morning show in the United States and, though few would know it until December 2013, a lesbian. In the few minutes they talked, the political landscape in which America's discussion of marriage equality would unfold changed forever. Reminding listeners of his record on gay rights, the president stressed that in embracing marriage equality he had traveled the same path as millions of Americans. "Marriage" is a loaded word that "evokes very powerful traditions, religious, beliefs, and so forth," he admitted respectfully. "It's just that—maybe they haven't had the experience that I have had in seeing same-sex couples, who are as committed, as monogamous, as responsible—as loving a group of parents as any heterosexual couple I know." The logic, the president contended, is inescapable. "If a soldier can fight for us, if a police officer can protect our neighborhoods, if a firefighter is expected to go into a burning building," can we then say to them "Oh, but by the way, we're going to treat you differently?" He spoke movingly of young people in general, and of his daughters Malia and Sasha in particular, comfortable with the idea that some of their friends were being raised by same-sex parents. "It wouldn't dawn on them that somehow their friends' parents would be treated differently. It doesn't make sense to them. And frankly," the president admitted, "that's the kind of thing that prompts a change of perspective."

Robin Roberts must have struggled to maintain her professional face as President Obama proclaimed that "At a certain point, I've just concluded that for me personally—it is important for me to go ahead and affirm that I think same-sex couples should be able to get married."[16] Though both men wished that President Obama had spoken out earlier, thought that perhaps California's Proposition 8 might never have passed if the president's position on same-sex marriage had evolved more quickly, they were ecstatic to have his voice behind them now.

Nor had President Obama been alone, Mark and Vic knew, in driving away the threatening clouds that hovered over their home state. In an op-ed piece that appeared in the *Washington Post* in March 2013, former President Clinton had turned his back on the Defense of Marriage Act. Though he had signed DOMA into law in 1996—claiming at the time that it was the lesser of two evils and expressing hope in a signing statement that it would not "provide an excuse for discrimination"—he had since concluded that "the law itself is discriminatory" and "should be overturned." Suggesting that Americans looking back to a time before the Nineteenth Amendment gave women the right to vote would find that world "not unusual or old-fashioned but alien," President Clinton went a step further. "I believe," he said, "that in 2013 DOMA and opposition to marriage equality are vestiges of just such an unfamiliar society."[17] Perhaps better still, the woman Mark and Vic hoped would follow Barack Obama as president, Hillary Clinton, had come out in favor of same-sex marriage. Less than two months after stepping down as Secretary of State, she added her voice to the growing chorus. "LGBT Americans are our colleagues, our teachers, our soldiers, our friends and loved ones," she said; "they are full and equal citizens and deserve the rights of citizenship. That's why I support marriage for lesbian and gay couples. I support it personally and as a matter of law."[18]

In addition to endorsements from presidents—past, present, and, they hoped, future—Mark and Vic recognized that other powerful voices had risen to stand with them against Texas. In August 2013 Justice Ruth Bader Ginsburg presided at the same-sex wedding of an old friend; in September 2014 Justice Elena Kagan did the same for a former law clerk. Symbolic gestures to be sure, but important symbolic gestures. More substantive, and therefore more reassuring, was Justice Ginsburg's much-heralded interview with *Bloomberg Business* in February 2014. Asked if she thought a Supreme Court decision finding a constitutional right for same-sex couples to marry would be accepted nationwide, Justice Ginsburg answered directly. "The change in people's attitudes on that issue has been enormous," she observed. "In recent years, people have said, 'This is the way I am.' And others looked around, and we discovered it's our next-door neighbor—we're very fond of them. Or it's our child's best friend, or even our child." We've come to realize, she contended, that "they are one of us." As a result, she suggested, accepting marriage equality "would not take a large adjustment."[19]

Mark and Vic knew that none of the nine justices would be directly influenced by public opinion. The outcome of *Obergefell v. Hodges* would be determined by their reading of the Fourteenth Amendment, almost certainly in light of precedents in *Romer* (1996), *Lawrence* (2006), and *Windsor* (2013). But they knew as well that in controversial cases the Court is reluctant to get ahead of public opinion. That polling numbers in recent years had confirmed Justice Ginsburg's assessment of the national mood further reassured them. A bi-partisan study of polling data commissioned by Freedom to Marry in 2011 (conducted by Joel Benenson and Jan van Lohuizen, respected pollsters who worked for President George W. Bush and President Barack Obama respectively) had shown support for same-sex marriage growing modestly: 1 percent a year—between 1996 and 2009. But in the two years between 2009 and 2011 it had leapt ahead at the rate of 5 percent annually, an increase professionals accustomed to the usually glacial pace of change on social issues found astonishing.

Benenson and Lohuizen had stressed in their report that by 2011 national polls consistently showed a majority of Americans in favor of marriage equality: Gallup (53 percent), ABC/Washington Post (53 percent), Public Religion Research Institute (51 percent), CNN/ORC (51 percent). They also predicted that support would continue to rise. A Williams Institute study released as the Court was about to sit went so far as to predict that by 2016 support would rise to 60 percent.[20] In fact, attaining a 60 percent supermajority didn't take that long. A Gallup poll underway as Mark and Vic stood on the steps of the Court revealed that 58 percent of Americans wanted a ruling that would make same-sex marriage legal nationwide.[21] Gallop's next poll, released on May 19, showed support for marriage equality at 60 percent.[22] Together with Nicole and Cleo in Texas, with the nearly 600 plaintiffs in same-sex marriage cases across the country, with the thirty plaintiffs set to go before the Court in *Obergefell v. Hodges*, with the millions of gays and lesbians who had chosen to live openly, their good and productive lives bringing family and friends, neighbors and co-workers into the fold, with the hundreds of lawyers who had worked so hard for so many years to bring about marriage equality—Mark and Vic had helped win the battle for hearts and minds in America.

Since the *Windsor* decision in June 2013, the floodgates had opened. Nearly sixty state and federal courts at every level short of the Supreme Court had ruled in favor of marriage equality, only five against. Same-sex marriage was legal now in thirty-seven states and the District of Columbia. Plaintiffs in same-sex marriage cases had suffered only five losses, the most significant coming in the Sixth Circuit Court of Appeals, the case that split the circuit courts and sent marriage equality to the highest court in the land. Setting that one defeat in context, Mark and Vic saw signs of hope. The Sixth Circuit *had* overturned lower-court rulings from Kentucky, Michigan, Ohio, and Tennessee, but courts in the Fourth, Seventh, Ninth, and Tenth Circuits had ruled in favor of marriage equality. Moreover, Judge Jeffrey Sutton's opinion was—as Ilya Somin, a conservative columnist writing for The Volokh Conspiracy in *The Washington Post*, observed—"not very strong . . . unlikely to persuade or even give much pause to anyone who doesn't already agree with its conclusions."[23]

In a withering and sure-footed dissent, Judge Martha Craig Daughtrey—like Mark, a graduate of Vanderbilt Law School—attacked the majority opinion as little more than "an engrossing TED Talk or, possibly, an introductory lecture in Political Philosophy. But as an appellate court decision," she added, "it wholly fails to grapple with the relevant constitutional question in this appeal: whether a state's constitutional prohibition of same-sex marriage violates equal protection under the Fourteenth Amendment." She identified a key flaw in Judge Sutton's argument: "The majority sets up a false premise—that the question before us is 'who should decide?'—and leads us through a largely irrelevant discourse on democracy and federalism." Perhaps more important, she identified an attitudinal problem that had warped the legal judgment of the judges in the majority:

In the main, the majority treats both the issues and the litigants here as mere abstractions. Instead of recognizing the plaintiffs as persons, suffering actual harm as a result of being denied the right to marry where they reside or the right to have their valid marriages recognized there, my colleagues view the plaintiffs as social activists who have somehow stumbled into federal court, inadvisably, when they should be out campaigning to win "the hearts and minds" of Michigan, Ohio, Kentucky, and Tennessee voters to their cause.

Where the others saw "political zealots trying to push reform on their fellow citizens," Judge Daughtrey saw "committed same-sex couples, many of them heading up *de facto* families," seeking no more than "a civil right that most of us take for granted."[24]

In a Facebook post hours after the decision appeared online, Mark had angrily denounced as "absurd" Judge Sutton's assertion that the court "cannot 'infer from history that prejudice against gays led to the traditional definition of marriage in the same way that we can infer from history that prejudice against African Americans led to laws against miscegenation.'" When the anger subsided, he and Vic were gladdened by Judge Martha Craig Daughtrey's dissent, particularly by her reference to Justice Anthony Kennedy's defense of "personhood" in *Lawrence* and *Windsor*, the denial of which had troubled them since they were old enough to understand that people were willing to cast them aside, to deny their essential humanity, because of their sexual orientation.[25]

Stunned that her colleagues would accept arguments that had been dismissed by the Fourth, Seventh, Ninth, and Tenth Circuits—the alleged need to encourage "responsible procreation" or to "wait and see" before changing historical norms—she could find only one explanation for their ruling against marriage equality. Is it possible, she wondered, "that the majority has purposefully taken the contrary position to create the circuit split regarding the legality of same-sex marriage that could prompt a grant of *certiorari* by the Supreme Court and an end to the uncertainty of status and the interstate chaos that the current discrepancy in state laws threatens?"[26]

***

With his and Vic's future riding on the outcome, Mark-the-Attorney had immersed himself in the details of same-sex marriage litigation in general and of *Obergefell v. Hodges* in particular. Though the number of *amicus* briefs submitted, 149 in all (seventy-seven supporting the petitioners who were seeking marriage equality, sixty-seven supporting the respondents), was almost overwhelming, he read the more important briefs carefully, skimmed the rest. What he found as page gave way to page was reassuring. As the states seeking to uphold marriage bans lost case after case, attorneys arguing on their behalf had discarded argument after argument. When Court convened on Tuesday, Mark and Vic knew supporters of marriage equality would hear once again slightly recast versions of the tattered remnants: federalism and the right of the states to define "marriage," the supposed need to allow the "democratic process" to take its course, the states' interest in encouraging "responsible procreation" and assuring that children are raised in "optimal" families, the value of tradition and the need for caution in "changing the nature of marriage." But they knew from earlier court victories and from the briefs that no creditable arguments against marriage equality remained unanswered.

The seventy-seven briefs filed on behalf of the petitioners in *Obergefell v. Hodges* covered a wide range of legal issues; predictably, Mark and Vic had their favorites. The Commonwealth of Virginia, for example, submitted what amounted to an apology to James Madison, George Mason, and Thomas Jefferson for losing sight of the "equality-of-right principle" they enshrined in the Declaration of Independence, the Virginia Declaration of Rights, and the Bill of Rights. Having argued on the wrong side of previous landmark cases—*Brown v. Board of Education, Loving v. Virginia, United States v. Virginia* (excluding female cadets from the Virginia Military Institute)—the State had once maintained that federalism coupled with "history and tradition . . . justify segregation and anti-miscegenation laws." In a stunning *mea culpa*, the brief admitted "Virginia's government was wrong then, and the four States that reprise modern-day versions of those failed arguments are wrong here."[27] Why, Mark and Vic wondered, could Texas not have found its way to a similar *mea culpa* in 2003 after *Lawrence* was decided?

The Brief of the Human Rights Campaign, popularized on the internet as the "People's Brief" to which, as a gesture of support, more than 200,000 Americans committed to marriage equality added their signatures below that of Edith Windsor, focused on the constitutionally impermissible *animus* that had prompted anti-gay legislation in Michigan, Ohio, Kentucky, and Tennessee. Building on *Windsor*, the catalyst that brought on the last stage of the campaign for marriage equality, Roberta Kaplan, the Counsel of Record, reminded the Court of the principle underlying that decision: "that gay people have dignity, and that the Constitution mandates that this dignity be respected equally under the law." Hence, laws based on *animus*, she and her co-authors,

Dale Carpenter and Steve Sanders pointed out, laws that grew from "a bare desire to harm," or even from a "want of careful, rational reflection"—must be set aside. Examining the text of the laws under scrutiny ("familiar tropes characterizing gay people as 'other,'" additional language that "played to voters' fears by reviving . . . demonic stereotypes of homosexuals"), the political and legal context in which the laws had been passed, the impact of the laws on people in the real world, and the absence of legitimate rationales for the states' arguments against same-sex marriage, the HRC brief exposed the ill-concealed *animus* behind the bans and convincingly laid bare the poverty of the state's arguments.

Two additional briefs that responded in innovative ways to the issues raised in *Obergefell v. Hodges* further reassured Mark and Vic. Back in Texas two organizations—Texas Competes and the Texas Association of Business—were busily spreading the word that discrimination was bad business and the Brief of 379 Employers and Organizations Representing Employers made it clear that employers across the country shared their conclusion. In their brief, Susan Baker Manning, the Counsel of Record, and Meghan Rhea turned early in their arguments to the all-important human dimension. "When same-sex couples are married," they maintained, "just as when opposite-sex couples are married, they serve as models of loving commitment to all." As a result, employee morale and productivity improve. But the core of their argument was pure nuts and bolts practicality: good business sense. The "fractured legal landscape" created by the handful of states holding out against marriage equality "hampers economic growth and impedes innovation by forcing businesses to work hard, and invest more, to achieve the same return on our investments." Administrative burdens imposed by unequal access to marriage were, they estimated, costing private sector businesses $3.5 million a day. Moreover, being forced to discriminate, the businesses argued, "goes against our core values and principles . . . we want the jurisdictions where we operate to recognize the need to enable all married persons to "live with pride in themselves and their unions" and to honor the "personal dignity and autonomy of all our employees."[28]

Mark and Vic found particular comfort in the Brief of Amici Curiae Kenneth B. Mehlman et al. They knew Mehlman's history as a much-respected

Republican operative, a man who knew better than most not just how conservatives think but how to move them to action. They knew he had worked as field director of George W. Bush's successful campaign for the presidency in 2000 and that he spent the next four years close to the center of power as director of the White House Office of Political affairs. They knew that in 2004, the first election cycle after the Supreme Judicial Court of Massachusetts made same-sex marriage legal, stampeding frightened conservatives across the country into passing constitutional amendments in thirteen states, Mehlman had managed President Bush's campaign for re-election and had at least tacitly approved of the strategy by which the GOP had driven frenzied evangelicals to the polls with feverish visions of societal collapse.

Rumors that Mehlman was gay had circulated as early as 2004, causing Mark and Vic to wonder why he would betray his deepest self by orchestrating attacks on the LGBT community. By 2010 when he was at last ready to speak the truth—the *New York Times* dubbed him at the time "the most prominent Republican official to come out"—Mehlman was contrite and determined to use his high profile to negate what gay rights advocates saw as his "incredibly destructive" legacy.[29] Mark and Vic, closeted in their professional lives long after they came out to friends and family, were ready to forgive and to welcome his help.

Mehlman began by using his extensive contacts to raise money for LGBT causes—more than $4.5 million. He got to know Ted Olson, raised funds for the American Foundation for Equal Rights (AFER), and filed a brief signed by more than a hundred Republicans in support of the lawsuit to overturn Prop 8 in California. Chad Griffin, who with Kristina Schake founded AFER and instigated the Prop 8 challenge, had been effusive in his praise. "When we achieve equality," he said of Mehlman in 2010, he will be one of the people to thank for it."[30]

For *Obergefell v. Hodges*, the earlier brief had been updated and augmented—and this time more than three hundred prominent Republicans, "social and political conservatives, moderates, and libertarians," had signed on. Returning time and time again to Republican-friendly words and phrases— "limited government," "individual freedom," "family values," "personal liberty," "responsibility," "fidelity," "commitment," "stability"—Seth P. Waxman as

Counsel of Record crafted an argument calculated to appeal to conservatives on their own terms. Bans against same-sex marriage, the brief declared, are "inconsistent with amici's understanding of the properly *limited role of government.*" Judicial restraint is to be admired, judicial activism to be condemned. But the Mehlman brief courageously recognized, in terms that would resonate with conservatives, circumstances in which the Constitution demands that courts intervene. When legislatures or popular majorities "pose significant threats to *individual freedom* . . . courts have the power to—and should—intervene . . . to protect our most *cherished liberties* against *overreaching by the government* . . . When *personal liberty* is at stake, the Constitution cannot continue to enshrine previously unexamined societal assumptions once new facts and information come to light." Conservatives should embrace marriage equality, the brief concludes, not in spite of their values, but because of them.[31]

Mark and Vic were proud that Akin Gump leapt into the fray with a brief on behalf of the American Historical Association and leading historians of marriage, discrediting the States' claim that marriage is "a static institution . . . rooted in 'tradition'" tied through history to the State's desire to encourage "procreation or the rearing of biological children." Rather, Akin Gump contended, "marriage has remained a vital institution because it is not static." Citing changes in laws governing coverture, rape within marriage, and inter-racial marriage, Pratik A. Shah as Counsel of Record—currently a partner at Akin Gump, formerly an assistant to the U. S. Solicitor General for whose office he led the drafting of the United States' challenge to the Defense of Marriage Act in *Windsor*—demonstrated that "states have, over time, altered many of [marriage's] dimensions to adapt to economic change and to shifting social and sexual mores."[32]

By the time the Supreme Court granted cert in *Obergefell v. Hodges*, Mark and Vic had become so emotionally invested in the cause of marriage equality that they wanted more than anything to play a role in what they hoped would be the last stage of the struggle. A call to Serge Benchetrit, a partner in the New York office of Willkie Farr & Gallagher with whom Mark had worked for almost twenty years, resulted in a path forward. Richard Bernstein, a straight man who once clerked for Justice Scalia, and Wesley Powell—who with his husband had adopted a son in Texas, only to have the State refuse to recognize the adoption—agreed to head up a team that would tell Mark and Vic's story, arguing that as plaintiffs in Texas where social and political pressures weighed heavily against same-sex marriage, Mark and Vic would never marry in their home state unless a court ruled in their favor.

The scope of the Willkie Farr brief changed, however, when at Mark's suggestion Powell talked with Mary Bonauto. She loved the premise and suggested that adding *amici* from other states where, as she wrote in an e-mail, "it is obviously ridiculous to think about a marriage bill passing out of a legisla-ture and being signed by a governor" would give the brief more weight. In the end ninety-two plaintiffs from fifteen states—Alabama, Alaska, Arkansas, Indiana, Kansas, Louisiana, Mississippi, Missouri, Montana, Nebraska, North Carolina, North Dakota, South Carolina, South Dakota, and Texas (a veritable rogues' gallery of opposition to marriage equality)—added their voices to Mark's and Vic's, a chorus that drew strength from numbers.

Knowing that Justice Kennedy would once again hold the swing vote, Willkie Farr set out to provide him with a legal standard he could use to argue against leaving the decision to the states without being accused of judi-cial activism. Bernstein encouraged his colleagues to employ the principles of originalism which he absorbed while clerking for Justice Scalia, its fore-most proponent on the Court. In his days as a clerk Bernstein had come to know Steven Calabresi, another of Justice Scalia's clerks in the 1987-88 term and now a prominent conservative scholar of originalism, who had recently joined with Hannah Begley in writing "an originalist argument for same sex marriage." Examining the historical context—"state constitutions prior to 1868 . . . contemporary speeches, articles, and dictionaries"—to deter-mine "the original public meaning" of the Equal Protection Clause, they had concluded that "it bans systems of caste and class-based discrimination," a perfect premise for the argument Bernstein and his colleagues wanted to make as they turned the language and theoretical framework most often asso-ciated with the Court's most conservative justices against them.[33]

The men who framed the Equal Protection Clause in 1868, Willkie Farr asserted, sent a message about its original meaning when they "rejected narrower versions barring only unequal treatment 'because of race, color or previous servitude,'" drafting and redrafting until they arrived at a "final, far more expansive definition of equal protection [that] 'abolished all class legislation in the States and d[id] away with *the injustice of subjecting one caste of persons to a code not applicable to another* ' " (emphasis in original). Another key word in the brief, "dynamic," was taken "on loan" from Justice Scalia. By chance, in the year of his clerkship, Bernstein had been assigned to write the first draft of *Business Electronics Corp. v. Sharp Electronics Corp.* (1988), a seldom-cited case he claims has been virtually forgotten. Still, in the moment of need twenty-five years later he remembered a critical passage construing the Sherman Act. Writing for the Court, Justice Scalia had "held that the term 'restraint of trade' had inherently *'dynamic potential'* which enabled the courts to *change* what practices the statute barred and permitted based on 'varying times and circumstances'" (emphasis in original).[34]

Like "caste" and "class," "dynamic" became foundational. The framers of the Equal Protection Clause "understood that recognition of what government practices violated the dynamic concept of equality had changed in the 81 years since the 1787 Constitution" and—another indication of original meaning—deliberately chose language that "left it to the courts over time to determine which laws impermissibly subjected a caste or class of citizens to unjustifiable discrimination." Repeated precedents from the Court, they argued, confirm the historical record "that the Equal Protection Clause is dynamic." Willkie Farr's deliberate use of Justice Scalia's language and originalist principles, so often deployed in arguing against marriage equality, sounded a refreshingly ironic note in Mark's and Vic's ears.

Remembering that the question of "Who decides?" had been the linchpin of Judge Sutton's opinion in the Sixth Circuit—and was, therefore, critical to their clients—Bernstein and his colleagues turned once again to history and legal precedent to undermine the argument that marriage law should be left to the states. Though moderate Democrats before the Civil War had advanced the doctrine of "Popular Sovereignty," the idea "that on divisive issues such as slavery, decisions should be left to the majority of voters in each state" had been discredited by no less a figure than Abraham Lincoln who had condemned it as a "living, creeping lie from the time of its introduction to today." The post-war generation that produced the Fourteenth Amendment had put such ideas behind them as relics incompatible with their evolving understanding of equality.[35]

Because their clients came from states where "hostility to the rights of gay men and lesbians" had led to the kind of "unapologetic *animus*" likely to influence the Court, Willkie Farr wanted to include state-by-state examples.[36] Offered early drafts of the brief for comment—half a dozen or more as Wesley Powell remembers—Mark pitched in with information drawn from his journal and his legal experience. "Working with Mark was very different from working with the usual *pro bono* client," Powell observed. "He's a lawyer and a smart guy who's lived and breathed these issues for years while the Texas case made its way through the courts. He had a lot to contribute."

For years Mark had chafed at the fact that though *Lawrence v. Texas* decriminalized gay sex in 2003, the Texas Health and Safety Code stubbornly, almost irrationally insisted that in Texas schools course materials in sex-ed classes must emphasize "in a factual manner and from a public health perspective that homosexuality is not a lifestyle acceptable to the general public and that homosexual conduct is a criminal offense under Section 21.06, Penal Code"—a sure sign of *animus*.[37] Because Vic had served in the Air Force for nearly twenty-three years, Mark took particular umbrage at Texas's mistreatment of gay servicemen and veterans. He sent Willkie Farr the story of offensive remarks by then-Governor Rick Perry at a 2005 event sponsored by the Calvary Cathedral International Church in Fort Worth, a gathering described in the *Star-Telegram* as "part state-government ceremony and part healing revival." Referencing Texas's 2005 constitutional amendment banning same-sex marriage, a reporter asked the governor what he would say to gay and lesbian veterans returning from the war in Iraq. Perry's reply was heavy with *animus*: "I'm going to say Texas has made a decision on marriage, and if there's a state with more lenient laws than Texas, then maybe that's where they should live."[38]

Though Mark and Vic understood that as individuals many Republicans supported marriage equality, they saw in the party's official position—platform statements issued nationally and in Texas—repeated signs of *animus* that they felt would strengthen the brief. As early as 1980 Democrats included protection from discrimination on the basis of "sexual orientation" in their platform; by 2004 the Democratic platform called for "full inclusion of gay and lesbian families in the life of the nation." Republicans avoided the issue entirely until 1992 when they spoke against granting "preferential status" on the basis of "sexual preference" (the term in itself an insult to the LGBT community). Recognizing in gay rights a wedge issue that could be used to rally the evangelical base, Republicans raised the level of rhetoric to almost hysterical heights as they moved from one platform statement to the next, often railing against "judicial activists" as in 2004 when they condemned "a few judges and local authorities" for "presuming to change the most fundamental institution of civilization, the union of a man and a woman in marriage."

In addition, Republicans had long opposed expanding anti-discrimination laws to include gays and lesbians, opposed ending the ban on gays in the military, opposed allowing gays and lesbians to adopt, and opposed spousal benefits of any kind for same-sex couples. They endorsed the Defense of Marriage Act repeatedly as court challenges mounted, and in 2004 they endorsed President George W. Bush's proposal for a constitutional amendment prohibiting same-sex marriage.[39] As oral arguments in *Obergefell* approached, the Republican platform still proclaimed that "The union of one man and one woman must be upheld as the national standard."[40] With the Republican establishment adamantly opposed to LGBT rights in general and marriage equality in particular, Mark and Vic thought it important to highlight their plight by pointing out that legislatures in all fifteen of the states represented in the Willkie Farr brief were controlled by Republicans and that governors in twelve of those states were Republicans as well.

Richard Bernstein agreed. "When a client has ideas about what should be included," he said, "those ideas should be incorporated whenever possible," adding that Mark played a significant role in shaping the brief. Powell concurred. "It was clear from the start that the brief was important to Mark and Vic. They had been key players in the Texas case. We knew how important it was to them to be heard at the national level. For those of us at Willkie Farr, it was satisfying to play a role in *Obergefell*, to provide some sense of relief for Mark and Vic and the 90 other plaintiffs included in the brief whose experience in states so strongly opposed to marriage equality was so very different from what those of us living in New York experienced."

On March 6, the morning the brief was filed, Mark thanked Willkie Farr & Gallagher in a Facebook post, noting that "Vic and I have been fortunate to be represented by great law firms, first Akin Gump in the district and 5th Circuit courts, now Willkie Farr before the Supreme Court."[41]

In briefs and in oral arguments, good lawyers tell stories that will appeal to juries and to judges. Mark and Vic knew that the legal story their side had told in the briefs was compelling. They knew that in oral arguments Mary Bonauto and Solicitor General Donald B. Verrilli would represent them and the LGBT community ably. They knew that momentum was on their side. Since *Windsor* court rulings had consistently gone their way; only thirteen states now prohibited same-sex marriage. Better still, they saw in the Court's "October Surprise," the Justices' decision not to stay favorable decisions involving five states from the Fourth, Seventh, and Tenth Circuit Courts of Appeals (Virginia, Indiana, Wisconsin, Utah, and Oklahoma), a sign that enough Justices were leaning their way and would make their marriage possible.

That since granting cert in *Obergefell* the Court had broken with precedent and refused to issue a stay in the contentious Alabama case, *Strange v. Searcy*, sweetened their imaginations still further. Justice Scalia's enraged dissent from that decision pointed out that "When state courts declare state laws unconstitutional and enjoin state officials from enforcing them, our ordinary practice is to suspend those injunctions from taking effect pending appellate review. . . This acquiescence may well be seen," he continued, "as a signal of the Court's intended resolution of that question."[42] For once, Mark and Vic agreed with Justice Scalia. With the end game about to begin, Mark and Vic were confident, 90 percent sure they told friends on Facebook and via e-mail. But always, there was the tiny voice, deep inside, wondering, questioning, struggling to move to 100 percent surety.

* * *

For the morning of the hearing, Mark and Vic set an alarm to wake them at 4:45 a.m. But, true to form, Mark tossed and turned through the night, too restless to sleep. By 4:30 he was up and about, ready to give up any pretense of rest. A few minutes before six o'clock he and Vic emerged from a cab in front of the Supreme Court and, finding their line-standers, Michael and Caitlin, half-awake in the muddle of tarps and blankets and fast-food wrappers that had been their East Capitol Street "home" for two days, took their places in line, confident that within the hour they would walk together into the Supreme Court of the United States. Setting off for a few hours of rest, Michael carried with him Mark's cell phone and camera. He knew lockers would be available inside, but wanted to avoid even the smallest delay in the hope of getting the best seats possible.

Within minutes the line began to collapse, accordion-like, as friends carried away chairs and cots, blankets and coolers, and the people headed into the courtroom drew closer together. Toward 7:30—the waiting seemed endless—a uniformed officer of the Supreme Court Police made his way along the line, tolling the numbers and handing out official tickets as he greeted the lucky few: forty-six, forty-seven, forty-eight, forty-nine . . . fifty. That was the moment when, as Vic would write later on Facebook, he felt a knife go into his heart. The number on his ticket was fifty, not forty-nine as he had expected. Mark, not he, should have been holding the last ticket, but the officer's arm had come down to stop Mark in place and his hand was terrifyingly empty. "In thirty seconds," Vic remembered later that day, the pain still in his voice, "my world collapsed. We were about to be ushered into the building and Mark would not be there." He pushed their one ticket at Mark. This was, after all, his dream as a lawyer, to sit in the Supreme Court for oral arguments. That this case would shape their future together made the dream that much more meaningful.

Everyone in the line knew his or her number; Mark's was fifty. "Someone's cut into the line!" he protested. Though the officer was sympathetic, his reply—"Nothing I can do"—was chilling. In his mind's eye, Mark saw the culprit slipping into the seat in which he had imagined himself since January. For eighteen years he and Vic had shared everything, but they would not share this quintessential moment.

Mark pushed the ticket back into Vic's hand and shoved him in the direction of the line, already moving away. "It'll be okay," he said, tears welling in his eyes. "Go. Go. Go!" He watched as Vic rejoined their friends in line, his feet moving slowly toward the entrance, his head turned back and his eyes still on Mark.[43] Held back at the base of the first set of steps leading to the plaza, Mark looked up at the motto carved into the west pediment—"Equal Justice under Law"—and wondered.

Alone outside, Mark struggled to compose himself. Clutching at straws, he thought of being admitted to the short-term seats for a bittersweet, three-minute stay. He'd have, at least, a glance of Vic from behind though Vic would almost certainly be oblivious of his presence. Later, Mark would see his most vulnerable moment again on a television newscast. Karina Kling and a cameraman from Time Warner Cable News were on the scene and recording at the very moment he was denied a ticket. Seeing the officer approach, Mark looks excitedly at the camera. "Here come the tickets, right now!" he exclaims. And then, surprised when nothing comes his way, he holds up a finger as if to freeze the officer in place. Rocking back on his heels, his cry of joy slips into a question he hardly dares ask. "Forty-nine . . . and fifty?" The camera closes in on the ticket in Vic's hand; on the sound track the audience hears Mark's cry of pain.

"Those were their numbers," Kling tells the camera, "but someone jumped the line and kept one of the pair from getting in." The camera pans from protestor to protestor, pauses on a man with a bullhorn reading from a bible, behind him a man with a biblical passage warning against homosexuality spread across a large banner. Moments later we catch a glimpse of two more signs. A young woman holds one, professionally printed with sharp, well-drawn black letters: "A child needs a mother and a father." Standing next to her is a young man whose sign reads "I have 2 moms and life is good." His sign, done in the rainbow colors of the gay pride flag, is very much handmade. The letters loop and swirl with the joy in his life. When the clip shifts to a new shot, the viewer sees Mark through the line of people headed into the court, hands in his pockets, tears in his eyes as he watches helplessly.

"I'm a little frustrated and disappointed," he tells Kling; "I'm sorry that I'm not with Vic." Minutes later, Emmarie Huetteman of the *New York Times* appeared at Mark's side. Word of what had happened was spreading rapidly. His eyes still red from the struggle to hold back tears, his voice unsteady, Mark told the story for the first of many times. But as he spoke, his usual calm began to return. He knew that across the country people in the LGBT community were being beaten every day, sometimes murdered; he knew that many had lost, or could not find jobs because of who they were; he knew that many had been cast out by their families. Not getting into the hearing was hurtful, but in comparison a small hurt. "The important thing," Mark told Huetteman, "is not that we're in the Court together, but that the Court rules the right way so we can spend the rest of our lives together."[44]

Inside, Vic set to work. Though stunned and angry, outraged by what had happened, he saw no way to rectify the injustice done. He had donned his Service Dress uniform for the day and knew from years of training that he couldn't allow what he was feeling to diminish the uniform. He turned first to one of the Supreme Court policemen standing nearby. "The man could see," Vic would tell friends later, "that this was tearing me up inside and his compassion was a credit to him and to the entire force."[45] Perhaps the uniform of an Air Force major helped as well. An hour after he and Mark had been driven apart, Vic talked a security guard into walking with him back to spot on the plaza where he had been separated from the man he loved. Again, Vic implored Mark to take the ticket. Again, Mark refused. Vic suggested that they remain outside together, but Mark would have none of it. And for the second time that day, they parted company as Vic, the security officer still at his side, returned sadly to take the one place that had been left to them.

In Vic's absence, others inside, aided by the Supreme Court Police, had set about a bit of detective work. Most had spent days—and nights— socializing to pass the time and knew which ticket number was theirs; even those who had paid line-standers had visited often enough to know who belonged where. They had discussed the possibility that someone might try to jump the line, had compiled a list of names from one to fifty to prevent foul play. Collectively, they had a better than good idea where Mark's ticket had gone. Tattered and frayed after three days exposed to the elements, the hand-written list told the story. Tracy Hollister, on the list as ticket #20, was the first to figure out what had happened. Faith in Action, a religious lobbying group that claims to represent 80,000 conservative Christians and operates out of offices just behind the Court, had maintained a presence in the line so its director would have a seat in the courtroom. The woman who worked as his second-in-command, the Chief of Program at Faith in Action, had supervised two paid line-standers who spotted each other from time to time to hold one seat. Talking to pass the time on the sidewalk, Tracy had come to know the young man in front of her, the woman's nephew, the primary line-stander for Faith in Action. She knew ticket #19 was his.

But on Tuesday morning as line-standers gave way to their patrons, the Chief of Program at Faith in Action replaced her nephew and the director stood by her side. Puzzled, reluctant at first to cause a scene, Tracy finally summoned the courage to pop the question. "Which of you," she asked, "is going inside the Court?" The director's reply—"We both are"—was as unsettling as the "self-assured air of entitlement" she heard in the tone of his voice.[46] Shocked, she fell for some minutes into silence. She knew that her friends Mark and Vic held the last two tickets. She knew their story. She knew the pain being separated on this of all days would bring them.

Tracy was still wondering what to do when the Supreme Court Police moved along the line distributing tickets. Faith in Action's Chief of Program took #19. When the policeman attempted to give ticket #20 to the director, Tracy objected. "I had strongly identified with that number since Friday," she wrote; "no one was going to take it from me." He accepted ticket #21. With the line stopped just before the entrance to the building, Tracy once again found her tongue. "I am feeling uncomfortable here," she said to her antago-nists; "I think you cut in line." Glaring at her, the director told her to take her concerns to the police.[47]

Vic's first impulse on being told what had happened was to take the suspects by the lapels and shake them until they admitted guilt. But again, the uniform; as an officer in the armed forces of the United States of America he couldn't do that. Fortunately, he didn't have to. Seeing Vic inside, seeing his pain, Tracy and others went quickly to work. Knowing they might need to identify him later, Eddie Rey had snapped a picture of the director as the line approached the entrance. His face is turned to the camera, his mouth open in protest that anyone would dare to challenge what he had done. To his left, Tracy looks on sadly, still not quite believing what had happened. Inside, Tracy challenged the guilty pair again, lowering her voice to avoid causing a disturbance. "Is this what your religion teaches," she asked? "To lie? To steal?" Twice the director threatened to have her removed from the line.

Tracy, Eddie, and his friend, Thalia followed the director and his assistant into the cafeteria, snapped another picture as they sat at a table. The director's head is bowed in prayer, a way of avoiding the eyes of his accusers; the Chief of Program looks up suspiciously, her mouth set in a hard line. This time Eddie spoke first, his words at once an indictment and a challenge. "As a member of a religious organization" he told the culprits, "you lied. You've cut in line and you need to give up your spot. There's a member of the military inside who fought for our country, our rights and your freedom, and his partner is outside. You're splitting him and his partner up."[48] Finally, Faith in Action agreed to give up the ticket they had accepted under false pretenses. Mark's ticket firmly in hand, Tracy persuaded a Supreme Court Policeman to take her outside where she knew her friend would be waiting. With minutes to spare before their group headed to the courtroom, they raced back into the building, barely slowing to pass through security. A photo of Mark and Vic's emotional reunion, taken by Chad Griffin, the president of the Human Rights Campaign, shows the two of them locked in a long embrace. Mark's eyes are closed. On his face, a broad smile. In his left hand, the salmon-colored ticket he almost didn't get, highlighted against the back of Vic's uniform. According to Kathleen Perrin, another of those who had helped to expose the line-jumper, "Every single person who witnessed their meeting, especially those of us who knew Mark and Vic, cried."[49] They had been cautioned to wait quietly before being taken upstairs, but when Mark and Vic were finally reunited, the entire line burst into spontaneous applause. Vic's final Facebook post before surrendering his phone summed up the experience perfectly: "Here inside SCOTUS with my best friend in the whole world."[50]

Once the dust had settled and calm had returned, Mark looked back to the once-frightening affair of the purloined ticket and discovered in it an allegory, a best case scenario of the way he hoped the marriage equality movement would play out. Like tens of thousands of same-sex couples, he and Vic had asked for nothing more than the right to marry and spend their lives together, but opponents on the religious right had employed every possible trick to keep them apart. "Our community," Mark asserted, "went to work to persuade religious types that they were wrong." And, ultimately, in Mark's hopeful imagining, "they backed away; we will be united."[51] That seemed to have happened in just the past few hours.

The couple from Faith in Action also looked back to reimagine the incident. Not long after oral arguments had concluded, Faith in Action posted a YouTube video filmed on the steps of the Supreme Court which claimed that their Chief of Program had played the role of peacemaker, giving up a ticket that was rightfully hers.[52] When later in the summer Tracy Hollister reached out to the director, hoping to talk with him about the humanity of people in the LGBT community, he admitted the truth. "I was not at my best morally or ethically," he admitted of that morning. "Not once did I think of the person that was crowded out of the courtroom by that crafty maneuver of mine."[53]

Tracy's efforts to reach out rather than lash out helped propel the director to a new place. Seated by chance next to Jim Obergefell in the courtroom, he had reached out to speak of how touched he had been by Jim's story of love lost to death. By summer's end he was ready to admit in correspondence with Tracy that "homosexual people seek intimate companionship for the same reasons that heterosexual people do, including the longing for commitment, shared life experiences, family bonds, and, most fundamentally, reciprocating love," and that the love gays and lesbians feel for one another "is just as real and genuine as the love I have for my wife of thirty-eight years." His view of same-sex marriage had evolved. "If you want to out me," he told Tracy, "out me," adding in language familiar to anyone in the LGBT community, "It's better to err on the side of being authentic than inauthentic."[54]

Getting into the courtroom together had been a struggle, but once inside Mark and Vic's luck changed for the better. Chance brought them seats on an aisle, Mark one row in front of Vic, on several banks of wooden chairs placed just behind the last row of permanent seating. Though flanked by pillars, they had an unobstructed view of the bench and were surrounded by some of the leaders of the marriage equality movement. Chad Griffin sat directly in front of Mark, next to him Sarah Warbelow, legal director for the HRC, and next to her two of the Michigan plaintiffs, Frank Colasonti, Jr. and James Ryder. Evan Wolfson and Marc Solomon were two rows in front of

Mark. Senator Cory Booker of New Jersey, a strong supporter of gay rights with whom Vic and Mark had narrowly missed a meeting the day before, sat next to Vic. They had hoped to thank Senator Booker who had risen two weeks earlier on the Senate floor to speak in praise of James Obergefell and his partner. "Their story," he told his colleagues that day, "is heartbreaking. It is inspiring. But unfortunately, it is all too common."[55] Now they took advantage of their chance to thank the senator and, with him, to express their hope that today's proceedings would put an end to such stories.

Further away—too far for conversation considering how often the security guards had insisted on decorous quiet inside the courtroom—were Jayne Rowse and April DeBoer, the Michigan plaintiffs whose wedding Mark and Vic would later attend. Like Mark and Vic they had become accidental activists. Nurses by profession, caring people by nature, they had together adopted four children, two with special needs. But in the eyes of the law, Jayne had adopted two children and April the other two since second-parent adoption in Michigan was prohibited to same-sex couples.

That each had no legal rights to the other's children, a legal reality that tore at their sense of family, was driven home on a snowy winter's day in Ohio when one or both nearly died. A truck attempting to pass entered their lane. The head-on collision that seemed momentarily inevitable was avoided only at the last moment when the truck veered off the road and into a field. Realizing that their family might have been shattered, driven apart both literally and legally, they filed a lawsuit challenging Michigan's adoption laws— and switched only when U. S. District Court Judge Bernard A. Friedman advised them that they would have a better chance of winning if they challenged Michigan's ban on same-sex marriage.

Planning for *DeLeon v. Perry* with Cleo and Nicole and the legal team at Akin Gump, Mark and Vic had hoped for a full trial on the merits. Akin Gump had prepared for that by submitting hundreds of pages of expert testimony. Jayne and April's case, *DeBoer v. Snyder*, was one of only three same-sex marriage cases to go to a full trial and Mark and Vic were grateful that the evidence presented on issue after issue discredited the arguments against same-sex marriage. Even before they knew the women personally, they had sung their praises in interview after interview. "By the lives they lead,"

Marks insists, "they help to break down barriers. They're exactly the kind of people you want representing you before the Supreme Court."[56]

Watching from afar, their intuition confirmed when at last they met in person, Mark and Vic sensed in Jayne and April other versions of themselves, ordinary people who couldn't imagine a life apart from the person they loved, determined to support and protect each other and to do good in the world. Waiting in the courtroom for oral arguments to begin, Mark and Vic could see the stress written on the faces around them, could feel it when they listened to their own bodies. And yet, they felt the comfort of being among friends who shared their vision and their values. Outside, hundreds more had gathered. Around the country millions more were waiting to hear what would happen in the next hour and a half. Soft conversation drifted this way and that until at last the Marshal called the Court to order.

"Oyez, oyez, oyez." Out of respect for the nine justices, the hundreds who had crowded into the courtroom stood. Court was in session.

Chapter 7

Justice That Arrives Like a Thunderbolt

All persons born or naturalized in the United States, and subject to the jurisdiction thereof, are citizens of the United States and of the state wherein they reside. No state shall make or enforce any law which shall abridge the privileges or immunities of citizens of the United States; nor shall any state deprive any person of life, liberty, or property, without due process of law; nor deny to any person within its jurisdiction the equal protection of the laws.

—The Fourteenth Amendment to the Constitution, Section I

Inside and out, Cass Gilbert designed the Supreme Court to impress. Moving through the doors, visitors are visually stunned by the Great Hall with its double rows of columns, coffered ceiling, and marble niches with busts of former chief justices. The massive courtroom—"almost bombastically pretentious" one justice quipped years ago—eighty-two by ninety-one feet, its ornate ceiling forty-two feet above supported by an additional twenty-four marble columns—is still more impressive.[1] Dwarfed by the size and majesty of Gilbert's architecture, most who venture inside fall under its spell. Decorous behavior comes naturally. Seconds after the Marshal called the Court to order, the floor to ceiling red-velvet curtains at the front of the room parted and the justices entered in groups of three, the Chief Justice and senior associates in the center, a group of three on either side. They swept theatrically to their places behind the huge mahogany bench, purposefully higher than the attorney arguing at the lectern, close enough to make eye-contact and intimidate.

The room fell silent and Mary Bonauto, whose long experience arguing for marriage equality had made her the obvious choice, rose to argue the first of the two questions defined by the Court at the end of February: "Does the Fourteenth Amendment require a state to license a marriage between two people of the same sex?"

Bonauto's first words—"Mr. Chief Justice, and may it please the Court: the intimate and committed relationships of same-sex couples . . . provide mutual support and are the foundation of family life in our society"—made clear the essentials of her argument: love is love, marriage is marriage, and family is family, whatever the sex of the partners. All deserve equal treatment and equal protection under the law as required by the Fourteenth Amendment. Hoping to influence Justice Kennedy, universally acknowledged as the all-important swing vote, her second sentence echoed the ideas underlying the Court's decision in *Windsor*, including what emerged there as the key concept, "dignity." Deny marriage to same-sex couples, she asserted, and their children will be hurt because "the stain of unworthiness that follows on individuals and families contravenes the basic constitutional commitment to equal dignity."[2] That was as far as Bonauto was allowed to go before, as is usual in Supreme Court proceedings, the justices began to pepper her with questions.

Justice Ginsburg, thought by most to be a supporter of marriage equality, spoke up first. "What do you do," she asked, "with the *Windsor* case where the court stressed the Federal government's historical deference to States when it comes to matters of domestic relations?" Bonauto took advantage of Justice Ginsburg's question to clear the legal air. "States do have primacy over domestic relations," she told the Justices, "except that their laws must respect the constitutional rights of persons."[3]

Court-watchers had almost universally predicted that no new arguments against marriage equality would emerge at the Supreme Court, that the conservative justices and attorneys arguing for the respondents would once again "round up the usual suspects." They were not disappointed.

Chief Justice Roberts, Justice Kennedy, and Justice Alito challenged Bonauto early on about the value of tradition and historical precedent. Advocates of same-sex marriage, the Chief Justice argued, are "not seeking to join the institution . . . you're seeking to change what the institution is." More than a few advocates of same-sex marriage, Mark and Vic among them, felt their hearts skip a beat as Justice Kennedy added his voice. "The word that keeps coming back to me in this case is—millennia, plus time . . . this definition has been with us for millennia. And it—it's very difficult for the Court to say, oh, well, we—we know better." Like the rest of the country, they knew that Justice Kennedy was likely to be the deciding vote and what they read as skepticism was making them nervous—extremely nervous.

Conservative justices on the Supreme Court are by nature reluctant to credit cultural and legal precedents from other countries. During his confirmation hearing in 2006, Justice Samuel Alito made his disposition clear in response to a question from Senator Tom Coburn. "I don't think," he told the senator and other members of the Senate Judiciary Committee, "that we should look to foreign law to interpret our Constitution."[4] Aware of his consistent reluctance to look for precedent in international law, Mark found Alito's sudden willingness to look abroad to bolster his objections to same-sex marriage more than a little ironic. Why is it, Justice Alito asked, that "until the end of the 20th century, there was never a nation or a culture that recognized marriage between two people of the same sex?" Later, he returned to the same line of argument. "There have been cultures that did not frown on homosexuality . . . Ancient Greece is an example . . . but did they have same-sex marriage in ancient Greece?" Justice Antonin Scalia joined his conservative colleague in his new-found respect for traditions from abroad. "Do you know of any society," he asked, "prior to the Netherlands in 2001, that permitted same-sex marriage?"[5]

Justice Breyer was the first to raise both the caution argument and the related argument that the democratic process ought to be allowed to run its course. That marriage should be reserved for heterosexual couples, he asserted, "has been the law everywhere for thousands of years . . . and

suddenly you want nine people outside the ballot box to require States that
don't want to do it to change . . . Why cannot those States at least wait and
see whether in fact doing so in the other States is or is not harmful?" What
seemed Justice Breyer's unexpected advocacy of the "wait and see" argument was seconded—again, surprisingly—by Justice Kennedy. "Part of the
wait," he suggested, "is to ascertain whether the social science, the new studies are accurate . . . if we're not going to wait, then it's only fair for us to say,
well, we're not going to consult social science."

That Chief Justice Roberts agreed on the value of moving more slowly
was less surprising—though his ultimate rationale for caution made many
wonder. "One of the things that's truly extraordinary about this whole
issue," he said to Mary Bonauto, is how quickly same-sex marriage has been
accepted "across broad elements of society." Citing the example of Maine,
where voters changed their minds on same-sex marriage, rejecting it in 2009,
approving it in 2012, the Chief Justice warned that too quick a victory would
in the end hurt the cause of same-sex marriage. "There will be no more
debate," he argued, and "closing of debate can close minds . . . it will have a
consequence on how this new institution is accepted."[6]

Listening to the opening minutes of oral arguments was gut-wrenching for
Mark and Vic. Hard questions from conservative justices were to be expected.
But for two men deep into planning a fall wedding, bundles of tension made
more tense by what had happened with Faith in Action, Justice Ginsburg's first
question was frightening. Justice Kennedy had followed that with yet another
surprising challenge, and now Justice Breyer's questions suggested he too
had serious doubts about marriage equality. "Good God," Mark thought in a
moment of panic. "We're going to lose! Perhaps we did move too quickly to
bring marriage equality to the Supreme Court." His mind raced, thinking about
what would happen if the decision went against them, about more years working to change minds. He thought about all he and Vic had done to prepare
for their wedding, the contracts they had signed, the thousands of dollars in
checks they had written, the emotional energy they had invested. The thought
of having to cancel everything pulled him down.

Reaching far into the bag of objections to same-sex marriage, Justice
Alito wondered if approving same-sex marriage would put the courts on the

slippery-slope to approval of group marriage or polygamy. And as Bonauto's time before the Court came to an end, Justice Scalia raised a surprisingly naïve version of the religious rights argument that seemed almost willfully to ignore long-established First Amendment rights. Same-sex marriage, he pointed out, will be "unpalatable to many of our citizens for religious reasons." Once it has been written into constitutional law, he asked, "is it conceivable that a minister who is authorized by the State to conduct a marriage can decline to marry two men if indeed this Court holds that they have a constitutional right to marry?"[7]

With the same quiet assurance that brought victory in Massachusetts in 2001, and with the Equal Protection Clause of the Fourteenth Amendment held close at hand, Bonauto turned back every question. Is same-sex marriage a new idea? Does the "traditional" concept of marriage preclude same-sex marriage? "The place of gay people in our civic society is something that has been contested for more than a century," Bonauto argued, citing issues with immigration law, public employment, and Federal service. More than forty years have elapsed, she pointed out, since same-sex marriage first reached the Supreme Court in *Baker v. Nelson*; the consideration of same-sex marriage in Hawaii more than twenty years earlier generated a great deal of public discussion as did the legalization of same-sex marriage in Massachusetts ten years earlier. "The American people have been debating and contesting this," she maintained; "it has been exhaustively aired." Asked why no nation or culture had recognized same-sex marriage before the twentieth century, Bonauto responded with the Court's own words in *Lawrence*. "Times can blind," she maintained, repeating the phrase twice in less than a minute. "It takes time to see stereotypes and to see the common humanity of people who had once been ignored or excluded." Before she could elaborate, Justice Ginsburg made it clear that the day of "skim milk marriages"—a phrase she had used during oral arguments in California's Prop 8 case—was coming to an end. She launched her own withering attack on the notion that "traditional marriage" had existed unchanged for millennia. "A millennium ago," she argued, marriage involved "a dominant and a subordinate relationship." When a man and a woman married, the woman's person was legally subsumed by the man's; he made all the important decisions. In recent years, Justice Ginsburg pointed out, marriage has changed to become more "egalitarian."[8]

Should the Court exercise caution in the face of societal change some find disturbing? Should it "wait and see," allowing time for people to change their minds and for the democratic process to work itself out as it did in Maine? Warned that cutting off debate on same-sex marriage would "close minds" and delay acceptance, Bonauto calmly pointed to "serious structural problems" in the Chief Justice's argument. Unlike voters in the states still contesting marriage equality, voters in Maine did not have to overcome "a constitutional amendment that really largely shuts down the process." What "really shuts down the debate," she argued, are constitutional amendments and state legislatures reluctant to accept social change. But the real problem with "wait and see," Bonauto pointed out, lies in continuing the harms done to couples denied the fundamental right to marry. "The effect of waiting is not neutral," she warned in turn; "it . . . consign[s] same-sex couples to this outlier status." Summoning the weight of precedent, she reminded the Court that "Wait and see by itself has never been considered a legitimate justification, a freestanding justification under the Fourteenth Amendment."[9]

Bonauto dismissed without so much as breaking stride Justice Alito's supposed fear that legalizing same-sex marriage would throw open the door to polygamy and group marriage. Returning to the definition of marriage with which she began, she asserted that "marriage . . . is [based] on the mutual support and consent of two people." In multi-party relationships, she argued, there would inevitably be "concerns about coercion and consent and disrupting family relationships" which the states would have difficulty answering. Justice Scalia's supposed fear—that making same-sex marriage a constitutional rather than a statutory right would infringe on religious rights by forcing unwilling ministers and rabbis to perform marriages that ran counter to their beliefs—evoked a storm of protest from the liberal justices who refused to let Bonauto's reminder of rights guaranteed by the First Amendment—"the Constitution will continue to apply"—stand alone. Justice Sotomayor coached Bonauto into pointing out that even in states with laws that barred discrimination against gays and lesbians no one had been forced to perform marriages against his or her will. Justice Kagan quietly undercut Justice Scalia by suggesting that she must have misunderstood the question, the answer being so obvious. "There are many rabbis that will not conduct marriages between Jews and non-Jews, notwithstanding that we have a constitutional prohibition against religious discrimination," she noted. Though Justice Scalia had been answered—and answered again—Justice Breyer felt compelled to add his bit. "It's called Congress shall make no law respecting the freedom of religion," he muttered.

No fireworks, no grand rhetorical gestures, just quiet competence. As her thirty minutes before the Court wound down, Mary Bonauto added a final word, reassurance that in deciding in favor of same-sex marriage the Court need not seem adversarial. "It's not about the Court versus the States," she suggested. "It's about the individual making the choice to marry and with whom to marry." And with that her work was done.

Given the unsettling nature of the initial questions she faced, not to mention questions about ancient culture more fit for a classicist than a lawyer, Mark and Vic felt that Mary Bonauto had done all she could. As the end of her arguments, they knew—mostly—where they stood with each of the nine justices. Any hope that Chief Justice Roberts would support marriage equality had slipped away. Justices Alito and Scalia were clearly opposed and Justice Thomas, though he had remained characteristically silent, would no doubt join them. Justices Ginsburg, Kagan, and Sotomayor were safely on board. Mark had begun to relax—his and Vic's hands had been joined since the proceedings began and Vic could feel the pressure lessen—but he was still looking for a clear sign from Justice Kennedy[10] Until that came, he'd teeter on the edge of his seat.

* * *

"Thank you, counsel," Chief Justice Roberts said respectfully as Mary Bonauto, saving a few minutes for rebuttal, wrapped up the case for marriage equality she had begun in 2003 when she argued and won *Goodridge et al. v. Department of Public Health* before the Supreme Judicial Court of Massachusetts. As she moved away from the lectern to make way for Donald Verrilli, the Solicitor General of the United States to whom the Court had granted fifteen minutes to speak on question one, the unthinkable happened. A lone protestor rose from his seat.

"The bible teaches," he screamed, "that if you support gay marriage you will burn in hell! It's an abomination." Startled eyes turned from every corner of the room toward the noise, searching to discover what sort of madman had dared to raise his voice in the country's highest court. Already quiet spectators grew more quiet still as his voice boomed across the room. "The nation will," he yelled, "earn God's wrath." Sitting just a few rows behind the trouble-maker, Mark and Vic reacted viscerally to the man's angry rant. They could hear someone or something being thrown around, they craned their necks to see, but they knew they couldn't stand up to look more closely without being ejected themselves. Security guards dragged the man from the courtroom in a matter of seconds, but he was determined not to go quickly—or quietly. A big man, he fought every step of the way, arms windmilling to keep the officers at a distance, legs braced against the floor to keep from being pushed out the door. Eighteen seconds passed before the doors closed behind him.

Lane Hudson, an LGBT activist in line for a short-term seat in the court-room, was caught off guard. "The doors burst open . . . There was a guy yelling and security guys dragging him out, and he was resisting and flailing and refusing to go. They had to drag him out and subdue him right outside the doors and cuff him."[11]

Charles Massey, co-founder of the Personal Stories Project, was close enough to hear the "crunch" as the guards forced the protestor to the marble floor, to hear the "zip" as the plastic ties closed around his wrists. "It was chaos. I could hear, could almost feel his screams," Massey said; "they echoed through the building for what seemed like twenty minutes." They are, he remembered almost a year after the moment, "still etched in my memory." The man's face was a twisted mask; his eyes blazed in a way that would in another era have suggested demonic possession. "I have never before been so close to such a clearly demented display of raw hatred," Massey recalled with a sigh of relief that the moment had become a memory, "to such bigotry and intolerance, not just to my people, but to any people. I hope never to witness anything of the sort again."[12]

Later, most would learn the identity of the man whose disrespect for the Court had knocked them on their heels—Rives Miller Grogan. They would learn as well that Grogan graduated from a bible college in Mansfield,

Texas, a city fewer than fifty miles from Mark and Vic's home in Plano—and yet another sign of the animus they faced in north Texas. Now the pastor of the New Beginnings Christian Church in Los Angeles, Grogan had in the past few years amassed a long record of arrests for disruptive behavior. By October 10, 2012—when he was arrested for running onto the field with an anti-abortion/vote Romney poster, delaying for three minutes the start of the third game in the Cincinnati-San Francisco divisional playoff series—he had already accumulated two convictions for disrupting oral arguments at the Supreme Court and another for shouting from the Senate gallery. Deadspin, Gawker Media's "sports with a twist of humor" website, dismissed Grogan as "the idiot on the field," but most inside the Court found little to laugh at and nothing they were willing to dismiss. As Lane Hudson told *The Advocate*, "I'm not above heckling or protesting, but the Supreme Court is the one place you don't do it."[13]

After the ballpark episode, barely a month passed before Grogan was arrested again, this time in Lima, Ohio, for heckling President Obama at a campaign rally. A compulsive repeat offender, on January 20, 2013, the day of President Obama's second inauguration, Grogan was arrested yet again, this time for climbing a tree and shouting anti-abortion slogans from his perch—and for climbing higher still when police arrived with ladders. Facing yet another charge for disorderly conduct, he was banned from the District of Columbia until his hearing at the end of February. Somehow, in spite of his long record, Grogan managed to make his way one more time into the Court to stage one more spectacle. This time he'd be charged with—and convicted of— using "loud, threatening or abusive language in the Supreme Court Building" and for "demonstrating with the intent of interfering with the administration of justice."[14]

Uncomfortably close to the scuffle, like those sitting around them, Mark and Vic were unsettled when Grogan began to scream, surprised when ten minutes later his screams from outside the courtroom were still loud enough to compete with Donald Verrilli's arguments, the volume rising and falling as the door opened and closed. "One thought that went through my head," Mark commented, "was that the guy actually made our case for us. People like him are the reason why marriage equality went to the Supreme Court."

Earlier, Justice Alito had suggested that anti-gay-marriage sentiment did not grow from *animus*. Ancient Greece, he argued, was gay-friendly, but didn't recognize gay marriages. Why must we conclude, Justice Alito asked, that people disapprove of gays when in fact they disapprove only of gay marriage? For Mark and Vic, Grogan's outburst countered that reading. "What poured from his mouth," Mark concluded, "was a perfect demonstration of the kind of *animus* gays and lesbians face every day."[15]

But in the end Mark and Vic were more startled by Justice Scalia's questionable joke than Grogan's invective. "It was rather refreshing, actually," Justice Scalia quipped, breaking the silence that hung over the room and spurring a ripple of soft laughter that spread across the rows of spectators.

Though long wary of Justice Scalia's antagonistic attitude toward same-sex marriage, aware that he is sometimes dubbed "the Catholic Justice," at other times "the Fox News Justice," Mark and Vic joined for a shocked moment in the general laughter, a release from the nervous tension generated both by the hearing itself and Rives Grogan's disruption. Until they began to think about the implications of what the Justice had said, the barely coded message his few words had sent to the plaintiffs. "Would he have said such a thing," Mark wondered, "if the man had started screaming 'Catholics are an abomination?'" Rives Grogan's imprecations were not just an insult to the Court; they were an insult to, even a verbal attack on the gays and lesbians who had come to the Supreme Court in search of justice. Grogan was clearly a fanatic with a long history of anti-social behavior. Dismissing his rants was easy. Antonin Scalia, an Associate Justice of the Supreme Court of the United States, was less easy to dismiss. As Jeffrey Toobin suggested in the *New York Times*, Justice "Scalia probably did agree that the directness of the protestor was bracing—'refreshing' . . . there's every reason to believe that Scalia more or less shared the protestor's view of the immorality of homosexuality, and that he regards the Court's toleration of gay people as one of the great disasters of his nearly three decades as a Justice."[16]

"I found it telling of Justice Scalia's view," Mark said after the arguments, "that he found the incident more funny than appalling."

***

When Chief Justice Roberts first offered Donald Verrilli a moment to compose himself, the Solicitor General accepted, then immediately changed his mind. "If the Court is ready," he offered in turn, and accompanied by the protestor's shouts, muffled now, but still audible, began his argument. Like Mary Bonauto's opening gambit, Verrilli's was a set piece composed to appeal to Justice Kennedy. "The opportunity to marry is integral to human dignity," Verrilli argued. "Excluding gay and lesbian couples from marriage demeans the dignity of these couples. It demeans their children, and it denies both the couples and their children the stabilizing structure that marriage affords." Before giving way to the first interruption, the Solicitor General returned four more times to key phrases that echoed Justice Kennedy's decision in *Windsor*—twice to "demeaning," twice to "equal dignity." Clearly, concisely, Verrilli laid out three reasons why the Court should reject the states' desire to "wait and see" and approve marriage equality now. Delay would in effect constitute an admission that the second-class citizenship afforded same-sex couples in non-marriage states "is consistent with the equal protection of the laws." It would create an embarrassingly awkward parallel to "the nation as a house divided that we had with *de jure* racial segregation." Finally, it would saddle same-sex couples "with enormous costs that this Court thought were costs of constitutional stature in *Windsor*."[17]

Justice Kennedy's earlier reference to the "millennia" during which marriage had been restricted to opposite-sex couples had so frightened advocates of marriage equality that many missed his almost immediate qualification, a first indication of the weight *Lawrence v. Texas* carried in his mind. "On a larger scale," he had suggested to Mary Bonauto, "it's been about the same time between *Brown* and *Loving* as between *Lawrence* and this case"—a signal that perhaps the time had come to extend marriage equality to the remaining states. When Justice Kennedy first broke into Verrilli's argument, he used the landmark 2003 case to open a door through which the Solicitor General could walk to victory. "Haven't we learned a tremendous amount," he asked, "since *Lawrence*, just in the last ten years?"[18] In that simple question Mark found the sign he had been hoping for from Justice Kennedy. Marriage equality would win. Once again, Vic felt a slight pressure as Mark's hand tightened on his—but this time he realized, the squeeze he felt was a quiet signal of celebration.

Quick to seize the offered grace, Verrilli saluted *Lawrence* as "an important catalyst that has brought us to where we are today." Since 2003, he argued, gay and lesbian couples have been able to live openly, start and raise families, join in public life without fear—and as that happened society discovered "that gay and lesbian people and gay and lesbian couples are full and equal members of the community." Recognizing what was afoot, the Chief Justice tried to shut the door; *Lawrence* required only that the states not intrude on personal relationships, he argued; *Obergefell* would require that the state "sanction" those relationships. Verrilli refused to be deterred, charged ahead to connect the Court's 2003 ruling with the equal protection case at hand. The full weight of *Lawrence*, he argued, is that it "put gay and lesbian couples, gay and lesbian people, in a position for the first time in our history to be able to lay claim to the abiding promise of the Fourteenth Amendment . . . this is about equal participation, participation on equal terms in a State-conferred status."[19]

Asked by Justice Alito to lay out "the essential elements of marriage," Verrilli echoed the definition Mary Bonauto had put forth earlier. Marriage, he suggested, involves "the obligations of mutual support and responsibility and the benefits surrounding marriage that State law provides to ensure that there is an enduring bond." But where Bonauto had spoken generally of "family life," the Solicitor General was more specific. "Certainly," he added, quietly steering the Court toward the road that would allow him to turn the states' "wait and see" argument on its head, "childrearing is bound up in all that." The states, he began, "want to exercise an attitude of caution [about same-sex marriage] because of concern about the welfare of children raised in same-sex households." Three times Verrilli noted the staggering number of children involved: "hundreds of thousands." He cited briefs from "all of the leading organizations" as proof that they are doing well, easily deflecting Justice Scalia's reference to arguments from fringe groups that had submitted *amicus* briefs. The prep work done, the Solicitor General lowered the boom, a simple statement with a question tucked inside: "What Respondents' position and Respondents' caution argument leads you to," he observed, "is the conclusion that those hundreds of thousands of children don't get the stabilizing structure and the many benefits of marriage." For Mark and Vic, for the clear majority of those who had come in hope, the logic of the government's position was unassailable, the answer to the implied question undeniable.

But what they remembered best when Donald Verrilli's too-brief appearance before the Court ended was the logic and the humanity of his closing. "In a world in which gay and lesbian couples live openly as our neighbors, raise their children side by side with the rest of us, contribute fully as members of the community," he declared, "it is simply untenable to suggest that they can be denied the right of equal participation in an institution of marriage, or that they can be required to wait until the majority decides that it is ready to treat gay and lesbian people as equals." For Mark and Vic the moment was momentous. Less than twenty-four hours earlier Valerie Jarrett had stood before them and two-hundred other plaintiffs in same-sex marriage cases brought together by Freedom to Marry, assuring them that they had the full support of the Obama administration; now, just a few feet from their seats, the president's top lawyer stood before them arguing eloquently for their rights before the nation's highest court, arguing that their claim to "the promise of the Fourteenth Amendment" should be honored "now." In the moment, neither could have uttered a word. They had begun to believe, really to believe that the dignity for which they had waited so long was at last within reach.

* * *

As John Bursch moved to the podium, arguing for the ninth time before the Supreme Court and hoping to regain the initiative for the states, Mark and Vic thought again, and with no little satisfaction, of the disadvantages he faced given shopworn arguments that had failed so often in lower courts, of the larger difficulties the states had faced in finding top-flight attorneys willing to argue the increasingly unpopular case against marriage equality. Appointed Solicitor General of Michigan in February 2011, Bursch had returned to private practice with Warner, Norcross & Judd at the end of 2013. As the Chief Justice signaled that the Court was ready to hear his arguments, Mark and Vic couldn't but wonder. They knew Bursch's firm had declined to stand behind him and wondered to what extent the distance they had created might bother him.

"This case isn't about how to define marriage," he began, echoing the language of Judge Sutton's majority opinion in *DeBoer v. Snyder*. "It's about who gets to decide that question." Pitting the people and the democratic process against the alleged tyranny of the federal courts, Bursch implored the Court "to affirm every individual's fundamental liberty interest in deciding the meaning of marriage." Within seconds the Court's liberals made it clear they were eager to talk about fundamental liberties—though they clearly differed on whose liberties should be affirmed. Justice Sotomayor allowed Bursch only four sentences before contradicting him. "We're not taking anybody's liberty away," she protested. Rejecting beforehand arguments based on tradition and religious rights, Justice Breyer reminded the states' attorney that the Court had long since declared marriage a fundamental right. "As the States administer it," he began, directing attention to the legal burden Bursch would have to bear, marriage "is open to vast numbers of people." Only one group of people has been excluded, he continued; "They have no possibility to participate in that fundamental liberty. That is people of the same sex who wish to marry. And so," Justice Breyer concluded, "We ask, why?" Knowing from the briefs how Bursch would respond—with a refer-ence to the states' alleged interest in regulating procreation that "same-sex marriage doesn't advance"—Justice Kagan joined the fray to express her own skepticism. "Are you saying," she asked, "that recognizing same-sex marriage will impinge upon that State interest?"[20]

"The marriage view on the other side here," Bursch began, "is that marriage is all about love and commitment . . . but the State doesn't have any interest in that." For a moment, Mark and Vic thought themselves back in New Orleans listening to Texas's arguments in *DeLeon v. Perry*. As Mary Bonauto would suggest in her closing remarks, "One casualty of the marriage litigation [has been] an impoverished view of what marriage is."[21] Where attorneys arguing in favor of marriage equality took their cues from Justice Kennedy, those arguing against looked to conservatives on the Court for guidance. Bursch's argument was hatched from two passages in Justice Alito's dissent in *Windsor*. In the first, Justice Alito argues that "changes in family structure and in the popular understanding of marriage and the family can have profound effects"; they are "complex, involving the interaction

of numerous factors, and [tend] to occur over an extended period of time."
In the second he distinguishes between the "traditional view" of marriage as
"an exclusively opposite-sex institution . . . inextricably linked to procreation and biological kinship" and a "newer view . . . the 'consent-based' vision
of marriage that primarily defines marriage as the solemnization of mutual
commitment—marked by strong emotional attachment and sexual attraction—
between two people" that had come to dominate "popular culture."[22]

Bringing together Justice Alito's two observations, Bursch laid out his
argument: Although marriage is a fundamental right, the state has a right
to exclude gays and lesbians from marriage because if same-sex marriage
becomes legal the definition of marriage will shift more and more from a
child-centric model based on biological kinship and the needs of children
to a consent-based model that turns away from children to focus on the
physical and emotional needs of adults. Over generations, children raised
in such marriages, dissatisfied with their lot, will be less inclined to marry.
As a result, more children will be born outside of marriage and the state
will bear the cost for many of those children. Absent proof that the causal
links in the argument are valid—that same-sex marriage is necessarily adult-
centered, that adult-centered marriage will lead to a decline in the marriage
rate, and that a declining marriage rate will send out-of-wedlock births spiraling
upward at the expense of the state—the argument is inherently flawed. Worse
yet, in oral argument Bursch could not clearly articulate his position and left
openings through which the liberal justices reached to shred the fabric he was
trying to sew together.

Asked repeatedly about the link between binding parents and children
together and the prohibition of same-sex marriage, Bursch seemed stuck in
an endless loop playing the same ineffectual one-note samba:

- It has to do with the societal understanding of what marriage means
  . . . when you change the definition of marriage to delink the idea that
  we're binding children with their biological mom and dad, that has
  consequences.
- The reason why there's harm if you change the definition [is] because, in
  people's minds, if marriage and creating children don't have anything to

do with each other, then what do you expect? You expect more children outside of marriage.

- We're talking about something that's going to change the meaning of the institution [of marriage] over generations . . . Think about two couples that are identically situated. They've been married for five years, and they each have a 3-year old child. One grows up believing that marriage is about keeping that couple bound to that child forever. The other couple believes that marriage is more about their emotional commitment to each other . . . A reasonable voter . . . could believe that there would be a different outcome if those two marriages were influenced by two different belief systems.

- . . . the two couples that I just described, one believing that marriage is all about staying with their kids, the other one believing it's all about emotion and commitment, could have different results.

- If you're changing the meaning of marriage from one where it's based on that biological bond to one where it's based on emotional commitment, then adults could think, rightly, that this relationship is more about adults and not about the kids . . . over decades, when laws change, when societal views on marriage change, there are consequences to that.

- If you change the societal meaning of what marriage is—and society has already started to move away from what we always understood marriage to be, that linkage between kids and their biological mom and dad. The more that link is separated, the more likely it is that when you've got an opposite-sex couple, that link will not be maintained, because it's more adult-centric, and it's less child-centric.

Bursch never succeeded in taking the Court sequentially through the stages of his argument; he asserted causal relationships but offered no proof of causation. For the nine justices looking down from their elevated bench there were incoherent echoes of Justice Alito's dissent in *Windsor*. For others in the courtroom there was only the mystery of a labyrinthine argument that wound this way and that only to come up, time after time, against the same wall.[23]

Justice Sotomayor interrupted after Bursch's initial attempt to explain the states' argument, bringing him up short with a crucial question. "How does withholding marriage from one group, same-sex couples," she asked, "increase the value [of marriage] to the other group?" Justice Kagan returned to the problem Justice Breyer had raised at the outset. "Before something as fundamental to a society and to individuals as marriage, before an exclusion of this kind can be made in that institution," she importuned, "the State needs some reason for that exclusion. What is the reason for the exclusion?" How can it be, Justice Breyer asked, that you acknowledge that marriage is a fundamental right, that you recognize that the Fourteenth Amendment prohibits depriving a person of liberty without due process of law, and yet you "take a group of people where so little distinguishes them from the people you give the liberty to . . . and don't let them participate in this basic institution?"[24]

Though the liberal justices hammered at Bursch from every side, pressing him to do more than to rephrase his last response, questions early in the argument were delivered in a reserved, even tone. But as Bursch failed time after time to explain how same-sex marriage would harm conventional marriages, Justice Kennedy's word choice betrayed his growing frustration. "How do we get from what I just said," he asked the former Solicitor General, "to some kind of rational or important distinction?" Recognizing that the alleged link between the legalization of same-sex marriage and potential harms done to heterosexual marriage was more a matter of intuition than of evidence, Justice Sotomayor changed her tone as well. "Why would that feeling, which doesn't make any logical sense, control our decision-making?" she asked. With the states' attorney floundering, unable to offer anything beyond formulas he had committed to memory, Justice Sotomayor issued another blunt challenge. "The problem is," she protested, "I don't actually accept your starting premise. The right to marriage is, I think, embedded in our constitutional law. It is a fundamental right." Impatience seeping more and more into her voice, she told Bursch, "The issue is you can't narrow it down to say, but is gay marriage fundamental . . . The issue was starting from the proposition of, is the right to marry fundamental? And then is it compelling for a State to exclude a group of people? . . . And that, for me," she concluded, "is as simple as it gets."[25]

Justice Kennedy continued the Court's corrosive attack on premises. Challenging the states' assertion that only opposite-sex couples could bond with their children, he told Bursch "That was very interesting, but it's just a wrong premise." Justice Kagan agreed. "This is what I think is difficult for some people with your argument," she said, further eroding the ground on which Bursch was struggling to find his footing; "it's hard to see how permitting same-sex marriage discourages people from being bonded with their biological children." Justice Breyer added his voice to the swelling chorus, exasperated that Bursch would not or could not answer "as simple as it gets." "What directly is your response," he demanded to know, "to the fact that if we assume a basic purpose of marriage is to encourage an emotion and rearing bond between parents and children, that allowing gay people to marry will weaken it?" Listening one more time to the states' often-repeated hypothetical—"If you de-link marriage from creating children"—Justice Breyer grew almost censorious. "What's the empirical part of what you just said . . . I just heard you say it, but I didn't follow it."[26]

The first time John Bursch tried to set aside any connection between the "dignity" of the LGBT community and marriage, Justice Kennedy took little notice, perhaps because the states' modest assertion was only that "the marriage institution did not develop to deny dignity or to give second class status to anyone." But when the State implied that same-sex couples in a "consent-based marriage" would inevitably focus on their own emotional needs, relegating their children to second-class status, Justice Kennedy struck back. The idea that "same-sex couples could not have the more noble purpose" was foreign to him. As he had done so often in the past, he spoke on behalf of the LGBT community. "Same-sex couples say, of course, we understand the nobility and the sacredness of marriage. We know we can't procreate, but we want the other attributes of [marriage] in order to show that we, too, have a dignity that can be fulfilled."[27]

When still later Bursch returned to the link between dignity and marriage—an attempt to turn the Court's attention from his failure to prove the causal relationships crucial to his argument—Justice Kennedy allayed any remaining doubt that he was firmly on the side of marriage equality. What advocates of marriage equality are asking the Court to do, Bursch maintained, "is to take an institution, which was never intended to be dignitary bestowing, and make it dignitary bestowing [*sic*]." "I don't understand this not dignity bestowing," Justice Kennedy retorted; "I thought that was the whole purpose of marriage . . . It's dignity bestowing and these parties say they want to have that same ennoblement." With the forty-five minutes allotted to the States drawing to an end, the Kennedy/Bursch exchange on "dignity" made it clear the endgame had arrived. Justice Kagan delivered the death-blow, a return to the essential question that had hung over the states' argument from its very beginning. "We just said," she reminded Bursch, "there's a right to marry, that is fundamental and that everybody is entitled to it unless there's some good reason for the State to exclude them." Referencing one more time the landmark case brought before the Supreme Court in 2003, *Lawrence v. Texas*, she summed up the problem with which Bursch had struggled unsuccessfully since Justice Breyer first raised the issue. "Once we understood that there was a right to engage in intimate activity, it was a right for everybody." What you are doing, she told Bursch, is "defining constitutional rights in terms of the kinds of people that can exercise them. And I don't think we've really ever done that."[28]

Having listened for an hour-and-a-half as though their lives depended on it—and in a very real sense, they did—Mark and Vic knew the Court wasn't going to do now what it had never done before. They knew they had won. The premise of the second question set by the Court—"Does the Fourteenth Amendment require a state to recognize a marriage between two people of the same sex when their marriage was lawfully licensed and performed out-of-state?"—supposed that they had lost on the first question. That they had not was confirmed by Justice Kennedy's relative silence when after a brief recess oral arguments resumed. Mark listened with one ear, but turned his attention to making notes for a speech he had been asked to make at the Freedom to Marry rally outside. Vic relaxed.

* * *

Because of Faith in Action Mark and Vic had entered the Supreme Court building separately, Vic first, Mark following. When they left, they walked together, hand and hand through the doors and into the sunlight, their hands still joined, their faces covered in smiles. Thrilled at the way oral arguments had gone, they paused to look out at the crowd that had taken over the plaza, realizing that they would never again be part of something like what was happening.

After watching the press conference outside the Court, Mark and Vic stood on the sidewalk, gathering their thoughts, talking with friends. Around them the frenetic activity that had begun almost at first light continued, part carnival, part protest rally, part religious revival. Steps away a dozen or so Orthodox Jews held a banner that read "LGBT Marriage, Rebellion Against God"; another banner threatened gays and lesbians with horrible punishments. One friend proposed confronting them. Mark discouraged him. He had already been through one tense confrontation since leaving the courtroom and had no taste for another.

He and Vic had barely stepped outside when a religious zealot broke into an interview with a reporter from China to confront Vic, pushing against him, angrily telling him he was a disgrace to the uniform he was wearing. Understanding that when in uniform he was a representative of the officer corps of the United States Air Force, Vic reacted with moderation. Mark, no uniform to moderate his behavior, justly proud of Vic's status as a veteran, shoved the man aside. But that one moment was enough. Back to his usual self, Mark turned away. He wanted to find Emmarie Huetteman, the *New York Times* reporter who talked with him after his morning brush with Faith in Action, offered him comfort when everything seemed to have gone wrong. He wanted to let her know everything had worked out and to thank her for a moment's much-needed kindness. Vic wanted to find and thank the Supreme Court policeman who escorted him outside when he tried to get Mark to use the one ticket left them after Faith in Action stole the other. In the end they found neither, but Karina Kling of Time-Warner Cable News found them. Asked "What happens now?" Mark used the opportunity to make one more appeal to the circuit court in New Orleans where *DeLeon v. Perry* had stalled. "The Fifth Circuit should not wait now," he said. Asked for his assessment of their day in court, Vic spoke from the perspective of a man who had served his country for twenty-three years. "Equality is something that we live for. Sometimes it's something we die for," he pointed out; "I think we're going to see equality come to pass."[29]

* * *

Though sure of victory, in the long two months before the decision Mark and Vic watched and listened compulsively as, day after day, pundits read the tea leaves. Up today, down tomorrow, but mostly up. Finally, on June 15 a few minutes before the Court convened at 10:00 a.m. to announce which decisions would be released that day, the national watch party began. Most of those watching closely knew that the Court often held the most important, the most controversial decisions until the end of the month—but no one wanted to risk missing "the moment" when the news broke. On Facebook Marc Solomon posted an early morning photo of the conference room at Freedom to Marry in New York. Behind Evan Wolfson at the head of the table a television glows against the darker walls, already turned on, ready to bring images of raucous celebration into the quiet room. On the back wall above the television, spreading along the wall on the right, are rows of framed newspaper articles memorializing good days in the fight for marriage equality. There is space on the wall, room for a few more pages, and everyone is hoping that papers carrying the news from today will fill one of those spaces. With the exception of Evan Wolfson, everyone at the long, narrow table—the digital whiz-kids he likes to call them—is focused intently on a computer screen, cursors set on the refresh button, ready to update the feed.[30]

For Jim Obergefell, increasingly anxious as the Supreme Court's scheduled "Decision Days" drew closer, checking on the internet from the home he had shared with John Arthur in Cincinnati was never an option. The favorable decision he expected would change millions of lives, would make history. But for Jim Obergefell, this was personal. The struggle to have his marriage with John recognized, to live in Ohio and to call the man he had loved for twenty years "husband," even posthumously, to have the most important relationship of his life recognized on John's death certificate, had become much of who he was. And so, on the morning of June 15 he stood at the head of the line waiting to enter the Supreme Court, hoping that on moving inside he would hear his name and be handed a copy of the Court's decision. He wanted to be there, listening to the voices with which the justices spoke, watching the expressions on their faces, when all was decided.

In Texas Mark and Vic were no less focused on "Decision Day." At the insistence of the public relations firm Akin Gump brought in to deal with the press, Mark had reluctantly prepared a statement to be released in the devastating event of a loss. We are "disappointed," he wrote, "saddened." "The fight for full equality, including marriage equality," he planned to assert, "will continue, and one day America will acknowledge what our founders declared in the Declaration of Independence, that 'all men are created equal.'"[31] Of course, neither Mark nor Vic believed for a minute they would have to continue anything. What they did believe, more and more with each passing day, was that they and millions of others in the LGBT community would soon be able to put anticipation behind them and get on with celebrating.

With Nicole and Cleo, their companions in *DeLeon v. Perry*, and the legal team from Akin Gump, they had agreed to appear at a press conference at the LBJ Library in Austin just hours after the Supreme Court announced its decision. And so, on June 15, the first possible day for the Supreme Court to rule, they rose before dawn, fed the beagles, and left the house at 6:30. At Love Field they boarded the only flight that would get them to Austin in time for the press conference—a flight scheduled for take off before news from the Supreme Court would be available—only to discover on arriving that this would not be "the day."

Disappointed, they caught the first flight back and immediately booked tickets to Austin for the remaining "Decision Days"—the eighteenth, twenty-second, twenty-fifth, and twenty-sixth of June—happy now to discover that the airline's schedule would allow them time in the terminal to discover on SCOTUSblog what decisions had been handed down before boarding another plane. On the eighteenth and the twenty-second their routine was much the same: rise early, feed the dogs, drive to the airport, endure the rigors of checking in, settle restlessly into a seat at Bruegger's Bagels to await news of a decision. But after a week of walking on broken glass he hoped wouldn't morph into broken dreams, Mark's patience was wearing thin. "Wide awake since about 3 am this morning in anticipation of SCOTUS possible ruling today," he told Facebook friends a little before 5:00 a.m. on the morning of the twenty-second.[32] That morning he dragged Vic out of the house so early that they sat for an hour in the car at Love Field before going into the terminal. And still, no decision. Later that day Mark posted again on Facebook: "SCOTUS is torturing us!"

On June 24 the story of Jim Obergefell's impatience led *The Washington Blade's* article on waiting—"Plaintiff couples on pins and needles awaiting ruling"—but Mark and Vic, along with Maurice Blanchard and Dominique James, and friends Jayne Rowse and April DeBoer, Joce Pritchett and Carla Webb, were featured as well—and their input changed the tone. Collectively, they admitted to anxiety, tension, emotional exhaustion—but what came through most clearly was that they expected to win and were excited to see that happen. Mostly, they talked of things positive—plans for news conferences, for celebrations with family and friends and, most of all, of wedding plans. Mark and Vic were no exception, mentioning that they had no plans to rush to a courthouse at the first opportunity because they were looking forward to "a more traditional wedding" that would take months of preparation. But, Mark added, fearful that even a ruling from the Supreme Court would not be enough to move extreme elements back home, "We're getting a license in case Texas tries to muck things up—like call a special session of the legislature."[33]

The next day *USA Today* ran a front page, human interest story on the varying ways five same-sex couples were looking ahead to marriage. Once again, Mark and Vic were featured. The front-page story began just below the fold with a photo of Mark and Vic that drew readers both to text and to an easily readable graphic indicating that national support for same-sex marriage had risen to 60 percent. Eyes that followed the story to the back page of the front section were drawn there to an oversized photo of Mark and Vic, part of Braden Summers's "All Love Is Equal" series. Intended to challenge the concept of iconic love in a setting that shouted "Texas," the photo showed Mark and Vic sipping coffee on a chilly morning at a ranch just outside Big Bend State Park, the horses they had been riding tethered a few feet away. Encouraged by the way their case had gone before the Fifth Circuit, the article noted, they had begun planning for their wedding in earnest, but had been taken aback when they sat in the Supreme Court and listened as Justice Kennedy "noted that marriage has been an opposite-sex union for 'millennia.'" Forgetting for a moment the uncertainty, the stress of waiting, Mark joked about seeing "dollars flying out the window!"[34]

Friends rushed to buy copies. One, Dana Lopez, commented on Facebook that Mark and Vic had become "the poster boys for gay marriage."[35] From far-away Europe, a former fraternity brother, Tim Warning, sent a congratulatory e-mail in the same vein.

> Having breakfast at my hotel in Hamburg, Germany looking at a picture of you and Vic on the front page of the *USA Today International Edition.* There is an even bigger picture of the two of you in the full-page spread on page 6. Just thought you would like to know you are the face of SSM in the US and globally on the day SCOTUS will hand down their decision. All the best to you and Vic on this big day.[36]

Seeing the articles, reading their friends' comments, Mark and Vic smiled—and the knots in their stomachs relaxed just a bit.

On Thursday, June 25 Mark and Vic headed again to Dallas-Love Airport, joking about Mark's friend's remark and their newfound notoriety, hoping as before that their day had come. They knew, however, that this day would be different, with or without a decision. Having learned of their morning ritual—rise before dawn, feed the dogs, drive to the airport, log on to SCOTUSblog and wait to see what decisions had come down that day—the local CBS affiliate had asked permission to add another element. Understanding that as two of the Texas plaintiffs Mark and Vic had assumed high-profile roles they never sought, knowing that Texans gay and straight would be interested in what happened, CBS wanted to be on hand to record their first reactions when the Supreme Court finally ruled. For today's vigil newsmen and plaintiffs would meet at Bruegger's Bagels airport location where, under the watchful eye of television cameras and the bemused eyes of a few patrons, Mark and Vic would log on to SCOTUSblog, refreshing their screens until the answer came, talking all the while with Jack Flink, an Emmy-winning reporter for KTVT-TV.

By the twenty-fifth three possible "Decision Days" had passed. Every day without a decision stretched already strained nerves closer to the breaking point; every day without a decision also raised the level of public interest to new heights. On Monday the twenty-second SCOTUSblog recorded

47,000 pageviews; three days later the number of page views had risen to almost 1.2 million.[37] But on June 25 the nine justices who held the fate of millions in their hands were unmoved by all the attention. Once again, Mark and Vic returned to their home wondering.

When they woke again, ready to run through their now familiar ritual one more time, Mark and Vic found on Facebook a reminder from Freedom to Marry; June 26 was "the anniversary of two momentous Supreme Court Decisions . . . 2003: *Lawrence v. Texas*, affirming the freedom of intimate conduct, and 2013: *Windsor v. United States,* striking down [the] core of [the] so-called Defense of Marriage Act." In bold letters, the meme proclaimed "It's Time: America is ready for another historic decision on the freedom to marry nationwide."[38] Not that either man needed reminding. Knowing that only one non-argument day remained on the Court's calendar, Mark posted his own reminder on Facebook. "50/50 chance today's the day." He and Vic were ready. Back at Bruegger's, they settled in, holding hands to steady themselves, watching SCOTUSblog one more time as the crew from KTVT turned the lights and camera on their table. One of them compulsively refreshed the screen every few seconds. Frustrated, Mark posted a lament on Facebook: "OMG this is torture." Minutes later he posted again, "I am getting nervous and excited and emotional."[39] From time to time he dabbed at his eyes, embarrassed that the camera would catch the tears that threatened to slide down his face.

Is it possible, Mark and Vic wondered, to measure how long they had waited? When did their wait for the right to marry begin? At the moment when they first knew they were gay? From the day of their first date in 1997 when they started down the seemingly impossible road to marriage? In the fall of 2004 with Mary Bonauto's victory in *Goodridge v. Department of Public Safety* before the Supreme Judicial Court of Massachusetts? In the fall of 2013 when they joined with Cleo DeLeon and Nicole Dimetman and filed suit against Texas? On the January day in 2015 when the Supreme Court granted cert in *Obergefell*, or on the April day when the justices sat for oral arguments? Whatever the measure, the wait had been long, and as the original Complaint in *DeLeon v. Perry* pointed out, with each day that passed the harms done by unjust laws seemed more galling.

Minutes after 9:00 a.m. Amy Howe's entries on SCOTUSblog made it clear that the endgame had arrived:

- Four boxes today, everyone. That could mean a lot of opinions, long ones, or both.
- Four boxes—FOUR!
- Here's Lyle with the first opinion.
- Marriage.
- Kennedy has the opinion.
- Holding: The Fourteenth Amendment requires a state to license a marriage between two people of the same sex.
- And to recognize a marriage between two people of the same sex when a marriage was lawfully performed out of state.
- It's 5-4.[40]

When Mark and Vic read "Kennedy has the opinion," they suspected they had won. Justice Kennedy had written the landmark opinions in *Romer*, *Lawrence*, and *Windsor*—and the conventional wisdom for months had been that if he wrote again the news would be good.

But for a few moments they didn't dare allow themselves to believe that the long wait was over. Mark feared that Amy Howe's "Holding" post signaled a win only on "recognition." Even Howe's next post—"And to recognize"— was not quite enough to reassure him. "We were on an emotional roller-coaster," he said; "it seemed like an eternity before we were sure."[41] Line after line they read what popped onto their screen, eleven interminable posts, until—at last—a link to the decision gave them access to Justice Kennedy's text. Only then did they recognize the enormity of their win.

In an instant, their eyes filled with tears. They rose to their feet, hugged, fumbled to put away Vic's laptop and gather their belongings, their fingers so thick with emotion they seemed beyond control. On just their second day at the airport KTVT got the footage for which they had hoped—a long-held shot of Mark and Vic leaving the bagel shop hand in hand, struggling in vain to hold back the tears welling in their eyes. Vic's mouth opens and his chest heaves as he takes a deep breath, trying to fill his lungs with air that had been sucked away. With his free hand Mark fumbles self-consciously with his glasses, gets them, somehow, into the breast pocket of his sport jacket. Vic presses Mark's other hand to his heart. Tickets in hand, they make their way toward and then by the camera, their faces set in a sober mask, afraid that if they look directly into the lens they will break down, until a friendly remark from Jack Flink, a reporter for KTVT-TV—"This is it, guys!"—brings a strained smile to their faces and they slip out of sight. Minutes later the video appeared on the CBS Dallas-Fort Worth website with an understated descriptor: "Mark Phariss & Vic Holmes overcome with emotion after SCOTUS rules same-sex couples have the right to marry. They're now headed to Austin to celebrate with other same-sex couples."

* * *

The routine of the TSA checkpoint, so often the source of petty annoyance, seemed on this morning a relief, a gift of time to compose themselves. Once on the other side, Mark returned to Facbeook to post the acknowledgment of victory he and Vic had prepared in advance:

Vic and I are overjoyed by today's Supreme Court decision. After almost 18 years together, we can soon exchange vows, place rings on each other's finger, look each other in the eye and say "I do"—all at a wedding surrounded by family and friends. We can't wait! In fact, in anticipation of today's decision we have scheduled a wedding for November and have booked a facility, a photographer, a videographer, a band, a florist and a cake baker.

On behalf of ourselves and all Texas' gay and lesbian citizens, we thank the Supreme Court for the best wedding gift one could ever receive, the ability to marry. Today's decision reaffirms the American principles of freedom, justice and equality for all. Let freedom ring![42]

Still too moved for speech, they downloaded the decision so they could read it *en route* to the press conference at the LBJ Library in Austin. Before boarding Mark found time for a final post. "Crying through the airport," he wrote over a photograph of himself and Vic standing in front of the Texas capitol taken months earlier when they still hoped for a win in the Fifth Circuit Court of Appeals. In the picture their faces are exultant smiles. Each has a hand raised in the famous "V for victory" gesture Mark learned as an undergrad at Westminster College in Fulton, Missouri, where Churchill delivered his "Iron Curtain" speech. Their other hands are also raised, joined to frame between them the dome of the capitol building—as the suit they filed with Nicole and Cleo had come to frame the argument for marriage equality in Texas.

For the first hour-and-a-half of marriage equality their world would be two narrow seats on a plane sweeping them to Austin. What they wanted most was to be alone together with their thoughts, but the experience of the past two years told them to prepare for the press conference toward which they were heading. No sooner had they settled into their seats than Vic opened his computer. Alone together, with Justice Kennedy as a genial third, they read the decision that had changed their lives. And the dissents.

Mark and Vic knew that around the country tens of thousands in the LGBT community were reading the same words at the same time. Still, as they read, they couldn't shake the idea that Justice Kennedy somehow knew their lives, their experiences, their thoughts and emotions. He was speaking, or so it seemed, directly to them. Having struggled as boys and young men to create authentic selves, for the right to be who they were in a culture that too-often disapproved, having longed for personhood, for the right to have others accept them as full-fledged human beings, Mark and Vic found in the opening words of the decision a soothing ointment to spread on old wounds: "The Constitution promises liberty to all within its reach, a liberty that includes certain specific rights that allow persons, within a lawful realm, to define and express their identity." Ten pages later when Justice Kennedy brought that guiding principle to bear on the question of same-sex marriage—"these liberties extend to certain personal choices central to individual dignity and autonomy, including intimate choices that define personal identity and beliefs"—they recognized in the inclusion of "dignity" how fully he understood the world of pain society had inflicted in the years gays and lesbians were compelled to wear masks that concealed their real selves, to deny the full truth of who they were.

Reading further, Mark and Vic found that, thanks to an uncanny ability to see into, to slip into the lives of an oppressed minority, Justice Kennedy had been able to speak with surety of what they longed for in the life they envisioned together. Given the freedom to marry, he wrote, "two persons together can find other freedoms, such as expression, intimacy, and spirituality. This is true for all persons, whatever their sexual orientation." Prohibited from marrying, gays and lesbians "are consigned to an instability . . . opposite-sex couples would find intolerable . . . [banning same-sex marriage] has the effect of teaching that gays and lesbians are unequal in important respects. It demeans gays and lesbians for the State to lock them out of a central institution of the Nation's society."

Seventeen pages into the decision, they found the definitive legal statement they craved: "The right to marry is a fundamental right inherent in the liberty of the person, and under the Due Process and Equal Protection Clauses of the Fourteenth Amendment couples of the same-sex may not be deprived of that right and that liberty." But beyond the legal declaration, itself so meaningful, Justice Kennedy seemed to understand what they had suffered for half a lifetime. He wrote knowingly, feelingly of the pain they had felt growing up gay, forced into secret lives on the margins of society—and the Court promised at last the right to intimacy, authenticity, and dignity.

Sentence after sentence, paragraph after paragraph, Mark and Vic made their way through the decision, more pleased with every page. In the now famous final paragraph, they discovered Justice Kennedy's greatest gift. As children discovering they were "different" they had been terrified by society's reaction to that difference. As young men learning every day that what they felt was "wrong," that society would not tolerate their desire to be with another man, they had suffered an incurable loneliness. Now, writing for the Court, Justice Kennedy was promising "no more":

No union is more profound than marriage, for it embodies the highest ideals of love, fidelity, devotion, sacrifice, and family. In forming a marital union, two people become something greater than once they were. As some of the petitioners in these cases demonstrate, marriage embodies a love that may endure even past death. It would misunderstand these men and women to say they disrespect the idea of marriage. Their plea is that they do respect it, respect it so deeply that they seek to find its fulfillment for themselves. Their hope is not to be condemned to live in loneliness, excluded from one of civilization's oldest institutions. They ask for equal dignity in the eyes of the law. The Constitution grants them that right.[43]

By the time their plane touched down in Austin they were ready to meet the press. Ready to begin a whole new phase of their lives together.

Like their friends, Jack Evans and George Harris, already surrounded at the Dallas County Clerk's Office by hundreds of euphoric couples waiting to get marriage licenses, Mark and Vic "would have been blown away" by the wave of unadulterated joy gays and lesbians around the country rode in the minutes after the decision was announced, sweeping them to places they had only dreamed of going. As the men made their way to Austin, messages from family and friends, even from perfect strangers congratulating them, thanking them for the part they had played in the struggle for marriage equality, poured in to their e-mail and Facebook pages. Everyone was crying. Steve Rudner, Chairman of the Board of Equality Texas, the father of a gay son and a friend who knew their story well, reached out with an understated message he knew they would understand: "Thank you, Mark and Vic, for everything. For all of us." Others were more effusive.

So happy for you both! Thank you for all you have done to advance equality for us all. Your work and your sacrifices have been instrumental. (Richard Farias)

I am so incredibly happy for you! I have watched and followed your journey and have ABSOLUTELY no idea how you feel, but know that you have fought hard for this and have shown us all that the system can work! Congratulations to both of you and I can't wait to see the wedding photos. (Tish Willis)

Tracy Hollister, instrumental in prying Mark's purloined ticket to the *Obergefell* hearing from the hands of Faith in Action, reached out to celebrate the courage they had shown and the authentic selves they had forged in their two-year battle for marriage equality. "Yes!!" she wrote, "Thanks for all you have done and all you are!!"[44] In a sign of how completely the world had turned, Jamie Haskins, an openly gay woman who had married Sarah Klaasen in 2012 and served now as chaplain of Westminster College where Mark once feared that he would be forced to leave were anyone to discover he was gay, posted a picture of herself holding a cake emblazoned with the hashtag of the day—"#Love Wins." "In the Klaskins' house," she added, "we celebrate good news with ice cream cake. We didn't waste any time today."[45]

In the District of Columbia advocates of same-sex marriage who had returned to the Supreme Court for the decision—Mary Bonauto and Douglas Hallward Driemeier, who had argued the two questions set by the court; Susan Sommer of the Lambda Legal Defense and Education Fund, Paul M. Smith and Pamela S. Karlan of Stanford Law School; a sampling of plaintiffs from Ohio, Jim Obergefell, Georgia Nicole, and Pamela Yorksmith, and two from Kentucky, Gregory Bourke and Michael DeLeon, side by side with their teenage children—sat wiping tears from their cheeks as Justice Kennedy summarized his argument, hanging on every word as he read key passages that would be lodged forever in their memories. Though anxious to join the ecstatic crowd that had assembled outside—so many people that some had been forced from the sidewalk onto the plaza where, as Mark Walsh wrote, "demonstrations of any kind are officially forbidden" but this one was somehow "allowed to run its course"—decorum demanded that they listen, however impatiently, to Chief Justice Roberts's summary of his dissent and, finally, to Justice Scalia's decision in an unrelated case before joining the celebration.[46]

Trapped in their seats, they missed what one comic labeled "the running of the interns," young people bursting at breakneck speed from the Supreme Court building, copies of the decision fluttering in their hands. They missed the first televised reports, Peter Williams of NBC proclaiming "total victory for the advocates of same-sex marriage" and Jan Crawford of CBS describing "a passionate opinion from Justice Kennedy." "You cannot imagine," she told viewers, "the roar of this crowd when it became evident that the first decision the Court was going to announce today was the landmark ruling that this crowd has been waiting for, that the nation has been waiting for."[47] They missed the moving moment in which the Gay Men's Chorus of Washington, D. C.

gathered to sing the national anthem—perhaps the only thing that could have quieted the euphoric crowd, even momentarily—their hands over their hearts, the crowd roaring its approval as they finished.

Back in Texas, Dennise Garcia, presiding judge of the 303ʳᵈ District Court in Dallas, changed her plans for the day when news of the decision reached her. "I'm headed to court right now to perform ceremonies," she tweeted at 10:17 a.m. "Since I'm on vacation, no docket, I'll be there as long as needed." Jack Evans, eighty-five, and George Harris, eighty-two, together for fifty-four years, were the first couple to stand before her—and the first of 170 same-sex couples to marry in Dallas County that day. Like Mark and Vic, whom they had befriended when they learned of *DeLeon v. Perry*, they had met at a house party thrown by a friend—and like Mark and Vic they had steadfastly refused to marry outside of Texas. Like Mark and Vic, they had suffered as young men from the shame heaped on them by the straight world, had suffered and been harmed by discrimination. As a young man managing the men's shop at Neiman Marcus, Jack saw sales rise but was forced to resign when his bosses discovered he was gay. "They were afraid I would be blackmailed into stealing from them," Jack remembers. George had been in the army, served briefly with the CIA, but was sent to Leavenworth and routed out of the service when his superiors discovered his sexual orientation. "It undermined me tremendously," he remembered, adding that it took him thirty-two years to admit even to himself that he was gay.[48]

Like Mark and Vic, Jack and George got into the struggle for gay rights early in life—though they did so in the early sixties when police in Dallas regularly went out of their way to harass gays and lesbians, even to the extent of setting up sting operations. A power lunch across the street from the real estate office they ran together for thirty-eight years led to the founding of the North Texas GLBT Chamber of Commerce in 2005. As *DeLeon V. Perry* and *Obergefell* worked their ways through the courts, Jack and George worked with the University of North Texas to launch The Dallas Way, an archive intended to preserve and document the history of the local LGBT community. "These young kids don't know we've got a history here," George suggests, to which Jack adds, "They don't know you haven't always been able to walk down the street holding hands."[49]

Church was an important part of life for the Phariss family, pictured here on Easter Sunday in 1962. (Back, L to R) Greg Phariss, Yona Kathryn (Willis) Phariss, Joe Kendall ("Kent") Phariss, and Joe Elmer Phariss; (Front, L to R) Mark Phariss and Marsha Phariss. *(Courtesy of Mark Phariss)*

Pictured here with his mother and father after the awards ceremony at St. Paul's Methodist Church in Lawton, Oklahoma, Mark earned the Boy Scout's God and Country Award at fourteen. *(Courtesy of Mark Phariss)*

Mark's mother smiles proudly in May 1985 as she holds his diploma from Vanderbilt University Law School. *(© 1985 Joan A. Lawson)*

Vic (left), nine years old, stands with his sister and brother, Tanya and Nicky Joe Rednour, in the dusty yard of their home in Apache Junction, Arizona, in August 1979. *(Courtesy of Vic Holmes)*

Lt. Col. Katrina Glavan-Heise (USAF) awards a Commendation Medal to Captain Vic Holmes at Sheppard Air Force Base, Wichita Falls, Texas, in October 2009. Vic earned the award for (among other things) organizing a Holocaust Remembrance Service, being the squadron Fitness Leader, and earning the title of Master Instructor. (*Courtesy of Vic Holmes*)

Vic Holmes (left) and Mark Phariss (right) pictured with former Texas Governor Ann Richards at the 10th Annual San Antonio Black Tie Dinner on October 24, 1998. Working through a friend, Lukin Gilliland Jr., Mark had recruited Governor Richards as the keynote speaker. (*Courtesy of Mark Phariss and Vic Holmes*)

Traveling for vacations, Vic (left) and Mark favored far-away destinations like Uluru Rock in Kata Tjutu National Park (Australia) where no one was likely to report the "credible evidence of homosexuality" that could have ended Vic's career. *(Courtesy of Mark Phariss and Vic Holmes)*

In December 2012 Vic (left) and Mark traveled to Antarctica. Unable to resist a challenge, they took the famed Polar Bear Plunge on Christmas Day into waters six degrees below freezing—good training, for plaintiffs in a marriage equality case. *(Courtesy of Mark Phariss and Vic Holmes)*

Betsy, one of their three beagles, slips away as Mark and Vic relax in the yard of their weekend house. The photo was taken for a *USA Today* feature on the way a small Texas town had come to accept the presence of two gay men. *(© 2014 Mei-Chun Jau Photography.)*

Sunsets on Cedar Lake in Gun Barrel City, Texas, are spectacular, but in this photograph from a *USA Today* feature Mark (left) and Vic have eyes only for each other. *(© 2014 Mei-Chun Jau Photography.)*

Mark and Vic are never far from the beagles with whom they share their lives. Here, Betsy has climbed comfortably onto Mark's lap and Jake onto Vic's as they relax at home. Abby, independent and camera-shy, has absented herself. (© 2014 Vernon Bryant/Dallas Morning News.)

On a chilly January evening at a ranch near Big Bend National Park, Texas, Mark (left) sips a beer while Vic tends to steaks grilling over an open fire. (© 2015 Braden Summers Photography.)

Savoring warm coffee on a cold morning, Mark (left) and Vic share a quiet, reflective moment far from their busy lives in Plano. (© 2015 Braden Summers Photography.)

Strolling in front of the iconic Palace Theater in Marfa, Texas, Vic (left) and Mark enjoy the echoes of those long ago days when *Giant* was filmed just outside of town. A favorite from their February 2015 shoot with Braden Summers, this photograph appeared later on their wedding invitations. (© 2015 Braden Summers Photography.)

Vic (left) and Mark laugh as they walk to the John H. Wood, Jr. Federal Courthouse in San Antonio for the February 12, 2014, hearing on the Motion for a Preliminary Injunction before Judge Orlando Garcia. (© 2014 AP Photo/Eric Gay)

After the hearing in San Antonio, Vic (far left) and Mark (center left) relax over lunch with their co-plaintiffs, Cleopatra DeLeon (center right) and Nicole Dimetman (far right) at the nearby Liberty Bar. *(© 2014 Lisa Krantz/San Antonio Express-News/Zuma.)*

Cleopatra DeLeon (far left), Nicole Dimetman (center left), Mark (center right) and Vic (far right) are all smiles after Judge Orlando Garcia issued a Preliminary Injunction barring Texas from enforcing its ban on same-sex marriages. *(© 2014 Lisa Krantz/San Antonio Express-News/Zuma.)*

At the Spirit of Texas Brunch in June 2014, Vic (far right) and Mark (center right) and their co-plaintiffs, and Cleopatra DeLeon (far right) and Nicole Dimetman (center left), shared the 2014 Anchor Award. The legal team from Akin Gump, represented here by Neel Lane (center left) and Frank Stenger-Castro (center right), was honored with the Vanguard Award. *(© 2014 Susan Risdon.)*

The Texas plaintiffs—Cleopatra DeLeon (far left), Nicole Dimetman (center left), Mark Phariss (center right) and Vic Holmes (far right)— pose for a photograph after the press conference on January 8, 2015, at the Cathedral Creative Studios in New Orleans for plaintiffs from Louisiana, Mississippi, and Texas. The women were expecting their second child, and Cleopatra's hand rests affectionately on Nicole's "baby-bump." *(© 2015 Susan Risdon.)*

As Mark (right) prepares to speak at the press conference following the January 9, 2015 hearing at the Fifth Circuit Court of Appeals, Vic reaches out affectionately to stroke his cheek. (© 2015 AP Photo/Stacy Revere.)

(Left to right): Vic, Mark, Nicole, and Cleopatra leave the Fifth Circuit Court of Appeals hand in hand--a show of solidarity. (© 2015 AP Photo/Stacy Revere.)

February 2014: Darren Braun, sent by *Texas Monthly* to shoot photos of Vic (back) and Mark to accompany Chris Kelly's article on their fight for marriage equality, suggested they dress in tuxedos. Two of their three beagles, Jake (left) and Betsy, thought it a good idea. Abby, the shy one, always independent, absented herself. Kelly's article ran in the February edition just days before their first appearance in court. (© 2014 Darren Braun.)

Cleopatra DeLeon and Nicole Dimetman, co-plaintiffs in the Texas case, were pictured with their son on the cover of the March 2015 edition of *Texas Monthly*. Nicole is visibly pregnant with their second child. (© 2015 *Texas Monthly*)

Two days before oral arguments in *Obergefell v. Hodges*, Mark and Vic struck up a friendship with Michiganders April DeBoer (center left) and Jayne Rowse (center right), named plaintiffs in *Obergefell*, when they met in front of the U. S. Supreme Court. *(Courtesy of Mark Phariss and Vic Holmes)*

On April 26, 2015, Mark (far left) and Vic (far right) stood on the steps of the Supreme Court in solidarity with Sandy Stier (center left) and Kris Perry (center right), two of California's Prop 8 plaintiffs. *(Courtesy of Mark Phariss and Vic Holmes)*

Arriving in Washington, D. C. several days before oral arguments in *Obergefell*, Mark (left) and Vic were able to catch up with a good friend from San Antonio, U.S. Air Force General Counsel Gordon Tanner, in his office at the Pentagon. *(Courtesy of Mark Phariss and Vic Holmes)*

The evening before oral arguments in *Obergefell v. Hodges* plaintiffs in same-sex marriage cases since the early 1970s gathered at the offices of Holland & Knight to celebrate how far their cause had come. Vic (left) and Mark paused that evening for a photograph with Evan Wolfson, the godfather of same-sex marriage and the founder of Freedom to Marry. *(© 2015 Judy G. Rolfe)*

On the morning of April 28, 2015, Mark (left) and Vic arrived early at the Supreme Court to take their places in line. A friend, Tracy Hollister, photographed them standing hopefully on the steps with the Supreme Court building glowing behind them in the dim light. *(Courtesy of Tracy Hollister)*

On June 26, 2015, the day the Supreme Court announced its decision in Obergefell, Vic (left) and Mark flew to Austin for a press conference at the LBJ Library with their co-plaintiffs, Cleopatra DeLeon and Nicole Dimetman, and Neel Lane, the lead attorney on their case. Vic surprised everyone with a formal proposal: "I'm not sure that it's ever been said," he remarked as he turned from the cameras to look in Mark's eyes, "so I'm saying it now. Will you marry me?" *(© 2015 Robert Daemmrich Photography Inc.)*

Mark Phariss (far left), Vic (center left), Cleopatra (center right), and Nicole (right)—join with their lead attorney, Neel Lane, raising their hands in Churchill's "Victory" sign after the press conference at the LBJ Library on June 26, 2015. *(© 2015 Susan Risdon)*

From the press conference in Austin, Mark (left) and Vic rushed back to Dallas to speak at the evening celebration of marriage equality at the Cathedral of Hope. Introduced as two of the plaintiffs who had fought for the right to marry in Texas, they received a standing ovation. (© 2015 2nd2Nunn Photography)

On June 29, 2015, Vic (left) and Mark returned to Austin to celebrate the U.S. Supreme Court marriage equality decision with Jim Obergefell, the first-named plaintiff in the case, at the Texas Capitol. (© 2015 AP Photo/Eric Gay)

Chad Griffin, President of the Human Rights Campaign (far left), and Jim Obergefell (center left), celebrate the decision at the Texas Capitol with Mark (center right) and Vic (far right). *(© 2015 AP Photo/Eric Gay)*

"Love Wins," the familiar sign proclaims, as Vic (left) and Mark kiss at the rally at the Texas Capitol in Austin. *(© 2015 Robert Daemmrich Photography, Inc.)*

With help from U. S. Senator Harry Reid, Vic (left) and Mark obtained a flag that flew over the U.S. Capitol the day the Supreme Court ruled in favor of marriage equality. Donated to the Dallas Black Tie Dinner and auctioned on November 14, 2015, the flag sold for a whopping $16,500. (© 2015 Lauren Mutti)

In the fall of 2013 Mark (left) and Vic traveled to San Antonio where they applied for—and were refused—a marriage license at the offices of Gerard ("Gerry") Rickhoff, the County Clerk. Two years later Gerry Rickhoff, a supporter of marriage equality whose freedom to act had been restricted by Texas law, greeted them in the lobby and smiled approvingly as Mark and Vic, beaming with happiness, held the license in their hands for the first time. (© 2015 Scott D. Smith)

Mark (left) and Vic pose for a formal wedding portrait in the lounge of the Westin Stonebriar Hotel, Frisco, Texas, minutes before the November 21, 2015, ceremony that would unite them in marriage. (© 2015 Scott Hager)

When they began to think seriously about their wedding, Mark and Vic realized that the guest list would be large. The wedding party—twenty-one people, gathered here in a lounge at the Westin Stonebriar Hotel wearing the RayBans® provided by the grooms as a "thank you" for participating—was proportionately large. (L to R: Brian Smith, David Sovell, Neal Chadwick, Greg Phariss [Best Man], Merritt Clements, Mark Phariss, Daylin McAnulla, Cathan Brice [front], Eva Cole [Best Woman], Vic Holmes, Austin McAnulla, Dan McKim, Christopher Gregory, Jeff Thomas, Jeremy Greshin, Robert Cruz, Mike Carnahan, Richard Garcia, and Stephen Wells.) (© 2015 Scott Hager)

Diana Finfrock-Farrar (far left) beams her approval as Mark great nephew, Cathan Brice, and Mark's cousin, Emily Polen, carry the wedding rings on two U.S. flags. One flew over the U.S. Capitol on April 28, 2015, when the U.S. Supreme Court held hearings on marriage equality, the other on June 26, 2015, when the U.S. Supreme Court ruled in favor of marriage equality. (© 2015 Scott Hager)

When a smiling Charlie Gonzalez, pronounced Vic (left) and Mark "married under the laws of the State of Texas and the Constitution of the United States," guests roared their approval and the newlyweds raised their arms in triumph. (© 2015 Scott Hager)

Mark and Vic hold up their wedding certificate, witnessed by (L to R) Neel Lane, Charles A. Gonzalez, Cleopatra DeLeon and Nicole Dimetman, Frank Stenger-Castro, and Michael Coolely. *(© 2015 Scott Hager)*

Mark (left) and Vic swing through their first dance as a married couple, backed up by IceHouse, the band that performed at their wedding. *(© 2015 Scott Hager)*

Wanting a lasting memento of their day, Mark (left) turned to San Antonio artist Pauline Howard to create a formal wedding portrait in pastels as a surprise wedding present for Vic. *(© 2015 Scott Hager)*

Mark and Vic cut into a cake designed specifically for them—six tiers, with a blue ribbon encircling every other tier, a reminder of Vic's nearly twenty-three years in the Air Force, topped by miniatures of Mark and Vic and their three beagles. *(© 2015 Scott Hager)*

At the insistence of Margaret Gragg of Dallas Affaires, Mark and Vic opted for a grooms' cake in the shape of Texas with the state flag on top, covered in part by a copy of the Constitution of the United States. *(© 2015 Scott Hager)*

Susan Risdon and Angela Hale, owners of Red Media Group, a media relations firm in Austin, Texas, helped with public relations in *DeLeon v. Perry*. From left to right: Susan Risdon, Mark Phariss, Vic Holmes, and Angela Hale. *(© 2015 Scott Hager)*

Mark's family: Left to right: Kristen Johnson (niece), Austin McAnulla (great nephew), Nikki Brice (niece), Kyle Brice (nephew-in-law), Cathan Brice (great nephew), Mark Phariss, Vic Holmes, Cynthia Mason Phariss (sister-in-law), Greg Phariss (brother), Daylin McAnulla (great nephew), Christopher Mason (nephew). *(© 2015 Scott Hager)*

Vic's family: Left to right: Guy Wills (brother-in-law), Tanya Rednour Wills (sister), Mark Phariss, Vic Holmes, Debonna Gregory (sister-in-law), Nicky Joe Rednour (brother), and Christopher Gregory (nephew). *(© 2015 Scott Hager)*

George Harris (left) and Jack Evans (right) were the first same-sex couple to marry on Decision Day in Dallas County, Texas. Grateful for their friendship, Mark announced their presence to the wedding guests. *(© 2015 Scott Hager)*

Bruce and Molly Beth Malcolm (far left, center left) brought a special gift to the wedding, a pocket-sized copy of the Constitution of the United States of America under which the Supreme Court declared same-sex marriage legal. *(© 2015 Scott Hager)*

At a gathering on March 12, 2016, in Dallas, Texas, Mark (left) and Vic seized the opportunity for a photograph with President Barack Obama. (© 2016 Kristin Bowman)

At a reception on June 3, 2015, Mark (left) and Vic were photographed with Secretary of State Hillary Rodham Clinton in Dallas, Texas. (© Barbara Kinney/Hillary for America)

November 10, 2015

Maj Victor Holmes, USAF (Ret)
  and Mr. Mark Phariss
Plano, Texas

Dear Major Holmes and Mr. Phariss:

Congratulations on your wedding! As you celebrate this joyous occasion and look forward to continuing your journey together, please know we are extraordinarily grateful for your service.

Thanks to brave Americans like you who stood up and fought for progress, our country is becoming more just and compassionate. We hope you take great pride in your contributions, and we wish you as much happiness and adventure in your marriage as we have known in ours. May your love for one another guide you in all you do, and may your bond grow stronger with each passing year.

Sincerely,

Michelle Obama

Letter from President and Mrs. Barack Obama congratulating Vic for his years of service in the United States Air Force and both men on their upcoming wedding. *(Courtesy of Mark Phariss and Vic Holmes)*

November 21, 2015

Mr. Mark Phariss
  and Mr. Victor Holmes
3400 Westover Drive
Plano, TX 75093

Dear Mark and Vic:

Congratulations on your wedding day!

As you begin this exciting new chapter in your life together, I join your family and friends in wishing you the very best, and I thank you, from the bottom of my heart, for your commitment to making this day possible for so many other loving couples across the country.

Your lives will be richer and happier because you have chosen each other. May the coming years bring you laughter in the good times, courage in the tough times, growing wisdom, and an enduring love.

With warm regards, I am

Sincerely yours,

Hillary

Hillary Rodham Clinton

Post Office Box 5256, New York, NY 10185 · www.hillaryclinton.com
Contributions or gifts to Hillary for America are not tax deductible.

 Paid for by Hillary for America

On November 21, 2015, Hillary Rodham Clinton sent a letter congratulating Mark and Vic on their wedding. *(Courtesy of Mark Phariss and Vic Holmes)*

Vic (left) and Mark walk through the surf at Playa Conchal, Guanacaste Province, Costa Rica on their honeymoon. (© 2015 *Photoventura Costa Rica*)

In 2014, afraid that one of them would die before same-sex marriage came to Texas, they "married" in defiance of Texas law. The Reverend Bill McElvaney, a sympathetic friend whose terminal cancer had made him fearless, joined them in a religious ceremony everyone present knew would mean nothing in a court of law but meant everything to Jack and George. For his kindness, the Reverend McElvaney was promptly sanctioned by the Methodist Church—ironically, the denomination to which Mark had once belonged. Now, on the morning of the twenty-sixth of June, realizing that the state-sanctioned marriage they had wanted for so many years was at last possible, they rushed to the offices of John Warren, the Dallas County Clerk. For three hours they waited as Warren's legal counsel dithered. Finally, a few minutes before noon, the much-coveted license to marry legally in Texas was put into their hands. Marrying them was "a huge honor for me," Judge Garcia told bystanders; "I had to fight back tears, tears of joy." Sharing their first kiss as a married couple, Jack and George made no attempt to hold back their tears.

Like the scores who followed in rapid succession, George was ecstatic. "It's wonderful," he proclaimed; it's really the highlight of our lives. It's the greatest thing that has ever happened to us."[50]

"You would have been blown away by the crowd there," Jack told friends after he and George were pronounced husband and husband. "There must have been 450 people there, people waiting to get married. It was amazing. Just amazing."[51]

Jack would have been even more amazed had he been caught up in the delirious throng outside the Supreme Court, a crowd that continued to grow for two hours after news of the decision broke, spilling from the plaza to the sidewalk and ultimately onto First Street where police were forced to shut down a lane of traffic. Couples marrying on the spot drew cheers. Lorence Wenke, once a Republican and a state representative in Michigan, stood smiling behind a giant shield inscribed with his wish for the future: "Our Constitution is our shield against Bible based discrimination toward our gay friends & neighbors." Ikeita Cantú held aloft a sign that summed up the mood perfectly: "Not just gay . . . Ecstatic."[52]

Judges who worked with Judge Tonya Parker had agreed in advance that she would be the first to perform a same-sex marriage ceremony in Dallas on the day the decision came down. A lesbian, she had announced in February 2012 that she would perform no more marriages until everyone was allowed to marry—and her colleagues wanted to reward her tenacious, principled stance. Unaware of their promise, Judge Garcia married Jack Evans and George Harris early in the day, but Parker's friend, Judge Eric Moyé, was determined she would have a "first" on Decision Day. He strode through the door of her courtroom and approached the bench, interrupting ongoing proceedings—highly unusual behavior for a judge known for his formality. He had told her earlier that he would be the first to celebrate with her on Decision Day, and as he approached her chair he spread his arms wide for a congratulatory hug. Flabbergasted, thrilled at the support from her colleagues, Judge Parker remembered the moment when she spoke at the Cathedral of Hope a year later. "I tried to continue with business as usual, but eventually, it got to the place that I had to accept that history was being made and it was okay for me to take the docket down." Later, Judge Parker's remaining colleagues, dressed in their judicial robes, took seats in the jury box in her courtroom as she made a little history of her own, officiating at the first same-sex marriage in the George L. Allen, Sr. Courts Building. "They wanted to be sitting in the jury room in their robes," Judge Parker told the crowd, "to symbolize to this community and all of our community that they stood in solidarity . . . not with me, but with the decision and the ideology that underlies it."[53]

Online the mood was equally jubilant. On the Facebook page of the case that brought marriage equality to Florida, *Huntsman v. Heavilin*, Mark Ebenhoch changed the cover photo to an artist's vision of a nuclear explosion—a visual sign of how the world had changed. "Aaron Huntsman gave that to me eight months ago," he explained later; "I could have posted it after the Florida ruling, but that wasn't big enough. I was saving it for the 'Big Win'—and when that came I had it up in five seconds."[54] After tense months waiting for the Court's decision, activist Mike Wallace couldn't resist a little online fun. He posted a formal photo of the nine justices photoshopped to show bursts of steam coming from Justice Antonin Scalia's ears.[55]

Marc Solomon posted a new version of the photo of the conference room at Freedom to Marry on Facebook—staffers sitting around the table as they had just days ago, but this time smiling broadly, their arms raised to hold aloft glasses for a ceremonial toast.[56] Fittingly, Evan Wolfson had been the first to see the news. "We were ready with the champagne, we did a quick toast," he said, "and then we hit the battle stations." Reading the decision in his office, paragraph after paragraph, Wolfson found himself in tears as decades of memories rushed over him.[57] Slate.com posted the "Map of the States Where Same-Sex Marriage Is Legal" advocates had seen so many times as the battle for marriage equality entered its final stages—and for the first time ever every state appeared in the same color. The first comment, posted by a professor of Political Science at Mark's undergraduate college, caught perfectly the reaction of most Americans: "This sure makes things easier. And more humane, logical, ethical, intelligent, equitable . . . Today represented a necessary affirmation of natural law and a comforting demonstration that we can actually continue to make progress and improve as a nation."[58]

* * *

Susan Risdon's Facebook post moments after the decision was announced unabashedly mixed business and pleasure. "We Won!!!!!!!!!!" she exulted. "News conference at 11:30 at the LBJ Library in Austin in the Brown Room." Though Mark and Vic arrived late, nobody—not Neel Lane who had argued *DeLeon v. Perry* in San Antonio and New Orleans, not Chuck Smith, Chief Executive Officer of Equality Texas, not the dozen or so journalists who had gathered to cover the story, certainly not Nicole and Cleo—seemed to care. Someone called up Kool & the Gang's "Celebration" on a phone. People who had spent a lot of time together since the case began sang along and smiled. And laughed. And danced. When Mark and Vic charged breathlessly into the room—"Sorry we're late," Vic whispered with a smile—Neel Lane waited patiently while hugs went round.

When he spoke, his words were in part a summary of what had happened, in part a warning shot fired across the bow of government officials in Texas who had already announced their intention to resist the Supreme Court's ruling in *Obergefell*. "Today is a wonderful day in America," he began, the happiness he shared with the plaintiffs bubbling up in his voice; "The Supreme Court of the United States recognized that marriage is a fundamental right for every citizen regardless of sexual orientation." But his tone changed quickly. Judge Orlando Garcia—who had declared Texas's ban against same-sex marriage unconstitutional in February 2014, but stayed his order pending Texas's appeal—had lifted the stay just hours earlier. "As of right now, officials in Texas are enjoined from enforcing restrictions on same-sex marriage in the state of Texas," Lane warned, his voice suddenly edgy as if spoiling for a fight; "they will do so at their peril, subject to the penalties under federal law that are provided if they deny constitutional rights to citizens of this state. We intend to guard vigilantly our clients' rights to the institution of marriage."

His work done, Lane passed the microphone to Cleo, who slid it along the table to Nicole. Before the press conference began she had been dancing in her seat. "Sometimes it's good to cause a little trouble," she said with a twinkle in her eye. "My mom—she's no longer with us, but she'd be so proud of me today," she began, adding as she turned to Cleo, "she'd be so proud of us. She always said, 'You've gotta be a good girl, you've gotta follow the rules, but sometimes it's good to cause a little bit of trouble." The "trouble" she and Cleo, Mark and Vic, Neel and the legal team at Akin Gump had raised had helped to bring marriage equality to Texas—and Nicole made it clear that she could hardly wait to join the happy crowds lining up for marriage licenses at the clerk's office.

Mark too was thinking of family. When Vic passed the microphone to him, he spoke first of his parents. "If they were alive today," he said, "they would have celebrated their 74th wedding anniversary last Monday." Remembering his parents, wishing they could have lived to share his happiness, Mark's voice cracked with emotion. He paused for a moment, until he felt Vic's steady hand on his. "The last anniversary they celebrated was their 46th. Vic and I never dreamed we would celebrate a wedding anniversary. And now we can thanks to the Supreme Court. The only downside," Mark added impishly, "is that they took so long that I'll be 101 before I can celebrate my 46th."

Everyone laughed, happy for a moment's relief from the intense emotions crowding the room. But when Vic spoke, the intensity returned. "I've heard it said," he began, "that two people can't change two millennia of tradition. But when that tradition involves discrimination on this level . . . that has to change. Two people," he continued—and, turning to Nicole and Cleo, corrected himself—"four people, it doesn't really matter. It isn't the quantity of people, it's the heart, the determination to correct something that was wrong." Turning to Mark, he began again. "The man I'm sitting next to, you can see him, but you can't *see* him the way I do. I can't tell you how much I love him, how much I want you all to know how much I love him." From the beginning, Vic spoke slowly, deliberately. Now he paused ever so slightly, and when he began again the words came even more slowly, the vocal equivalent of words carved in stone. "This matters. It matters that I love him. That's not a trivial thing. It's not something to be brushed aside as if it were nothing." The people listening in the Brown Room of the LBJ Library felt for a moment as though time had stopped. And then Vic carried his audience along on the last step. "This has been a long fight. I'm glad that it has come to the point where now I can marry the man that I love, legally, where I can tell everybody that this man and this man only is the one for me."

As Nicole had done in speaking of her mother, as Mark had done in speaking of his parents, Vic pushed his audience to the edge of an emotional cliff with his simple declaration of love—and caught them before they pitched over. "I'm not sure that it's ever been said," he continued as he turned from the cameras to look in Mark's eyes, "so I'm saying it now. Will you marry me?" People laughed as they had before the press conference began; they applauded. And Vic's mic-drop surprise—even Mark was taken aback—was recorded on tape for all time. Mark needed only two words—"Well, yes!"—to reply. Chuck Smith began to speak about the work to be done, the need for laws that would protect gays and lesbians and transgender people from discrimination in housing and in the workplace. People tried to pay attention, but few could turn their eyes from Vic, his head resting now on Mark's shoulder, his eyes closed, a smile on his face.

Earlier, Mark had reached out to reassure Texans unable to accept the Supreme Court's ruling on marriage equality. "We respect your right to oppose," he told them, "we do not want any church to have to marry anyone they don't want to marry and under the First Amendment they don't have to. All we ask is that they recognize our state marriage as we would recognize theirs." As the press conference drew to a close, Nicole reached out as well. "I feel for you," she said to Texans opposed to marriage equality, "because in your heart today you're very sad. I understand that your beliefs are genuine, that many of you are not opposed because you hate me personally. I'm sorry that my happiness today causes you distress. You don't have to approve, necessarily, of my family. The only thing that has changed today is that from a civil point of view Cleo's and my family is not going to be discriminated against."

Neel Lane, however, followed up quickly to distinguish between private individuals and government officials—and reissued the challenge with which the press conference had begun:

> I understand that individuals may have problems . . . But when you are a state official in the state of Texas, you swear an oath to uphold the Constitution of the United States of America, in addition to the laws and the Constitution of Texas. If your personal beliefs prevent you from keeping that oath, then you need to step down. You do not have a religious right to violate the oath you took as an official of the state of Texas. There are consequences if in violation of that oath you deny constitutional rights to citizens who live in your state—and there will be lawyers who will hold you to that oath.

The last question of the press conference was less contentious, more humorous: Will Greg Abbott be invited to your wedding? Mark's answer was almost drowned out by the laughter that swept across the room.

"I wish more people would remember how to listen," Lane would write the next day in response to a photo Mark posted on Facebook—himself, Mark and Vic, Cleo and Nicole, smiles on their faces, their hands raised in Churchill's "V for Victory" sign. "I could not have asked for more humane, beautiful companions," he added, celebrating the impulse that led Mark and Nicole to extend an olive branch. "You guys made me tear up during the press conference."[59] But for those reluctant to listen, his message to comply fully with the holding of the Supreme Court had been clear.[60]

Tightly scheduled—in the two years since *DeLeon v. Perry* was filed busy-ness had become a way of life, but not one that came easily—Mark and Vic sprinted for the airport as soon as the press conference was over.

They had hoped on Decision Day to get their much overdue marriage license. But they had also agreed to speak at the Dallas Day of Decision rally at the Cathedral of Hope and realized there was no way they could get to the Dallas County Courthouse, stand in line, and still get to the Cathedral of Hope on time. Celebrating close to home with friends who had supported them through difficult times was their top priority. By the time they arrived a crowd well in excess of the Cathedral's nominal capacity of 1200 had settled into the pews or found places in the aisles. Settled, that is, but for the tendency to break spontaneously into jubilant cheers and to sing wedding-themed songs like "Chapel of Love"—with special emphasis on the part that promises the happy couple will "never be lonely anymore." When The Reverend Neil Cazares-Thomas introduced Mark and Vic as two of the plaintiffs who had challenged Texas in *DeLeon v. Perry*, the congregation rose to their feet for a prolonged ovation.

Flanked by two floor-to-ceiling stained-glass windows on either side of the sanctuary, Mark returned to the theme he had set in Austin, thanking the Supreme Court for "the best wedding present we could have . . . the opportunity to celebrate anniversaries like everyone else." Behind him, an outsized cross soared to the highest point in the cathedral, drawing the crowd's eyes upward as Mark raised their spirits. As he had done so often during the last two years, he spoke of the past, the history of the marriage equality movement, showering thanks on those who had worked so hard for so many years to make the moment of victory possible. Vic looked to the future. "What happened today didn't happen for us," he told the crowd. "Look to your left or right and you'll see a young person. That is who this decision is for."

More than a dozen pastors beamed their approval as the Reverend Cazares-Thomas moved to the capstone of the evening, the marriage of two couples, Debbie Johnson and Zante Barica, and Marlon Cortez and Shannon Baily. When he choked up trying to say what he had never before been able to say to a gay couple—"by the power vested in me by the state of Texas"—the crowd cheered. When he regained control and added—"and by the U. S. Constitution"—they cheered more loudly still.[61]

The rally over, Mark and Vic paused in the lobby to talk with friends, then fell in with the crowd behind a multi-colored Dallas Day of Decision banner—"Marriage for all, y'all" written in an exuberant script—for the mile-plus march along Cedar Springs to the Monument of Love. Walking hand in hand, they sought comfort, shedding their sport jackets in the 95-degree heat. Unfortunately, they couldn't shed the uncomfortable dress shoes they had chosen for the day. His feet hurting more and more with each step, Mark thought of the African Americans who for more than six months walked miles to and from work during the Birmingham bus boycott in 1955. "My feets is tired," one man said then, "but my soul is rested." Watching the clouds gathering above their heads, wondering when the rains would come, they stood with a thousand others at the Monument of Love and cheered as Paul Castillo of Lambda Legal fired up the crowd one more time. Until, that is, torrents of rain sent them running to the Green Papaya, their Vietnamese restaurant of choice. There, and later at the Round-up Saloon, crowds of well-wishers showered them with thanks, pulled them close for commemorative selfies, offered to buy them drinks. They had come a long way since October 2013 when *DeLeon v. Perry* was filed, had learned a lot about how to deal with the spotlight. And yet, they continued to be surprised when someone picked them out in a crowd.

That night in Dallas, Mark and Vic and hundreds of others danced the night away at the Round-Up; 1200 miles away in the nation's capital the White House glowed in the night, decked out for the occasion in the colors of the rainbow flag—giving new meaning to Valerie Jarrett's assertion that "We are the beacon for the world." Minutes after eleven o'clock that morning, President Obama had called across town to congratulate Jim Obergefell, so emotionally overwhelmed, so flustered that he struggled for words to thank the president. Later, speaking in the Rose Garden, Obama reached out to congratulate "our LGBT brothers and sisters" and the American people. Sometimes, he began, progress on the journey toward full equality comes "in small increments . . . [despite] the persistent effort of dedicated citizens. And then sometimes there are days like this, when that slow, steady effort is rewarded with justice that arrives like a thunderbolt." Wrestling with events that threatened to drive Americans apart—as the president spoke, a helicopter warmed up on the south lawn for the trip to Charleston where he was to eulogize the Reverend Clementa Pinckney, pastor of the Mother Emmanuel African Methodist Episcopal Church, cut down with eight members of his congregation in a hail of gunfire from a white supremacist who had joined their bible study—the president spoke slowly, struggling to control the emotion in his voice. He praised "the countless small acts of courage" of the millions, gay and straight, who risked so much for so long for equality.

But most of all, he spoke of unity. Extending the freedom to marry to "loving, same-sex couples," he declared, signaled "a victory for America" because "When all Americans are treated as equal, we are all more free." Recalling his second inaugural address—"if we are truly created equal, then surely the love we commit to one another must be equal as well"—President Obama echoed the themes of "One Today," the poem Richard Blanco, America's first openly gay, first Latino inaugural poet, read that day. We trace our roots to different cultures, Blanco asserts in "One Today"; we follow in our individual lives an infinite number of storylines. But in the end we share all that is important—"one sun," "one light," "one ground," "one wind," "one sky"—and in the alchemy of sharing we become "one country." Recognizing the possibility that Americans would be driven apart by the day's events, the president challenged his listeners to adopt Blanco's sense of oneness. "For all our differences," he claimed, "we are one people, stonger together than we could ever be alone. That's always been our story."[62]

The White House wasn't alone in taking on the colors of the rainbow flag on June 26. Long before the lights went on at 1600 Pennsylvania Avenue, the internet lit up in the same explosion of color as corporation after corporation took to Facebook, Instagram, and Twitter in a show of support for marriage equality. Not that corporate support for the LGBT community was a new thing in the spring of 2015. The list of companies that had featured same-sex couples in their advertising was already lengthy: Amazon, Barney's, Coca-Cola, The Gap/Banana Republic, Honey Made, IKEA, Tiffany's, Microsoft, J. C. Penney, Ray-Ban, Target, Tylenol, Wells Fargo. Kimberly Clark had already approached Mark and Vic about doing a commercial for Kleenex centered on their wedding day; Jack Evans and George Harris had been recruited to do a commercial for Necco's candy hearts in the year of their fifty-fifth Valentine's Day together.

As the possibility of adverse public reactions receded—reactions like the bomb threat at an IKEA store in Hicksville, New York, after the company ran an ad featuring two men shopping for a new dining room table (1994), or the boycott organized by the anti-gay group "One Million Moms" after J. C. Penney hired Ellen DeGeneres as its spokesperson (2012)—more and more companies began to air heartwarming ads only Kim Davis, the Rowan County, Kentucky, clerk who defied a federal court order to issue marriage licenses to same-sex couples, or Franklin Graham, president and CEO of the Billy Graham Evangelistic Association, could resist. A Wells Fargo ad showcased two soon-to-be moms learning sign-language so the hearing impaired little girl they were adopting would be comfortable with them from the start. Though the ad cost the bank some business—Graham moved the accounts of the association bearing his father's name and urged his followers to do the same—company spokesman Ruben Pulido was unapologetic. "Our marketing programs and content," he told the *San Francisco Business Times*, echoing the argument of Ken Mehlman's *amicus* brief, "reflect our company's values."[63]

What *was* remarkable about the reaction of corporate America to the Supreme Court's decision was its intensity. Everyone wanted to be a part of the history-making moment. American Airlines ran a photo of an empty cabin in a widebody jet, every screen, row after row, lit up to show their logo against the rainbow flag. "We're all on board," the text proclaimed; "Diversity strengthens us all." Ben & Jerry's, which rebranded "Chubby Hubby" as "Hubby Hubby" when the Vermont legislature made same-sex marriage legal (2009), praised the Supreme Court's action as "a tremendous win for all Americans who believe in love, liberty, and equality." Two women in their meme held up a pint container of "I Dough, I Dough," Chocolate Chip Cookie Dough reimagined for the occasion. In white text centered in a black rectangle, Airbnb asked "Dear Scotus, Are you free this weekend? Because there's a big party, and you can be our guests of honor." The note was signed with a heart—red—made from two thumbprints. "It's official now," Coca-Cola wrote above a line of six iconic Coke bottles in bright, rainbow colors. "Proud to celebrate marriage equality," Expedia tweeted, above an illustration that showed a stylized white plane angling into a rainbow sky. Finding an expressive way to express their approval of the Supreme Court decision was easy for Yahoo. Against the background of the rainbow flag they posted the company's name in white caps, followed by an exclamation point. "That's a lot of brands for bigots to boycott," one man wrote when Queerty.com posted their fifty-three favorites. Another noted that "The wrong side of history will be a very lonely place."[64]

As they waited to board a plane for Austin on the twenty-sixth, Mark and Vic sent a hopeful message to friends on Facebook: "We won. The Supreme Court ruled in our favor. All of it. Now we can return to normal life. 100%. Just-like-everyone-else normal life." Physically and mentally exhausted by Friday's non-stop celebrations, they spent the weekend at their house in Gun Barrel City, a first attempt at "normal." Try as they might, however, they couldn't separate from what had happened. Saturday morning a friend sent Mark a recording of Woody Guthrie's "This Land Is Your Land" and he caught fire once again, posting the lyrics to his Facebook page. "How appropriate, huh?" he asked, adding "Can you tell I am still stoked!" Sunday night he logged on again to praise the lawyers who had labored for years on *DeLeon v. Perry* and in *Obergefell* submitted a brief for the Historians of Marriage that set before the Court critical information Justice Kennedy cited in his decision. "I think that they—Neel Lane, Matthew Pepping, Frank Stenger-Castro, Michael Cooley, Andrew Newman, Barry Chassnoff, & Pratik Shah—deserve our thanks," he wrote, "not just for their work in Texas but also for their work before SCOTUS!!!!!"[65]

Monday marked a new beginning for Mark and Vic—if not of "normal," then at least of what would soon become their "new normal" where the line between private life and public advocacy would become even more blurred than it had been in the past two years. Off yet again to Austin, they joined with Cleo and Nicole—"L Style G Style" had just branded the plaintiffs as "our own Texas heroes"—with Jim Obergefell, Chad Griffin, and Chuck Smith for a rally on the north steps of the Capitol.[66] Another opportunity for Equality Texas, the Texas Freedom Network, the ACLU, and the HRC to celebrate and to direct attention to the upcoming battle for protections in employment and housing. And, as it turned out, to have a little fun at the same time. When Mark recited the lyrics to Guthrie's "This Land Is Your Land," the crowd broke into song to wind up the rally.

Returning to work on Tuesday morning, Mark had barely settled at his desk when a delivery arrived, flowers from the Westin Stonebriar Hotel and Golf Club, the site for the wedding and reception, a second arrangement from their florist, 21 Parc. Better even than the flowers was the heartfelt note from Shannon Walker, wedding coordinator at the Westin Stonebriar:

> What an amazing day in history! I wanted to just send my congratulations, and say how sincerely happy I am for the two of you. You believed that this day would come in Texas and the world around us, and I am proud to be a part of this amazing moment in your life.
>
> Come November, friends and family will surround you as you commit your lives together. This celebration will be one of the most special events I have ever been a part of, and I appreciate you allowing us to join in your celebration of love, life and equality.
>
> Congratulations again from deep within my heart.

Confirmation, Mark and Vic thought, that in choosing the Westin Stonebriar and 21 Parc they had chosen wisely. But Shannon's note reminded them, one more time, that in the past two years their public and private lives had become conjoined twins, something they never wanted, never intended to happen. Their new, comfortable-but-not-quite-comfortable normal.

* * *

Early in July Evan Wolfson wrote to supporters of Freedom to Marry, a final note that looked in two directions: a celebration of "America's win" and an acknowledgement "that there's still much work to do." "As I read the Supreme Court decision," he said, "I followed the stories across the country of couples getting married . . . I cried and cried."[67] Like Evan, Mark and Vic shed their tears and followed the national story. But their own story, still unfolding, demanded attention as well. Same-sex couples in Texas had begun to marry on the morning of June 26 after Judge Orlando Garcia lifted his stay in *DeLeon v. Perry*. By the time Evan Wolfson sent his letter of thanks on the second day of July, Texas had issued nearly a thousand marriage licenses to gay and lesbian couples. And yet, maddeningly, despite the wave of change sweeping across Louisiana, Mississippi, and Texas, the Fifth Circuit Court of Appeals had taken no action. From New Orleans, Mark and Vic, Cleo and Nicole had for almost six months heard only the frustrating sounds of silence. That the Fifth Circuit had heard but failed to act on appeals in same-sex marriage cases from the three states within its jurisdiction might, they feared, be construed by some as a procedural roadblock opponents could use in delaying implementation of *Obergefell* in Texas.

On June 29, the Fifth Circuit Court of Appeals stirred at last, like a latter-day Rip Van Winkle emerging from a long sleep. What do we need to do, what should we do, in light of the Supreme Court's decision? Both parties in the cases from Louisiana, Mississippi, and Texas were instructed to submit "letter advisories" by July 1, a common practice when a higher court issues a decision directly on point after briefing and oral argument have already occurred. Akin Gump's response was quick and thorough—two and a half pages, thick with precedent, but the endgame could not have been more clear:

> this Court may, in light of *Obergefell*, direct the District Court to enter judgment in favor of Plaintiffs, issue a permanent injunction to enjoin Defendants from enforcing Article I, Section 32 of the Texas Constitution, any related provisions in the Texas Family Code, and any other laws or regulations prohibiting a person from marrying another person of the same sex or recognizing same-sex marriage; and take any and all steps necessary to enforce the judgment and permanent injunction.[68]

Texas's response to the Fifth Circuit's request was shorter, less than a page that echoed the conclusions in Akin Gump's letter. Elated that Texas had been able to conjure up no further roadblocks, Mark posted the letter to Vic's timeline.

On July 1 the agonizing months of waiting came at last to an end. The Fifth Circuit Court of Appeals finally issued Judge Jerry E. Smith's decision.

> Because, as both sides now agree, the injunction appealed from is correct in light of *Obergefell*, the preliminary injunction is AFFIRMED. This matter is REMANDED for entry of judgment in

favor of the plaintiffs. The court must act expeditiously on remand and should enter final judgment on the merits (exclusive of any collateral matters such as costs and attorney fees) by July 17, 2015, and earlier if reasonably possible.

Though delighted by Judge Smith's plain statement that the plaintiffs had carried the day, Mark was less happy at the way he had framed, perhaps even qualified the decision. In Mark's eyes the phrasing seemed almost to invite lawsuits from the religious right:

> *Obergefell*, in both its Fourteenth and First Amendment iterations, is the law of the land and, consequently, the law of this circuit and should not be taken lightly by actors within the jurisdiction of this court. We express no view on how controversies involving the intersection of these rights should be resolved but instead leave that to the robust operation of our system of laws and the good faith of those who are impacted by them.[69]

"There was no reason beyond Judge Smith's conservative leanings," Mark maintained, "for him to introduce the possibility of First Amendment challenges to LGBT rights. Like Ken Paxton in Texas, he's reaching out to encourage conservatives to stir up what trouble they can."[70]

Vic was no less impatient with the Fifth Circuit's inaction, no less concerned with what seemed like Judge Smith's ham-handed attempt to limit the impact of *Obergefell*. But in writing to friends on Facebook he couched his objections in humor. "The language of Judge Smith's opinion is startlingly reminiscent of Abbott's and Paxton's comments," he observed; "they're not nearly as funny as Abbott and Costello though they are—in my opinion—just as bungling." Mostly, characteristically, he was happy. "The end of the story is that the story has not one, but two happy endings. After a tough day in clinic, I emerge to gasp some air and it is unexpectedly sweet! The opinion from the Fifth Circuit has remanded our case back to Judge Orlando Garcia's court for a decision in favor of the plaintiffs . . . And I get to marry the handsome prince and we will live happily ever after."[71]

Mark took longer to get to the lighter side, but he did get there. Four weeks after marriage equality triumphed in court he was finding "a lot to celebrate." "Vic's and my wedding is less than 4 months away," he wrote on Facebook. "Wow!" Wedding invitations from same-sex couples ready to tie the knot were pouring in. And there is, he noted with his usual wry, tongue-tucked-firmly-in-cheek humor, "other good news as well." Reacting to lists of engagements, weddings, and births in the *Dallas Morning News*, he mocked what had once been the core argument of the forces arrayed against marriage equality: that if same-sex couples were allowed to marry, heterosexual marriage would be so debased that heterosexuals would cease to marry and cease to have children, thereby bringing on the end of civilization as we know it. "Look!" he wrote, "heterosexuals are still getting engaged and married and, I suspect, 9 months from now there will still be babies born. The world has not come to an end. Lots to celebrate."[72]

* * *

Neel Lane didn't have to wait long to make good on his threat to pursue government officials reluctant to recognize that marriage equality had come to Texas. For years Mark and Vic had been acutely sensitive to stories of same-sex couples who had been separated by death, their life together demeaned by Texas's refusal to name the surviving spouse as "husband" or "wife" on a death certificate. It could have happened to them. It did happen to Dan Graney whose partner of thirty-six years, husband of one year, Roberto Flores, died in September 2010. Debating in the summer of 2013 whether to sign on to *DeLeon v. Perry*, Mark and Vic remembered what had happened to Dan and Roberto. That the state had refused to respect their love became one more reason to accept the risks involved in a lawsuit. After the Supreme Court's decision in *Obergefell*, after Judge Orlando Garcia lifted the stay on his order declaring Texas's ban on same-sex marriage unconstitutional, what happened to Dan and Roberto and too many others should have been over. Forever. But it wasn't. Not, at least, according to Kirk Cole, Interim Director of the Texas Department of State Health Services and Attorney General Kenneth Paxton.

John Stone-Hoskins knew on Decision Day that the cancer ravaging his body would end his life in a matter of months. For whatever time remained, he had only one goal: to force the state of Texas to amend his late husband's death certificate. Though married for just under a year when James died in January 2015, the two had been together for a decade— and for much of that time James had been confined to his bed by Sjögren's syndrome. John, the man who loved him, who cared for him year after year, wanted for himself and James, and for thousands of LGBT couples, the dignity of being recognized as spouses. The day after marriage equality came to Texas, John called the Department of State Health Services to ask for an amended certificate. When his request was refused—despite the fact that *Obergefell* was a retroactive recognition case, despite the fact that Judge Garcia's ruling in *DeLeon v. Perry* had struck down Texas's restrictions on same-sex marriage a year and more before the Supreme Court ruled, Attorney General Ken Paxton argued against all logic that the Supreme Court's decision need not be applied retrospectively—John called Akin Gump and asked for Neel Lane.

On August 4 Matt Pepping of Akin Gump advised the plaintiffs in *DeLeon v. Perry* of what was afoot. "Your lawsuit," he began, "will continue to be a vehicle of good."

> We were recently contacted by a terminally ill man, John Stone-Hoskins, to help him have his spouse's death certificate amended. His husband died in January this year, and since the rulings in our case he has been petitioning the state to amend the death certificate to list him as the surviving spouse. The state has refused. Tomorrow we will file a motion to intervene and for contempt against the AG and the Commissioner of the Department of State Health Services. Due to Mr. Stone-Hoskins precarious condition, we will file it as an emergency motion.

Understanding the precarious state of John's health, Judge Garcia granted Akin Gump's motion the day it was filed. Kirk Cole was ordered to "immediately" issue an amended death certificate for James Stone-Hoskins. Ken Paxton and Kirk Cole, having violated Judge Garcia's order resolving *DeLeon v. Perry*, were ordered then to appear in court on August 12 "to determine whether Defendants should be held in contempt for disobedience of this Court's July 7, 2015 order, permanently enjoining Defendants from enforcing any [of] Texas's laws that prohibit or fail to recognize same-sex marriage."[73] Chastened, the Texas Department of State Health Services issued an amended death certificate for James H. Stone-Hoskins the next day, belatedly recognizing that at the time of his death he had been "married," granting John the dignity of "husband."

Two days later, Mark was moved to tears when a touching message popped onto his screen. "This is John (Jay) Stone-Hoskins. Neel is handling my case and I wanted to thank you for being one of the plaintiffs that led to the original case."[74] Neel was in fact still "handling" the state's reluctance to comply fully with Judge Garcia's order, joined now by lawyers from Lambda Legal and a private law firm whose clients' requests for amended death certificates had not yet been honored. Though the State argued that Paxton could not be held in contempt for providing legal advice to a state agency, in a telephone conference on August 10 lawyers for the state capitulated, advising the Court that "in the next couple of days, . . . in conjunction with the State Department of Health Services, [the Attorney General's Office] would issue policy guidance related to the recognition of same-sex marriage in death and birth certificates" and assuring that "the State and its agencies will fully be in compliance with [this Court's] final judgment that was issued on July 7th."[75] To ensure that discrimination against same-sex marriage couples would no longer be possible in Texas, at least with regard to death and birth certificates, Judge Garcia appointed Neel Lane to review whatever the state proposed.

For once the state acted quickly. New guidelines issued on August 13 ordered that in the future:

- Birth certificates would include the names of both parents, regardless of their genders, provided they are married;
- Death certificates would include the name of surviving same-sex spouses;
- Same-sex couples would be allowed to adopt as a couple, provided they are married, and birth certificates for adopted children would include the names of both parents;
- Gestational agreements would be available to all married couples, regardless of the genders of the couple.

John Stone-Hoskins, whose battle with Ken Paxton and Kirk Cole ushered in a new day for gays and lesbians in Texas, lost his battle with cancer on October 10, 2015. Lamenting the loss of a client and a friend, Neel Lane celebrated John's life and legacy. "In his last days," Neel told friends, [John] told me how happy he was that he helped secure relief to thousands of Texas residents who sought amended death certificates that recognized their marriages."

Learning of John Stone-Hoskins' quarrel with Texas, Mark saw immediately where it would end. "Texas will lose this fight," he wrote, "and waste thousands of dollars of taxpayer's money in the process." As the bills for conservative attempts to deny rights to LGBT couples around the nation came due—South Carolina, Pennsylvania, Wisconsin, Virginia, Oregon, Colorado, and North Dakota had already agreed to pay millions in fees—taxpayers in Texas *were* compelled to pay dearly for the state's intransigence. For work in *DeLeon v. Perry* that spread over nearly two years, Akin Gump was awarded more than $605,000 in legal fees and costs—a penalty Texas appealed. For their work defending the constitutional rights of gays and lesbians in Texas, Neel Lane and the legal team supporting him collected accolades as well. In his order setting the amount of the award, Judge Orlando Garcia praised the plaintiffs' attorneys for "excellent and commendable skill in prosecuting the case." At the Spirit of Texas Brunch in June 2014, Equality Texas presented Akin Gump with the Vanguard Award, given annually to "an exemplary business that has demonstrated a commitment to LGBT equality in the state of Texas through fair employee policy and community advocacy." In 2015 *Texas Lawyer* named Neel Lane as a finalist for Texas Attorney of the Year.

* * *

With the manic rush of Decision Day behind them and the loose ends of *DeLeon v. Perry* at last resolved, Mark and Vic looked forward to the familiar rituals of summer they hoped would bring them again to the "100% just-like-everyone-else normal life" they missed so much. But when they arrived at their lake house in Gun Barrel City for the Fourth of July weekend, they discovered that the new normal—good elements of the new normal—had arrived before them. Taped to the front door they found a poster-sized note from their neighbors, Mats and Martha Roos, fashioned by Emma, their daughter. "CONGRATS, newlyweds, Mark and Vic" the sign read in letters that echoed the colors of the rainbow and were surrounded by hearts. The card was signed "with love." Breakfasting the next morning at the Huddle House—where customers had on occasion asked the management not to serve them—they discovered when they asked for the tab that someone had recognized them and paid for their meal.

As the summer progressed, they worked hard to "get away." A family photo from great-nephew Cathan's fifth birthday party in Broken Arrow, Oklahoma, shows Mark smiling a little nervously at the eight-foot python draped across his shoulders—and the moment seems almost a wry comment on his and Vic's life since *DeLeon v. Perry* was filed. The summer unfurled in that newly discovered space between two worlds where public and private, business and pleasure overlap. On a trip to New York, they toured the Metropolitan Museum of Art and the Museum of Modern Art, enjoyed *Beautiful: The Carole King Musical* and *Fun Home*, and "walked on the wild side"— Vic's description of Times Square at night. But the real reason for their visit to New York was to appear as part of Willkie Farr's Diversity Speaker Series, a way of saying thanks to the firm that had briefed their case before the Supreme Court. Wes Powell, a friend at Willkie Farr, would later describe their presentation as the most anticipated and best attended program in years. They enjoyed a dinner with Roberta Kaplan—a chance to reflect on parallel life experiences and all they had shared since oral arguments before the Fifth Circuit Court of Appeals in January 2015—and talked at lunch the next day with Kaplan's associates and law clerks about their case.

As the summer slipped away and the date of their wedding drew closer, Mark and Vic paused on August 9, the anniversary of their first date—for too many years they had feared it would be their only anniversary—to reflect on Facebook on their eighteen years as a couple. "In 3 months I get to marry Vic and call him my husband," Mark wrote, "something I never dreamed possible when we first met. While I will have another anniversary then, August 9, 1997 will always be a day I will cherish and celebrate." He wrote about being nervous on the night of their first date—he was coming out that night to his cousin, Rita Polen and her husband, Jerry; he was to give a speech in front of "the brilliant Elizabeth Birch and the wonderful Betty DeGeneres"—but mostly he wrote of loving Vic, about being "blessed to have Vic in my life, to call him my partner and best friend."[76]

Vic was both funny and touching. "It's hard to believe," he began, "that this is the last time this date will be our anniversary. It's hard to believe I live now in a world in which our next anniversary will be a wedding anniversary. But it is not, nor has it ever been," he added. "hard to believe that I'm sharing this world with the man who has made every day of those eighteen years special." Thinking back to their first date, he too remembered being nervous—though the source of his concern could not have been further from Mark's. Learning that they'd be attending a classy HRC fundraiser at Guillermo Nicolas' showplace home, Vic's concerns were sartorial. "I'm a computer geek," he wrote in his post, "I'm a workaholic. I'm fashion disadvantaged." Happy moving between his Air Force uniform and blue jeans, he had no idea what middle ground was appropriate and Mark's suggestion that he wear khakis was little help. "I had no idea what khakis were back then," Vic continued, enjoying the opportunity to poke fun at his younger self, "and even less idea which belt I needed to match my New Balance 691s." The list of his "faults" went on. "I cry when I see puppies hurt. I don't always think before my heart acts." But Vic's post was really a cry of triumph. "For all of these flaws," he wrote, "I have one single strength that gets me through. I am not alone." Switching audiences, turning from his Facebook friends to address Mark directly, he concluded with the simple truth that had brought him from "Khakis?" to confidence, a declaration of love that in its simple truth reached beyond poetry: "Eighteen years have sped past and you are inextricably, inexplicably, and undeniably a part of me I know I cannot live without. Wherever I am, wherever you are, I will always love you."[77]

With the anniversary of their first date behind them, the wedding that had seemed so impossibly distant when the Supreme Court made same-sex weddings possible was suddenly less than three months away. Hoping that distractions would make the time pass more quickly, Mark and Vic kept busy—not that there was any real chance of doing otherwise. Twice a week there were dance lessons with Arthur Murray—and always, mounting pressure, self-imposed, to "get it right." During Homecoming Weekend at Vanderbilt, Mark's law school, Mark was invited to speak on *DeLeon v. Perry* and the two-year struggle with Texas. His law school classmate and one-time friend, Greg Abbott, was invited to share the program with him. He declined. As attorney general, Abbott had defended Texas's ban on same-sex marriage and, more recently, as governor of Texas he had responded to the *Obergefell* decision by directing state agencies to protect Texans' "religious rights." Still, the governor's refusal to talk saddened Mark. When in July a passenger in an airport waiting room verbally attacked Abbott for his anti-LGBT actions, told him to "Go to Hell," Mark had reacted with his usual good sense. "I'm all for reaching out to Governor Abbott, shaking his hand and telling him why the right to marry was so important to the LGBT community and whey he's wrong on marriage equality," he told friends. "However, we must be respectful in doing so." Mark's hope for a rational—and mutually respectful—exchange of views was displaced one more time by another of the governor's political gestures.[78]

There was a trip to Michigan, in part to visit with Vic's brother and his family, in part to attend the wedding of April DeBoer and Jayne Rowse, two of the *Obergefell* plaintiffs, another to Washington, D. C. to attend the HRC's national dinner where they reveled in Vice-President Joe Biden's declaration. "The shrill voices in the national political arena trying to undo what has been done will not succeed. Don't worry about it," he told the faithful who had gathered to celebrate; "the American people have moved *so* far beyond them and their appeals to prejudice and fear and homophobia." They laughed, let the tensions of the past years slip away, when the Vice-President poked fun at the sometimes frightening leaders of the Republican Party. "Oh, there's homophobes still left!" he quipped; "Most of 'em are running for president, I think." When the Vice-President praised the enormous courage of the men and women who had risked so much to achieve marriage equality—jobs, livelihoods, physical well-being—they thought of Cleo and Nicole who had shared the burden with them in Texas and of the hundreds of other plaintiffs around the country they so much admired.

But what moved Mark and Vic most that evening was Vice-President Biden's story of himself as a teenager and his first encounter with two men in love. Driving into town with his father—on his way to pick up an application for summer work as a lifeguard—a very young Joe Biden looked to his right when the car stopped at a red light. What he saw surprised him. Two men, conservatively dressed, embraced, kissed, and then set off in different directions for a day at work. Confused, he looked back at his father. "I will never forget what my dad said to me," the Vice-President remembered. "He said, 'Joey, they are in love with each other. It's that simple.'"[79] On the huge screens to his left and right, the image of the Vice-President looked out at the crowd as he waited for the applause to die down, a smile on his face. Mark and Vic looked at each other. Some couples in the room had loved each other more than the eighteen years they had spent together, but they were sure none loved more deeply.

Listening to Vice-President Biden, two years to the day from their first attempt to obtain a marriage license, less than two months from the day they would marry, Mark and Vic couldn't help but look back on the road they had traveled. Their love had been "that simple." Their first attempt to obtain a wedding license had, however, been anything but. And yet, as they sat at dinner in Washington, D. C., the coveted license to marry denied on October 3, 2013, had been granted. So much had changed, and with Cleo and Nicole they had been part of the change.

* * *

Time is funny. Or, rather, our experience time is funny. For the flight from Dallas to San Antonio airlines schedule a short seventy minutes; real time in the air is usually less. But the truth is, of course, that "real time" isn't real at all. When important business waits at the end of a trip, life-changing business, each new minute seems longer than the last. Time slows, bends back on itself, like a soft watch in a Dali painting. Rushing through the air at more than 200 miles an hour, Mark and Vic felt nothing so strongly as the relativity of time. Needing to work through the morning, they had booked a mid-afternoon flight to San Antonio. With wheels-down at 3:25 p.m. and an appointment in town just thirty-five minutes later, they had splurged on first-class tickets so there would be no delay getting off the plane and into the airport. Time would, they knew, be tight, but they would make it. Then the bell signaling an announcement rang and the pilot's voice came over the intercom. Thunderstorms ahead, detour to avoid turbulence, possible delay. Sorry.

Already nervous, more than nervous, breathless at the prospect of what lay ahead, Mark and Vic exchanged knowing glances. "Of course there'd be thunderstorms," Mark grumbled, "today of all days, when we have zero time for delays." In the two years since they had been denied a marriage license at the Bexar County Courthouse in San Antonio, the state had placed obstacle after obstacle in their way. Now, September 25, 2015, returning to San Antonio to claim what was rightfully theirs, they knew, as Mark had asserted at a press conference in New Orleans, that they were "on the right side of the law." Earlier he had checked in from the airport with a friend. 'We're getting kind of giddy," he admitted when asked how he felt; "we're less than four hours from getting our license."

"That's how it is," his friend responded. "When you've lived your life believing that certain things are barred to you and, suddenly, the wheel turns, embracing that brave new world takes just a little while."[80] And yet, with every minute now the gap was closing. Compared to the barriers Texas had set in their way, maneuvering around something as natural as a thunderstorm seemed an easy thing.

In the end their flight touched down on time, and when the crew opened the cabin door they were among the first up the gangway. Still, they felt, too many minutes had slipped away; they had scheduled too closely. Determined to get to the courthouse on time, they left their luggage spinning on the carousel, by-passed the booth where they were to pick up a car, and hailed a cab.

In the foyer of the Paul Elizondo tower downtown, County Clerk Gerry Rickhoff, named two years earlier as a defendant in *DeLeon v. Perry*, greeted them with hugs. A longtime supporter of same-sex marriage, he had been "taken aback by the requirement that I violate their civil rights . . . I had to deny them," he asserted, "but that was Texas speaking, not Gerry Rickhoff." For Tea Party types who expected him as a Republican to oppose marriage equality, he had developed a standard response. "I have to explain to them," he says, "that I'm a human being first."[81] "I definitely wanted to be here in support of them today," he told the small crowd that had assembled to support Mark and Vic.

"We wanted to come back to the same clerk's office that turned us down," Mark added for the reporters present. "We knew Gerry was supportive previously and wanted to give him the chance to actually issue the license."[82]

Gerry Rickhoff—in a line-up of country clerks nationwide he'd stand apart as the anti-Kim Davis—had prepared well in advance to welcome Mark and Vic back to his office. A month before the Supreme Court made same-sex marriage legal in Texas, he ordered gender specifications removed from marriage licenses in Bexar County. As decision day approached he put out word to the media that extra judges would be ready—and that his office would stay open "24 hours a day, 7 days a week" if necessary. "That was a fun way," he adds, "to say that I embrace everybody."[83] On Decision Day he joined the plaintiffs in a motion asking Judge Orlando Garcia to lift the stay he issued on February 26, 2014. He also issued an invitation to same-sex couples in counties not yet issuing marriage licenses:

> My message is always, if there's reluctance or hesitation by the clerk, just get in your car and drive down to Bexar County. We're going to embrace you, and we're going to make sure that you're served, and we'll stay open after hours to accomplish that if that's what's required."[84]

Determined to make things right, Rickhoff had looked forward to the day he could issue a license to the men who had started it all in Texas.

Waiting for Mark and Vic inside the office were two old friends ready to celebrate with them—Frank Stenger-Castro, the Akin Gump attorney who had accompanied Mark and Vic to the County Clerk's office two years earlier, and Charlie Gonzalez, a friend who had served Texas for fourteen years in the U. S. House of Representatives. This time Mark didn't have to explain why he and Vic were there. This time, like the heterosexual couples surrounding them, he and Vic sat with a clerk who walked them through the application for a marriage license. Leaning forward eagerly, they answered her questions, one by one. No one could stop smiling. Not Mark. Not Vic. Not Sylvia Lopez, the clerk. At her direction Mark and Vic raised their right hands and swore that the information they had given was correct. Standing inches behind them, Gerry Rickhoff had their backs, literally and symbolically. When Ms. Lopez placed an official seal on the license, a circle of silver with two red ribbons descending, Vic, overcome with emotion, reached for Mark's hand.

"This was something I never thought I was going to see," he said. "Ever. This has really helped me to have a lot more hope."

"Now I get to put a ring on his finger and start calling him spouse, husband," Mark added. "That means so much to me."[85] Holding the license by their fingertips only, almost as if were a sacred object they hardly dared touch, they held their newly issued license aloft and smiled into the cameras.

Relieved that a wrong done on behalf of the state had been righted at last, that events in his office had come full-circle, Gerry Rickhoff was delighted. "I'm just thrilled that same-sex marriage is now the law of the land," he said, "glad to be on the right side of history."[86] When the next day Mark posted to Facebook a picture of himself and Vic, their hands raised, broad smiles on their faces, a very happy county clerk hovering over them, he couldn't resist poking a bit of fun at a county clerk in Kentucky who had *not* come down on the right side of history: "Sorry, Kim Davis!" he wrote. But he wasn't sorry. Not at all.

After handshakes and high-fives and hugs, many who had come to bear witness followed Mark and Vic to the eighth floor where former State Senator José Menendez and his wife, Cehlia, were ready with more hugs. "This is the culmination of a very long relationship—they've had a long road," he told the press. "Finally, Mark and Vic have a committed relationship recognized by society."[87]

Michelle Casady, who covered the afternoon's events for the *San Antonio Express*, wrote the perfect lead: "Before they were catapulted onto the national stage as plaintiffs in a marriage equality suit against the state of Texas, and before they were denied a marriage license in Bexar County two years ago, the love story of Mark Phariss and Vic Holmes began right here in San Antonio 18 years ago."[88] With the return to San Antonio, their story had come full circle. Like the figures from literature and film, they had gone in search of new worlds and come home with the golden fleece. Full circle. Even to the point that they would spend their San Antonio night at the home of Keith Stanford and Chris Hammet at whose house they met in the spring of 1997.

The rest of the weekend would, they feared, go by like a whirlwind leaving little or no time to reflect on the journey of the past two years. And it did. License in hand, Mark and Vic rushed back to the airport to retrieve their abandoned luggage and wait in line to pick up their rental car. A quick stop to change and then off to celebrate the wedding of two close friends, Marci Marmor and Sherrill Oldham, together for thirty-five years and finally able to marry. On Saturday, a shower in their honor given by Merritt and Karen Clements and David and Mary Belan Doggett that would reunite them with friends from their days in San Antonio—quiet music from a guitarist playing in the background, Mexican food, mimosas, and laughter. Finally, a quick drive to Austin where 300 people waited to honor the four plaintiffs in *DeLeon v. Perry* at The Real M Word: A Celebration of Marriage Equality.

That night in Austin, rising to give thanks, Mark sounded one more time the same notes he had struck at every opportunity in the two-year fight for marriage equality he and Vic, Cleo and Nicole, had waged in Texas:

- We all—gay and straight alike—come from the same common stardust and will return to that same dust,
- We all—gay and straight alike—share common DNA,
- Our differences are less significant—far less significant—than our commonalities, and
- We all want to love and to be loved.

And as ever, the note that rang most clear and true—the note that prompted a standing ovation from the 600 who had come to celebrate—spread credit for the victory to the entire community:

> Our battle for marriage equality—and by that I mean the LGBT community's nationwide battle—was not won by fantastic lawyers and great legal arguments (though the lawyers *were* fantastic, their arguments formidable, and their sacrifices immense). It was won because our community—in this room and around the country—reminded others, and sometimes ourselves, of our common humanity.

All that remained, or so they thought, was to get married. And plans for that were far along.

Chapter 8

Backlash in Texas

The arts of power and its minions are the same in all countries and in all ages. It marks a victim; denounces it; and excites the public odium and the public hatred, to conceal its own abuses and encroachments.
—Henry Clay, Speaking in the Senate, March 14, 1834

At the White House Pride Reception in June 2016, not quite a year after the monumental Supreme Court decision that made marriage equality the law of the land, President Obama paused to look back—and ahead. He thanked the activists and the organizers, the lawyers and the families who had accepted LGBT members. When at the end of the list, the place of honor, he concluded with thanks to "Every brave American who came out and spoke out, especially when it was tough," Mark and Vic felt a little tinge of pride. The president celebrated the generation coming of age to which his daughters, Malia and Sasha, belonged. We live now, he enthused, "in an America where the laws are finally catching up to the hearts of kids and what they instinctively understand." There is, he acknowledged, work to be done; he reminded his audience of Bayard Rustin, the civil rights leader who proclaimed that "We need in every community a group of angelic troublemakers." Taking his appreciative audience back to the day of the *Obergefell* decision, he shared a treasured memory:

> One of the most special moments of my presidency was that warm summer night last June when we lit up the White House out there. It was a powerful symbol here at home, where more Americans finally felt accepted and whole, and that their country recognized the love that they felt. It was a beacon for people around the world who are still fighting for those rights. It was a reminder that when the change we seek comes, and when we move a little bit further on our journey toward equality and justice, we still have a responsibility to reach back and help pull up others who are striving to do the same.

But in the midst of the celebration, the president sounded as well a note of warning. Change is possible, progress is possible, he said. "It's not inevitable, though. History doesn't just travel forward; it can go backwards if we don't work hard."[1]

Not everyone shared President Barack Obama's warm memories of the night the White House was bathed in the colors of the rainbow flag. Not everyone was as ready as the president to celebrate the work of "angelic troublemakers." In the days immediately after the decision, too many government officials were determined to make good on President Obama's warning and to shift the machinery of state—and history—into reverse. Justice Kennedy had no sooner finished reading key passages from his decision than Governor Greg Abbott, faced with yet another decision from the nation's high court that extended individual rights where Texas had denied them, launched a counterstrike long on rhetoric, short on legal reasoning. "The Supreme Court has abandoned its role as an impartial judicial arbiter," he blustered, "and has become an unelected nine-member legislature. Five Justices on the Supreme Court have imposed on the entire society their personal views on an issue that the Constitution and the Court's previous decisions reserve to the people of the United States." Texans whose conscience dictated "that marriage is only the union of one man and one women" would, he asserted, be protected by the constitutional guarantee of religious liberty.[2]

In a directive to the heads of all state agencies, Governor Abbott wrapped himself piously in the robes of the founders "who sought a place to worship God according to the dictates of conscience and free from government coercion." Relying ironically on the kind of "legalistic argle-bargle" Justice Scalia condemned in his dissent to the *Windsor* decision, he referenced the First Amendment, Article I of the Texas Constitution, and chapter 110 of the Texas Civil Practice and Remedies Code (the Texas Religious Freedom Restoration Act) in a high-sounding attempt to mask the fact that he was encouraging lawlessness in Texas. "As government officials," he concluded, "we have a constitutional duty to preserve, protect, and defend the religious liberty of every Texan . . . I expect all agencies under my direction to prioritize compliance with the First Amendment to the United States Constitution."[3]

Realizing that the Supreme Court was poised to strike down marriage bans remaining in Texas and a handful of other states, Lieutenant Governor Dan Patrick had launched a pre-emptive strike the day before the decision was announced. "County clerks and Justices of the Peace," he lamented, "could be forced to subjugate their sincerely held religious beliefs" if the Court ruled in favor of same-sex marriage; expecting the Court would do just that, he had asked Attorney General Paxton "to provide guidance to county clerks and Justices of the Peace who face this conflict of conscience."[4] In a press release after the decision was distributed, the Lieutenant Governor blasted the Supreme Court's decision as "unconstitutional" and warned that it "threatens to undermine the First Amendment protections from the government interfering with the free exercise of religion." To preclude that, he had asked the Attorney General to expand the scope of the recently passed SB 2065 Pastor Protection Act "to include County Clerks, Judges, and Justices of the Peace who may be forced to issue a marriage license or preside over a wedding that is against the free exercise of their religion."[5]

In May 2015 Attorney General Kenneth Paxton was still settling into his new job when Alysin Camerota of CNN asked him in a live interview how Texas would respond to a Supreme Court ruling legalizing same-sex marriage: "Texas would have to conform to the federal law, yes?"

His response left little doubt that Texas would in fact do all it could to defy the federal government. Demonstrating his loyalty to the Tea Party conservatives who elected him, Paxton answered first with a burst of "word salad" gibberish that left Camerota looking puzzled. When she asked again, he fell silent. Her third try to elicit a comprehensible response—"Meaning Texas would have to conform to the Supreme Court?"—pushed Paxton into another "bob and weave" non-statement. "We would have to see how it worked," he told her; "we would have to see how that opinion is written, versus how this law is passed."[6]

Given Paxton's well-known loyalties, Mark and Vic were not surprised when his posturing regarding the *Obergefell* opinion exceeded that even of the governor and lieutenant governor. The tone of his press release was aggressive and his criticism of the Court unrestrained:

> Friday, the United States Supreme Court again ignored the text and spirit of the Constitution to manufacture a right that simply does not exist. In so doing, the Court weakened itself and weakened the rule of law, but did nothing to weaken our resolve to protect religious liberty and to return to democratic self-government in the face of judicial activists attempting to tell us how to live."

Faced with what he called "a lawless decision by an activist Court," Paxton clung to a legal technicality. "There is not," he opined, "a court order in place in Texas to issue any particular license whatsoever—only the flawed direction by the U. S. Supreme Court on Constitutionality and applicable state laws." But for all the bravado, he protected himself by warning state officials that defying the Supreme Court would almost certainly lead to trouble. "It is important to note," he admitted, "that any clerk who wishes to defend their religious objections and who chooses not to issue licenses may well face litigation and/or a fine."[7] Opinion No. KP-0025, sent to the Lieutenant Governor the same day, was in reality no less tentative:

> County clerks and their employees retain religious freedoms that *may* allow accommodation of their religious objections to issuing same-sex

marriage licenses. The strength of any such claim depends on the particular facts of each case. (emphasis added)

And once again, he included the cautionary admission: "It is conceivable that an applicant for a same-sex marriage license may claim a violation of the constitution."[8]

Though in setting the date of their wedding Mark and Vic had worried that Texas would do what it could to resist the Supreme Court, watching the story unfold was nonetheless painful. "What strikes me most," Mark wrote, "is less what the comments [of Governor Abbott and Attorney General Paxton] say than what the comments do not say":

- There's an absolute lack of any mention of, or concern for, the constitutional rights and religious liberties of LGBT Texans.
- There's a lot of concern for and discussion about the constitutional rights and religious liberties of those who oppose marriage equality (important interests, no doubt), but not one word—literally, not one word—about the rights of those who support it.
- It is as if LGBT Texans do not exist. It's as if, in their minds, LGBT Texans are not Texans. It is as if they were not elected to be, and are not, the Governor and Attorney General for all Texans.[9]

Nor were Mark and Vic the only ones concerned with the follies of irascible government officials in Texas. Evan Wolfson of Freedom to Marry was equally troubled. "We've won the freedom to marry," he noted days after the Supreme Court delivered on the dream that had been his life's work; "But now we want to take that conversation to places where it's only just beginning, like Texas and Alabama."[10] Sarah Warbelow, Legal Director of the Human Rights Campaign, wrote directly to Governor Abbott.

We urge you to take immediate action to ensure that Judges or Justices of the Peace begin issuing marriage licenses to all eligible Texas couples immediately. We also urge you to take affirmative steps to communicate the meaning and reach of this case to all government officials tasked with performing and recognizing marriages, including those performed outside of the state of Texas.[11]

Chad Griffin, President of the Human Rights Campaign, flew to Texas to lead a rally at the statehouse in Austin.

* * *

Conservative elements in Texas had not, of course, waited for the Supreme Court to legalize same-sex marriage before striking out at the LGBT community. More afraid with each passing day that they had lost control of the narrative, that the polls had turned against them and that the Court would add its voice against them before the end of the current term, opponents of marriage equality in conservative bastions across the country began with the new year to look desperately for ways, however hateful, to stave off the inevitable. Determined not to be outdone by anti-gay forces in Oklahoma, Alabama, Arkansas, and Indiana—that the dome of the Texas State Capitol rises eight feet higher than the dome of the U. S. Capitol in Washington, D. C. is no accident—members of the 84th Legislature submitted a record number of anti-LGBT bills. Of the twenty-three such bills introduced before the March 13 filing deadline, twenty were framed intentionally as attacks on the LGBT community, three would have brought unintended negative consequences.

Granted, change was in the air. With Judge Garcia's decision in February 2014, same-sex marriage had been declared legal in Texas; had he not stayed his decision same-sex marriages would have been taking place before the 84th Legislature opened for business. But the change Mark and Vic so welcomed was, they realized, by some strange paradox the root of a new problem. As marriage equality arrived in more and more states, as even the most dyed-in-the-wool conservatives realized that the Supreme Court was likely to rule in favor of marriage equality, many in the Texas legislature found themselves uncomfortably at sea—and committed to fighting a rearguard action. "I think the opponents of equality are seeing the world wake up to the reality of the discrimination faced by the LGBT community," Daniel Williams, a legislative specialist with Equality Texas suggested. They "are increasingly finding themselves on the wrong side of history, and that's a very uncomfortable place to be."[12]

Asked specifically about Cecil Bell, an anti-LGBT firebrand who authored no fewer than four discriminatory bills, more than any other legislator, Williams spoke almost kindly. "Cecil is genuinely pursuing what he perceives as a threat to his well-being and the well-being of his constituents," he said. "He's not crazy and he's not a frothing at the mouth bigot. He's just frightened by a world that is far broader and more diverse than anything his life has prepared him for."[13] Whatever the reasons, the pace at which anti-LGBT legislation was introduced into the Texas legislature increased with each passing month—more bills in January 2015 than in all of 2014, more in February than in January, more in March than in February—until legislators had marched down every possible avenue.

With so many determined to grab a share of the anti-gay spotlight by locking in discrimination for as long as possible, bills with similar goals were often stacked two, three, and even four deep. Among the measures proposed:

- Bills attempting to prevent same-sex couples from marrying by: 1) revoking the salaries and benefits of government employees who issue marriage licenses to same-sex couples or recognize their marriages, 2) preventing "rogue" county clerks from issuing marriage licenses to same-sex couples by taking the power to issue licenses from them and placing it with the Secretary of State who would authorize local authorities to issue marriage licenses only as long as they complied with his or her reading of the law, 3) defying a likely Supreme Court decision in favor of same-sex marriage by declaring that the Supremacy Clause of the Constitution does not apply in Texas, 4) refusing to fund government offices that might be required by court order to issue marriage licenses to same-sex couples;
- "Religious Freedom" bills that: 1) allow individuals and businesses to refuse goods and services to Texans, including LGBT Texans, where doing so would violate their religious beliefs and, 2) allow an employee disciplined for creating a work environment hostile to LGBT people or discriminating against LGBT customers to sue his or her employer, 3) allow faith-based welfare organizations to refuse services to LGBT people;
- Bills prohibiting municipalities from passing or enforcing local anti-discrimination ordinances to protect LGBT people from discrimination in employment, housing, and services;

- So-called "Bathroom Surveillance Bills" that: 1) criminalize transgender Texans by making it illegal for them to use facilities appropriate to their gender identity or expression, 2) make it a felony for business owners to allow transgender people to use appropriate bath and locker rooms, 3) promote harassment and bullying by creating a reward of up to $2,000 for students who report transgender students using the "wrong" bath or locker rooms;
- A bill that strips same-gender spouses of pension plan benefits guaranteed under the Employee Retirement Income Security Act (ERISA).

In the practiced eye of Daniel Williams, not since 2005 when the state's marriage amendment passed and a proposal to prevent LGBT people from serving as foster parents was narrowly defeated on the House floor had gay rights been so often and so seriously attacked in Texas.

As the battle to pass anti-LGBT legislation began, Sara Warbelow, legal director of the HRC, predicted that most bills would fail. "There is not an appetite among moderate Republicans," she suggested with just a touch of irony, "to pass bills that are so blatantly unconstitutional."[14] But fringe elements in the Texas legislature, egged on by Governor Greg Abbott, Lt. Governor Daniel Patrick, Attorney General Kenneth Paxton, and Cecil Bell and Molly White in the House of Representatives, Tea Baggers all, were not about to let political realities interfere with their need to provide fuel for the fires that would bring the deeply held biases of their core voters to the boiling point.

Two days after the Supreme Court heard arguments in *Obergefell v. Hodges*, Governor Greg Abbott issued a call to action, doubling down on the states' rights argument and willfully ignoring the historical role of the federal courts in adjudicating disputes. "Texans voted overwhelmingly to define marriage in this State as the union of one man and one woman," he proclaimed in a press release. "As Texas' attorney general, I defended the definition of marriage in the Texas Constitution against court challenges and I commend Attorney General Paxton for continuing that work. Texans—not unelected federal judges—should decide this important question for their State."[15] Mark and Vic were furious when, as HB 4105 came to the floor, perhaps the most dangerous of Cecil Bell's four bills, Governor Abbott made a rare appearance on the floor of the House, many feared to lobby for its passage. The fight was getting personal, frighteningly personal. "This bill," Mark wrote in an angry Facebook post, "is blatantly unconstitutional . . . if passed and signed, it will force more litigation, cost the state more legal fees . . . and may delay Vic's and my wedding."[16]

Cecil Bell hinted strongly at the possibility of outright defiance. "The sovereignty of the states is not something to be taken lightly," he intoned; "the leap to assume that Texas moves with [a Supreme Court ruling] is just that—a leap. History is replete with cases where Supreme Court precedent isn't immediately embraced and in some cases isn't ever embraced."[17] Jonathan Saenz, the outspoken president of Texas Values, infamous in the LGBT community for his use of language that is both hurtful and inflammatory, threatened dire consequences for state employees tempted to comply with a favorable ruling from the Court. "If you're a government actor or an official of the state," he warned, "you should exercise extreme caution before making a decision based on a U. S. Supreme Court decision."[18] Hubris, it would seem, is never in short supply in Texas where, for some at least, arrogance is a way of life.

A practicing attorney for thirty years, accustomed to working with legal realities that will stand up in court, Mark could hardly believe what he was hearing from Texas's power elite. "I am amazed that there are officeholders and others in Texas (and elsewhere)," he wrote on Facebook, "who really believe that if the Supreme Court rules in favor of same-sex marriages in the KY, OH, TN, and MI cases SCOTUS heard just yesterday, the decision isn't binding upon Texas. For those who supposedly love the Constitution, there is a little thing called the Supremacy Clause." Usually tactful, inclined to treat opposing voices kindly in the hope that today's opposition will become tomorrow's ally, he gave voice at last to his frustration with politicians more interested in rhetoric than reality. "I really don't know how to get my head around such stupidity at high levels. The earth is not flat. The sun does not revolve around the earth. There are billions of galaxies. And Texas is not at the center of any of them."[19]

Steve Rudner of Equality Texas—another attorney accustomed to working with legal realities—was equally appalled. And equally blunt. "Here in Texas our biggest enemy is willful ignorance . . . a State Rep says that history is replete with cases where Supreme Court precedent isn't immediately embraced and in some cases isn't ever embraced. He isn't talking about public opinion. He is talking about the legislature refusing to follow a Supreme Court ruling." Turning to Jonathan Saenz's ruthless threat against state employees willing to follow the law, Rudner ratcheted up his own response. "The head of Texas Values," he wrote, "takes stupidity to another level, arguing that because the Supreme Court case involved the 7th Circuit, their decision doesn't have to be followed here in Texas. Will the grown-up Texas Republicans who went to law school please reach out to your leadership and explain to them how our federal court system works? Because we will look awfully stupid if the President has to send in the National Guard to enforce the Court's decision."[20]

For months Mark and Vic watched in pain and anger as supporters of anti-gay legislation shamelessly manipulated public hearings to trot out one more time the same offensive scare stories and emotional rhetoric Anita Bryant had relied on to inflame conservatives in the 1970s: homosexuals are pedophiles; same-sex marriage is bestiality; ministers will be forced to conduct polygamous marriages. But in the end Sara Warbelow's prediction proved correct. Thanks to the combined efforts of Equality Texas and allied organizations—the Human Rights Campaign, the Texas Association of Business, the ACLU, and the Texas Freedom Network—of the twenty-three anti-LGBT bills introduced during the 84th Legislature, only one was passed and signed into law. HB 3567, the so-called Pastor's Protection Act, emerged in a much-amended, toned-down version that neither Equality Texas nor the Human Rights Campaign opposed because it did no more than to enumerate in statute the already existing rights of religious institutions to set their own standards for which marriages they will recognize.

The best reactionaries in the Texas legislature could manage was a condemnatory letter from House Republicans and a parallel resolution by Senate Republicans. Though full of high-sounding language "solemnly proclaim[ing] that the institution of marriage is clearly established in Article 1

Section 32 of the Texas Constitution as a union consisting of one man and one woman," neither had any legal force. Few were fooled, especially Steve Hotze who busies himself as president of the Conservative Republicans of Texas when not practicing alternative medicine or hawking his own line of vitamins. Senate Resolution 1028, he grumbled, has "no significance and no effect—it carries exactly the same weight as Senate Resolution 997, recognizing March 26, 2015 as John Wayne Day."

Through the winter and spring Mark and Vic suffered as bigots in the legislature did all they could to demean and to undermine the rights of the LGBT community; in the first part of the summer, Greg Abbott, Dan Patrick, and Ken Paxton had enthusiastically picked up where the legislators had left off and prolonged their pain. But as summer gave way to fall, Mark and Vic found themselves more and more able to stand apart from the fray, more and more content with what they had done and all that had happened.

On the twenty-first of November 2015 they would stand together, husband and husband for the first time.

Chapter 9

Married at Last, Deep in the Heart of Texas

I believe all Americans, no matter their race, no matter their sex, no matter their sexual orientation, should have that same freedom to marry . . . I am not a political person, but I am proud that Richard's and my name is on a court case that can help reinforce the love, the commitment, the fairness and the family that so many people, black or white, young or old, gay or straight, seek in life. I support the freedom to marry for all. That's what *Loving*, and loving, are all about.

—Mildred Loving reflecting on *Loving v. Virginia*

Writing in early June 2015, three weeks and more before the Supreme Court announced its decision in *Obergefell v. Hodges*, Professor Audrey Remley, a friend Mark had made in his undergraduate years at Westminster College, wondered about the Save-the-Date card that had appeared in her mailbox. "Are you that confident that the law will change," she asked, "or are you just saying 'the hell with it, this is what we want to do?'"[1] He and Vic *were* sure, had been 90 percent sure since October 2014 when the Supreme Court refused to hear appeals in same-sex marriage cases from the Fourth, Seventh, and Tenth Circuits. They looked that fall at one venue for their wedding, but abruptly put on the brakes. Same-sex marriage *would* become legal, but until the Supreme Court accepted a case one all-important question remained: When? Choosing a venue, setting an exact date seemed too "iffy."

In early January oral arguments in same-sex marriage cases from Louisiana, Mississippi, and Texas before the Fifth Circuit Court of Appeals went well, whetting their appetites once again. With the smell of victory in the air, Mark and Vic found their patience dwindling. Eight days later, January 16, 2015, the Supreme Court granted *cert* in *Obergefell v. Hodges*. Though the date for oral arguments would not be set until the end of February, "iffy" had given somehow way at last to "almost certain." Preparations began in earnest.

As Mark and Vic first sat down to talk seriously about their wedding, they knew—or quickly discovered— three things they wanted. The first was that neither had any desire to marry the moment the question was settled. "Let's do it the way we want to do it," Vic said, "not just because we can."[2] They knew they wanted an outdoor wedding after the heat of the Dallas summer had passed—September, October, perhaps even November—time enough to plan carefully. When you wait eighteen years to marry, you want to be more than usually sure that you've gotten everything right. The second of their three "wants" came home to Mark one afternoon as he sat talking with Ron Chapman, an attorney and an old friend. Discouraged that the Fifth Circuit had failed to rule quickly on *DeLeon v. Perry*, Mark and Vic worried in their darker moments that they had not done enough to bring marriage equality to Texas. When Mark revealed his fears over lunch, his old friend scattered the clouds.

"Nothing?' Ron said, surprised at Mark's self-reproach. Like many another, he was amazed at what Mark and Vic, Nicole and Cleo had achieved in their two years' struggle. They had spread the banner of same-sex marriage and rallied the community in Texas to the cause. Faced with criticism, even with occasional hatred, they had reacted publicly with moderation, even with good humor. "It's been so classy," Ron told him. "So classy. You and Vic have been good emissaries for the cause." Reassured, Mark and Vic resolved that Ron Chapman's "classy" would become the keynote for their wedding, the guiding principle that would shape their decisions. Finally, they were determined to include in their wedding all the rituals that have marked weddings since time immemorial, determined to show the world that their love was like any other, to hasten the day when no one would feel the need to distinguish between "marriage" and "same-sex marriage."

Not surprisingly, their first struggle was with the guest list. They knew the statistical averages—that most couples invite about 180 people, that just under 140 of those invited attend. But they knew as well that beyond the friends they had shared for years each was part of a wider circle, and that in addition to old friends many of the people who had offered help and support were hoping, even expecting to be invited. Their wedding, they realized quickly, would have to be a bit larger, perhaps as many as 250 invitations with 200 acceptances. And then, reality set in. The guest list grew by leaps, and then it grew by bounds—and the number invited grew to 415. In the end, on November 21, 325 people would gather around them as they pledged their lives to one another—and settled in for a Texas-sized celebration.

Anyone who has planned a wedding knows how many decisions are involved, how easy it is to sink under the weight of choices. For Mark and Vic, perhaps because it seemed at first an easier decision than so many of the others, finding the perfect spot for a honeymoon rose quickly to the top of the list. That and finding the perfect place for the ceremony and the reception.

Hearing that a wedding was in the works, Bob Craycraft, the CEO of Safety-Kleen, once Mark's boss, now a friend, sent a note of congratulations. "It has been a long time coming," he wrote—and remembering the couple's penchant for travel, he asked about the honeymoon. "Knowing you," Bob quipped, "it's probably some wild National Geographic trip, a dense rain forest or something."[3] He knew his man. On January 16, 2015, the day the Supreme Court agreed to hear *Obergefell*, Mark sent Vic a "short list" of possible National Geographic expeditions: a tour of Nepal, a wildlife safari in India, another that would take them to the slopes of Mt. Kilimanjaro in Tanzania, a trip to the Falklands and Antarctica, a private expedition to Patagonia.

For two weeks the discussion swung this way and that. What ultimately determined their choice was the desire to photograph mountain gorillas.

But when gay men travel together in Africa, things can get complicated quickly, even dangerous. Homosexuality is illegal in Uganda, punishable by up to fourteen years in jail. Even getting to East Africa could be dangerous. Most flights from the United States go through Qatar, another state that criminalizes homosexuality. When at the beginning of April they put down a deposit on the honeymoon, they were booked with National Geographic for Tanzania and, perhaps, Rwanda as well. What they didn't know was that in the end, after still more complications, they'd exchange the rain forests of Africa for the rain forests of Costa Rica. Adventure with a touch of luxury: transfers via white-water raft to the Pacure Lodge in Arenal National Park, trekking in the Chato Hill rainforest, zip-lining through the forest canopy, waterfall hikes, hanging bridge tours— sites and occasions for a thousand photographs and memories.

Putting one decision behind them, however, served only to make clear how much remained to be done. By the middle of February both men felt overwhelmed by the number and difficulty of the tasks before them—and they were worried as well. Stories of vendors refusing to work with same-sex couples—bakeries, and florists, even the occasional pizza parlor—had become a media staple. With every visit they feared that, sooner or later, they would be turned away. But as Mark revealed in a Facebook post, he and Vic experienced nothing of the sort:

> Over the last six months, Vic and I have spoken with numerous wedding photographers, cake bakers, florists, venue operators, bands, ring makers, etc. In each instance we pretty quickly told them we were a same-sex couple and that we wouldn't say a word if that was an issue for them.
>
> I am pleased to report that, so far, not one person or company we've spoken with said it would be an issue. Several didn't know that same-sex marriages weren't yet legal in Texas, and several apologized for the fact that we felt we had to ask.[4]

Two decades earlier, searching for bands to perform at Human Rights Campaign events in San Antonio, Mark had too often felt the sting of rejection. Realizing that attitudes had changed, even among conservatives in Texas, reassured both men.

As the time to commit to a space for the ceremony and reception drew near, the Dallas Museum of Art rose to become the odds-on favorite. Conscious that a gay wedding might draw unwanted attention, especially the wedding of the men who had sued Texas to make same-sex marriage possible, Mark and Vic were concerned about privacy, even security. The idea of enclosed spaces to which access could easily be controlled—the Sculpture Garden for the wedding and cocktails, the Hamon Atrium for the reception—seemed a good idea. But on the date of the wedding, November 21, parts of the Dallas Museum of Art would be under construction, and as the number of guests rose steadily it became apparent that the seating capacity of the Sculpture Garden would be stretched beyond any reasonable limit.

They turned to the Westin Stonebriar where Shannon Walker, the wedding specialist, was more than usually accommodating. Realizing Mark and Vic were concerned about disruptions and uncomfortable with the openness of the hotel, she agreed to take special measures to ensure that the deluxe rooms overlooking the terrace where the wedding would take place would be reserved for wedding guests at no extra charge, to hire a security guard who would control access to the rooms set aside for the cocktail hour and the reception. She made it clear as well that the hotel would take special care with aesthetics: a floral arch to frame the wedding party on the terrace, enhanced decorations for the buffet tables. "We know this is going to be a high profile, highly publicized event," she said; "the Westin Stonebriar prides itself on customer satisfaction and we want to make sure the experience we provide is 'above and beyond.'"[5]

Walker wasn't alone in realizing that Mark and Vic's wedding would be a high profile event. Learning that the men were considering another venue, Olga King, a special events manager at the Dallas Museum of Art, urged them to reconsider. The day they married would, of course, be a high point in their "personal history," but she recognized that much more was involved. "The history of the Texas legislature and the Texas community," she wrote, "will be affected by your event in an unprecedented manner. Appreciating your work and all efforts on this very important matter, I'd love to see if we can have the honor of providing a venue for it."[6] Mark and Vic were touched by the acknowledgment of what they had done, but the ever-increasing number of guests they were expecting made the change impossible.

For ten months, mid-January to mid-November, they rode the whirlwind of wedding preparations. Tuesday and Thursday evenings they set aside for lessons at the Arthur Murray Studio in Plano—a hundred hours of lessons— prepping for what they knew would be a closely watched first dance. Like any other couple, they settled on the wording and style for save-the-date cards, invitations, and programs, chose "just right" photographs, and checked for errors on what seemed an endless succession of proofs. They found Joe Pacetti, a jeweler whose craftsmanship they admired, and set him to work incorporating two diamonds from a ring Mark inherited from his father—he had saved them for twenty-nine years after his father's death, hoping someday he would be able to marry—into simple but elegant wedding rings.

In July a friend sent a flag, obtained with the help of Senator Harry Reid's office, that had flown over the nation's Capitol the day the Supreme Court heard oral arguments in *Obergefell*. The men quickly arranged with Senator Reid for a second flag, one that would fly over the Capitol building the day the Supreme Court announced its decision, intending to use the pair as pillows the ring bearer would use to carry their rings down the aisle on the day they married. About the same time, Mark found himself joking with a friend. "The wedding," he laughed, "is getting totally out of hand!"—in part a reference to the steady and never-ending stream of things to be done, in part a reference to mounting costs, the belated discovery that putting the word "wedding" in front of any goods, any services, doubles or triples the price.[7]

By some miracle of perseverance, every detail was eventually wrestled into submission. Everything got done. Save-the date cards went out on May 26, a month before the Supreme Court ruled on *Obergefell v. Hodges*. Wedding invitations were sent on August 10, invitations to the rehearsal dinner two weeks later. All three were mailed with "forever" stamps—in the foreground an American flag waving in the breeze, in the background bursts of fireworks, fitting symbols of how deeply in love these old friends and soon-to-be newlyweds had fallen and the triumph of American values that had allowed them at last to marry. No detail signaling that to the world seemed too small to deserve attention. For their wedding, eighteen years in the making, Mark and Vic were determined not to miss a beat.

Guests arriving at the Westin Stonebriar, friends and family who had looked forward for months, even years to celebrating with Mark and Vic, were presented at check-in with a bottle of champagne from the award-winning Windsor Vineyards in Sonoma County, a *Blanc de Blanc* from the winery's Platinum Series. A perfect way to get the party started and a harbinger of good things to come. Marking each bottle, a specially printed commemorative label:

Mark and Vic

Thank you for coming to our wedding

Love Won!

11.21.2015

Tucked into the bottom of the gift bag was a package of Texas Trail Mix, it too labeled for the occasion: "Mark + Vic = 1 on 11/21." Riding the elevators to their rooms, everyone smiled.

* * *

Shadows on the golf course just beyond the French doors had stretched to their limits and begun to fade when the wedding party gathered in the lounge just off the main lobby, ready for the rehearsal and the rehearsal dinner, ready to get the celebration started. A function, perhaps, of Mark and Vic's many years accumulating friends, the wedding party was large: twenty people. Drawn from the various stages of the men's lives—mutual friends from their early days in San Antonio and their years in Plano, friends Vic made in the Air Force and at his current job at the University of North Texas, Mark's friends from his undergraduate years at Westminster College and law school at Vanderbilt University, relatives of both men, young and old, many of those gathered had never before met. Arriving for the rehearsal, most stepped first to the huge French doors for a peek at the Terrace Garden where the ceremony would take place and then joined a conversational group. Smiles and handshakes and the low murmur of conversation went around the room.

Spirits were running high, and there was just a moment's hesitation when Charlie Gonzalez, a former judge and congressman, now a good friend who had agreed to perform the ceremony, and Rachel Burt, the wedding coordinator, first sought to move the group through the half-light and into the tent set up to shelter guests. Lisa Krantz, the photographer from the *San Antonio*

News Express who had followed Mark and Vic's story since they filed suit against Texas in the fall of 2013, looked on as Charlie walked his jubilant group through the ceremony.

Twilight had given way to darkness by the time the rehearsal was over. Guided by the glow of underwater lights from the nearby pool, guests made their way to the Restaurant Terrace just a few steps away for the rehearsal dinner. Warmed literally by propane heaters, warmed in spirit by gaslight that flickered from antiqued, wrought-iron lanterns and danced across the light sandstone pillars and walls, they found their seats and settled in. Their glasses filled, they bowed their heads as the Rev. Arthur Murphy, a friend Mark met in law school who had switched professions, offered a prayer, as Mark and Vic offered thanks for the ties of family and friendship that had brought everyone together for a bit of magic. Two years of struggle, two years of being whirled about by the legal system, every move, every thought exposed to the public eye, had brought them at last to this comfortable moment.

Invitations to the rehearsal dinner had included a second invitation: "Let's Get to Know Each Other!" a small insert suggested. Understanding that we are bound together by stories of shared experiences, Mark and Vic encouraged an evening of story-telling. "Your story," the card read, "can be light-hearted, touching, funny, or serious. It can be about how you met Vic and/or Mark, what you have done with them, or what connects you with them." The only limits: "Keep it short, and keep it clean!" Almost thirty people rose to the challenge with stories celebrating love and family and friendship, the courage Mark and Vic had shown in squaring off against the state of Texas and, perhaps most of all, their status as "the perfect couple, made for each other."

Teenagers spoke with the kind of openness only the young can muster about human needs Mark and Vic helped to fill, about the simple pleasures of visiting back and forth with much-loved "cool uncles" who had become role models. Friends and relatives who rose to speak expressed their affection in good-natured teasing. Vic's talent with computers repeatedly called up visions of the quirky, but brilliant and lovable nerd unable to part with the stuffed animals that accompanied him everywhere. Mark's too-good-to-be-true disposition drew similar teasing. The kind, open-hearted kid childhood friends remembered had been singled out in law school as the one guy in the class with a heart-of-gold, Dory swimming among sharks. What no amount of gentle humor could hide, what most often inspired the humor, was how much the lucky few gathered for the rehearsal dinner loved and respected Mark and Vic, how much they admired their courage and determination.

No one spoke more knowingly or with more conviction of the courage Mark and Vic had shown in their two years' struggle for marriage equality in Texas than Charlie Gonzalez—lawyer, judge, legislator, longtime friend— the man they had asked to marry them:

> It's so important what you guys have done. And you did it with great style. You did it as a party. My hat is off to both of you for having the absolute courage, the honesty of your convictions and, of course, your feelings, to put your names on that pleading. I think that courage will truly define your relationship going forward. What you've done has tremendous consequences for many, many people.

For a long moment, Charlie paused. His eyes played across the crowd, waiting for the full import of what he had said to sink in. Understanding somehow that he was not quite done, no one spoke, no one moved. A smile crossed his lips, and he began again. "Who would even think," he asked quietly, "that the Constitution didn't protect everyone?" A wave of laughter swept round the room, people murmured their approval. And the smile Charlie had begun passed from person to person.

Jeremy Greshin, another of Mark's friends from Vanderbilt, drew a direct line between his father's work in the mid-sixties as a lawyer fighting for the civil rights of African Americans and what Mark and Vic had done fighting for the civil rights of gays and lesbians in Texas. Though a young man with two children at home, struggling to establish a law practice on Long Island, his father had packed his bags and headed to Tennessee and Mississippi to defend African Americans—succeeding in a murder trial to the point that bigots repeatedly hurled bricks through his window. "It was a pretty tense time," Greshin said with a rueful smile, remembering the dangers his father had faced. "When we heard about what Mark and Vic were doing," he added, "we felt that this was the civil rights issue of this generation. We wanted our children to know about how much courage and conviction they had . . . they served as great role models for our children."

Even more than family and friendship, even more than courage, what the people who rose to speak at the rehearsal dinner most wanted to celebrate was the extraordinary, "made for each other" love Mark and Vic had shared for over eighteen years, the sense that each completed the other. From childhood Gwen Jones had wanted nothing but the best for Mark, wanted him "to be with someone special." And then, she said, "I met Vic—handsome, smart, courtly, that military bearing, and he so interested in everything Mark said and did. I knew Mark had found that 'someone special.'" Merritt Clements, a partner at a law firm where Mark once worked who had become a friend, recognized that same "chemistry." "They're just a perfect match for one another," he claimed as heads nodded affirmatively around the room. "They are as dedicated and committed and married a couple as they could be except for one small thing," Merritt joked, "and that will be remedied tomorrow."

Given the audience at the rehearsal dinner, people who had known Mark, or Vic, or Mark and Vic for decades, people who knew what they had endured before they met, the depth of their love and the frustration of the years they lived apart, the pressure-cooker that had been their lives during the two years of their legal battle with Texas, tears welled up as one story gave way to another. No stories brought the audience so close to tears as those told by Torri Cruz and Greg Phariss, tears of laughter from Torri, tears of another sort from Greg.

A petit woman whose eyes sparkle when she laughs, Torri had gotten to know Mark in the early nineties when she and her husband, Robert, were still dating. When Vic came on the scene, Mark brought him into the circle, and over two decades the couples' friendship deepened. They moved within a few years of one another from San Antonio to Dallas; Torri and Robert gave birth to two children. The two couples spent many a Christmas morning opening presents together, shared half a lifetime of experiences and fell over the years into the comfortable relationship of old friends who can be counted on to help out as necessary. And yet, Torri admitted, she had found herself just a little shocked as she and her boys walked from the pool one day with Vic at her side.

"Vic informed me that I was his girlfriend," Torri began, clearly enjoying the opportunity to tease guests who didn't know the story with her deadpan humor. "When Mark called, my picture would show up on his phone." She paused for a moment to let that much sink in, then took the story up another notch. "A little later I was informed that we were engaged," she said. Needing to hide his relationship with Mark from colleagues in the Air Force, Vic had substituted Torri's picture for Mark's. Photos of Torri sat atop Vic's desk at work. He led his colleagues to believe that in time he planned to move to Dallas to marry a beautiful, young divorcée and help raise her two boys. But, Torri lamented, the story ended with a tragic reversal. "When Vic retired from the military, he dumped me, informed me he would not be moving to Dallas to adopt the kids." No one laughed harder than Rob, Torri's husband, unless it was Mark. "She is absolutely," he joked, "my favorite of Vic's exes."

By far the most touching story of the night came from Greg Phariss, Mark's younger brother. Down from Walters, Oklahoma for the wedding, he hadn't driven many miles. And yet, in every way that really mattered few people at the rehearsal dinner had traveled further. "As you can see," he began, gesturing at Mark, "we're about as opposite as we can be. And I mean opposite. And yet we're brothers." Mark was dressed in khaki slacks, a striped, button-down shirt, and a camel hair blazer, Greg in blue jeans and a sweatshirt. But style was only the beginning of their differences. A former school administrator, a former wrestling and football coach who looks the part, Greg Phariss is a man cast in the classic male mold. That Mark would be gay had never occurred to him; it simply wasn't within the realm of possibility. When his ex-wife phoned him, told him Mark had been seen at the Texas State Fair with other men who "looked gay." Greg told her she was "full of it." Not possible. Then he called Mark.

"Are you gay?" he asked.

"Yes," came the reply.

For a beat, two beats, three beats, the line fell silent. Finally, Greg found his voice.

"I don't care," he told Mark, "I don't understand, but I don't care."

Whatever tension might have hung in the air fell away as the brothers laughed together.

"Why didn't you tell me?" Greg had demanded that night on the phone. Mark, admitted that, like many another, he had hidden the truth from his family as long as he could, afraid of losing what mattered most in the world.

"I wasn't a basher," Greg confided, "but I was pretty bad. You have to understand the dramatic turnaround I made in my beliefs." Mark's revelation had stopped Greg dead in his tracks, but it forced him to think. Over time, Mark told his brother about his work with the Human Rights Campaign. He took him to a birthday party where most of the guests were gays and lesbians—"shell-shock," Greg admitted. In time, Greg met—and accepted—Vic. And in time, he embraced marriage equality. "His being my brother, that opened up my eyes, allowed me to see not only him, but the whole issue of equality in a different light." Turning to Mark and Vic, Greg spoke for a moment as though the rest of the guests had dropped from sight. "To me," he said, "the couple I see here . . . I really don't think of them any differently than I do my wife and me." Turning again to the rest of the room, Greg continued. "I'm proud of them for what they've done, and more than that, I'm proud of Mark because he's my brother."

Toward the beginning of the rehearsal dinner the wedding coordinator, had passed a hat with numbers that would determine the order in which guests would tell the stories linking them to Mark and Vic. Greg Phariss hadn't bothered to take a number. As recently as that afternoon, driving from their home to Frisco, he had confided to his wife, Cynthia, that he didn't intend to speak. Listening to others talk of Mark and Vic, realizing how much they were loved, had changed his mind. And in fact, his rightful place among the story-tellers was at the end. No story could have brought the evening to a more perfect close than his account of the journey by which he had come to accept Mark as a gay man, a journey driven by familial love and even a little courage on his part—and had carried him to places he never thought to go. After Greg's final, triumphant declaration—love for his brother, pride in what Mark and Vic had done, the recognition that all marriages are equal—a hush fell over the crowd, a respectful silence. Then the applause began—and continued—further celebration of the love and courage that had moved Greg to accept his brother and Vic for who they were.

"Family are the people who support you," Vic said as he rose to bid the crowd good-night and struck one more time the chord that had resonated through the evening. "They're the people who are there for you when no one else is. They're the people in our lives that we turn to and think about, that call, write, Skype. You are the people who are important to us." Looking from table to table, his eyes settling now on this group, now on another, he continued. "We want all of you to know one another because you are all part of our family. Thank you," he concluded, "thank you very much for being who you are."

* * *

The rehearsal dinner was no sooner over than John Holstead and his crew from 21 Parc set to work on the floral arch that would frame the wedding the next morning. Working by the glow of iPhone flashlights, they zip-tied manzanita branches to the structural elements of the tent and wove baskets of flowers, one by one, into the open spaces. With the smell of fresh eucalyptus hanging in the air, Holstead gave a quiet thanks for the chill that would keep his flowers fresh. He was concerned about the wind, already picking up and expected to increase through the night, but he needn't have worried. Though the winds howled, waking more than a few concerned guests, his work proved as solid as the love that had sustained Mark and Vic through eighteen years and given them the courage to change the course of history in Texas. For those who had followed the story closely, the noise of the wind that morning was drowned out by the chorus of voices that had risen to sing the praises to two quiet men from Plano, accidental activists who, together with Cleo and Nicole and the legal team from Akin Gump, had done what many thought impossible.

"They led the fight for same-sex couples to marry in Texas and all across the country," Jason Wheeler told viewers in the Dallas-Fort Worth area watching the news on the day of the wedding; "Mark Phariss and Vic Holmes became two of the best known faces in the fight for marriage equality."[8] Before the day of the ceremony President and Mrs. Barack Obama sent a letter of congratulations. "We are extraordinarily grateful for your service," they wrote alluding to Vic's nearly twenty-three years in the Air Force. But the main thrust of their letter was the service Mark and Vic had performed as a couple: "Thanks to brave Americans like you who stood up and fought for progress, our country is becoming more and more compassionate."[9] A second congratulatory letter conveying "warm regards" arrived from former Secretary of State Hillary Clinton. "I thank you from the bottom of my heart," she wrote, "for your commitment to making this day possible for so many other loving couples across the country."[10] Celia Israel, a Texas State Representative, brought the matter home in her letter. "You have put yourselves on the frontlines on behalf of our state and so many Texas families, like yours and mine. Thank you for being a part of the change that zapped us into the 21st century. What a thrill to know both of you. Not only are you history makers, but you are also such good men . . . Thank you for being so willing to represent the very best of what Texas has to offer."[11]

Yet another congratulatory note came from Evan Wolfson, founder of Freedom to Marry and one of the chief architects of the marriage equality movement.

A million lesbian and gay people have gotten legally, joyously married since we won the freedom to marry nationwide in June—and among them now are Mark and Vic. They worked hard for this day, and today their love for, and commitment to each other as well as our country shine bright deep in the heart of Texas, their home.[12]

Steve Rudner, Chairman of the Board of Equality Texas, sent another:

On their wedding day, we reflect on the sacrifices made and the courage exhibited by Mark and Vic in their pioneering roles in the fight for marriage equality. A love so deep it could not be constrained or denied by the State of Texas, and a love so strong that even the Supreme Court of the United States could feel its power, is certainly one to which we should all aspire.[13]

A million lesbian and gay couples married since *Obergefell*, each special and unforgettable in their own way, as Steve Rudner suggested, to people in love whatever their sexual orientation. But on the morning of November 21, 2015, none seemed as special as Mark and Vic.

* * *

Though early-morning temperatures refused to rise above a frosty forty-six degrees and the wind was blowing steadily at twenty-five-miles an hour, family and members of the wedding party were smiling, laughing as they gathered in the lounge for the usual round of photographs. A little chill, a little wind seemed no more than apt reminders of the hardships their friends had endured to bring marriage equality to Texas. As the guests were seated outside, Mark and Vic posed with group after group for an endless succession of formal pictures; the Metro Chamber Players opened with light-hearted show tunes that had most humming along, "Get Me to the Church on Time" and "What a Wonderful World." For their wedding Mark and Vic wanted serious, but not fusty—a bit of playful whimsy here and there that would call to mind the human beings beneath the formal wear. Their gifts to the members of the wedding party included matching ties *and* classy Ray-Ban sunglasses to wear in a funky, wide-angle group shot that stretched the width of the lounge and included nineteen smiling people, their thumbs raised in affirmation of what was to come.

Ring bearers Cathan Brice and Emily Polen picked their way carefully down the steps to the tent, mindful of the rings on the folded flags they carried; the groomsmen at the end of the procession, Mike Carnahan and Dan McKion, each held, carefully and reverentially, one of the stuffed alligators that go everywhere with Vic, Harry and Crikey. Another touch of that whimsy—and one neither Mark nor the waiting crowd was aware of until the doors swung open one last time to reveal him and Vic, hand in hand. Vic appeared in his Air Force Service Dress uniform, tailored to accentuate his lean, athletic build. Mark had decided on black tie—and had shed forty pounds for the wedding. In his pocket Mark carried a tiny copy of the Constitution and related documents—bound in black leather and embossed with gold letters, "M & V"—a gift from Molly Beth Malcolm, the former chair of the Texas Democratic Party. She had placed a marker at Section 1 of The Virginia Declaration of Rights which preceded the Constitution by more than a decade. "All men are by nature equally free and independent," the text there proclaims, "and have certain inherent rights, of which, when they enter into a state of society, they cannot, by any compact, deprive or divest their posterity; namely, the enjoyment of life and liberty, with the means of acquiring and possessing property, and pursuing and obtaining happiness and safety."[14]

But for several quiet, almost veiled references to the years of struggle that had led to this moment—passing references to "their determination to be married" and "the victory of their love"—the Reverend Arthur Murphy's opening prayer might have served to begin any wedding, a sign that the day when "gay weddings" will become simply "weddings" is not so very far off. When he had finished, Mark and Vic, standing a foot apart, turned to Gwen Jones and Steve Olivares as they sang "I've Dreamed of You." And then, one of those perfect, unscripted moments that sent a quiet murmur of satisfaction through the crowd. "I prayed one day/That your arms would hold me tight," Gwen and Steve sang. Listening to the lyrics, ready to live them, Mark stepped back, Vic forward, and their hands came together.

Understanding how important music was to Mark and Vic—they had spent hours choosing "just right" songs for the ceremony, the reception, and even the wedding video—the Honorable Charles Gonzales began the ceremony with lines borrowed from Andrew Lloyd Webber's *Aspects of Love*. "Love changes everything," Gonzales reminded his audience of believers, "hands and faces, earth and sky." Allow love into your life, he suggested, and it "will turn your world around . . . that world will last forever." Eighteen years ago, he pointed out, Mark and Vic had their first date—and discovered soon thereafter that their worlds were spinning a bit differently. "Love conquers all," Charlie continued, "Sometimes the fears and doubts of those falling in love" and—a subtle message to Texans still adjusting to the idea of same-sex marriage—"the fears and doubts of others." "This is a wonderful day," he asserted, a challenge to those reluctant to accept change, "for the world to acknowledge and respect."

At the end of what the program referred to as "Words of Wisdom," he cited the now famous last paragraph of Justice Anthony Kennedy's *Obergefell* decision. "No union is more profound than marriage, for it embodies the highest ideals of love, fidelity, devotion, sacrifice, and family. In forming a marital union, two people become something greater than once they were." From the way they looked at one another, no one doubted Mark and Vic were ready for "something greater."

With Vic commenting as his too-busy schedule allowed, Mark had labored for weeks to perfect the vows they would make to each other. As a tribute to Edith Windsor and Thea Spyer, pioneers in the struggle to legalize same-sex marriage, he took a key passage from the vows they exchanged in May 2007. Another short passage came from W. H. Auden's "Stop the Clocks," a poetic tribute to Auden's lover and long one of Mark's favorite poems. Over time, Mark had knit the strands seamlessly together.

Warning the crowd that he might stumble, Vic spoke first. "I don't recall," he told Mark, his voice cracking with emotion, "the instant you were more than the world to me, but I know it must have happened because I can no more envision a world without you than a world without gravity." Recalling the frightening moment at the end of April when they had been separated as they headed into the Supreme Court, Vic spoke of his panic. "The gravity that held everything together came undone . . . I felt like I was tumbling with neither an anchor nor a guide. When we were reunited, I felt the world rebalance and restore itself." Despite his fear, Vic's execution was flawless—though more than a few of those looking on felt their lips tremble with emotion.

Mark's offering to Vic was no less touching—but he couldn't resist adding a bit of self-deprecating humor, a touch or two of that whimsy with which the morning had begun. "Since the first day I saw you," he told Vic, "I was smitten . . . You are my best friend, my lover, my soul-mate, the shoulder I lean on and the one I sometimes cry on. I love your laughter, your smile, your intellect, your kindness." But as he went on, adding more and more reasons why he had grown to love Vic, family and friends broke into smiles. "I love you," Mark repeated, because of "the way you care for our family, our friends, and our four-footed children," because "you'll traipse through a cemetery with me to research family trees," because "you'll fix my computer and printer without complaining," because "you ignore my singing and backseat driving (generally, without complaining)," and because "you enjoy my so-so piano playing."

And then, the vows and the exchange of rings:

On this day, in the presence of our family and friends, I, Vic Holmes, take you, Mark Phariss, to be my lawfully wedded husband and with this ring I thee wed. From this day forward as in all days past you shall be my North, my South, my East and West, my working week and my Sunday rest, my noon, my midnight, my talk, my song. I will love you forever and forever be yours.

His face glowing, his voice cracking with emotion, Mark took his turn. The moment for which they had waited so many years had come at last.

"I finally found someone, someone to share my life," Gwen Jones and Steve Olivares proclaimed in another song, a perfect expression of the love Mark and Vic shared; "You're exceptional, I can't wait for the rest of my life." And then, the moment Mark and Vic had hoped for through eighteen years together. A smile on his face, exultation in his voice, Charlie Gonzalez spun the magic that changed everything.

Since Mark and Vic have consented to be married and have expressed their love and pledged their lives before this company, by joining hands, the exchanging of vows, and the giving of rings, I pronounce that they are married under the laws of the State of Texas and the Constitution of the United States.

"Married under the laws of the State of Texas and the Constitution of the United States"—everyone understood the significance of the formula, the message being sent to Greg Abbott, Dan Patrick, Kenneth Paxton, and their allies in the state legislature. Guests cheered, Mark and Vic raised their arms in triumph, pumping their fists. A kiss for luck, a selfie for fun, and they were on the way down the aisle and into the rest of their lives. Years of emotional turmoil, years of hiding their relationship from family and friends, from Mark's employers and Vic's colleagues in the U. S. Air Force, years of legal battles in Texas and beyond—the dark times were over. Part of a nationwide struggle to legalize same-sex marriage, they had led the way in Texas—and won.

* * *

Guests sipping flutes of champagne hardly knew where to look first as they entered the Stonebriar Ballroom for the reception. Pinlights suspended from the ceiling drew most eyes to oversized floral centerpieces on each of the thirty tables spread about the room. Like any couple getting married, Mark and Vic had thought long and hard about a color scheme, choosing in the end colors that supported blue to represent Vic's years of service in the United States Air Force—chrysanthemums, lime green Cymbidium orchids, blue Dutch hydrangeas, and a variety of roses. When work on the flowers began, John Holstead of 21 Parc was aware that the Supreme Court had legalized same-sex marriage, but didn't know that in Texas "Mark and Vic were spearheading the movement." As more and more guests confirmed they were coming and the demand for flowers grew, he realized that the Phariss-Holmes wedding would be "a monumental, historic event"—and he grew more and more determined that everything would be top-of-the-line. Pre-planning spread over several months. Ten people worked for four days to put together the arrangements. Installation stretched over a twenty-hour day. In the end the effect was dazzling.[15]

As the reception began, the band, Icehouse, rocked the crowd with "Uptown Funk." Then Kenya Gilstrap, a vocalist with the band, jumped into an Etta James classic and everyone knew they had come home: "You smiled/ and then the spell was cast,/And here we are in heaven, for you are mine . . . At last." For more than a few in the crowd, only one response was possible, the title of another Etta James classic: "All I Could Do Was Cry."

Word had spread that there was "something special" about the wedding cake and the grooms' cake, and most guests stopped by the table where they were displayed before taking their seats. The wedding cake by Dallas Affaires Cake Co. was spectacular: six-tiered with a blue ribbon marking every other tier—that "Air Force" theme again— and fresh flowers cascading down the sides. But it was the cake-topper, designed by Concarta of Los Angeles, the firm that provided the cake-topper for the wedding of Jessse Tyler Ferguson of *Modern Family* fame, that drew "oohs and aahs" from guests. Working from photographs and measurements, Concarta created two six-inch-high figures: "Vic" in his uniform, accurate down to the tiny medals on his chest, and Mark in his tuxedo. At their feet sat the "four-footed children" to whom Mark had referred in his vows to Vic: Abby, Betsy, and Jake, the beagles who are their constant companions.

The design of the grooms' cake prompted smiles of approval. In contrast to the handful of bakers around the country who refused to provide services for same-sex weddings, Margaret Gragg of Dallas Affaires had no trouble getting into the spirit of things. Mark and Vic had imagined their grooms' cake as a square with a copy of the Constitution spread across the top. A statement. Margaret proposed a cake in the shape of Texas with the state flag on top, the flag covered in part by a copy of the Constitution of the United States. A bigger, more provocative statement. When the men hesitated, afraid her proposal might be a bit "too much," Margaret put her foot down. "Since you were the Texas plaintiffs," she wrote in an e-mail, "I would like for you to reconsider. Texas shape cake with Texas flag on top, double rings on the flag's star and Constitution draped over the cake, coming down its side like a document. When you look back on this years from now, you'll realize that the cake tells the story."[16] In the end, she got her way, and guests snapping photos could not have been more pleased that she did.

In the two years of their battle for marriage equality in Texas, Mark and Vic had read dozens of briefs and decisions from every level of the federal judicial system. Hoping to remind their guests how many plaintiffs had shared in the struggle, how many attorneys had worked into the night to present their arguments in the best possible light, how many court cases had been won—and occasionally lost—they chose thirty of their favorite passages, one for each table, and set them in frames for guests to ponder. Predictably, they balanced the "serious" and "thought-provoking" with the whimsical. Remembering the fuss that ensued when Memories Pizza in Walkerton, Indiana, leapt into the national spotlight by declaring they would not cater gay weddings, Mark and Vic apologized to their guests. Though they had arranged for four serving stations with a wide variety of foods, they had failed to include pizza among the choices. But as Mark quickly pointed out—tongue tucked firmly in cheek—they had placed on each table a gift-card for pizza "in case anyone feels the need." "Trailblazers . . . proponents of edible diversity," Frederick Miller proclaimed of Mark and Vic on Facebook, joining in the fun, "marital equality and freedom of choice. Together at last!"[17]

Signaling that the time had come to begin the program, Icehouse broke into an up-tempo version of "Deep in the Heart of Texas"; Yutaka Meyers, the band's leader, stepped to the microphone and introduced Mark and Vic as "newlyweds and husbands for life." When the applause had subsided—and that took no little while—Mark turned to the crowd, one question on his lips. "I remember there were some politicians who declared that this day would never occur; I think they might have said it would be a cold day in hell," he said, the satisfaction evident in his voice. "Well, we just had a cold day, we just got married, and it was fantastic. Who would have believed eighteen years ago when Vic and I first met, or even five years ago, that Vic and I would be married one day 'Deep in the Heart of Texas'? Now we are!"

Remembering that some friends, even some members of his and Vic's families had chosen not to attend their wedding, Mark's welcome to their guests began exactly where Vic had left off at the rehearsal dinner the night before—with a celebration of the "family of choice" that had rallied to surround and support them. Wishing that time would have allowed him to recognize each guest, Vic bowed to necessity and singled out only the members of the wedding party. Mark introduced a small group of special guests that included Gordon Tanner, General Counsel of the U. S. Air Force; Chuck Smith, Executive Director of Equality Texas; Steve Rudner, Chairman of the Board of Equality Texas; Chris Hammet at whose home he and Vic met. Next he introduced Nicole Dimetman and Cleo DeLeon, co-plaintiffs in *DeLeon v. Perry*, and members of the Akin Gump legal team that had carried them to victory: Neel Lane, Frank Stenger-Castro, and Michael Cooley. One by one, they bent over a small table to sign copies of the opinions and court orders that brought marriage equality to Texas: Judge Garcia's opinion from February 2014, the Fifth Circuit Court's order to Judge Garcia directing him to lift his stay, and Judge Garcia's final judgment in *DeLeon v. Perry*, a ceremonial end to the two years they had stood, shoulder to shoulder, against the State of Texas. That done, Mark and Vic bent to sign the marriage license the legal papers had made possible—and, in a final gesture to the team that had battled for marriage equality in Texas since October 2013, lawyers and plaintiffs posed for one more triumphant photograph, a visible sign of the kind of the "family of choice" Mark celebrated in his welcome.

Charlie Gonzales, Neel Lane, Neal Chadwick, and Eva Cole, Vic's "Best Person" in the wedding party, offered toasts. Not surprisingly—the theme had surfaced time many times during the wedding weekend—Eva spoke of family. Not surprisingly, she mixed deeply felt emotion with humor. She had met Vic at the gym at a time when she was recruiting softball players. "He's tall, good looking, and well built," she thought on first seeing Vic. "I'll bet this guy can play ball!" Turns out, he couldn't. Though he arrived for the first game looking the part—"great shoes, great glove, the whole shebang"— he swung the bat like a cricket player and in his first appearance at the plate drove the ball all of six inches. Still, they remained friends and in time she came to know and love Mark. Together, she argued, they had evolved into the prefect couple. "For every ying there is a yang . . . When you have a guy like Vic who travels with two stuffed animals, Crikey and Harry, you have to have a solid individual who has the ability to see Crikey and Harry as people and remain supportive."

Growing more serious, she celebrated "the union of Mark and Vic" as the making of a new family: "When I look at this gorgeous couple and the beautiful people in this room, I see nothing but family made up of friends, supporters, co-workers, and relatives brought together by love." Raising her own glass, she led everyone in the room to believe they had been admitted to a charmed circle. "From everyone here, Crikey, Harry, and the Beagles, we wish you love, light, and happiness." Beaming, Mark and Vic raised their own glasses, appropriately engraved. "Today," they read, "I marry my best friend."

Two rituals that would link Mark and Vic with millions upon millions of married couples, straight and gay, remained: the ceremonial cutting of the cake and the traditional first dance. For the first ritual, the cake-cutter, suitably engraved—"Life with you is a piece of cake"—and the cake-server— "You're the icing on my cake!"—were ready. For the latter, Mark and Vic were ready. Mark had come to love dancing when in high school he and other members of the debate team would slip over the Texas border on weekends to enter dance contests in one honkytonk or another. Vic had considerably less experience—until, that is, they enrolled for months of twice-weekly lessons with Arthur Murray. Mark's weekly updates on Facebook had created high expectations. For two years they had stepped carefully, dancing around the legal obstacles Texas set in their way; now Texas had been ordered to measure its steps by theirs. Mark and Vic were ready to shine in that momentous first dance as husband and husband.

Dancing to a rock medley that began with the Spinners' "Could It Be I'm Falling in Love?" they began by circling the floor, hand in hand, smiling, until they were once again center stage. Then Vic spun into Mark's arms for a dip, a surprise opening, and Mark leaned in for what turned out to be the first of many kisses, each of which drew applause from appreciative friends. For a few moments they settled into a rhythmic rhumba until they swung away from each other, each with an arm extended in classic *Dancing with the Stars* fashion. There were dips and twirls, bits of the rhumba and the jitterbug intertwined. But in fact the audience cared less about what they did than how they did it. For almost five minutes Mark and Vic looked into each other's eyes and sang to each other, enjoying every moment. That was the real treat for friends aware of all they had been through, watching Mark and Vic together like any couple who just happen to be head over heels in love, dancing in a room with over three-hundred people whose presence they hardly recognized. Any time the dance led to an embrace and a kiss— and it often did—the crowd cheered. When Mark wagged his finger, beckoning Vic closer, Vic patted his chest as if to still his beating heart—and the crowd roared.

"I Wanna Dance with Somebody," the soundtrack suddenly proclaimed, jumping from the Spinners to Whitney Houston, "with somebody who loves me." Moving now to a faster song, a harder beat, the men circled the room, each in a different direction, clapping their hands and encouraging the crowd to join in the clapping to match their rising energy. They fell into a classic jitterbug rock-step—more movement, more twirls, spins with every step. They stepped up the kissing, two at a time now. As a tribute to Mark's honkytonk dance days in the late seventies—more of the whimsy that marked the day from start to finish—they worked in, to the delight of the crowd, a sampling of John Travolta's classic *Saturday Night Fever* moves at the end. Dance bands love good dancers according to Yutaka Meyers, the leader of Icehouse. They inspire the musicians to raise the level of their performance. Watching Mark and Vic, they got exactly what they needed to drive them in their second set. "How about a big round of applause?" Meyers asked as the men bowed to each other, to the crowd, and one more time to each other. "That was fantastic." It was. Jack Evans, who had waited fifty-four years to marry the man he loved, was delighted with the dance and the day. "Could *Dancing with the Stars* be far behind?" he wondered as Mark and Vic finished with a final kiss.[18]

The rituals completed, one big moment remained, a surprise gift months in the planning that Mark had carefully kept from the man he loved—and perhaps the ultimate memory of their wedding. After months considering the possibilities, Mark settled at last on the perfect memento. Turning to Pauline Howard, a San Antonio artist who had done work for them before, he commissioned a new portrait as a wedding gift for Vic. Working from photographs, she drew Mark and Vic, dressed for the wedding, standing proudly in front of the Texas Capitol, the dome rising behind their heads, Abby, Betsy, and Jake at their feet. In the last moments of the reception, he presented it to a thunderstruck Vic as a wedding gift.

* * *

The idea of Mark and Vic as champions of civil rights and makers of history was hardly new to the people they had welcomed to their wedding as family. But as the weekend wore on that idea sprung more and more often into the minds of more and more people, happy to have been included in their family of choice. One guest, remembering too well the frosty tempera-tures with which the day had begun, wrote in a note of thanks that "We may have shivered a bit during the ceremony, but we shivered as a part of history as Mark Phariss and Vic Holmes got married."[19] Angela Ellis was still more effusive. "What a pleasure it was," she wrote, "to witness something so beautiful. Not just an ordinary wedding, this was part of Texas history. These two became part of U.S. history by standing up for their rights to be married just like anyone else who's in love."[20] Bess Morrison, a friend Mark and Vic met on an expedition to Antarctica in 2012, summed up the day perfectly as "a wedding and a victory party all in one."[21] Pauline's portrait, Mark and Vic in the foreground, dressed as they were for the wedding, dominating the Texas Capitol behind them, was the perfect representation of what they had done.

One word on everyone's lips was "honored"; another was "grateful." Lynne Perry understood exactly what Mark and Vic had achieved on the way to marriage. "Once you guys make a friend," she wrote by way of thanks, "she's a friend for life—you make it so! I'm honored and blessed to have both of you in my life and think of you as brothers . . . Your wedding was spectacular in taste and execution, a first-class event to be cherished forever."[22] Corie Olivares, a friend of twenty years, so close that she traveled to New Orleans to offer support when the Fifth Circuit Court heard oral arguments in *De Leon v. Perry*, summed it up perfectly in a Facebook post: "I've been to a lot of weddings, but I've never been to one where absolutely every single guest was overwhelmed with the joy of the day. Every guest was excited and happily greeting others sharing stories of our friendship, love, and pride to be among the blessed to be called your friends."[23]

A few days before the wedding, six months after the Supreme Court ruled in favor of marriage equality, Mark took his triumphant mood to Facebook. "There were many dire predictions about allowing same-sex marriage" he wrote, "and none of them—not one!—has come true."

> Ted Cruz said it was a "threat to our liberty" when, in fact, it extended liberty to the LGBT community. The State of Texas argued that marriage equality had to be denied in order to encourage straight couples to marry and have children . . . And yet straight people continue to marry and have children, and all the married straight couples haven't headed for the divorce courts.

"Wow!" he continued, warming to more sarcasm, "I guess gay marriage wasn't the end of procreation and civilization after all."[24] A couple of weeks later, a year to the day after he and Mark sat in the Fifth Circuit Court in New Orleans listening to oral arguments in same-sex marriage cases from Louisiana, Mississippi, and Texas, Vic posted his own reflection on Facebook.

Speaking intimately, as if his audience did not stretch beyond the close circle of friends with whom he and Mark had shared the joys and sorrows of that day, he reached out as well to the wider circle so often in his thoughts over the past two years, young people just discovering their sexual orientation. "I would," he began, "without reservation or question—do it again."

> as painful as it was to sit there and listen to people who knew nothing about myself or my compatriots elaborate on why we should not be equal, it was that very pain that would compel me to do it again. No one should have to sit through that, let alone live that way each day. Yes, I would do it again because those of you who remember living that way and remember the pain of being pushed into the shadows . . . we lived that way. But the children who will come after us should never be subjected to that pain.

He and Mark and Cleo and Nicole, together with hundreds of otherwise ordinary people who had signed on as plaintiffs in marriage equality cases across the country, had endured crippling heartbreaks and overcome once-impossible legal barriers. Collectively, they had fought their way to a new civil right—a new future. But theirs was more than a narrow legal victory. Much more. What they had really won was the right to be who they were, to live authentic lives in full view of friends and family, neighbors and coworkers—the surest way to win the hearts and minds of people unfamiliar with what it means to be LGBT.

Vic thanked the plaintiffs from Louisiana, Mississippi, and Texas "whose courage could power a small city." He thanked the lawyers "whose brilliance brought an amazing victory." But most of all, he thanked Mark "who has stood with me since 1997 and will now stand with me forever."[25]

Love won.

Table of Cases

Baehr v. Miike, 910 P.2d 112, 80 Haw. 341 (1996).

Baker v. Nelson, 191 N.W.2d 185, 291 Minn. 310 (1971), *appeal dismissed*, 409 U.S. 810, 93 S.Ct. 37, 34 L.Ed. 2d 65 (1972).

Baker v. Vermont, 744 A.2d 864 (Vt. 1999).

Baskin v. Bogan, 766 F.3d 648 (7th Cir. 2014).

Bowers v. Hardwick, 478 U.S. 186, 106 S. Ct. 2841, 92 L. Ed. 2d 140 (1986).

Brown v. Board of Education, 347 U.S. 483, 74 S. Ct. 686, 98 L. Ed. 873 (1954).

Bush v. Gore, 531 U.S. 98, 121 S. Ct. 525, 148 L. Ed. 2d 388 (2000).

Business Electronics Corp. v. Sharp Electronics Corp., 485 U.S. 717, 108 S. Ct. 1515, 99 L. Ed. 2d 808 (1988).

Campaign for Southern Equality v. Bryant, 64 F. Supp. 3d 906 (S.D. Miss. 2014), *affm'd* 791 F.3d 625 (5th Cir. 2015).

Campaign for Southern Equality v. Bryant, 791 F. 3d 625 (5th Cir. 2015).

Chambers v. Florida, 309 U.S. 227, 60 S. Ct. 472, 84 L. Ed. 716 (1940).

DeBoer v. Snyder, 973 F. Supp. 2d 757 (E.D. Mich. 2014), *rev'd*, 722 F. 3d 388 (6th Cir. 2014), *rev'd* 576 U.S. ____ (2015).

DeBoer v. Snyder, 772 F.3d 388 (6th Cir. 2014), *rev'd* , 576 U.S. ____ (2015).

DeLeon v. Abbott, 791 F.3d 619 (5th Cir. 2015).

De Leon v. Perry, 975 F. Supp. 2d 632 (W.D. Tex. 2014), *aff'd & remanded sub nom, DeLeon v. Abbott*, 791 F.3d 619 (5th Cir. 2015).

Geiger v. Kitzhaber, 994 F. Supp. 2d 1128 (D. Or. 2014).

Gill v. Office of Personnel Management, 682 F.3rd. I.

Goodridge v. Department of Public Health, 440 Mass. 309, 798 N.E.2d 941, 798 N.E. 941 (2003).

Griswold v. Connecticut, 381 U.S. 479, 85 S. Ct. 1678, 14 L. Ed. 2d 510 (1965).

Harris v. Ramey, 339 S.W.2d 479 (Ky. Ct. App. 1960) (per curiam).

Hollingsworth v. Perry, 133 S. Ct. 2652, 570 U.S., 186 L. Ed. 2d 768 (2013).

Kitchen v. Herbert, 755 F.3d 1193 (10th Cir. 2014), *cert. denied*, 135 S. Ct. 265, 190 L. Ed. 2d 138 (2014).

Pedersen v. OPM, 881 F. Supp. 2nd 294 (D.Conn. 2012).

Perry v. Schwarzenegger, 704 F. Supp. 2d 921 (N.D. Cal. 2010). *Affm'd sub nom, Perry v. Brown*, 671 F.3d 1052 (9th Cir. 2012), *vacated & remanded sub nom, Hollingsworth v. Perry*, 133 S. Ct. 2652, 570 U.S., 186 L. Ed. 2d 768 (2013); *Huntsman v. Heavilin*, 21 Fla. L. Weekly Supp. 916a (Fla. 16th Cir. Ct. July 17, 2014).

Perry v. Schwarzenegger, 704 F. Supp. 2d 921 (N.D. Cal. 2010). *Affm'd sub nom, Perry v. Brown*, 671 F.3d 1052 (9th Cir. 2012), *vacated & remanded sub nom, Hollingsworth v. Perry,* 133 S. Ct. 2652, 570 U.S., 186 L. Ed. 2d 768 (2013).

Huntsman v. Heavilin, 21 Fla. L. Weekly Supp. 916a (Fla. 16th Cir. Ct. July 17, 2014).

Lawrence v. Texas, 539 US 558 (2003).

Loving v. Virginia, 388 U.S. 1, 87 S. Ct. 1817, 18 L. Ed. 2d 1010 (1967).

McNosky v. Perry, No. 1:13-CV-631-SS (W.D. Tex. filed July 29, 2013).

Nuckols v. Perry, No. 3:13-CV-245 (S.D. Texas July 7, 2013) (order dismissing without Prejudice).

Obergefell v. Hodges, 135 S. Ct. 2071, 576 U.S.____, 191 L. Ed. 2d 953 (2015).

Planned Parenthood of Southeastern Pa. v. Casey, 505 U.S. 833, 112 S. Ct. 2791, 120 L. Ed. 2d 674 (1992).

Robicheaux v. Caldwell, 2 F. Supp 3rd 910 (E.D. LA 2014), *rev'd,* 791 F.3d 616 (5th Cir. 2015).

Robicheaux v. Caldwell, 791 F.3d 616 (5th Cir. 2015).

Roe v. Wade, 410 US 113, 93 S. Ct. 705, 35 L. Ed. 2d 147 (1973).

Romer v. Evans, 517 US 620, 116 S. Ct. 1620, 134 L. Ed. 2d 855 (1996).

Schuette v. Coalition to Defend Affirmative Action, 134 S. Ct. 1623, 572 US __, 188 L. Ed. 2d 613 (2014).

Silverman v. United States, 365 US 505, 81 S. Ct. 679, 5 L. Ed. 2d 734 (1961).

Smith v. Allright, 321 US 649, 64 S. Ct. 757, 88 L. Ed. 987 (1944).

St. Joesph Abbey v. Castile, 712 F. 3d 215 (5th Cir. 2013).

Strange v. Searcy, 135 S. Ct. 940, 191 L. Ed. 2d 149 (2015).

Sweatt v. Painter, 339 US 629, 70 S. Ct. 848, 94 L. Ed. 1114 (1950).

Texas v. Johnson, 491 US 397, 109 S. Ct. 2533, 105 L. Ed. 2d 342 (1989).

United States v. Windsor, 133 S. Ct. 2675, 570 US 12, 186 L. Ed. 2d 808 (2013).

West Virginia v. Barnette, 319 US 624, 63 S. Ct. 1178, 87 L. Ed. 1628 (1943).

Zablocki v. Redhail, 434 US 374, 98 S. Ct. 673, 54 L. Ed. 2d 618 (1978).

Zahrn v. Perry. No. 1:13-CV-955-SS (W.D. Tex. filed October 31, 2013).

Endnotes

Notes for Author's Preface

1. Cleve Jones, *When We Rise: My Life in the Movement* (New York: Hachette, 2016), 53.
2. Obergefell v. Hodges, 576 U.S.__ (2015), transcript at 58.
3. Michelangelo Signorile, *It's Not Over: Getting Beyond Tolerance, Defeating Homophobia, and Winning True Equality* (New York: Meridian, 2015), 1–3.
4. Barack Obama, "Remarks by the President at the LGBT Pride Reception, June 9, 2016," https://obamawhitehouse.archives.gov/the-press-office/2016/06/09/remarks-president-lgbt-pride-reception. Accessed January 23, 2017.
5. "Saying William Pryor Is the 'Most Demonstrably Antigay Judicial Nominee in Recent Memory,' Lambda Legal Opposes Nomination to Federal Appeals Court," April 26, 2005, http://www.lambdalegal.org/news/ny_20050426_william-pryor-is-most-demonstrably-antigay-judicial-nominee. Accessed January 15, 2017.
6. Brief of the States of Alabama, South Carolina, and Utah as *Amici Curiae* in Support of Respondent, *Lawrence v. Texas*, 539 US 558 (2003) at 17, 19, 25, 27.

Notes for Introduction

1. *United States v. Windsor* was a tax case that challenged Section 3 of the so-called Defense of Marriage Act (DOMA) which specified that for federal purposes the words "marriage" and "spouse" applied only to heterosexual unions. After the death of her spouse, Thea Spyer, the Internal Revenue Service denied Edith Windsor's claim to the exemption for surviving spouses and compelled her to pay $363,053 in estate taxes. Represented by Roberta Kaplan of Paul, Weiss, Rifkind, Wharton & Garrison, Windsor filed a lawsuit in the U.S. District Court for the Southern District of New York on November 9, 2010. After wins before the district court and the Second Circuit Court of Appeals, the case was appealed to the Supreme Court which heard oral arguments on March 27, 2013. The implications of *Windsor* for the marriage equality movement are more fully explored in Chapter 2.

   Hollingsworth v. Perry was a frontal assault on the constitutionality of California's ban on same-sex marriage. In May 2008 the California Supreme Court ruled that the state's statutes prohibiting same-sex marriage violated the California Constitution. Same-sex couples in California were able to wed until the following November when voters passed Proposition 8, a constitutional amendment that once again banned same-sex marriage. On May 23, 2009, David Boies and Ted Olson, rivals on *Bush v. Gore*, joined forces to file suit on behalf of the American Foundation for Equal Rights (AFER) in the U.S. District Court for the Northern District of California. After wins before the district court and the Ninth Circuit Court of Appeals, the case was appealed to the Supreme Court which heard oral arguments on March 26, 2013.

2. Joshua Alston, "Pro Bono Firm of 2014: Akin Gump," *Law 360*, September 29, 2014, https://www.law360.com/articles/581772/pro-bono-firm-of-2014-akin-gump. Accessed January 05, 2014.
3. Conversation with the author, December 7, 2014.

Notes for Chapter 1

1. Ibid.
2. Kevin P. Phillips, "Poll Deals Homosexuals a Reverse," *The Lawton Constitution*, October 12, 1973, p. 10.
3. Eugene E. Levitt and A. D. Klassen, "Public Attitudes toward Homosexuality: Part of the 1970 National Survey by the Institute for Sex Research," *Journal of Homosexuality* 1.1 (1974): 29–43, Fall 1974.
4. Kathy Gilbert, "GC2016 Tackling 44-Year Stance on Homosexuality," April 27, 2015, The People of the United Methodist Church, http://www.umc.org/news-and-media/gc2016-tackling-44-year-stance-on-homosexuality. Accessed September 11, 2016.
5. Conversation with the author, December 7, 2014.
6. Dudley Clendinen and Adam Nagourney, *Out for Good: The Struggle to Build a Gay Rights Movement in America* (New York: Simon and Schuster, 1999), 303.
7. A. J. Angulo, *Miseducation: A History of Ignorance-Making in America and Abroad* (Baltimore: Johns Hopkins UP, 2016), 64.
8. Conversation with the author, December 7, 2015.
9. Mark Phariss, E-mail to the author, January 15, 2015.
10. Conversation with the author, December 7, 2014.
11. Joyce Murdoch and Deb Price, *Courting Justice: Gay Men and Lesbians v. the Supreme Court* (New York: Basic Books, 2002), 199–200.
12. George Hodgman, *Bettyville* (New York: Viking, 2015), 130.
13. Clendinen and Nagourney, *Out for Good*, 487–8.
14. Conversation with the author, November 4, 2015.
15. Conversation with the author, January 15, 2015.

16. Mark Phariss, E-mail to the author, November 15, 2015.

17. Bowers V. Hardwick, 478 U.S.___(1986) at 197, citing 4 W. Blackstone, Commentaries *215.

18. John Calvin Jeffires, *Justice Lewis F. Powell, Jr.* (New York: Fordham University Press, 1994), 530.

19. Bowers, 478 U.S.___(1986) at 199, citing Olmstead v. United States, 277 U.S. 438, 478 (1928) (Blackmun, H. dissenting).

20. Lawrence v. Texas, 539 U.S.___(2003) (O'Connor, S., concurring).

21. Lawrence v. Texas, 539 U.S.___(2003) at 6, 18, 17.

22. Mark Phariss, E-mail to the author, January 15, 2015.

23. Conversation with the author, December 7, 2014.

24. Conversation with the author, October 20, 2015.

25. Ibid.

26. Conversation with the author, December 7, 2015.

27. David Dunlap, "Survey Details Gay Slayings around U.S.," *New York Times*, December 21, 1994, http://www.nytimes.com/1994/12/21/us/survey-details-gay-slayings-around-us.html. Accessed September 14, 2016.

28. Conversation with the author, October 16, 2015.

29. Conversation with the author, October 17, 2015.

30. Conversation with the author, September 25, 2016.

31. Conversation with the author, October 18, 2015.

32. Ibid.

33. Ibid.

34. Ibid.

35. Conversation with the author, September 25, 2016.

36. Conversation with the author, October 16, 2015.

37. E-mail to the author, October 25, 2015.

38. Conversation with the author, October 16, 2015.

39. Conversation with the author, October 18, 2015.

40. Conversation with the author, October 18, 2015.

41. Ibid.

42. Ibid.

43. Conversation with the author, December 7, 2014.

44. Conversation with the author, October 16, 2015.

45. Conversation with the author, October 17, 2015.

46. Conversation with the author, December 7, 2014.

47. Betty DeGeneres, *Love, Ellen: A Mother/Daughter Journey* (New York: Harper, 1999), 35.

48. Betty DeGeneres, Letter to Mark Phariss, March 9, 1999.

49. Barbara C. Jordan, "Statement on the Articles of Impeachment," (delivered July 25, 1974). *American Rhetoric.* http://www.americanrhetoric.com/

speeches/barbarajordanjudiciarystatement.htm. Accessed December 30, 2016.

50. Francis X. Clines, "Barbara Jordan Dies at 59; Her Voice Stirred the Nation," *New York Times*, January 18, 1996, http://www.nytimes.com/1996/01/18/us/barbara-jordan-dies-at-59-her-voice-stirred-the-nation.html. Accessed October 27, 2015.
51. Bruce Handy, "He Called Me Ellen DeGenerate?" *Time Magazine*, April 14, 1997, http://time.com/348943/he-called-me-ellen-degenerate. Accessed October 29, 2015.
52. Conversation with the author, October 13, 2015.
53. Handy, "Ellen DeGenerate?".
54. "Ellen Update: Episode When She Comes Out of the Closet," *Religious Tolerance*, http://www.religioustolerance.org/hom_0043.htm. Accessed January 6, 2017.
55. Maria F. Durand, "Supporters Come Out for Ellen," *San Antonio Express-News*, May 1, 1997, 1B. http://nl.newsbank.com/nl-search/we/Archives?p_action=doc&pdocid...rname=refuser&_accountid-AC0114051613534812474&s_upgradable=no. Accessed: February 21, 2016.
56. ABC News 20/20, "Sexual Assault in the Air Force, Celebrities, and Serial Killers, Season 25, Episode 11," ABC, February 13, 2004, http://abcnews.go.com/2020/story?id=124308&page=1. Accessed January 6, 2017.
57. Christopher Anderson, "Gay-Hiring Proposal Draws Big Reaction," *San Antonio Express News*, January 28, 1998, http://nl.newsbank.com/nl-search/we/Archives?p_action+doc&p_docid...rname=refuser&_account=AC11405613534812474&s_upgradable=no. Accessed February 21, 2016.
58. Rick Casey, "Prayer, Politics, and Perfidy at City Hall," *San Antonio Express News*, February 2, 1998, http://nl.newsbank.com/nl-search/we/Archives?p_action+doc&p_docid...rname=refuser&s_account=AC11405613534812474&s_upgradable=no. Accessed February 21, 2016.
59. Lillian Faderman, *The Gay Revolution: The Story of the Struggle* (New York: Simon & Schuster, 2015), 511.
60. Conversation with the author, December 7, 2014.
61. Conversation with the author, November 15, 2015.
62. Conversation with the author, October 16, 2015.
63. "Resolution on Homosexuality: 1976," Southern Baptist Convention: 1976, http://www.sbc.net/resolutions/606. Accessed September 14, 2016.

64. "Resolution on Commendation of Anita Bryant: 1978," Southern Baptist Convention: 1978, http://www.sbc.net/resolutions/search/results.asp?query=anita+bryant. Accessed September 14, 2016.

65. "Resolution on Homosexuality: 1985," Southern Baptist Convention: 1985, http://www.sbc.net/resolutions/year/1985. Accessed September 14, 2016.

66. "Resolution on Homosexuality, Military Service, and Civil Rights: 1993," Southern Baptist Convention: 1993, http://www.sbc.net/resolutions/613/resolution-on-homosexuality-military-service-and-civil-rights. Accessed September 14, 2016.

67. "Resolution on Christian Citizenship: 2004," Southern Baptist Convention: 2004, http://www.sbc.net/resolutions/1136/on-christian-citizenship. Accessed September 14, 2016.

68. Resolution Regarding Activist Judges," Southern Baptist Convention: 2004, http://sbtexas.com/am-site/media/2004-resolutions.pdf. Accessed November 11, 2015.

69. *Prestonwood Intern Ministry: Intern Manual*, http://www.prestonwood.org/docs/default-source/site-downloads/intern-manual.pdf?sfvrsn=2. Accessed November 11, 2015.

70. Janet Elliott, "Gay Marriage Ban Approved," *Houston Chronicle*, November 9, 2005, http://www.chron.com/news/houston-texas/article/Gay-marriage-ban-approved-1925874.php. Accessed September 13, 2016.

71. Rob Boston, "Texas Governor Holds Bill Signing at Fort Worth Church School in Bid to Corral Evangelical Voters," Americans United for Separation of Church and State, July/August 2005, https://www.au.org/church-state/julyaugust-2005-church-state/featured/religious-right-roundup. Accessed September 13, 2016.

72. "Southern Baptists Urged to Reject any Laws Legalizing Gay Marriage," Fox News, June 17, 2015, http://www.foxnews.com/opinion/2015/06/16/southern-baptists-urged-to-reject-any-laws-legalizing-gay-marriage.html. Accessed September 25, 2015.

73. "Dallas-Area Churches React to Supreme Court Gay Marriage Ruling," *Dallas Morning News*, June 26, 2015, http://dallasmorningnews.com/news/local-news/20150626-dallas-area-churches-react-to-supreme -court-gay-marriage-ruling.ece. Accessed October 26, 2015.

74. Ibid.

75. Ibid.

76. Conversation with the author, December 7, 2015.

77. Ibid.

78. Conversation with the author, September 11, 2016.

79. Ibid.

80. Conversation with the author, September 25, 2016.

Notes for Chapter 2

1. Vic Holmes, conversation with the author, December 7, 2014. Civil unions, regarded by some as a stepping-stone on the way to marriage, arose as a way of recognizing a legal relationship between unmarried same-sex partners in states that prohibited them from marrying. Not quite three years after Mark and Vic's first date, Vermont became the first state to offer civil unions. In December 1999 the State Supreme Court ruled that none of the state's arguments in Baker v. State of Vermont "provides a reasonable and just basis for the continued exclusion of same-sex couples from the benefits incident to a civil marriage under Vermont law," but left implementation of their decision to the state legislature. Supporters of same-sex marriage were disappointed when the legislature stopped short of marriage and legalized civil unions. As Mary Bonauto suggests in *Love Unites Us*, "None of us had imagined an artificial splitting of 'marriage' into two components, tangible benefits on the one hand, and the dignity and status of marriage on the other. The dignity of married status was itself one of the benefits of marriage" (76). As their relationship deepened, Mark and Vic realized they could not have agreed more.

   The level of rights and benefits varied from state to state. Because they originated in the states, civil unions did not provide access to benefits conferred by the federal government and did not have to be recognized in other states. Article 1, Section 32 of the Texas Constitution specifically prohibited the state or any political subdivision thereof from creating or recognizing any legal status similar to marriage.

2. Mary Bonauto in oral arguments for Goodridge v. Department of Public Health, 798 N. E. 2nd. 941 (Mass. 2003), cited in Mark Solomon, *Winning Marriage: The Inside Story of How Same-Sex Couples Took on the Politicians and Pundits—and Won*. Lebanon, NH: ForeEdge, 2014.

3. "Fighting Marriage Discrimination in Texas: Mark Phariss and Vic Holmes, Plano, Texas," April 2014, www.freedom tomarry.org/stories/entry/fighting-marriage-discrimination-in-texas. Accessed June 6, 2014.

4. "Plano Couple Files Lawsuit Challenging Marriage Ban," *Dallas Voice*, November 1, 2013, http://www.dallasvoice.com/plano-couple-files-law-suit-challenging-marriage-ban-10160630.html. Accessed June 6, 2016.

5. "Akin Gump Named Among Law360's Pro Bono Firms of the Year for Second Consecutive Year," Akin Gump Strauss Hauer & Feld, September 29, 2014, http://www.akingump.com/en/news-insights/akin-gump-named-among-law360-s-pro-bono-firms-of-the-year-for.html. Accessed October 3, 2014.

6. Pam Coloff, "To Love and to Cherish," *Texas Monthly*, March 2015, 182.

7. Elaine Ayala, Guillermo Contreras and Melissa Fletcher Stoeltje, "Couples Sue over Ban on Same-Sex Marriage," *San Antonio Express News*, October 28, 2013, http://www.expressnews.com/news/local/article/Couples-sue-over-ban-on-same-sex-marriage-4934103.php. Accessed March 2, 2015.
8. Bowers v. Hardwick, 478 U.S. at 194.
9. Ibid. at 196–7.
10. Romer v. Evans, 517 U.S. at 620.
11. Ibid. at 626, 633, 635, 632, 634, 635.
12. Ibid. at 636, 639, 644. (Scalia, A., dissenting.)
13. Ibid. at 638, 644. (Scalia, A., dissenting.)
14. Ibid. at 640, 641, 642, 644. (Scalia, A., dissenting.)
15. Conversation with the author, December 7, 2014.
16. Don Temples, "In His Honor: Shepard Family Creates Foundation," *HRC Quarterly*, Summer 2015, 9.
17. Andrew Sullivan, "Here Comes the Groom," *The New Republic* (August 28, 1989): 22.
18. Ibid.
19. Evan Wolfson, "Same-Sex Marriage and Morality: The Human Rights View of the Constitution," Freedom to Marry, http://www.freedomtomarry.org/pages/publications. Accessed May 15, 2016.
20. Lauren McGaughy, "Unlikely Gay Marriage Pioneers Tied Knot in Houston," *The Houston Chronicle*, November 28, 2014, http://www.houstonchronicle.com/news/politics/texas/article/Unlikely-gay-marriage-pioneers-tied-knot-in-5923174.php. Accessed August 31, 2016.
21. Ibid.
22. Robert Barnes, "40 Years Later, Story of a Same-Sex Marriage in Colo. Remains Remarkable," *The Washington Post,* April 18, 2015, https://www.washingtonpost.com/politics/courts_law/40-years-later-a-same-sex-marriage-in-colorado-remains-remarkable/2015/04/18/e65852d0-e2d4-11e4-b510-962fcfabc310_story.html?utm_term=.61c67c69506a. Accessed January 26, 2016.
23. 74 Haw. 530, 852 P. 2nd at 68.
24. PBS Newshour, "Gay Marriage Debate: Wedded States," PBS, May 23, 1996, http://www.pbs.org/newshour/bb/law-jan-june96-gay_marriage_05-23/. Accessed January 27, 2016.
25. Defense of Marriage Act, Pub.L. 104–199, 110 Stat. 2419 (1996).
26. Solomon, 93.
27. U.S. House, *Report of the Committee on the Judiciary*, July 6, 1996. 104th Cong., 2nd sess., at 2, 4, 9, 10.
28. Goodridge v. Department of Public Health, 798 N. E. 2nd. 941 (Mass. 2003) at 312, 321, 339, 341.

29. Frank Phillips, "Weld Supports Gay Marriage Ruling," *The Boston Globe*, November 27, 2003, http://archive.boston.com/news/local/ articles/2003/11/27/weld_supports_gay_marriage_ruling/. Accessed January 26, 2016.

30. Dale Carpenter, *Flagrant Conduct: The Story of Lawrence v. Texas* (New York: W. W. Norton: 2012), xiv–xv.

31. U.S. Congress, *Report of the Committee on the Judiciary*, July 6, 1996. 104th Cong., 2nd sess., 16.

32. Lawrence v. Texas, 539 U.S. at 575.

33. Ibid. at 576, 571.

34. Ibid. at 578–9.

35. Ibid. at 567, 574.

36. Romer v. Evans at 646. (Scalia, A., dissenting).

37. Lawrence v. Texas, 539 U.S. at 578; 567.

38. Lawrence at 590; 602;604. (Scalia, A., dissenting).

39. Ibid. 593; 589; 599; 601.

40. Ibid. 604; 605.

41. Matt Coles and others, *Winning Marriage: What We Need to Do Now,"* https://s3.amazonaws.com/s3.documentcloud.org/documents/2108219/ final-marriage-concept-paper.pdf. Accessed: January 20, 2016.

42. Roberta Kaplan, *Then Comes Marriage: United States v. Windsor* (New York: Norton, 2015), 120.

43. Debra Cassens Weiss, "Justice Ginsburg: Roe v. Wade Decision Came Too Soon," *ABA Journal*, February 13, 2012, http://www.slate.com/articles/ news_and_politics/jurisprudence/2013/05/justice_ginsburg_and_roe_v_ wade_caution_for_gay_marriage.html. Accessed January 20, 2016.

44. United States v. Windsor, 570 U.S. at 22, 25, 13, 14.

45. Ibid. at 19, 14, 20, 26.

46. Ryan Grim, "Scalia Slams 'Legalistic Argle-Bargle,' 'Re-Argues 'Homosexual Sodomy' in Dissenting DOMA Rant," June 6, 2013, http:// www.huffingtonpost.com/2013/06/26/doma-scalia_n_3503706.html. Accessed April 2, 2015.

47. Vic Holmes, Conversation with the author, December 7, 2014.

48. Ibid.

49. Mark Phariss, Conversation with the author, December 7, 2014.

50. Vic Holmes, Conversation with the author, December 7, 2014.

51. Vic Holmes, Conversation with the author, October 16, 2015.

52. Frank Stenger-Castro, E-mail to Mark Phariss, September 6, 2013.

53. Guillermo Contreras Ayala and Melissa Fletcher Stoeltje, "Couples Sue," *San Antonio Express News*, http://www.expressnews.com/news/ local/article/Couples-sue-over-ban-on-same-sex-marriage-4934103. php. Accessed March 2, 2015.

54. Patrick Michels, "Two Couples Challenge Texas' Same-Sex Marriage Ban," *Texas Observer*, November 1, 2013, http://texasobserver.org/two-couples-challenge-texas-sex-marriage ban/. Accessed April 2, 2015.

55. Plaintiffs' Original Complaint for Declaratory and Injunctive Relief," DeLeon v. Perry 5:13-cv-982 at 9, 2–3, 12, 9–10, 13.

56. Vic Holmes, Conversation with the author, December 7, 2014.

57. Ibid.

58. Ibid.

59. Mark Phariss, E-mail to Elizabeth Birch, October 7, 2013.

60. Elizabeth Birch, E-mail to Mark Phariss, October 8, 2013.

61. Mark Phariss, Conversation with the author, December 7, 2014.

62. The Texas Lyceum, founded in 1980, brings together emerging leaders from across the state to share ideas in a non-partisan, non-political, non-adversarial setting. Membership on the Board of Directors is limited to 96 and past members include one president of the United States, three governors of Texas, and two United States Senators from Texas. Mark Phariss, the first openly gay man to serve on the Board, was elected to the class of 2002 and served two three-year terms.

63. Mark Joseph Stern, "The University of North Carolina's New President Is Shockingly Anti-Gay, *Slate*, October 27, 2015, http://www.slate.com/blogs/outward/2015/10/27/margaret_spellings_ new_unc_president_is_anti_gay.html. Accessed August 4, 2016.

64. Mark Phariss, Conversation with the author, August 25, 2016.

65. Mark Phariss and Vic Holmes, Conversation with the author, December 7, 2014.

66. Peter Myers, Text to Mark Phariss, October 26, 2013.

67. Mark Phariss, Facebook, October 28, 2013.

68. Mark Phariss, Facebook, October 29, 2013.

69. Mark Phariss, Facebook, October 31, 2013.

Notes for Chapter 3

1. Anna Waugh, "Plano Couple Files Lawsuit Challenging Marriage Ban," *Dallas Voice*, Nov. 1, 2013, http://www.dallasvoice.com/plano-couple-files-lawsuit-challenging-marriage-ban-10160630.html. Accessed November 18, 2014.

2. Mark Phariss, E-mail to Akin Gump, October 29, 2013.

3. Vic Holmes, E-mail to Plaintiffs and Akin Gump, October 31, 2013.

4. Mark Phariss, Journal, October 31, 2013 and November 20, 2013.

5. "Transcript of All Pending Matters before the Honorable Sam Sparks," January 9, 2014, Docket Nos. A 13-CA-631 SS and A 13-CA-955 SS, The United States District Court for the Western District of Texas.

6. Mark Phariss, E-mail to Neel Lane and Matt Pepping, January 30, 2014.
7. Vic Holmes, E-mail to Akin Gump legal team and Plaintiffs, October 31, 2013.
8. "Transcript," 4.
9. Mark Phariss, E-mail to Akin Gump Group, January 30, 2014.
10. Mark Phariss, E-mail to Akin Gump Group, February 1, 2014.
11. Plaintiff's Opposed Motion for Preliminary Injunction Enjoining Defendants from Enforcing Texas' Same-Sex Marriage Ban, DeLeon v. Perry 5:13-cv-982-OLG at 41, 1, 42.
12. Ibid., 3.
13. Ibid., 4.
14. Charlie Butts, "Pro-family Leader on Texas Lawsuit: Homosexuals Imposing Their Version of Morality," *News Now*, December 2, 2013, http://www.onenewsnow.com/legal-courts/2013/12/02/pro-family-leader-on-texas-lawsuit-homosexuals-imposing-their-version-of-morality#.Us7K82eA1Ur. Accessed September 4, 2016.
15. Mark Phariss, Journal, January 3, 2014.
16. Mark Phariss, E-mail to Akin Gump Plaintiffs Group, January 6, 2014.
17. Mark Phariss, Journal, November 1, 2013.
18. "UNTHSC Physician Assistant Makes House Calls for Disabled Adults," December 18, 2013, https://www.unthsc.edu/newsroom/story/unthsc-physician-assistant-makes-a%C2%80ahauhouse-calls-for-disabled-adults-3/. Accessed August 4, 2016.
19. Mark Phariss, Facebook, November 27, 2013.
20. Mark Phariss, Facebook, December 31, 2013.
21. Andrew Dial, Letter to Mark Phariss and Vic Holmes, February 27, 2014.
22. Christopher Kelly, "The Accidental Activists," *Texas Monthly*, February, 2014, 40.
23. "Plano Men at Center of Texas Gay Marriage Case That Opens Wednesday," *Dallas Morning News*, February 7, 2014, http://www.dallasnews.com/news/plano/2014/02/07/plano-men-at-center-of-texas-gay-marriage-case-that-opens-wednesday. Accessed November 18, 2014.
24. Ibid.
25. Mark Phariss, Journal, February 8, 2014.
26. Ibid.
27. Mark Phariss, Facebook, February 12, 2014.
28. Transcript of Preliminary Injunction Hearing before the Honorable Orlando L. Garcia District Court Judge," DeLeon v. Perry 5:13-982-OLG, United States District Court, Western District of Texas, San Antonio Division. February 12, 2014, at 2.
29. Transcript of Preliminary Injunction at 4–5, 8.
30. Matt Pepping, Conversation with the author, October 6, 2016.

31. Transcript of Preliminary Injunction at 10.
32. Ibid. at 22–23.
33. Ibid. at 22.
34. Ibid. at 29–31.
35. Ibid. at 32–33.
36. Ibid. at 33, 40, 42, 34.
37. Ibid. at 46.
38. Ibid. at 50.
39. Ibid. at 52, 57.
40. Ibid. at 59–60.
41. Mark Phariss, Journal, February 12, 2014.
42. Robert T. Garrett, "Federal Judge Hears Request to Block Texas Ban on Same-Sex Marriage," February 12, 2014, http://www.dallasnews.com/news/politics/headlines/20140212-federal-judge-hears-request-to-block-texas-ban-on-same-sex-marriage.ece. Accessed August 20, 2016.
43. Julian Castro and Evan Wolfson, "Seeking Freedom for Everyone," *The San Antonio Express Current*, February, 12, 2014, http://www.mysanantonio.com/opinion/commentary/article/Seeking-freedom-for-everyone-5225574.php. Accessed August 8, 2016.
44. Neel Lane, E-mail to Plaintiffs and Attorneys, February 25, 2014.
45. Barry Chasnoff, E-mail to Lawyers and Plaintiffs, February 26, 2014.
46. Victor Holmes, E-mail to the Author, August 10, 2016.
47. DeLeon v. Perry, 975 F. Supp. 2nd 632 (2014) at 12, 13, 30, 31, 32.
48. Matthew Pepping, E-mail to the Plaintiffs, February 26, 2014.
49. Elizabeth Birch, E-mail to Mark Phariss, February 26, 2016; Chad Griffin, E-mail to Mark Phariss, February 26, 2014.
50. Andrew Caine, E-mail to Mark Phariss, February 26, 2014.
51. Lauren Mutti, E-mail to Mark Phariss, February 26, 2014.
52. Debbie Jo Hauppert, E-mail to Mark Phariss, February 26, 2014.
53. Glen Maxey, Comment on the Facebook page of Mark Phariss, February 26, 2014.
54. Matthew Pepping, E-mail to the Plaintiffs, February 27, 2014.
55. Susan Kay, E-mail to Mark Phariss, February 27, 2014.
56. Shelly Kofler, "Greg Abbott Went to Law School with a Plaintiff in Gay Marriage Suit He's Fighting," KERA, February 27, 2016. http://keranews.org/post/greg-abbott-went-law-school-plaintiff-gay-marriage-suit-he-s-fighting. Accessed February 27, 2016.
57. Ibid.
58. Shelly Kofler, "Greg Abbott Faces Law School Friend as Plaintiff in Same-Sex Marriage Suit," KERA, February 28, 2014. http://keranews.org/post/greg-abbott-faces-law-school-friend-plaintiff-same-sex-marriage-suit. Accessed August 20, 2014. In time, Mark's persistence in sending Christmas cards brought the result for which

he had hoped. Days before Christmas 2016 a card arrived from Greg Abbott addressed now to "Mark Phariss and Vic Holmes."

59. Judge Barbara Nellermoe, Comment on Facebook, March 14, 2014.
60. "The Champions for Justice in Texas," *The Melissa Harris-Perry Show*, MSNBC, March 16, 2014, http://www.msnbc.com/melissa-harris-perry/watch/the-champions-for-justice-in-texas-197155395998. Accessed January 2, 2017.
61. "Fighting Marriage Discrimination in Texas: Mark Phariss and Vic Holmes, Plano, Texas," April, 2014, Freedom to Marry, April 2, 2014, http://www.freedomtomarry.org/stories/entry/fighting-marriage-discrimination-in-texas. Accessed August 22, 2016.
62. "Spirit of Texas Honorees on Frontline in Fight for Equality," *Q San Antonio*, May 15, 2014, http://qsanantonio.com/brunch14.html. Accessed August 8, 2014.
63. Motion to Advance Case for Hearing, Fifth Circuit Court of Appeals, No. 14-50196. October 6, 2014.
64. Mark Phariss, Facebook, November 2, 2014.
65. Mark Phariss, Facebook, March 20, 2014.
66. Mark Phariss, Facebook, September 29, 2014.
67. Mark Phariss, Facebook, October 1, 2014.
68. State Defendants' Answer and Affirmative Defenses to the Rummell Amended Complaint," District Court for the District of Oregon, February 20, 2014. No. 6:13-cv-01834-MC.
69. Geiger v. Kitzhaber, 19 May, 2014.No. 6:13-cv-O1834-MC at 26.
70. Mark Phariss, Facebook, November 15, 2014.

Notes for Chapter 4

1. Kelsey Davis, "Crowds Flock to Fifth Circuit Court of Appeals to Hear Arguments Regarding Same-Sex Marriage in Louisiana, Mississippi, and Texas," WDSU News, January 9, 2015, http://www.wdsu.com/news/local-news/new-orleans/crowds-flock-to-fifth-circuit-court-of-appeals-to-hear-arguments-regarding-samesex-marriage/30624316. Accessed January 12, 2015.
2. Ibid.
3. Ibid.
4. Ibid.
5. Mark Curriden, "Meet the Chief Judge of the Nation's Most Divisive, Controversial and Conservative Appeals Court," *ABA Journal*, February 1, 2014, http://www.abajournal.com/magazine/article/meet_the_chief_judge_of_the_nations_most_divisive_controversial/. Accessed December 9, 2014.
6. Dianna Wray, "Backstory: The Fifth Circuit Court Wasn't Always the Most Conservative Court Around," *Houston News*, November 6,

2014, http://www.houstonpress.com/news/backstory-the-fifth-circuit-wasnt-always-the-most-conservative-court-around-6715354. Accessed December 10, 2014.

7. Faderman, 312.
8. Mark Curriden, "Meet the Chief."
9. Chris Casteel, "Oklahoma Judge on 10th U.S. Circuit Court of Appeals Defies Expectations in Same-Sex Marriage Case," *The Oklahoman*, August 10, 2014, http://newsok.com/article/5143093. Accessed January 9, 2017.
10. Mark Curriden, "Judge Builds Respect through Years on the Bench," *The Dallas Morning News*, August 2014, http://www.dallasnews.com/news/news/2014/08/02/judge-builds-respect-through-years-on-the-bench. Accessed January 2, 2017.
11. Emma Margolin, Twitter, January 9, 2015, https://twitter.com/emargony/status/553584703555399680. Accessed January 12, 2015.
12. Chris Geidner, Twitter, January 9, 2015, https://twitter.com/search?q=MS%20and%20Tx%20arguments%20remain&src=typd. Accessed January 12, 2015.
13. Paul Weiss Rifkind Wharton & Garrison, "Roberta Kaplan," https://www.paulweiss.com/professionals/partners-and-counsel/roberta-a-kaplan.aspx. Accessed: January 9, 2017.

Notes for Chapter 5

1. Diane Anderson-Minshall, "Remembering the Worst Mass Killing of LGBT People in U. S. History," *The Advocate*, November 15, 2013, http://www.advocate.com/crime/2013/11/15/remembering-worst-mass-killing-lgbt-people-us-history. Accessed March 9, 2015.
2. Clendinen and Nagourney, 187.
3. Gordon Tanner, E-mail to Vic Holmes, December 11, 2014.
4. Transcript, DeLeon v. Perry, 14:50196 (5th Cir 2015) at 4, 49, 5.
5. Ibid. at 5.
6. Nina Totenberg, "Federal Judge Richard Posner: The GOP Has Made Me Less Conservative," NPR, July 5, 2012, http://www.npr.org/sections/itsallpolitics/2012/07/05/156319272/federal-judge-richard-posner-the-gop-has-made-me-less-conservative. Accessed January 15, 2015.
7. Baskin v. Bogan at 38.
8. Ibid. at 19–20, 37, 12, 12.
9. Transcript, DeLeon v. Perry at 16–7.
10. Ibid. at 8, 7,11, 7.
11. Vic Holmes, Facebook, January 9, 2016.
12. Transcript, DeLeon v. Perry at 11–12.

13. Ibid. at 22–4, 19.
14. Ibid. at 7, 23, 11, 14, 18.
15. Ibid. at 13.
16. Baskin v. Bogan at 9.
17. Transcript, DeLeon v. Perry at 14, 16.
18. Ibid. at 16, 19–20.
19. Ibid. at 21–22.
20. Ibid. at 24–27.
21. Ibid. at p. 28.
22. Ibid.
23. Ibid. at 33, 28.
24. Baskin v. Bogan at 2.
25. Transcript, DeLeon v. Perry at 29.
26. Ibid. at 29, 42–3, 30–31.
27. DeBoer v. Snyder at 56.
28. Baskin v. Bogan at 14.
29. Transcript, *DeBoer v. Perry* at 32.
30. Ibid. at 33, 39, 33.
31. Ibid. at 39.
32. St. Joseph Abbey v. Castile at 18.
33. Transcript, DeLeon v. Perry at 38.
34. Ibid. at 36, 40.
35. Ibid. at 42–3, 46–7.
36. Mark Phariss, Facebook, January 4, 2015.
37. Kristen Johnson, Text to Mark Phariss, January 13, 2015.
38. Jim Rainbolt-Bailey, Facebook Message to Mark Phariss, January 9, 2015.
39. "Thank You, Texas Plaintiffs," Texas for Marriage, January 28, 2015, http://texasformarriage.org/messages-of-support-for-texas-plaintiffs. Accessed January 28, 2015.
40. Conversation with the author, January 12, 2015.
41. Mark Phariss, E-mail to Attorneys and Plaintiffs, January 14, 2015.
42. "The Supreme Court and Gay Marriage" (editorial), *New York Times*, January 16, 2015, https://www.nytimes.com/2015/01/17/opinion/the-supreme-court-and-gay-marriage.html. Accessed January 16, 2015.
43. "It's Official: The Supreme Court Will Review the Freedom to Marry in 2015!" Freedom to Marry, http://www.freedomtomarry.org/blog/entry/its-official-the-supreme-court-will-review-the-freedom-to-marry-in-2017. Accessed January 16, 2015.
44. James Esseks, "The End Game for Marriage Equality is Here," *The Huffington Post*, January 15, 2015, http://www.huffingtonpost.com/james-d-exxeks/the-end-game-is-here-for_b_6489404.html. Accessed January 16, 2015.

45. David G. Savage, "Supreme Court Set to Decide National Debate on Gay Marriage," *Los Angeles Times,* January 16, 2016, http://www. freedomtomarry.org/blog/entry/its-official-the-supreme-court-will-review-the-freedom-to-marry-in-2017. Accessed January 16, 2016.
46. Mark Phariss, Facebook, March 5, 2015.
47. Neel Lane, E-mail to the plaintiffs, January 16, 2015.
48. "Lane:5ᵗʰ Circuit Court Should Still Rule," *The Dallas Voice*, January 16, 2015, http://www.dallasvoice.com/;ane-5th-circuit-court-rule-10188194. html. Accessed January 17, 2015.
49. "Plano Couple Optimistic about Future of Same Sex Marriage," CBS Dallas-Fort Worth, January 16, 2015, 2015, http://dfw.cbslocal/2015/01/ 16/plano-couple-optimistic-about-future-of-same-sex-marriage/. Accessed May 27.
50. "Join Us on Decision Day," Texas for Marriage, https://www. facebook.com/freedomtomarry.org/photos/a.215294370092. 270234.40484170092/10155192405760093/?type=1&theater. Accessed January 26, 2015.
51. Mark Phariss, "Repealing Plano's Equal Rights Ordinance Would Give City a Black Eye, Bad Reputation," *Dallas Morning News*, January 27, 2015, http://lgbtqblog.dallasnews.com/category/discrimination/page/2/. Accessed January 28, 2015.
52. Pamela Coloff, E-mail to the author, May 31, 2015.
53. Roar of the Crowd, *Texas Monthly*, April 2015, 8–10.
54. Veronica Zaragovia, "Gay Couples Ask Court to Lift Hold on Same-Sex Marriage in Texas," KUT.org, February 12, 2015, http://kut.org/post/ gay-couples-ask-court-lift-hold-same-sex-marriage-texas. Accessed February 12, 2015.
55. Coloff, "To Love and to Cherish," 179, 181.
56. Plaintiff's Opposed Motion to Lift Stay of Injunction for all Parties or, in the Alternative, for Order Re Birth of Child, *DeLeon v. Perry*, 14-50196, February 11, 2015, 4.
57. Calily Bien, "Couple Fighting for Same-Sex Marriage Rights Give Birth to Baby Girl," KXAN, March 23, 2015, http://kxan.com/2015/03/23/ couple-fighting-for-same-sex-marriage-rights-gives-birth-to baby-girl/. Accessed March 23, 2015.
58. "Texas Same-Sex Marriage Plaintiffs Endure 2ⁿᵈ Harrowing Birth with No Parental Rights," Towerload, March 24, 20135, http://www.towleroad. com/2015/03/texas-same-sex-marriage-plaintiffs-endure-2nd-harrowing-child-birth-with-no-legal-rights/. Accessed March 24, 2015.
59. Mark Phariss, Facebook, May 30, 2015.
60. Mark Phariss, Facebook, February 21, 2015.
61. Mark Phariss, E-mail to the author, March 21, 2015.
62. Conversaton with the author, June 15, 2015.

Notes for Chapter 6

1. Tony Adams, Interview with Mark Phariss and Vic Holmes, April 27, 2015.
2. Chris Johnson, "Marriage Plaintiffs Gather to Celebrate on Eve of Arguments," *Washington Blade,* April 28, 2015, http://www.washingtonblade.com/2015/04/28/marriage-plaintiffs-gather-to-celebrate-on-eve-of-arguments/. Accessed May 5, 2015.
3. Ibid.
4. Conversation with the author, April 27, 2015.
5. Ibid.
6. Jayne O'Donnell, "Line Sitters, Activists Keep It Civil before High Court's Gay Marriage Case. *USA Today*, Apr. 27, 2015, http://www.usatoday.com/story/news/politics/2015/04/27/supreme-court-line-sitters-activists-gay-marriage-case/26463081/. Accessed April 9, 2016.
7. "The Supreme Court of the United States: The Supreme Court Building," http://www.supremecourt.gov/about/courtbuilding.aspx. Accessed April 23, 2015.
8. Mark Phariss, Facebook, April 23, 2015.
9. Mark Phariss, E-mail to Mary Bonauto, March 31, 2015.
10. Jerry Orr, Letter to Mark Phariss, May 15, 1974.
11. Mark Phariss, Facebook. April 24, 2015.
12. Before the legal battle for marriage equality was over, DeLeon v. Perry would be cited as precedential 204 times. For a list of the citations, see Google Scholar: https://scholar.google.com/scholar?q=deLeon+v.+perry&hl=en&as_sdt=6&as_vis=1&oi=scholart&sa=X&ved=0ahUKEwjFrpijvbrRAhVB_mMKHeP8DicQgQMIGTAA. Accessed: January 11, 2017.
13. Daniel Rafter, E-mail to Mark Phariss, March 20, 2014.
14. Mark Phariss, Chronology, April 22, 2004.
15. *Meet the Press*, NBC News, May 6, 2012, http://www.nbcnews.com/id/47311900/ns/meet_the_press-transcripts/t/may-joe-biden-kelly-ayotte-diane-swonk-tom-brokaw-chuck-todd/#.WIDkkxsrJ1s. Accessed March 3, 2016.
16. Barak Obama, "Robin Roberts ABC News Interview with President Obama" (transcript), ABC News, May 9, 2012. http://abcnews.go.com/Politics/transcript-robin-roberts-abc-news-interview-president-obama/story?id=16316043. Accessed March 3, 2016.
17. William Clinton, "It's Time to Overturn DOMA," *Washington Post*, March 7, 2013, https://www.washingtonpost.com/opinions/bill-clinton-its-time-to-overturn-doma/2013/03/07/fc184408-8747-11e2-98a3-b3db6b9ac586_story.html. Accessed March 3, 2016.

18. "Hillary Clinton for HRC's Americans for Marriage Equality," March 18, 2013, https://www.youtube.com/watch?v=6RP9pbKMJ7c. Accessed April 9, 2016.

19. Ruth Bader Ginsburg, "Ruth Bader Ginsburg Thinks Americans Are Ready for Gay Marriage," interview by Greg Stohr and Matthew Winkler, *Bloomberg Business*, February 12, 2015, http://www.bloomberg. com/news/articles/2015-02-12/ginsburg-says-u-s-ready-to-accept-ruling-approving-gay-marriage-i61z6gq2. Accessed March 6, 2016.

20. Andrew R. Flores and Scott Barclay, "Trends in Support for Marriage for Same-Sex Couples by State," April 2015, http://williamsinstitute. law.ucla.edu/wp-content/uploads/Trends-in-Public-Support-for-Same-Sex-Marriage-2004-2014.pdf. Accessed March 20, 2016.

21. Carrie Dann, "Poll: Majority Wants Supreme Court to OK Same Sex Marriage Nationally," May 4, 2015, http://www.nbcnews.com/meet-the-press/poll-majority-wants-supreme-court-ok-same-sex-marriage-nationally-n353411. Accessed March 3, 2016.

22. Justin McCarthy, "Record-High 60% of Americans Support Same-Sex Marriage," May 19, 2015, http://www.gallup.com/poll/183272/record-high-americans-support-sex-marriage.aspx. Accessed May 19, 2015.

23. Ilya Somin, "Assessing the Sixth Circuit Decision Upholding the Constitutionality of Law Banning Same-Sex Marriage," *The Washington Post*, November 6, 2014, https://www.washingtonpost.com/news/volokh-conspiracy/wp/2014/11/06/assessing-the-sixth-circuit-upholding-the-constitutionality-of-laws-banning-same-sex-marriage/. Accessed March 20, 2016.

24. DeBoer v. Snyder, 973 F. Supp. 2d 757, 768 (EDMich. 2014) at 53. (Daughtrey, M. C., dissenting).

25. Mark Phariss, Facebook, October 6, 2014.

26. DeBoer v. Snyder at 43–4, 55.

27. Brief of the Commonwealth of Virginia as Amicus Curiae in Support of Petitioners, Obergefell v. Hodges, 576 U.S.__ (2015) at 3–4.

28. Brief of 379 Employers and Organizations Representing Employers as Amici Curiae in Support of Petitioners, Obergefell v. Hodges, 576 U.S.__ (2015) at 19, 17, 38, 20, 41–2.

29. Sheryl Gay Stoleberg, "Strategist Out of Closet and into Fray, This Time for Gay Marriage," *New York Times*, June 19, 2013, http://www.nytimes. com/2013/06/20/us/strategist-out-of-closet-and-into-fray-this-time-for-gay-marriage.html. Accessed March 28, 2016.

30. Marc Ambinder, "Bush Campaign Chief and Former RNC Chair Ken Mehlman: I'm Gay," *The Atlantic*, August 25, 2010, http://www.theatlantic.com/ politics/archive/2010/08/bush-campaign-chief-and-former-rnc-chair-ken-mehlman-im-gay/62065/. Accessed March 28, 2016.

31. Brief of Amici Curiae Kenneth B. Mehlman et al. Supporting Petitioners, Obergefell v. Hodges, 576 U.S.__ (2015) at 1–3, 6, 25, 1.
32. Brief of Historians of Marriage and the American Historical Association as Amici Curiae in Support of Petitioners, Obergefell v. Hodges, 576 U.S.__ (2015) at 1, 7, 2, 22.
33. Steven G. Calabresi and Hannah M. Begley, "Originalism and Same Sex Marriage," Northwestern Public Law Research Paper No. 14–51, http://papers.ssrn.com/sol3/papers.cfm?abstract_id=2509443. Accessed March 2, 2016.
34. Brief of Ninety-Two Plaintiffs in Marriage Cases in Alabama, Alaska, Arkansas, Indiana, Kansas, Louisiana, Mississippi, Missouri, Montana, Nebraska, North Carolina, North Dakota, South Carolina, South Dakota and Texas as Amici Curiae in Support of Petitioners, Obergefell v. Hodges, 576 U.S.__ (2015) at 6, 11.
35. Ibid. at 13–15.
36. Ibid. at 4, 20.
37. Texas Health and Safety Code §163.002. Instructional Elements. See also § Section 21.06, Penal Code; Tex. Health & Safety Code Ann. Sec. 85.007.
38. Bud Kennedy, "Perry Said If Gays Like Another State's Laws, 'That's Where They Should Live'," *Fort Worth Star-Telegram*, June 12, 2014. Reprinted from a column published on June 7, 2005, http://www.star-telegram.com/mobile/m-opinion/article3861668.html. Accessed April 4, 2016.
39. "The American Presidency Project: Political Party Platforms Receiving Votes: 1840–2012," http://www.presidency.ucsb.edu/platforms.php. Accessed April 4, 2016.
40. "Republican Platform 2015: Renewing American Values," https://gop.com/platform/renewing-american-values/. Accessed March 4, 2016.
41. Mark Phariss, Facebook, March 6, 2015.
42. *Luther Strange, Attorney General of Alabama v. Cari D. Searcy, et al: On Application for Stay*, 574 U.S. (2015) (Scalia, A., dissenting).
43. Vic Holmes, Facebook, April 28, 2015.
44. Emmarie Huetteman, "Outside the Court, Many Still Seek a Peek," *New York Times*, April 28, 2015, http://www.nytimes.com/live/supreme-court-same-sex-marriage-arguments/outside-the-court-many-still-seek-a-peak/. Accessed March 9, 2016.
45. Conversation with the author, April 28, 2015.
46. Tracy Hollister, Unpublished Memoir shared with the author. April 28, 2015.
47. Ibid.
48. Ibid.

49. Comment on Mark Phariss's post to Facebook, April 28, 2015.

50. Vic Holmes, Facebook, April 28, 2015.

51. Mark Phariss, conversation with the author, April 28, 2015.

52. www.youtube.com. Accessed June 1, 2015. The video has since deleted from YouTube.

53. Tracy Hollister, Unpublished Memoir.

54. Ibid.

55. "Booker Takes to US Senate Floor ahead of Same-Sex Marriage Arguments in Supreme Court Two Weeks from Now," CBS News. April 14, 2015, http://philadelphia.cbslocal.com/2015/04/14/booker-takes-to-us-senate-floor-ahead-of-same-sex-marriage-arguments-in-supreme-court-two-weeks-from-now/. Accessed May 19, 2015.

56. Mark Phariss, conversation with the author, March 19, 2015.

Notes for Chapter 7

1. "Supreme Court of the United States: The Court Building," http://www.supremecourt.gov/about/courtbuilding.aspx. Accessed April 23, 2015.

2. Obergefell v. Hodges, Transcript at 4

3. Ibid. at 4–5.

4. "U.S. Senate Judiciary Committee Hearing on Judge Samuel Alito's Nomination to the Supreme Court" (transcript), *The Washington Post*, January 11, 2006, http://www.washingtonpost.com/wp-dyn/content/article/2006/01/11/AR2006011101148.html. Accessed August 31, 2016,

5. Ibid. at 5, 6–7,9, 14, 12.

6. Ibid. at 16, 20, 21–2.

7. Ibid. at 23.

8. Ibid. at 7–8, 10–11.

9. Ibid. at 22, 20–1.

10. Ibid. at 23, 26, 27.

11. Neal Broverman, "Antigay Heckler Dragged Out of Supreme Court," *The Advocate*, April 28, 2015, http://www.advocate.com/politics/marriage-equality/2015/04/28/antigay-heckler-dragged-out-supreme-court. Accessed April 4, 2016.

12. Charles Massey, E-mail to the author, April 8, 2016.

13. Neal Broverman, "Antigay Heckler."

14. Kathleen L. Arberg (Public Information Officer, U. S. Supreme Court), E-mail to the author, May 20, 2015.

15. Mark Phariss, E-mail to the author, May 13, 2015.

16. Jeffrey Toobin, "Justice Scalia's Shameful Joke," *The New Yorker*, April 28, 2015, http://www.newyorker.com/news/daily-comment/on-gay-marriage-its-not-scalias-court. Accessed April 13, 2015.

17. Ibid. at 28–30.

18. Ibid. at 7, 30.
19. Ibid. at 30–31.
20. Ibid. at 41–2, 44.
21. Ibid. at 43.
22. United States v. Windsor at 8, 14. (Alito, S., dissenting)
23. Obergefell v. Hodges, Transcript at 45, 47–8, 51, 66, 70.
24. Ibid. at 47, 58–9.
25. Ibid. at 50–1, 61.
26. Ibid. at 65–7.
27. Ibid. at 43, 49.
28. Ibid. at 72–3, 80.
29. Karina Kling, "Supreme Court Hears Same-Sex Marriage Arguments," Time Warner News, April 28, 2015, http://www.twcnews.com/tx/texas/politics/2015/04/28/same-sex-marriage-case-before-supreme-court.html. Accessed June 6, 2016.
30. Marc Solomon, Facebook, June 15, 2015.
31. Mark Phariss, E-mail to the author, June 25, 2015.
32. Mark Phariss, Facebook, June 22, 2015.
33. Chris Johnson, "Plaintiff Couples on Pins and Needles Awaiting Ruling," *The Washington Blade*, June 24, 2015, http://www.washingtonblade.com/2015/06/24/plaintiff-couples-on-pins-and-needles-awaiting-ruling/. Accessed September 8, 2015.
34. "Gay Couples Count on Legal Blessing to Wed," *USA Today*, June 25, 2015.
35. Dana Lopez, Facebook, June 25, 2015.
36. Mark Phariss, Facebook, June 26, 2015.
37. Andrew Hamm, E-mail to the author, October 7, 2015.
38. Freedom to Marry, Facebook, June 26, 2015.
39. Mark Phariss, Facebook, June 26, 2015.
40. Amy Howe, SCOTUSblog, June 26, 2015, http://www.scotusblog.com/. Accessed June 26, 2015.
41. Conversation with the author, June 27, 2015.
42. Mark Phariss, Facebook, June 26, 2015.
43. Obergefell v. Hodges at 1–2, 10, 13, 28.
44. Comments on Mark Phariss' Facebook page, June 26, 2015.
45. Jamie Haskins, Facebook, June 26, 2015.
46. Mark Walsh, "A 'View' from the Courtroom: A Marriage Celebration, SCOTUSblog (Jun. 26, 2015, 6:13 PM), http://www.scotusblog.com/2015/06/a-view-from-the-courtroom-a-marriage-celebration/. Accessed June 27, 2015.
47. "Supreme Court Strikes Down Ban on Same-Sex Marriage—NBC News Special Report," April 26, 2015, NBC, https://www.youtube.com/watch?v=wFbl0DuCq6g; Special Report: CBS News, "Special Report: Supreme

Court Legalizes Same-Sex Marriage," CBS, April 26, 2015, https://www. youtube.com/watch?v=0L7HfOjivEQ. Accessed June 26, 2015.

48. Conversation with the author, December 7, 2015.

49. Ibid.

50. "Gay Marriage Arrives in Texas," *Texas Observer*, June 26, 2015, https:// www.texasobserver.org/supreme-court-upholds-same-sex-marriage/. Accessed June 26, 2015.

51. Diane Herbst, "First Same-Sex Couple Marries in Dallas County After 50-Year Wait," *Time*, June 26, 2015, http://time.com/3938782/jack-evans-george-harris-marriage-texas/. Accessed June 26, 2015.

52. C. R. Denning, "Impromptu Celebration Outside SCOTUS After Gay-Marriage Ruling," Hit & Rumble Blog, April 26, 2015, http:// reason.com/blog/2015/06/26/libertarians-join-celebration-outside-sc. Accessed June 27, 2015.

53. "Love Ignites: A One Year Anniversary Celebration for Marriage Equality," Cathedral of Hope, Dallas, June 26, 2016.

54. *Huntsman v. Heavilin*, Facebook, April 26, 2015.

55. Mike Wallace, Facebook, April 26, 2015.

56. Marc Solomon, Facebook, April 26, 2015.

57. Mark Joseph Stern, "How the Mastermind of Marriage Equality Felt," July 8, 2015 http://www.slate.com/blogs/outward/2015/07/08/evan_wolfson_how_the_marriage_equality_mastermind_felt_when_he_won. html. Accessed July 8, 2015.

58. Kali Wright-Smith, comment on the Facebook page of Slate.com, April 26, 2015.

59. Neel Lane, comment on Facebook post by Mark Phariss, June 27, 2015.

60. Proprietary video provided by Susan Risdon, Red Media Group.

61. Proprietary video provided by Susan Risdon, Red Media Group.

62. Barack Obama, "Remarks by the President on the Supreme Court Decision on Marriage Equality," June 26, 2015, https://www.whitehouse. gov/the-press-office/2015/06/26/remarks-president-supreme-court-decision-marriage-equality. Accessed June 26, 2016.

63. Mark Calvey, "Wells Fargo Unveils Its First National Ads Featuring Same-Sex Couple," *San Francisco Business Times*, April 24, http:// www.bizjournals.com/sanfrancisco/blog/2015/04/wells-fargo-lgbt-same-sex-tiffany.html. Accessed June 1, 2016.

64. "From Absolut to Zappos Major Companies Get Behind the Supreme Court Decision," *Queerty*, April 26, 2015. http://www.queerty.com/ from-absolut-to-zappos-major-companies-get-behind-the-supreme-court-decision-20150629/yahoo. Accessed June 29, 2015.

65. Mark Phariss, Facebook, June 28, 2015.

66. L Style G Style, Facebook, June 29, 2015.

67. Evan Wolfson, E-mail to Mark Phariss and Vic Holmes, July 2, 2015.

68. Neel Lane, Letter to the United States Court of Appeals for the Fifth Circuit, June 29, 2015.
69. United States Court of Appeals for the Fifth Circuit, Appeal from the United States District Court for the Western District of Texas. Case: 14-50196. Document: 00513102283. July 1, 2015.
70. Conversation with the author, May 24, 2015.
71. Vic Holmes, Facebook, July 1, 2015.
72. Mark Phariss, Facebook, July 24, 2016.
73. United States District Court for the Western District of Texas, San Antonio Division, Cause No. SA-13-CA—00982-OLG. August 11, 2015.
74. John Stone-Hoskins, E-mail to Mark Phariss, August 9, 2015.
75. United States District Court for the Western District of Texas, San Antonio Division. Case 5:13-cv-00982-OLG, Document 113. August 11, 2015.
76. Mark Phariss, Facebook, August 9, 2015.
77. Vic Holmes, Facebook, August 9, 2015.
78. Mark Phariss, Facebook, July 17, 2015.
79. "Vice President Joe Biden Addresses the 2015 HRC National Dinner," Oct. 3, 2015, https://www.hrc.org/videos/videos-vice-president-joe-biden-addresses-the-2015-hrc-national-dinner. Accessed December 20, 2016.
80. Mark Phariss, Facebook Messenger, October 3, 2015.
81. Conversation with the author, October 7, 2015.
82. Michelle Casady, "Texas Pair, Marriage Equality Plaintiffs, Get License to Wed," *San Antonio Express News*, September 25, 2015, http://www.mysanantonio.com/news/local/article/Plaintiffs-in-marriage-equality-suit-finally-get-6530847.php. Accessed September 26, 2015.
83. Conversation with the author, October 7, 2015.
84. "Gay Marriage Arrives in Texas," June 26, 2015, https://www.texasobserver.org/supreme-court-upholds-same-sex-marriage/. Accessed June 27, 2015.
85. Erin Nichols, "Same-Sex Couple Returns to Bexar County for Marriage License," Fox News, September 25, 2015, http://news4sanantonio.com/news/local-deprecated/same-sex-couple-returns-to-bexar-county-for-marriage-license. Accessed September 36, 2015.
86. Conversation with the author, October 7, 2015.
87. Casady, "Texas Pair," September 26, 2015.
88. Ibid.

Notes for Chapter 8

1. "Remarks by the President at LGBT Pride," Reception, June 19, 2016, http://obamawhitehouse.archives.gov/the-press-office/2016/06/09/remarks-president-lgbt-pride-reception. Accessed January 23, 2017.

2. "Governor Abbott Statement on Supreme Court Ruling on Same-Sex Marriage," June 26, 2016, http://gov.texas.gov/news/press-release/21131. Accessed September 7, 2016.

3. "Preserving Religious Liberty for all Texans," June 26, 2015, http://gov.texas.gov/files/press-office/State_AgencyHeads_SCOTUS_Rulin_06262015.pdf. Accessed September 8, 2016.

4. "Lt. Governor Patrick Requests Legal Opinion from Texas Attorney General in Preparation for Supreme Court Ruling," June 26, 2015, https://www.ltgov.state.tx.us/2015/06/26/lt-governor-patrick-requests-legal-opinion-from-texas-attorney-general-in-preparation-for-supreme-court-ruling/. Accessed September 9, 2016.

5. "Lt. Governor Patrick Statement on Supreme Court Ruling on Same-Sex Marriage," June 26, 2015, https://www.ltgov.state.tx.us/2015/06/26/lt-governor-patrick-statement-on-supreme-court-ruling-on-same-sex-marriage/. Accessed September 8, 2015.

6. Alysin Camerota, "Texas Prepares for Same-Sex Marriage Fight," CNN, May 13, 2015, https://www.youtube.com/watch?v=Xro9qU5ic0o. Accessed September 9, 2015.

7. "Attorney General Paxton: Religious Liberties of Texas Public Officials Remain Constitutionally Protected after *Obergefell v. Hodges*," June 28, 2015, https://www.texasattorneygeneral.gov/static/5144.html. Accessed September 7, 2015.

8. Kenneth Paxton, Letter to Lieutenant Governor Dan Patrick, June 28, 2015, https://www.texasattorneygeneral.gov/opinions/opinions/51paxton/op/2015/kp0025.pdf. Accessed September 7, 2015.

9. Mark Phariss, Facebook, July 1, 2015.

10. Stern, "How the Mastermind of Marriage Equality Felt."

11. "Without Delay: HRC Calls on State Officials to Remove Obstacles to Marriage Equality Immediately," June 26, 2015, http://www.hrc.org/blog/without-delay-hrc-calls-on-state-officials-to-remove-obstacles-to-marriage. Accessed June 27, 2015.

12. John Wright, "Equality Texas Optimistic Despite Record Number of Anti-LGBT Bills," *OutSmart*, 1 April, 2015, http://www.outsmartmagazine.com/2015/04/equality-texas-optimistic-despite-record-number-of-anti-lgbt-bills/. Accessed July 18, 2015.

13. Daniel Williams, E-mail to the author, July 20, 2015.

14. John Wright, "Texas Lawmakers File Record Number of Anti-LGBT Bills," *Texas Observer*, March 17, 2005, https://www.texasobserver.org/texas-lawmakers-file-record-number-of-anti-lgbt-bills/. Accessed July 15, 2015.

15. "Governor Abbott Statement on Supreme Court Same-Sex Marriages Cases."

16. Mark Phariss, Facebook, May 11, 2015.

17. Rick Jervis, "Texas Takes Defiant Stance as Gay Marriage Decision Looms," *USA Today*, April 29, 2015, http://www.usatoday.com/story/news/2015/04/29/texas-same-sex-marriage-supreme-court/26577219/. Accessed April 29, 2015.
18. Ibid.
19. Mark Phariss, Facebook, April 30, 2015.
20. Steve Rudner, Facebook, April 30, 2015.

Notes for Chapter 9

1. Audrey Remley, E-mail to Mark Phariss, June 2, 2015.
2. Conversation with the author, October 18, 2015.
3. Robert Craycraft, E-mail to Mark Phariss, November 19, 2015.
4. Mark Phariss, Facebook, April 17, 2015.
5. Shannon Walker, E-mail to the author, December 8, 2015.
6. Olga King, E-mail to Mark Phariss, April 23, 2015.
7. Conversation with the author, July 22, 2015.
8. "Same-Sex Marriage Advocates Finally Wed," WFAA, November 22, 2015, www.wffaa.com. Accessed Nov. 29, 2015.
9. President and Mrs. Barack Obama, Letter to Vic Holmes and Mark Phariss, November 10, 2015.
10. Hillary Clinton, Letter to Mark Phariss and Victor Holmes, November 22, 2015.
11. Celia Israel, Letter to Mark Phariss and Vic Holmes, November 21, 2015.
12. Evan Wolfson, E-mail to Mark Phariss, November 11, 2015.
13. Steve Rudner, E-mail to Mark Phariss, November 11, 2015.
14. "The Virginia Declaration of Rights," The Constitution Society, http://www.constitution.org/bcp/virg_dor.htm. Accessed December 8, 2015.
15. John Holstead, E-mail to the author, January 4, 2016.
16. Margaret Gragg, E-mail to Mark Phariss and Vic Holmes, July 7, 2015.
17. Frederick Miller, Facebook, November 22, 2015.
18. Jack Evans, Facebook, November 23, 2015.
19. David Collins, Facebook, November 22, 2015.
20. Angela Ellis, Facebook, November 21, 2015.
21. E-mail to the Author, September 12, 2016.
22. E-mail to Mark Phariss, November 22, 2015.
23. Corie Olivares, Facebook, November 25, 2015.
24. Mark Phariss, Facebook, November 9, 2015.
25. Vic Holmes, Facebook, January 9, 2016.

Bibliography

Abbott, Greg. "Governor Abbott Statement on Supreme Court Ruling on Same-Sex Marriage," June 26, 2016, http://gov.texas.gov/news/press-release/21131. Accessed September 7, 2016.

Abbott, Greg. "Preserving Religious Liberty for all Texans," June 26, 2015, http://gov.texas.gov/files/press-office/State_AgencyHeads_SCOTUS_Rulin_06262015.pdf. Accessed September 8, 2016.

"Akin Gump Named Among Law360's Pro Bono Firms of the Year for Second Consecutive Year," Akin Gump Strauss Hauer & Feld, September 29, 2014, http://www.akingump.com/en/news-insights/akin-gump-named-among-law360-s-pro-bono-firms-of-the-year-for.html. Accessed October 3, 2014.

Alston, Joshua. "Pro Bono Firm of 2014: Akin Gump," *Law 360*, September 29, 2014, https://www.akingump.com/images/content/3/2/v2/32179/Pro-Bono-Firm-Of-2014-Akin-Gump.pdf. Accessed October 3, 2014.

Ambinder, Mark. "Bush Campaign Chief and Former RNC Chair Ken Mehlman: I'm Gay," *The Atlantic*, August 25, 2010, http://www.theatlantic.com/politics/archive/2010/08/bush-campaign-chief-and-former-rnc-chair-ken-mehlman-im-gay/62065/. Accessed March 28, 2016.

"The American Presidency Project: Political Party Platforms Receiving Votes: 1840-2012," http://www.presidency.ucsb.edu/platforms.php. Accessed April 4, 2016.

Anderson, Christopher. "Gay-Hiring Proposal Draws Big Reaction," *San Antonio Express News*, January 28, 1998, http://nl.newsbank.com/nl-search/we/Archives?p_action+doc&p_docid...rname=refuser&s_account=AC11405613534812474&s_upgradable=no. Accessed February 21, 2016.

Anderson-Minshall, Diane. "Remembering the Worst Mass Killing of LGBT People in U. S. History," *The Advocate*, November 15, 2013, http://www.advocate.com/crime/2013/11/15/remembering-worst-mass-killing-lgbt-people-us-history. Accessed March 9, 2015.

Angulo, A. J. *Miseducation: A History of Ignorance-Making in America and Abroad*. Baltimore: Johns Hopkins UP, 2016.

Ayala, Elaine. "Couples Sue Over Ban on Same-Sex Marriage," *San Antonio Express News*, October 28, 2013, http://www.expressnews.com/news/local/article/Couples-sue-over-ban-on-same-sex-marriage-4934103.php. Accessed March 2, 2015.

Barnes, Robert. "40 Years Later, Story of a Same-Sex Marriage in Colo. Remains Remarkable," *The Washington Post,* April 18, 2015, https://www.washingtonpost.com/politics/courts_law/40-years-later-a-same-sex-marriage-in-colorado-remains-remarkable/2015/04/18/

e65852d0-e2d4-11e4-b510-962fcfabc310_story.html?utm_
term=.61c67c69506a. Accessed January 26, 2016.

Biden, Joseph, Interview with Chuck Todd, *Meet the Press*. NBC News,
May 6, 2012, http://www.nbcnews.com/id/47311900/ns/meet_the_press-
transcripts/t/may-joe-biden-kelly-ayotte-diane-swonk-tom-brokaw-
chuck-todd/#.WIDkkxsrJ1s. Accessed March 3, 2016.

Bien, Calily. "Couple Fighting for Same-Sex Marriage Rights Give Birth
to Baby Girl," KXAN, March 23, 2015, http://kxan.com/2015/03/23/
couple-fighting-for-same-sex-marriage-rights-gives-birth-to   baby-girl/.
Accessed March 23, 2015.

"Booker Takes to US Senate Floor ahead of Same-Sex Marriage Arguments
in Supreme Court Two Weeks from Now," CBS News. April 14, 2015,
http://philadelphia.cbslocal.com/2015/04/14/booker-takes-to-us-senate-
floor-ahead-of-same-sex-marriage-arguments-in-supreme-court-two-
weeks-from-now/. Accessed May 19, 2015.

Boston, Rob. "Texas Governor Holds Bill Signing at Fort Worth Church
School in Bid to Corral Evangelical Voters," Americans United for Separation of Church and State, July/August 2005, https://www.au.org/church-
state/julyaugust-2005-church-state/featured/religious-right-roundup.
Accessed September 13, 2016.

Brief of Amici Curiae Kenneth B. Mehlman et al. Supporting Petitioners,
Obergefell v. Hodges, 576 U.S.__ (2015) (Mehlman Brief).

Brief of the Commonwealth of Virginia as Amicus Curiae in Support of
Petitioners, Obergefell v. Hodges, 576 U.S.__ (2015).

Brief of Historians of Marriage and the American Historical Association as
Amici Curiae in Support of Petitioners, Obergefell v. Hodges, 576 U.S.__
(2015).

Brief of the Human Rights Campaign and ____ Americans Supporting Petitioners, Obergefell v. Hodges, 576 U.S.__ (2015) (The People's Brief).

Brief of Ninety-Two Plaintiffs in Marriage Cases in Alabama, Alaska, Arkansas,
Indiana, Kansas, Louisiana, Mississippi, Missouri, Montana, Nebraska, North
Carolina, North Dakota, South Carolina, South Dakota and Texas as Amici
Curiae in Support of Petitioners, Obergefell v. Hodges, 576 U.S.__ (2015).

Brief of the States of Alabama, South Carolina, and Utah as *Amici Curiae* in
Support of Respondent, *Lawrence v. Texas*, 539 US 558 (2003)

Brief of 379 Employers and Organizations Representing Employers as Amici
Curiae in Support of Petitioners, Obergefell v. Hodges, 576 U.S.__ (2015).

Broverman, Neal. "Antigay Heckler Dragged Out of Supreme Court,"
The Advocate, April 28, 2015, http://www.advocate.com/politics/
marriage-equality/2015/04/28/antigay-heckler-dragged-out-supreme-
court. Accessed April 4, 2016.

Butts, Charlie. "Pro-family Leader on Texas lawsuit: Homosexuals
Imposing Their Version of Morality," *News Now*, December 2, 2013,

http://www.onenewsnow.com/legal-courts/2013/12/02/pro-family-leader-on-texas-lawsuit-homosexuals-imposing-their-version-of-morality#. Us7K82eA1Ur. Accessed September 4, 2016.

Calabresi, Steven G. and Hannah M. Begley. "Originalism and Same Sex Marriage," Northwestern Public Law Research Paper No. 14-51. http://papers.ssrn.com/sol3/papers.cfm?abstract_id=2509443. Accessed March 2, 2016.

Calvey, Mark. "Wells Fargo Unveils its First National Ads Featuring Same-Sex Couple," *San Francisco Business Times*, April 24, http://www.bizjournals.com/sanfrancisco/blog/2015/04/wells-fargo-lgbt-same-sex-tiffany.html. Accessed June 1, 2016.

Camerota, Alysin."Texas Prepares for Same-Sex Marriage Fight," CNN, May 13, 2015, https://www.youtube.com/watch?v=Xro9qU5ic0o. Accessed September 9, 2015.

Carpenter, Dale. *Flagrant Conduct: The Story of Lawrence v. Texas.* New York: W. W. Norton: 2012.

Casady, Michelle. "Texas Pair, Marriage Equality Plaintiffs, Get License to Wed," *San Antonio Express News*, September 25, 2015, http://www.mysanantonio.com/news/local/article/Plaintiffs-in-marriage-equality-suit-finally-get-6530847.php. Accessed September 26, 2015.

Casey, Rick. "Prayer, Politics, and Perfidy at City Hall," *San Antonio Express News*, February 2, 1998, http://nl.newsbank.com/nl-search/we/Archives?p_action+doc&p_docid...rname=refuser&s_account=AC11405613 534812474&s_upgradable=no. Accessed February 21, 2016.

Casteel, Chris. "Oklahoma Judge on 10th U.S. Circuit Court of Appeals Defies Expectations in Same-Sex Marriage Case," *The Oklahoman*, August 10, 2014, http://newsok.com/article/5143093. Accessed January 9, 2017.

Castro, Julian and Evan Wolfson. "Seeking Freedom for Everyone," *The San Antonio Express Current*, February, 12, 2014. http://www.mysanantonio.com/opinion/commentary/article/Seeking-freedom-for-everyone-5225574.php. Accessed August 8, 2016.

Cathcart, Kevin M. and Leslie J. Gabel-Brett, eds., *Love Unites Us: Winning the Freedom to Marry in America.* New York: The Free Press, 2016.

"The Champions for Justice in Texas." *The Melissa Harris-Perry Show*, MSNBC, March 16, 2014, http://www.msnbc.com/melissa-harris-perry/watch/the-champions-for-justice-in-texas-197155395998. Accessed January 2, 2017.

Clendinen, Dudley and Adam Nagourney. *Out for Good: The Struggle to Build a Gay Rights Movement in America.* New York: Simon and Schuster, 1999.

Clines, Francis X. "Barbara Jordan Dies at 59; Her Voice Stirred the Nation," *New York Times*, January 18, 1996, http://www.nytimes.com/1996/01/18/

us/barbara-jordan-dies-at-59-her-voice-stirred-the-nation.html. Accessed October 27, 2015.

Clinton, William. "It's Time to Overturn DOMA," *Washington Post*, March 7, 2013, https://www.washingtonpost.com/opinions/bill-clinton-its-time-to-overturn-doma/2013/03/07/fc184408-8747-11e2-98a3-b3db6b9ac586_story.html. Accessed March 3, 2016.

Coles, Matt and others. *Winning Marriage: What We Need to Do Now*," https://s3.amazonaws.com/s3.documentcloud.org/documents/2108219/final-marriage-concept-paper.pdf. Accessed January 20, 2016.

Coloff, Pam. "To Love and to Cherish," *Texas Monthly*, March 2015, 86 ff.

Curriden, Mark. "Judge Builds Respect through Years on the Bench," *The Dallas Morning News*, August 2014, http://www.dallasnews.com/news/news/2014/08/02/judge-builds-respect-through-years-on-the-bench. Accessed January 2, 2017.

Curriden, Mark. "Meet the Chief Judge of the Nation's Most Divisive, Controversial and Conservative Appeals Court*," ABA Journal*, February 1, 2014, http://www.abajournal.com/magazine/article/meet_the_chief_judge_of_the_nations_most_divisive_controversial/. Accessed December 9, 2014.

"Dallas-Area Churches React to Supreme Court Gay Marriage Ruling," *Dallas Morning News*, June 26, 2015, http://dallasmorningnews.com/news/local-news/20150626-dallas-area-churches-react-to-supreme-court-gay-marriage-ruling.ece. Accessed October 26, 2015.

Dann, Carrie. "Poll: Majority Wants Supreme Court to OK Same Sex Marriage Nationally," May 4, 2015, http://www.nbcnews.com/meet-the-press/poll-majority-wants-supreme-court-ok-same-sex-marriage-nationally-n353411. Accessed March 3, 2016.

Davis, Kelsey. "Crowds Flock to Fifth Circuit Court of Appeals to Hear Arguments Regarding Same-Sex Marriage in Louisiana, Mississippi, and Texas," WDSU News, January 9, 2015, http://www.wdsu.com/news/local-news/new-orleans/crowds-flock-to-fifth-circuit-court-of-appeals-to-hear-arguments-regarding-samesex-marriage/30624316. Accessed January 12, 201

Defense of Marriage Act, Pub.L. 104–199, 110 Stat. 2419 (1996).

DeGeneres, Betty. *Love, Ellen: A Mother/Daughter Journey.* New York: Harper, 1999.

Denning, C. J. "Impromptu Celebration Outside SCOTUS after Gay-Marriage Ruling," Hit & Rumble Blog, April 26, 2015, http://reason.com/blog/2015/06/26/libertarians-join-celebration-outside-sc. Accessed June 27, 2015.

Dunlap, David. "Survey Details Gay Slayings around U.S.," *New York Times*, December 21, 1994, http://www.nytimes.com/1994/12/21/us/survey-details-gay-slayings-around-us.html. Accessed January 3, 2015.

Durand, Maria F. "Supporters Come Out for Ellen," *San Antonio Express-News*, May 1, 1997, 1B, http://nl.newsbank.com/nl-search/we/Archives?p_action=doc&pdocid...rname=refuser&_accountid-AC0114051613534812474&s_upgradable=no. Accessed February 21, 2016.

"Ellen Update: Episode When She Comes Out of the Closet," *Religious Tolerance*, April 27, 1997, http://www.religioustolerance.org/hom_0043.htm. Accessed January 6, 2017.

Elliott, Janet. "Gay Marriage Ban Approved," *Houston Chronicle*, November 9, 2005, http://www.chron.com/news/houston-texas/article/Gay-marriage-ban-approved-1925874.php. Accessed September 13, 2016.

Esseks, James. "The End Game for Marriage Equality Is Here," *The Huffington Post*, January 15, 2015, http://www.huffingtonpost.com/james-d-exxeks/the-end-game-is -here-for_b_6489404.html. Accessed January 16, 2015.

Faderman, Lillian. *The Gay Revolution: The Story of the Struggle*. New York: Simon & Schuster, 2015.

"Fighting Marriage Discrimination in Texas: Mark Phariss and Vic Holmes, Plano, Texas," April 2014, www.freedom tomarry.org/stories/entry/fighting-marriage-discrimination-in-texas. Accessed June 6, 2014.

Flores, Andrew R. and Scott Barclay. "Trends in Support for Marriage for Same-Sex Couples by State," April 2015, http://williamsinstitute.law.ucla.edu/wp-content/uploads/Trends-in-Public-Support-for-Same-Sex-Marriage-2004-2014.pdf. Accessed March 20, 2016.

"From Absolut to Zappos: Major Companies Get Behind the Supreme Court Decision," *Queerty*, April 26, 2015, http://www.queerty.com/from-absolut-to-zappos-major-companies-get-behind-the-supreme-court-decision-20150629/yahoo. Accessed June 29, 2015.

Garrett, Robert T. "Federal Judge Hears Request to Block Texas Ban on Same-Sex Marriage," *Dallas Morning News*, February 12, 2014, http://www.dallasnews.com/news/politics/headlines/20140212-federal-judge-hears-request-to-block-texas-ban-on-same-sex-marriage.ece. Accessed August 20, 2016.

"Gay Marriage Arrives in Texas, *Texas Observer*," June 26, 2015, https://www.texasobserver.org/supreme-court-upholds-same-sex-marriage/. Accessed June 26, 2015.

Gilbert, Kathy. "GC2016 Tackling 44-Year Stance on Homosexuality," April 27, 2015, The People of the United Methodist Church, http://www.umc.org/news-and-media/gc2016-tackling-44-year-stance-on-homosexuality. Accessed September 11, 2016.

Ginsburg, Ruth Bader. "Ruth Bader Ginsburg Thinks Americans Are Ready for Gay Marriage," interview by Greg Stohr and Matthew Winkler.

Bloomberg Business, February 12, 2015, http://www.bloomberg.com/news/articles/2015-02-12/ginsburg-says-u-s-ready-to-accept-ruling-approving-gay-marriage-i61z6gq2. Accessed March 6, 2016.

Grim, Ryan. "Scalia Slams 'Legalistic Argle-Bargle, 'Re-Argues 'Homosexual Sodomy' in Dissenting DOMA Rant," June 6, 2013, http://www.huffingtonpost.com/2013/06/26/doma-scalia_n_3503706.html. Accessed April 2, 2015.

Handy, Bruce. "He Called Me Ellen DeGenerate?" *Time Magazine*, April 14, 1997, http://time.com/348943/he-called-me-ellen-degenerate. Accessed October 29, 2015.

Herbst, Diane. "First Same-Sex Couple Marries in Dallas County after 50-Year Wait," *Time*, June 26, 2015, http://time.com/3938782/jack-evans-george-harris-marriage-texas/. Accessed June 26, 2015.

Hodgman, George. *Bettyville*. New York: Viking, 2015.

Howe, Amy. SCOTUSblog, June 26, 2015, http://www.scotusblog.com/. Accessed June 26, 2015.

Huetteman, Emmarie. "Outside the Court, Many Still Seek a Peek," *New York Times*, April 28, 2015, http://www.nytimes.com/live/supreme-court-same-sex-marriage-arguments/outside-the-court-many-still-seek-a-peak/. Accessed March 9, 2016.

Jeffires, John Calvin. *Justice Lewis F. Powell, Jr*. New York: Fordham University Press, 1994.

Jervis, Rick. "Texas Takes Defiant Stance as Gay Marriage Decision Looms," *USA Today*, April 29, 2015, http://www.usatoday.com/story/news/2015/04/29/texas-same-sex-marriage-supreme-court/26577219/. Accessed April 29, 2015.

"It's Official: The Supreme Court Will Review the Freedom to Marry in 2015!" Freedom to Marry, January 16, 2015, http://www.freedomtomarry.org/blog/entry/its-official-the-supreme-court-will-review-the-freedom-to-marry-in-2017. Accessed January 16, 2015.

Johnson, Chris. "Marriage Plaintiffs Gather to Celebrate on Eve of Arguments," *Washington Blade,* April 28, 2015, http://www.washingtonblade.com/2015/04/28/marriage-plaintiffs-gather-to-celebrate-on-eve-of-arguments/. Accessed May 5, 2015.

Johnson, Chris. "Plaintiff Couples on Pins and Needles Awaiting Ruling," *The Washington Blade*, June 24, 2015, http://www.washingtonblade.com/2015/06/24/plaintiff-couples-on-pins-and-needles-awaiting-ruling/. Accessed September 8, 2015.

"Join Us on Decision Day." Texas for Marriage, https://www.facebook.com/freedomtomarry.org/photos70092.270234.40484170092/10155192405760093/?type=1&theater. Accessed January 26, 2015.

Jones, Cleve. *When We Rise: My Life in the Movement*. New York: Hachette, 2016.

Jordan, Barbara C. "Statement on the Articles of Impeachment, July 25, 1974," American Rhetoric. http://www.americanrhetoric.com/speeches/barbarajordanjudiciarystatement.htm. Accessed December 30, 2016.

Kaplan, Roberta. *Then Comes Marriage: United States v. Windsor.* New York. Norton, 2015.

Kelly, Christopher. "The Accidental Activists," *Texas Monthly.* February, 2014, 27 ff.

Kennedy, Bud. "Perry Said If Gays Like Another State's Laws, 'That's Where They Should Live,' *Fort Worth Star-Telegram*, June 12, 2014. Reprinted from a column published on June 7, 2005, http://www.star-telegram.com/mobile/m-opinion/article3861668.html. Accessed April 4, 2016.

Kling, Karina. "Supreme Court Hears Same-Sex Marriage Arguments," *Time Warner News*, April 28, 2015, http://www.twcnews.com/tx/texas/politics/2015/04/28/same-sex-marriage-case-before-supreme-court.html. Accessed June 6, 2016.

Kofler, Shelly. "Greg Abbott Went to Law School with a Plaintiff in Gay Marriage Suit He's Fighting," KERA. February 27, 2016, http://keranews.org/post/greg-abbott-went-law-school-plaintiff-gay-marriage-suit-he-s-fighting. Accessed February 27, 2016.

Kofler, Shelly. "Greg Abbott Faces Law School Friend as Plaintiff in Same-Sex Marriage Suit," KERA, February 28, 2014, http://keranews.org/post/greg-abbott-faces-law-school-friend-plaintiff-same-sex-marriage-suit. Accessed August 20, 2014.

"Lane: 5th Circuit Court Should Still Rule," *The Dallas Voice*, January 16, 2015, http://www.dallasvoice.com/;ane-5th-circuit-court-rule-10188194.html. Accessed January 17, 2015.

Levitt, Eugene E. and A. D. Klassen. "Public Attitudes toward Homosexuality: Part of the 1970 National Survey by the Institute for Sex Research," *Journal of Homosexuality* 1.1 (1974): 29-43, Fall 1974.

Luther Strange, Attorney General of Alabama v. Cari D. Searcy, et al.: On Application for Stay, 574 U.S. (2015) (Scalia, A., dissenting).

McCarthy, Justin. "Record-High 60% of Americans Support Same-Sex Marriage," May 19, 2015, http://www.gallup.com/poll/183272/record-high-americans-support-sex-marriage.aspx. Accessed May 19, 2015.

McGaughy, Lauren. "Unlikely Gay Marriage Pioneers Tied Knot in Houston." *The Houston Chronicle*, November 28, 2014, http://www.houstonchronicle.com/news/politics/texas/article/Unlikely-gay-marriage-pioneers-tied-knot-in-5923174.php. Accessed August 31, 2016.

Michels, Patrick. "Two Couples Challenge Texas' Same-Sex Marriage Ban." *Texas Observer*, November 1, 2013, http://texasobserver.org/two-couples-challenge-texas-sex-marriage ban/. Accessed April 2, 2015.

Motion to Advance Case for Hearing, Fifth Circuit Court of Appeals, *DeLeon v. Perry*, No. 14-50196. October 6, 2014.

Murdoch, Joyce and Deb Price. *Courting Justice: Gay Men and Lesbians v. the Supreme Court.* New York: Basic Books, 2002.

Nichols, Erin. "Same-Sex Couple Returns to Bexar County for Marriage License," Fox News, September 25, 2015, http://news4sanantonio.com/news/local-deprecated/same-sex-couple-returns-to-bexar-county-for-marriage-license. Accessed September 26, 2015.

Obama, Barack. "Robin Roberts ABC News Interview with President Obama" (transcript), ABC News, May 9, 2012, http://abcnews.go.com/Politics/transcript-robin-roberts-abc-news-interview-president-obama/story?id=16316043. Accessed March 3, 2016.

Obama, Barack. "Remarks by the President at the LGBT Pride Reception, June 9, 2016," https://obamawhitehouse.archives.gov/the-press-office/2016/06/09/remarks-president-lgbt-pride-reception. Accessed January 23, 2017.

Obama, Barack. "Remarks by the President on the Supreme Court Decision on Marriage Equality," June 26, 2015, https://www.whitehouse.gov/the-press-office/2015/06/26/remarks-president-supreme-court-decision-marriage-equality. Accessed June 26, 2016.

O'Donnell, Jayne. "Line Sitters, Activists Keep It Civil before High Court's Gay Marriage Case, *USA Today*, Apr. 27, 2015, http://www.usatoday.com/story/news/politics/2015/04/27/supreme-court-line-sitters-activists-gay-marriage-case/26463081/. Accessed April 9, 2016.

Patrick, Daniel. "Lt. Governor Patrick Requests Legal Opinion from Texas Attorney General in Preparation for Supreme Court Ruling," June 26, 2015, https://www.ltgov.state.tx.us/2015/06/26/lt-governor-patrick-requests-legal-opinion-from-texas-attorney-general-in-preparation-for-supreme-court-ruling/. Accessed September 9, 2016.

Patrick, Daniel. "Lt. Governor Patrick Statement on Supreme Court Ruling on Same-Sex Marriage," June 26, 2015, https://www.ltgov.state.tx.us/2015/06/26/lt-governor-patrick-statement-on-supreme-court-ruling-on-same-sex-marriage/. Accessed September 8, 2015.

Paul Weiss Rifkind Wharton & Garrison, http://www.paulweiss.com. Accessed January 9, 2017.

PBS Newshour. "Gay Marriage Debate: Wedded States." PBS, May 23, 1996. http://www.pbs.org/newshour/bb/law-jan-june96-gay_marriage_05-23/. Accessed January 27, 2016.

Paxton, Kenneth. "Attorney General Paxton: Religious Liberties of Texas Public Officials Remain Constitutionally Protected after *Obergefell v. Hodges*," June 28, 2015, https://www.texasattorneygeneral.gov/static/5144.html. Accessed September 7, 2015.

Paxton, Kenneth. Letter to Lieutenant Governor Dan Patrick, June 28, 2015, https://www.texasattorneygeneral.gov/opinions/opinions/51paxton/op/2015/kp0025.pdf. Accessed September 7, 2015.

Phariss, Mark. "Repealing Plano's Equal Rights Ordinance Would Give City a Black Eye, Bad Reputation," *Dallas Morning News*, January 27, 2015, http://lgbtqblog.dallasnews.com/category/discrimination/page/2/. Accessed January 28, 2015,

Phillips, Frank. "Weld Supports Gay Marriage Ruling," *The Boston Globe*, November 27, 2003. http://archive.boston.com/news/local/articles/2003/11/27/weld_supports_gay_marriage_ruling/. Accessed: January 26, 2016.

Phillips, Kevin P. "Poll Deals Homosexuals a Reverse," *The Lawton Constitution*, October 12, 1973.

Plaintiff's Opposed Motion for Preliminary Injunction Enjoining Defendants from Enforcing Texas' Same-Sex Marriage Ban, *DeLeon v. Perry* 5:13-cv-982-OLG at 41, 1, 42.

Plaintiff's Opposed Motion to Lift Stay of Injunction for all Parties or, in the Alternative, for Order Re Birth of Child, *DeLeon v. Perry* 14-50196, February 11, 2015 at 4.

Plaintiffs' Original Complaint for Declaratory and Injunctive Relief," *DeLeon v. Perry* 5:13-cv-982.

Posner, Richard. "Federal Judge Richard Posner: The GOP Has Made Me Less Conservative," interview with Nina Totenberg, NPR, July 5, 2012, http://www.npr.org/sections/itsallpolitics/2012/07/05/156319272/federal-judge-richard-posner-the-gop-has-made-me-less-conservative. Accessed January 15, 2015.

Prestonwood Baptist Church, http://www.prestonwood.org.

"Republican Platform 2015: Renewing American Values," http://gop.com/platform/renewing-american-values/. Accessed March 4, 2016.

Roar of the Crowd. *Texas Monthly*, April 2015, 8-10.

"Same-Sex Marriage Advocates Finally Wed," WFAA, November 22, 2015, www.wffaa.com. Accessed Nov. 29, 2015.

Savage, David G. "Supreme Court Set to Decide National Debate on Gay Marriage," *Los Angeles Times,* January 16, 2016, http://www.freedomtomarry.org/blog/entry/its-official-the-supreme-court-will-review-the-freedom-to-marry-in-2017. Accessed January 16, 2016.

"Saying William Pryor Is the 'Most Demonstrably Antigay Judicial Nominee in Recent Memory,' Lambda Legal Opposes Nomination to Federal Appeals Court," April 26, 2005, http://www.lambdalegal.org/news/ny_20050426_william-pryor-is-most-demonstrably-antigay-judicial-nominee. Accessed January 15, 2017.

"Sexual Assault in the Air Force, Celebrities, and Serial Killers." ABC News 20/20 Season 25, Episode 11," ABC, February 13, 2004, http://abcnews.go.com/2020/story?id=124308&page=1. Accessed January 6, 2017.

Signorile, Michelangelo. *It's Not Over: Getting Beyond Tolerance, Defeating Homophobia, and Winning True Equality*. New York: Meridian, 2015.

Solomon, Marc. *Winning Marriage: The Inside Story of How Same-sex Couples Took on the Politicians and Pundits—and Won.* Lebanon, NH: ForeEdge, 2014.

Somin, Ilya. "Assessing the Sixth Circuit Decision Upholding the Constitutionality of Law Banning Same-Sex Marriage," *The Washington Post*, November 6, 2014, https://www.washingtonpost.com/news/volokh-conspiracy/wp/2014/11/06/assessing-the-sixth-circuit-upholding-the-constitutionality-of-laws-banning-same-sex-marriage/. Accessed March 20, 2016.

Southern Baptist Convention. http://www.scbc.net/resolutions. Accessed September 14, 2016.

"Southern Baptists Urged to Reject any Laws Legalizing Gay Marriage," Fox News, June 17, 2015, http://www.foxnews.com/opinion/2015/06/16/southern-baptists-urged-to-reject-any-laws-legalizing-gay-marriage.html. Accessed September 25, 2015.

"Special Report: Supreme Court Legalizes Same-Sex Marriage," CBS, April 26, 2015, https://www.youtube.com/watch?v=0L7HfOjivEQ. Accessed June 26, 2015.

"Spirit of Texas Honorees on Frontline in Fight for Equality," *Q San Antonio*, May 15, 2014, http://qsanantonio.com/brunch14.html. Accessed August 8, 2014.

State Defendants' Answer and Affirmative Defenses to the Rummell Amended Complaint," District Court for the District of Oregon, February 20, 2014. No. 6:13-cv-01834-MC.

Stern, Mark Joseph. "How the Mastermind of Marriage Equality Felt the Moment He Realized He'd Won," *Slate*, July 8, 2015, http://www.slate.com/blogs/outward/2015/07/08/evan_wolfson_how_the_marriage_equality_mastermind_felt_when_he_won.html. Accessed July 10, 2015.

Stern, Mark Joseph. "The University of North Carolina's New President Is Shockingly Anti-Gay," *Slate*, October 27, 2015, http://www.slate.com/blogs/outward/2015/10/27/margaret_spellings_new_unc_president_is_anti_gay.html. Accessed August 4, 2016.

Stoleberg, Sheryl Gay. "Strategist Out of Closet and into Fray, This Time for Gay Marriage," *New York Times,* June 19, 2013, http://www.nytimes.com/2013/06/20/us/strategist-out-of-closet-and-into-fray-this-time-for-gay-marriage.html. Accessed March 28, 2016.

Sullivan, Andrew. "Here Comes the Groom," *The New Republic*, August 28, 1989, 22.

"The Supreme Court and Gay Marriage" (editorial). *New York Times*, January 16, 2015, https://www.nytimes.com/2015/01/17/opinion/the-supreme-court-and-gay-marriage.html. Accessed January 16, 2015.

"The Supreme Court of the United States: The Supreme Court Building," http://www.supremecourt.gov/about/courtbuilding.aspx. Accessed April 23, 2015.

"Supreme Court Strikes Down Ban on Same-Sex Marriage—NBC News Special Report," April 26, 2015, NBC, https://www.youtube.com/watch?v=wFbl0DuCq6g. Accessed June 26, 2015.

Texas Health and Safety Code §163.002. Instructional Elements. See also § Section 21.06, Penal Code; Tex. Health & Safety Code Ann. Sec. 85.007.

Temples, Don. "In His Honor: Shepard Family Creates Foundation," *HRC Quarterly*, Summer 2015, 9.

"Texas Same-Sex Marriage Plaintiffs Endure 2nd Harrowing Birth with No Parental Rights," Towerload, March 24, 20135, http://www.towleroad.com/2015/03/texas-same-sex-marriage-plaintiffs-endure-2nd-harrowing-child-birth-with-no-legal-rights/. Accessed March 24, 2015.

"Thank You, Texas Plaintiffs," Texas for Marriage, January 28, 2015, http://texasformarriage.org/messages-of-support-for-texas-plaintiffs. Accessed January 28, 2015.

Toobin, Jeffrey. "Justice Scalia's Shameful Joke," *The New Yorker*, April 28, 2015, http://www.newyorker.com/news/daily-comment/on-gay-marriage-its-not-scalias-court. Accessed April 13, 2015.

Transcript of All Pending Matters before the Honorable Sam Sparks, January 9, 2014, Docket Nos. A 13-CA-631 SS and A 13-CA-955 SS, The United States District Court for the Western District of Texas.

Transcript of Preliminary Injunction Hearing before the Honorable Orlando L. Garcia District Court Judge," *DeLeon v. Perry* 5:13-982-OLG. United States District Court, Western District of Texas, San Antonio Division. February 12, 2014.

"UNTHSC Physician Assistant Makes House Calls for Disabled Adults," December 18, 2013, https://www.unthsc.edu/newsroom/story/unthsc-physician-assistant-makes-a%C2%80ahauhouse-calls-for-disabled-adults-3/. Accessed August 4, 2016.

U.S. House, *Report of the Committee on the Judiciary*, July 6, 1996. 104th Cong., 2nd sess.

"U.S. Senate Judiciary Committee Hearing on Judge Samuel Alito's Nomination to the Supreme Court" (transcript), *The Washington Post*, January 11, 2006, http://www.washingtonpost.com/wp-dyn/content/article/2006/01/11/AR2006011101148.html. Accessed August 31, 2016.

"Vice President Joe Biden Addresses the 2015 HRC National Dinner," Oct. 3, 2015, https://www.hrc.org/videos/videos-vice-president-joe-biden-addresses-the-2015-hrc-national-dinner. Accessed December 20, 2016.

"The Virginia Declaration of Rights," The Constitution Society, http://www.constitution.org/bcp/virg_dor.htm. Accessed December 8, 2015.

Walsh, Mark. "A 'View' from the Courtroom: A Marriage Celebration, SCOTUSblog, June 26, 2015, 6:13 PM, http://www.scotusblog.com/2015/06/a-view-from-the-courtroom-a-marriage-celebration/. Accessed June 27, 2015.

Waugh, Anna. "Plano Couple Files Lawsuit Challenging Marriage Ban," *Dallas Voice*, Nov. 1, 2013, http://www.dallasvoice.com/plano-couple-files-lawsuit-challenging-marriage-ban-10160630.html. Accessed November 18, 2014.

Weiss, Debra Cassens. "Justice Ginsburg: Roe v. Wade Decision Came Too Soon," *ABA Journal*, February 13, 2012, http://www.slate.com/articles/news_and_politics/jurisprudence/2013/05/justice_ginsburg_and_roe_v_wade_caution_for_gay_marriage.html. Accessed January 20, 2016.

Weiss, Jeffrey. "Plano Men at Center of Texas Gay Marriage Cast That Opens Wednesday," *Dallas Morning News*, February 7, 2014, http://www.dallasnews.com/news/plano/2014/02/07/plano-men-at-center-of-texas-gay-marriage-case-that-opens-wednesday. Accessed November 18, 2014.

"Without Delay: HRC Calls on State Officials to Remove Obstacles to Marriage Equality Immediately," June 26, 2015, http://www.hrc.org/blog/without-delay-hrc-calls-on-state-officials-to-remove-obstacles-to-marriage. Accessed June 27, 2015,

Wolfson, Evan. "Same-Sex Marriage and Morality: The Human Rights View of the Constitution," Freedom to Marry, http://www.freedomtomarry.org/pages/publications. Accessed May 15, 2016

Wray, Diana. "Backstory: The Fifth Circuit Court Wasn't Always the Most Conservative Court Around," *Houston News*, November 6, 2014, http://www.houstonpress.com/news/backstory-the-fifth-circuit-wasnt-always-the-most-conservative-court-around-6715354. Accessed December 10, 2014.

Wright, John. "Equality Texas Optimistic Despite Record Number of Anti-LGBT Bills," *OutSmart*, 1 April, 2015, http://www.outsmartmagazine.com/2015/04/equality-texas-optimistic-despite-record-number-of-anti-lgbt-bills/. Accessed July 18, 2015.

Wright, John. "Texas Lawmakers File Record Number of Anti-LGBT Bills," *Texas Observer*, March 17, 2005, https://www.texasobserver.org/texas-lawmakers-file-record-number-of-anti-lgbt-bills/. Accessed July 15, 2015.

Zaragovia, Veronica. "Gay Couples Ask Court to Lift Hold on Same-Sex Marriage in Texas," KUT.org, February 12, 2015, http://kut.org/post/gay-couples-ask-court-lift-hold-same-sex-marriage-texas. Accessed February 12, 2015.

Index

A

ABA Journal, 153

Abbott, Cecilia, 132–33

Abbott, Greg: as Attorney General, 10, 53, 88, 117, 209; encourages anti-gay legislation, 300–301, 303; first campaign, 133; friendship with Mark Phariss, 6, 53, 88, 117, 131–33, 272, 280, 287, 297; as Governor, 132, 139, 297, 211, 321; objects to *Obergefell* decision, 294–95, 300; paralyzed, 6, 88, 132.

ABC (American Broadcast Corporation), 6, 43–4, 205, 213

Above the Law, 160

Abzug, Bella, 154

ACLU (American Civil Liberties Union), 101, 142, 190, 199, 277, 302

Adams, Richard, 73, 200

Adams, Tony, 200

Advocate, The, 191, 243

AIDS (Acquired Immunodeficiency Syndrome), 22–23, 26, 190

Akin Gump Strauss Hauer & Feld LLD, 8, 10–11, 96–97, 110, 127–8, 134, 137, 139, 150, 152, 187–8, 226, 290, 316, 324; arguments in circuit court, 177–85; arguments in district court, 118–24; files brief in *Obergefell v. Hodges*, 221; Complaint in *DeLeon v. Perry*, 106–9; first meeting with plaintiffs, 90–3; honors and awards, 135, 284; legal maneuvering in *DeLeon v. Perry*, 101–6, 124–25, 136, 137–38, 141, 195–96, 233; letter of advisory to Fifth Circuit Court of Appeals, 279–80; pro bono representation, 62–3; recruiting plaintiffs, 64–5, 88, 89–93; represents John Stone-Hosking, 281–84

"All Love Is Equal," 257

Allen, Wright, 140

Alito, Samuel, 237–38, 240–44, 246, 248–50

Amendment 2 (Colorado), 66–8

Amendment 2 (Hawaii), 74

American Family Association, 43

American Lawyer, The, 160

American Psychological Association, 33

animus, 54, 67–69, 75, 77–78, 107, 157, 161, 275–77, 180–81, 192, 218–19, 224, 243–44

American Foundation for Equal Rights (AFER), 220

Apache Junction, Arizona, 30–31

Arnst, Tom, 95

Arthur, John, 189, 255

Arthur Murray Dance Studio, 286, 309, 325

Aspects of Love, 319

Auden, W. H., 320

Augustine, Alexius, 101

authenticity: denied to gays and lesbians, 56; desire/need for, 23, 262–64; Vic's understanding of, 32–33, 59–60, 262–64; made possible by Kennedy's *Obergefell* opinion, 329

Ayala, Elayne, 96

B

Baehr v. Lewin. See Baehr v. Miike

Baehr v. Miike, 73–75

Baehr, Ninia, 200–201

Baily, Shannon, and Marlon Cortez, 273

Baker, Jack, and Mike McConnell, 72

Baker v. Nelson: original case, 72; precedential value, 179–80, 189, 239

Balmelli, Edward, and Michael Horgan, 201

Barica, Zante and Debbie Johnson, 273

Barr, Bob, 74

Baskin v. Bogan, 169–71, 178, 180, 183

Begley, Hannah, 222

Bell, Cecil, 298, 300–301

Benchetrit, Serge, 221

Benenson, Joel, and Jan van Louhuizen, 215

Benishik, Michael, 29

Bernstein, Richard, 221–25

Beta Theta Pi (college fraternity), 20–21

Biden, Joe: on *Meet the Press*, 212–13; addresses HRC national dinner, 287–88

Bill of Rights, 218

Billington, Almareeta, 25, 27

Birch, Elizabeth, 40, 93, 128, 285

Black, Hugo, 98

Blackmun, Harry, 24

Blackstone, William, 24, 66

Blanco, Richard, 185–87, 275

Bloomberg Business, 214

Boggs, Luther, 165

Boies, David, 142

Bonauto, Mary, 201; prepares the way for same-sex marriage, 76, 83–4, 287; *Goodridge v. Office of Personnel Management*, 53, 76–77, 259; Mark's e-mail congratulating her, 207; Mark's Facebook homage to, 207; *Obergefell v. Hodges*, 190, 207, 222, 226, 236–41, 246, 248; rejection of civil unions, 61

Bonham Exchange, 27, 108–9

Booker, Cory, 233

Boston Globe, 77

Bourke, Gregory, 265

Bowers v. Hardwick, 23–25, 65–66, 68–69, 78–82

Bowie, James, 7

Breyer, Stephen, 79, 237–8, 241, 248–53

Brice, Cathan, 285, 318

Bridegroom, 110

Bridges, Ruby, 148

Broussard, Paul, 28

Brown v. Board of Education, 144, 218

Bryant, Anita, 17–18, 43–44, 51, 55, 193, 302

Burger, Warren, 24, 66, 68, 78

Bursch, John J., 208, 247–53

Burt, Rachel, 310, 315

Bush, George H. W., 102

Bush, George W., 70, 77, 94, 203–4, 209, 215, 220,225

Bush v. Gore, 209–10

Business Electronics Corp. v. Sharp Electronics Corp., *See* Scalia, Antonin

Butter & Binion, 132

Buzzfeed, 157–58, 161

C

CBS (Columbia Broadcasting System), 191, 258, 261, 265

Cabellero, Michael and Caitlin O'Hara, 206, 227

Cabaniss, Boyce, 192

Caine, Andy, 129

Cairo, Illinois, 29–30

Calabresi, Stephen, 222

California: 27, 28; Proposition 8, 175, 213, 220, 239; Proposition 8
    Plaintiffs, 142, 201

Calvary Cathedral International Church, 53, 224

Camerota, Alysin, 295–96

Cammermeyer, Margarethe, 247

Cantú, Ikeita, 267

Capehart, Jonathan, 134–35

Carnahan, Mike, 18, 20, 318

Carpenter, Dale, 77–78, 219

Carson, Ben, 54

Carter, Dean, 27–28

Casady, Michelle, 291

Casey, Rick, 46, 134

Cass, Gilbert, 206–7, 235

Castillo, Paul, 274

Castro, Julian, 125

Cathedral Creative Studios, 147–150, 202

Cathedral of Hope, 268, 273–74

"Catholic Justice, the," 244

Cazares-Thomas, Neil, 273

Chadwick, Neal, 23, 28, 325

Chang, Kevin, 74

Chapman, Ron, 305–6

Chapman, William, 17

Chasnoff, Barry, 97, 106, 111, 122, 127, 152; argues in district court, 119–
    21; asks Management Committee to take Texas Case, 62–63; hosts first
    meeting of attorneys and plaintiffs, 90, 92–93

Chisum, Warren, 53

Chivette, Brandi, 32

Chrysler Corporation, 43

Churchill, Winston, 185, 262, 272

civil unions, 61, 212

Clements, Merritt and Karen, 292

Clinton, Bill, 102, 110, 209; Defense of Marriage Act, 74, 213–14; Don't
    Ask, Don't Tell, 47; *Washington Post* op-ed, 213–14

Clinton, Hillary, 214, 317

CNN (Cable News Network), 215, 295

Coburn, Tom, 237

Cohen, Andy, 135–36

Colasonti, Frank, Jr., 232

Cole, Eva, 325

Cole, Kirk, 281–82, 284

Cooley, Michael, 109, 277, 324

Colloff, Pamela, 63, 192, 194

Colson, Charles, 44

Comprehensive Education and Training Act (CETA), 30

Concarta, 322

Congressional Record, 65

Conway, Jack, 140

Cooley, Michael109, 277, 324

Cooper, Chris, 93

Cornyn, John, 94–95, 211

Cortez, Marlon, and Shannon Baily. *See* Baily, Shannon

"Could It Be I'm Falling in Love?" 326

Crawford, Jan, 265

Craycraft, Bob, 306

Crockett, Davy, 7–8

Crutchfield, Finis, 166

Cruz, Ted, 54, 114, 192–93, 211, 328; dinner with Mark Phariss and Vic Holmes, 209–10; insensitivity, 210–11

Cruz, Torri and Robert, 57, 313–14

Curriden, Mark, 153

D

Dale, Candy W., 140

Dallas Affaires Cake Company, 322–23

Dallas Morning News, 111, 114–16, 124, 193, 281

Dallas Museum of Art, 308

Dallas Voice, 98

Dancel, Genora, 200–201

Dancing with the Stars, 326–27

Daughtrey, Martha Craig, 216–17

DeBoer, April, and Jayne Rowse, 140, 233–34, 257, 287

DeBoer v. Snyder, 189, 248

"Decision Day," 191, 255–56, 281, 284, 290; celebration at Cathedral of
    Hope, 272–73; checking SCOTUSblog, 260; congratulatory messages,
    264–65; corporate reaction, 275–77; jubilation in the District of
    Columbia, 265–66; jubilation online, 268–69; march to the Monument
    of Love, 273–74; marriages in Dallas begin, 266; Obama's Rose Garden
    speech, 274–75; press conference in Austin, 269–72; reading Kennedy's
    decision, 262–64; waiting at the airport, 259–61
Declaration of Independence: Texas, 63; United States, 218, 256
Defense of Marriage Act (DOMA), 78, 122, 157, 161, 212, 221, 225, 259;
    Clinton's repudiation of, 213–14; court cases challenging, 84; motivated
    by animus, 75–76; Obama refuses to defend, 213; rushed through
    Congress, 74–75, 82; provisions of Section 3, 83–84; nullified by *Windsor*,
    84–86; State Defense of Marriage Act, 192; Texas's "Mini-DOMA," 3
DeGeneres, Betty, 40–41, 285
DeGeneres, Ellen, 43–45, 276
DeLeon, Cleopatra, and Nicole Dimetman: legal battles resulting from
    childbirth and adoption, 89, 119, 139–40, 148–49, 166, 169, 177–78,
    185, 188, 194–96; married in Massachusetts, 64–65, 148, 195; on
    cover of *Texas Monthly*, 193–94; remarks at press conferences, 148–
    49, 185 (New Orleans), 269–72 (Austin); receive Anchor Award, 135;
    recognized at Mark and Vic's wedding, 324
DeLeon, Michael, 265
DeLeon v. Perry: arguments in circuit court, 166–83; arguments in district
    court, 119–2; ceremonial ending of *DeLeon v. Perry*, 324; dispute over
    venue, 102–23; district court decision, 128; in legal limbo, 139–43, 190–
    97, 278–79; Fifth Circuit order, 280; Motion for Preliminary Injunction,
    106–9; notices of recent authority, 110, 125; Plaintiff's Original Complaint
    for Declaratory and Injunctive Relief, 90–91; precedential value, 281–83;
    request for "letter advisories," 279; stay lifted, 278
Denison, John, 149
Dern, Laura, 44
Dial, Andrew, 113
difference v. sameness, 70–72, 80, 141, 161, 263, 275, 292
dignity: in *Goodridge*, 76; importance of/desire for, 3, 7, 35, 60, 137, 147–49,
    165–66, 183, 197, 247, 282–83; in Brief of 379 Employers, 219; in Brief
    of the Human Rights Campaign, 218; in *Campaign for Southern Equality
    v. Bryant*, 160, 162; in *DeLeon v. Perry*, 91, 108; in *Lawrence*, 79–80;
    in *Obergefell*, 236, 245, 252, 253 (oral arguments), 262–64 (Kennedy's
    decision); in *Windsor*, 85–87

Dimetman, Nicole. *See* DeLeon, Cleopatra, and Nicole Dimetman
DiSano, Samuel, xxii
Dobson, James, 22
Doggett, David, and Mary Belan, 292
Don't Ask, Don't Tell: learning to evade, 35, 47–48, 57–59; repealed by Barack Obama, 212; paranoia caused by, 35–37, 47, 59, 87
Driemeier, Douglas Hallward, 207
Driscoll, Mike, 44
Driving Miss Daisy, 26
Due Process Clause, 79–80, 91, 107, 124, 189, 211, 251, 263
Duncan, Kyle, 156–57, 161
Dunlap, David, 29
Dygert, Randall, 192–93

E

Earl, Nancy, 41–42, 55
Ebonhoch, Mark, 268
Ehret, Rich, 186–87
Employment Non-Discrimination Act (ENDA), 40, 46, 69
Equal Protection Clause, 73, 77, 91, 107, 125, 140, 210, 222–23, 239, 263
Equality Case Files, 205
Equality Texas, 135, 144, 146, 150, 192, 264, 269, 277, 284, 298, 302, 317, 324
Ert, William "Billie," 72–73
Esseks, James, 192
Evans, Jack and George Harris, 264, 266–68, 275, 327
Evelyn & Walter Haas Jr. Fund, 201
Expert Global Solutions, 4, 87, 131

F

Faith and Freedom Coalition, 54
Faith in Action, 229–31
Falwell, Jerry, 22, 43–44, 77
Family Research Council, 222
Farias, Richard 264
Federal Rule 53, 205
Federalism, 161, 216, 218
Ferguson, Jesse Tyler, 322

Few Good Men, A, 37

Fifth Amendment, 79, 84

Fifth Circuit Four, 153

Fisher, Thomas, 170

Flink, Jack, 256, 261

Flores, Roberto and Dan Graney, 88, 281

Flores, Roger, 45

Foley, Dan, 73, 201

For All of Us, One Today, 186, 275

Fourteenth Amendment, 77, 79–81, 91, 107, 122, 124, 140, 162, 177, 184, 189, 210, 215–16, 223, 236, 239–40, 246–47, 251, 253, 260, 263

Fox News, 117

"the Fox News Justice," 244

Frank, Barney, 74

Free, Mitch, 111

Freedom to Marry, 73, 75, 125, 134, 199, 201–2, 215, 247, 253, 255, 259, 268, 278, 297, 317

Frey, John, 187

Friedman, Bernard A., 140, 233

G

Gallup, Inc., 215

Garner, Tyron, 77, 134

Garcia, Denise, 266–68

Garcia, Michelle, 186

Garcia, Orlando, 125–28, 131, 134–36, 139, 167, 182, 188, 194, 196, 209, 211, 324; congratulates Akin Gump attorneys, 284; decision in *DeLeon v. Perry*, 127–28; *DeLeon v. Perry* remanded to his court, 280–82; hears *DeLeon v. Perry*, 118–24; lifting the stay, 138,195, 270, 278, 281, 290; Stone-Hoskins case, 281–84; venue dispute, 102–4, 105; schedules *DeLeon v. Perry*, 109–10, 115

Garcia, Richard, 133

Gay and Lesbian Alliance of North Texas, 135

Gay Men's Chorus of Washington, D. C., 265–66

Geidner, Chris, 157, 161

George L. Allen, Sr. Courts Building, 268

Gilbert, Cass, 206–7, 235

Gilstrap, Kenya, 322

Ginsburg, Ruth Bader, votes with majority in *Lawrence*, 79; on *Roe v. Wade*, 84; presides at same-sex wedding, 214–15; questions/comments in *Obergefell*, 236, 240–42; "sea-change" in equal rights law, 159; "skim milk marriage," 61, 239

GLAD (GLBTQ Legal Advocates and Defenders), 83, 142, 199, 201, 207

GLAAD, 44

Gonzalez, Charlie, as congressman, 290; presides at wedding, 301–11, 319, 321, 325; provides tickets to Obama inauguration, 208; remarks at rehearsal dinner, 312

Gonzalez, Lilah, 11

Good Hope Missionary Baptist Church, 42

Good Morning America, 213

Goodfriend, Sarah, and Suzanne Bryant, 192

Goodridge, Julie, 201

Goodridge et al. v. Department of Public Health, 52–53, 61, 76–77, 82, 201, 241, 259

Gragg, Margaret, 323

Graham, Franklin, 276

Graham, Jack, 51, 54–55

Graney, Dan and Roberto Flores, 88, 281

Graves, James E., appointed by Obama, 153; questions in *DeLeon v. Perry*, 167–69, 171, 173–74, 176, 179–180, 211; questions in *Campaign for Southern Equality v. Bryant*, 155–59

Gregory, David, 212

Greshin, Jeremy, 312

Griffin, Chad, congratulates Texas plaintiffs, 128, 142; founds AFER, 220; takes photo of Mark and Vic at Supreme Court, 231; in the Supreme Court for *Obergefell*, 232; attends post-*Obergefell* rally in Austin, 277, 298

Grim, Ryan, 86

Griswold v. Connecticut, 66

Grogan, Rives Miller, 205, 241–44

Guerrero, Debra, 40, 46

Guswha, Jenna, 187

Guthrie, Woody, 277

H

Hale, Angela, 100, 145, 151

Hallward-Driemeier, Douglas, 207, 265

Hammet, Chris, 13, 291, 324

Harris, Jack, and George Evans. *See* Evans, George and Jack Harris

Harris v. Rainey, 105

Harvard Law School, 71

Haskins, Jamie and Sarah Klassen, 265

Hauppert, Debbie Jo, 129

Hayburn, John G., II, 124–25

heightened scrutiny. *See* scrutiny, levels of

Helm, Mary, 18

Henderson, Russell, 69

Hennessy-Fiske, Molly, 132

Hennigan, Vicky, 187

Herbert v. Kitchen, 105, 110

"Here Comes the Groom," 70–71

Herman, Guy, 192

Herring, Mark, 124

Hickman, Cathy, 187

Higginbotham, Patrick E. 155, 167–69, 179; cites Richard Posner, 169, 171–72, 176; "cowboy common sense," 154; decision in *St. Joseph's Abbey*, 161, 181–82; humor, 159, 163; impatience with states' arguments, 158, 173–76; precedential value of *Baker v. Nelson*, 159, 179; Reagan appointee, 154; "sea-change," 162; as swing vote, 154, 157, 163; warns of animus, 174–76

Holland & Knight, LLP, 199

Hollingsworth v. Perry, 6, 142, 201, 220, 239

Hollister, Tracy, 229–32, 264

Holmes, Bobbi, 30

Holmes, Jerome, 154

Holmes, Mary, first marriage ends, 29; trains as a nurse, 30; remarries, 30; suspects Vic is gay, 33, 50; Vic comes out to her, 50–51

Holmes, Nicky Joe, 30

Holmes, Tanya, 29–30

Holmes, Vic: adolescence, 30–33; Cherokee heritage, 4; childhood, 29–30; coming out, 50–51; commissioning ceremony, 50; enlists in U.S. Air Force, 4, 33; faking heterosexuality, 32–35; fear of meeting with violence, 21, 37; fear of OSI, 35–36; legally changes his name, 30; as physician assistant, 5, 48, 50, 58–59; relationships with women, 32–34; standing ovation from physician assistant class, 131; suicidal thoughts, 36; Uniform Code of Military Justice, 33

Holmes, Vic, and Mark Phariss. *See* Phariss, Mark, and Vic Holmes
Holmes, William ("Billy Jo"), 30–33, 55, 111
Holstead, John, 316, 322
Homophobia, 21, 23, 32, 56, 287
Hotze, Steve, 303
House Judiciary Committee, 42, 75–76
Houston Chronicle, 72, 154
Houston Press, 153
Houston, Whitney, 326
Howard, Pauline, 2, 327
Howard University, 42
Howe, Amy, 260
Hudson, Lane, 242
Hudson, Rock, 23
Huetteman, Emmarie, 228–29, 254
Huffington Post, 86, 111, 132
Human Rights Campaign (HRC), 40, 70, 71, 128, 315; advocacy, 43, 70, 100, 218, 297–98, 302; Mark and Vic's association with, 39, 57, 138, 208, 209, 307; rates Akin Gump as 100% on Corporate Equality Index, 63
Huntsman v. Heavilin, 268
Hutchison, Kay Bailey, 69, 82
Hyde, Henry, 75

I

"I Wanna Dance with Somebody," 326
Icehouse, 322–24, 326–27
immutability, 108, 175
Israel, Celia, 317
"It's Time to Overturn DOMA" (Clinton), 213–14

J

Jarrett, Valerie, 203–4, 247, 274
J. C. Penney, 43, 275–76
Jefferson, Thomas, 218
John H. Wood, Jr. Federal Courthouse: architecture, 117
John Minor Wisdom Courthouse, 144, 147, 151, 160, 187, 197; architecture, 151–52, 155

Johnson, Debbie, and Zante Barica, 273
Johnson, Chris, 200
Johnson, Heather, 187
Johnson, Kristen, 50, 95, 111, 186
Johnson, Lyndon, 42
Johnson, Magic, 26
Jones, Gwen, 313, 319, 321
Jones, John E., 141
Jordan, Barbara and Nancy Earl, 41–43, 45, 55

K

Kagan, Elana: officiates at same-sex marriage, 214; questions/comment in
    oral arguments for *Obergefell*, 240–41, 248, 251–53
Kaplan, Roberta, 24, 62, 142, 285; winning *Windsor*, 84–87; oral arguments
    in *Campaign for Southern Equality v. Bryant*, 158–62, 172; influence on
    DeLeon v. Perry, 174, 177, 181; at press conference in New Orleans, 184;
    Brief of the Human Rights Campaign, 218
Karlan, Pamela, 24, 265
Katami, Paul, 142
Kay, Susan, 131
Kelly, Chris, 114
Kennedy, Anthony, 69, 156, 217; comments and questions in *Obergefell*,
    237–38, 241, 245, 251–53, 257; opinion in *Lawrence*, 25, 78–81, 222;
    opinion in *Obergefell*, 260, 262–63, 265, 277, 294, 319; opinion in *Romer*,
    67; opinion in *Windsor*, 84–86; referenced in Complaint in *DeLeon v.*
    Perry, 90–91; referenced in *Robicheaux v. George*, 156–57; referenced
    in *Campaign for Southern Equality v. Bryant*, 159–61; referenced in
    DeLeon v. Perry, 178, 182; referenced in *Obergefell*, 236, 245, 248; "times
    can blind," 25, 79, 84, 160, 239
KENS 5, 125
KERA, 131–34
Kern, Terrence C., 124
Kerry, John, 77, 210
King, Olga, 308
Kling, Karina, 228, 254
KLRN, 134
Kofler, Shelly, 131–33
Krantz, Lisa, 310
KTVT, 258, 261

L

L Syle G Style, 377

Lakey, David, 119

Lambda Legal, 101, 137, 142, 150, 155, 183, 199, 201, 265, 274, 283

Lane, Neel, 90, 92, 96–97, 103, 111, 116, 126–28, 137, 179, 190, 193, 277, 324–25; awards/praise earned pursuing *DeLeon v. Perry*, 284; *DeLeon v. Perry* as civil rights case, 11; delivers responsive argument in district court, 122; descent from Sam Maverick, 63; involvement in John Stone-Hoskins case, 281–84; as latter-day Walt Whitman, 108–9; Motion to Lift Stay in *DeLeon v. Perry*, 195–96; oral arguments before Fifth Circuit, 177–83; press conference in Austin, 269–70, 272; press conference in New Orleans, 184–85; recognized at Mark and Vic's wedding, 324' rebuts Motion to Consolidate, 104

Lane, Robin, 25–26

Lawrence, John, 137, 184

Lawrence v. Texas, 24–25, 52, 77, 122, 134, 180–81, 212, 224; Justice Kennedy's opinion, 78–82; key element in *Obergefell*, 245–46, 253, 259; cited before the Fifth Circuit, 180–181

Lawton Constitution, 15–16

Lee, Lewis, 46

Lee, Paul, 116–17

Leivitt, Eugene, and Albert Klassen, 15–16

Lella, Andy, 135–36

Liberty Counsel, 77

Liberty Institute, 193

Lincoln, Abraham, 223

Lopez, Dana, 258

Lopez, Sylvia, 290

Los Angeles Times, 129, 132

Love, Ellen: A Mother/Daughter Journey, 40–41

Loving, Richard and Mildred, 149

Loving v. Virginia, 90, 107, 149, 175, 179, 218, 245, 304

M

Madison, James, 218

Malcolm, Molly Beth, 318–19

Manning, Susan Baker, 219

Marbut, Robert, Jr., 416

Margolin, Emma, 157

Marmor, Marci and Sherrill Oldham, 292

Marriage Equality in:

Alabama, ???, 297–98; *Strange v. Scarcy*, 226

Alaska, 82, 222

Arkansas, 137, 140, 222, 298

California, 142, 178, 210, 213, 220, 239

Colorado,73, 80–82, 142, 200, 284

District of Columbia, 2, 109, 119, 141, 143, 190, 216

Florida, 268

Hawaii, 73–76, 200–1, 239

Idaho, 140

Illinois, 141

Indiana, 141, 157, 169–71, 175, 178, 180, 226, 298

Kansas, 17, 142, 222, 141–42

Kentucky, 124–5, 140, 142, 189, 216, 218, 276

Louisiana, 137–38, 140, 142, 189, 216, 218, 265, 276, 137–38, 145–47, 150, 202, 222, 278–79, 305, 328–29; oral arguments at the Fifth Circuit, 155–58, 161–62, 168–69, 176, 182; press conference after Fifth Circuit Hearing, 183–85, 188, 197

Maine, 102, 238, 240

Maryland, 102

Massachusetts, 201, 210, 239, 241, 259; precipitating factor in anti-marriage sentiment, 52–53, 82, 220; marriage of Cleopatra DeLeon and Nicole Dimetman, 64, 148, 177, 195; *Goodridge v. Department of Public Health*, 76–77

Michigan, 140, 142, 189, 205, 216, 218, 232–33, 248

Minnesota, 17, 72–73, 103

Mississippi, 137, 146, 188, 197, 202, 222, 278–79, 305, 328–29; Jose Pritchett at Cathedral Creative Studios, 147–48, 150' oral arguments at the Fifth Circuit, 158–63, 168–69, 171, 176, 179, 182; press conference in New Orleans, 183–85

Missouri, 222

Montana, 222

Nebraska, 82, 222

Nevada, 82, 124

New Mexico, 109

New York, 83–85, 157, 184

North Carolina, 142, 222

North Dakota, 222, 284
Ohio, 119, 142, 189, 216, 218
Oklahoma, 124, 141, 226
Oregon, 125, 140, 284
Pennsylvania, 141, 284
South Carolina, 142, 222, 284
South Dakota, 222
Tennessee, 142, 189, 216, 218
Texas. *See DeLeon v. Perry*
Utah, 105, 110, 119–120, 141, 154, 226
Vermont, 76, 276
Virginia, 105–6, 124, 140–41, 218, 226, 284
Washington, D. C., 2, 109, 119, 141, 143, 190, 216
Washington (state), 102
West Virginia, 120, 142
Wisconsin, 141, 169, 170, 226, 284
Wyoming, 142
Marshall, Margaret H., 76
Marshall, Thurgood, 207, 212
Martingale, Sherri, 34
Mason, George, 218
Massey, Charles, 242
Massey, Pam, 117
Masto, Catherine Cortez, 124
Matlovich, Leonard, 17
Matheson, Clayton, 8
Matthew Shepard and James Byrd Hate Crimes Prevention Act, 70
Matthews, Charles, 154
Matthews & Branscomb, 22, 25, 133
Maxey, Glen, 129–30
Mcanulla, Austin and Daylin, 6, 111, 134
McElvaney, Bill, 121
McKinney, Aaron, 69
McKion, Dan, 318
McManus, Adam, 46
McNosky, Chris, 101–2
McNosky v. Perry, 101–4, 106
McShane, Michael J., 140–42
Meet the Press, 212

Mehlman, Ken, 95, 219–20, 276
Melissa Harris-Perry Show, 134
Menendez, Jose and Cehlia, 40, 291
Methany, Justin, 158–60, 162–63
Metropolitan Community Church (MCC), 72, 165
Meyers, Yutaka, 323, 326–27
Miller, Frederick, 323
Milk, Harvey, 28
Minter, Shannon, 158
Mitchell, Jonathan, 168–178, 180
Modern Family, 193–4, 322
Molina, Antonio, 72–73, 181
Monument of Love, 274
Moon, Ronald, 73
Morrison, Bess, 327
Morrison, Cathy Hill, xxii
Moyé, Eric, 268
MSNBC, 99–100, 117, 134, 157
Muñoz, Henry, 8
Murphy, Arthur, 311, 319
Murphy, Michael, 105, 121–23, 152
Mutti, Lauren, 129
Myers, Peter, 95

N

NBC (National Broadcasting Company), 265
Nebraska, University of, 5
Nellermoe, Barbara, 134
Nelson, Linda, 44
New Beginnings Christian Church, 243
New Republic, 71
New York City Gay and Lesbian Anti-Violence Project, 29
New York Times, 29, 189, 220, 228, 244, 254
Newman, Andrew, 277
Nicolas, Guillermo, 39–40, 45, 286
Nicole, Georgia, 265
Nineteenth Amendment, 214
North Texas GLBT Chamber of Commerce, 266
Nuckols v. Perry, 101

O

Obama, Barack, 153, 186, 203–4, 212, 214–15, 243, 247, 274; comments on *Obergefell* decision, 274–75; declines to defend DOMA, 212; advocates repeal of Don't Ask, Don't Tell, 47, 212; signs Matthew Shepard and James Byrd Hate Crimes Bill, 70; sends letter of congratulations, 316–17; support for same-sex marriage, 203, 212–13, 274–75; White House Pride Reception 2016, 293–94

Obama, Malia and Sasha, 213

Obergefell, James, 189, 255, 257, 265, 274, 277

Obergefell v. Hodges: access to oral arguments, 205–6; amicus briefs: Brief of 92 Plaintiffs, 221–26, Brief of 379 Employers, 219; Brief of Amici Curiae Kenneth B. Mehlman, 219–21, Brief of Historians of Marriage, 221, Brief of the Human Rights Campaign, 218–19, Brief of the Commonwealth of Virginia, 218, corporate reaction to the decision, 275–77; oral arguments in, 236–41, 245–53; protestor interrupts, 241–44; public opinion at the time of oral arguments, 215–16; gathering of plaintiffs at Holland & Knight, 199–204; Supreme Court grants cert, 189, 305

"October Surprise," 141–42, 226

O'Connor, Brenda, 34

O'Connor, Sandra Day, *Lawrence v. Texas*, (O'Connor, S. concurring), 24

Office of Special Investigations (OSI)

Olivares, Corie, 328

Olivares, Steve, 319, 321

Olivia Cruises, 43

Olson, Theodore, 220

P

Pacetti, Joe, 309

Parker, Tonya, 267–68

Parsley, Rod, 53

Paxton, Kenneth, 280, 300, 303, 321; encourages resistance to *Obergefell* decision, 295–97; interview with Alysin Camerota, 295; faces contempt of court charges, 281–84

Pepping, Matt, 90, 92, 97, 103–6, 119, 128, 131, 134, 136, 188, 277, 282

Perrin, Kathleen, 205, 231

Perry, Kris, 142, 201

Perry, Lynn, 328

Perry, Rick: signs Proposition 2, 53; repudiates gay veterans, 224

Perry, Troy, 165–66, 197

Personal Stories Project, 242

personhood: denied under Don't Ask, Don't Tell, 59; longing for, 262; referenced in *DeBoer v. Snyder* (Daughtrey, M., dissenting), 262; referenced in *Lawrence*, 79–80; referenced in *Windsor*, (majority opinion), 84–86, (Scalia, A., dissenting, 86–87)

Pew Research Center, 6

Phariss, Greg and Cynthia, 15, 111; bachelor party, 56–57; learns Mark is gay, 49; Paris trip, 5; reaction to lawsuit, 95, remarks at rehearsal dinner, 313–16

Phariss, Joe Elmer, 15, 17, 25, 59, 191

Phariss, Kent, 18

Phariss, Mark: adolescence, 16–20; ancestry, 4; childhood, 14–16; college years, 20–23; coming out, 23–28, 40–45, 49; deaths in the family, 18; fear of meeting with violence, 19, 28–29; first house, 28–29; friendship with Greg Abbott, 6, 88, 117, 123, 131–33, 139, 287; love of family, 5; public service, 4; relationships with women, 25–26; suicidal thoughts/ depression, 16, 25–26, 28; hiding his homosexuality, 23–25, 28, 57; young adulthood, 20–28

Phariss, Mark, and Vic Holmes: application for a marriage license, 1, 6–11; denied a marriage license, 1, 8–10; fears/warnings of meeting with violence, 51, 53, 88, 95, 115, 127, 199, 308; first meeting, 13–14; first date, 39–41, 45; hearing before the Federal District Court for the Western District of Texas, 166–83; hearing before the Fifth Circuit Court of Appeals, 118–24; hiding their relationship, 47–48, 56–59; home in Plano, 2, 113; honeymoon, 191, 306–7; lawsuit announced on Facebook, 96–97; lease agreement, 47–48; line cutting incident at the Supreme Court, 227–32; marriage, 318–21; press conference in Austin, 269–72; publicity, reaction to, 65, 95–96, 98–101, 111, 114, 274; on *Watch What Happens Live with Andy Cohen*, 135–36; years living apart, 48–49

Phariss, Marsha: childhood evangelism, 15; coming out to, 49; lack of acceptance, 49–50; support for, 5

Phariss, Yona: death of, 25; religious nature, 15; views *Yentl* with Mark, 23

Phelps, Fred, 138

Phrasaveth, Sonemaly, 192

Piazza, Chris, 137, 140

Pinckney, Clementa, 274

Planned Parenthood of Southeastern Pa v. Casey, 79

Polaski, Adam, 134–35

Polen, Emily, 318
Polen, Rita and Jerry, 39, 45, 285–86
polling Results, 6, 15–16, 146, 215, 298
Poppe, Ryan, 96
Posner, Richard A., 157, 169–71, 175, 178–80
"Postcards from Buster" controversy, 94
Powell, Lewis, Jr., 24
Powell, Wesley, 221–22, 224–25, 285
Prestonwood Baptist Church, 51–55, 60
Priestly, William and Thomas, 153
Pritchett, Jocelyn (Joce), 147–50, 197, 202, 257
Proposition 2 (Texas), 52–53
Proposition 8 (California), 142, 175, 201, 213, 220, 239
Public Religion Research Institute, 215
Pulido, Ruben, 276
"Puppy Episode," 43–45

Q

Question 711 (Oklahoma), 124

R

Rafter, Dan, 135, 209
Rainbolt-Baily, Jim and Michael, 186–87
Raison, Randall, 187
Rasmussen, Buddy, 165
Ratchford, C. Brice (President of the University of Missouri), 20
rational basis review. *See* scrutiny, levels of
Reagan, Ronald, 66, 153–54, 158, 173
Red Media Group, 100, 111, 145
Rednour, Floyd, 29–30
Reed, Ralph, 54–55
Reeves, Carlton W., 150, 158
Rehnquist, William, 67–68, 209
Reid, Harry, 208–9, 309
Remley, Audrey, 304
Reskovac, Rev. John, 15
Rhea, Meghan, 219

Rickhoff, Gerard "Gerry," 8, 10, 118–19, 123–24, 289–91

Risdon, Susan, 100, 111, 145, 269

Roberts, John, 237–38, 241, 245, 265

Roberts, Robin, 213

Robertson, Pat, 44

Robicheaux v. George, 137–38, 152–53, 155–57, 183–84

Romer v. Evans, 69–70, 77, 80, 84, 122, 180, 215, 260; cited in *DeLeon v. Perry*, 107; majority opinion/Scalia's dissent, 66–69; reverses *Bowers*, 78

Romney, Mitt, 77

Roos, Mats, Martha, and Emma, 284–85

Rorex, Clela, 73

Rosenblum, Ellen, 125, 140

Ross, Billy, 111

Ross, Worth, 40, 94

Rowse, Jayne and April DeBoer. *See* DeBoer, April

Rozsa, Gabe, 208

Rubin, Jeanne, 135

Rudner, Steve: appears in El Paso with Mark and Vic, 192; congratulates Mark and Vic, 264, 317; dinner at Galatoire's, 150; reaction to Texas resistance to *Obergefell* decision, 302; rebuts Jonathan Saenz' attacks in New Orleans, 144–47; recognized at Mark and Vic's wedding, 324; responds to political backlash in Texas, 302

Rustin, Bayard, 293–94

Ryder, James, 232

S

Saenz, Jonathan, 109, 145–46, 302–2

Safford, Kathy and Barb Melzer, 89

Salas, Mario, 46

"Same-Sex Marriage: An Idea Whose Time Has Come?" 192

"Samesex Marriage and Morality: The Human Rights Vision of the Constitution," 71–72

Samuelson, Timothy, 170

San Antonio Baptist Association, 46

San Antonio Country, 22

San Antonio Current, 111

San Antonio Express News, 46, 65, 89, 96, 99, 111, 125, 291

Sanders, Andrea and Rebecca Bickett, 184

Sanders, Bernie, 192

Sanders, Steve, 219

Santibanez, Janette, 11

Saturday Night Fever, 326

Save Our Children Campaign, 17–18, 43

Scalia, Antonin: 268, 295; decision in *Business Electronics* used in brief for *Obergefell* plaintiffs, 221–26; dissents in: *Lawrence*, 78–82; *Obergefell*, 265; *Romer*, 67–69; *Windsor*, 86–87; questions/comments in oral arguments for *Obergefell*, 237, 239–41, 244, 246

Schafly, Phyllis, 44

Schake, Kristina, 220

Schanklin, Robert "Butch," 19–20

Schindler, Allen, 37

Schuette v. Coalition to Defend Affirmative Action, 156

Schulman, Steven, 63

Scott, Havard, 147, 183–84

SCOTUSblog, 256, 255–60

scrutiny, levels of

careful review/"rational basis with a bite," 159–60, 181–82

heightened scrutiny, 73, 159–60, 181–82

rational basis review: defined, 67; in *Campaign for Southern Equality*, 159, 161–62; in *DeLeon*, 90, 105, 120–23, 128, 168–69, 171–75, 181–82; in *Goodridge*, 76; in *Lawrence* (Scalia, A., dissenting), 81

September 11, 57–59

Shah, Pratik A., 221, 277

Shelby, Robert J., 110–11

Shepard, Judy, 70

Shepard, Matthew, 69–71, 78

Sherman Act, 223

Simpson, Andrew, 101

"skim milk marriage," 61, 239

Slate, 269

Smith, Chuck, 135, 269, 271, 277, 324

Smith, Jerry E., 155, 167–68; comments/questions in oral arguments for: *Campaign for Southern Equality*, 158–59, 162, 179; *DeLeon*, 168, 173–74, 176; *Robicheaux*, 157–58, 179; conservative background, 153–58, 179; Mark's discontent with post-*Obergefell* order in *DeLeon*, 279–80

Smith v. Allright, 212

Solomon, Marc, 75, 232, 255, 268–69

Somin, Ilya, 216

Sommer, Susan, 265

Sotomayor, Sonia, 240–41, 248, 251

Souter, David, 79

South Florida Gay News, 200

Southern Baptist Convention, 51–55

Southern Poverty Law Center, 22, 43

Sovell, David and Caroline, 26

Sparks, Sam, 102–6

Spellings, Margaret, 94–95

Spirit of Texas Brunch, 135, 284

Spyer, Thea. *See* Windsor, Edith

St. Joseph Abbey v. Castile, 161–62, 174, 182

St. Paul's Methodist Church, 15–16

Stanford, Keith, 13, 291

Stanford Supreme Court Litigation Clinic, 24

State Defense of Marriage Act, 192

Stenger-Castro, Frank, 94, 97, 117, 152, 277; accompanies Mark and Vic
   to apply for marriage license, 7–11, 290–91; compares Neel Lane to
   Walt Whitman, 108; gathering expert testimony to support Motion for
   Preliminary Injunction, 106–7; post-*Windsor* phone call with Mark,
   62–63; proposes lawsuit to Akin Gump, 63–64; recognized at Mark and
   Vic's wedding, 324; recruiting plaintiffs, 64–65, 89–90

Stern, Mark, 94

Stevens, John Paul, 79

Stier, Sandy Belzer, 142

Stone-Hoskins, John, 281–84

"Stop the Clocks," 320

Strange v. Searcy, 226

Strayhorn, Carole, 53

Streisand, Barbra, 22–23

Stricker, Sven, 101

Sullivan, Andrew, 70–71

Sullivan, Tony and Richard Adams, 73, 200

Summers, Braden, 191–92, 257

Supreme Judicial Court of Massachusetts, 76–77, 220, 241, 259

Sutton, Jeffrey S., 189, 216–17, 223, 248

Sweatt v. Painter, 212

T

Taft, William Howard, 206

Tanner, Gordon: answers query on rule governing retirees wearing uniforms, 167; arranges tour of the Pentagon for Mark and Vic, 208; recognized at Mark and Vic's wedding, 324

Taylor, Camilla, 155–57, 183–84

Taylor, Don and Bruce Jarstfer, 88

10/10/10/20 Plan, 83

Texas: Article 1, Section 32 (Texas Constitution), 62, in DeLeon, 3, 53, 107, 128, 181, 211, 224, 279, 303–4; first same-sex marriage, 72–73; first same-sex marriage, see Molina, Antonio; 63R HB 103, 73; minority rights in, 107, 212; post-*Obergefell* backlash in, 293–303; statutes prohibiting same-sex marriage, 3, 53, 181

Texas Association of Businesses, 219, 302

Texas Competes, 219

Texas for Marriage, 187–88, 191

Texas Freedom Network, 277, 302

Texas Health and Safety Code, 224

Texas Lawyer, 99, 284

"A Texas Love Story," 191

Texas Lyceum, 94–95, 135, 209–10

Texas Monthly, 63, 111, 114, 193–94

Texas Pastor Council, 54

Texas Public Radio, 96, 99, see also Poppe, Ryan

Texas Restoration Project, 52–53

Texas Tribune, 6, 125

Texas Values, 109, 145, 153, 301–2

The Real M Word: A Celebration of Marriage Equality, 292

"This Land Is Your Land," 277

This Week with Rick Casey. See Casey, Rick

Thomas, Clarence, 67

Thomas, Jeff, 133

Time Magazine, 17, 43

Time Warner Cable News, 228–29, 254

"times can blind," 25, 79, 84, 160–61, 239

Toobin, Jeffrey, 244

Travolta, John, 326

Twain, Mark, 3, 96–97

21 Parc, 278, 316, 322

U

Uniform Code of Military Justice. *See under* Holmes, Vic

United States v. Virginia, 218

United States v. Windsor, 6, 10, 24, 63, 64; 217, 221, 250, 295; referenced in: *Campaign for Southern Equality*, 158–62; *DeLeon*, 90, 107, 121–22, 171, 178, 180, 182; *Obergefell*, 236, 245, 248; *Robicheaux*, 156–57; states' right to define marriage, 121, 162; as stepping-stone to marriage equality, 62, 86–87, 142, 215–16, 188–89, 215–16, 218, 226, 259–60;

Upstairs Bar Fire, 164–66, 197

University of North Texas Health Science Center, 5, 59–60, 111, 131

Urbanski, Michael, 105

U.S. Court of Appeals for the Eighth Circuit, 21

U.S. Court of Appeals for the Fifth Circuit, 104, 106, 131, 134, 136–41, 144–45, 147, 149–53, 164, 184, 192–93, 257, 285, 305, 324; Motion to Lift the Stay, 195; oral arguments in: Campaign for Southern Equality, 158–63; DeLeon, 168–83; Robicheaux, 155–57; waiting for the court to rule, 188, 190–92, 196–97, 202, 211, 254, 261, 279–80, 305

U.S. Court of Appeals for the First Circuit, 84

U. S. Court of Appeals for the Fourth Circuit, 216, 226, 304

U.S. Court of Appeals for the Ninth Circuit, 216

U.S. Court of Appeals for the Second Circuit, 84

U.S. Court of Appeals for the Seventh Circuit, 216, 226, 304; importance of Judge Posner's decision, 157, 169–71, 175

U.S. Court of Appeals for the Sixth Circuit: Daughtrey's minority opinion, 180, 216; overturns district court rulings, 142, 189, 216; turning point in the battle for marriage equality, 223; "Who Decides" as key question in Willkie Farr's *Obergefell* brief, 223

U.S. Court of Appeals for the Tenth Circuit, 105, 110, 141, 154, 189, 216–17, 226, 304

U.S. District Court for the District of Utah, 105, 110, 120

U.S. District Court for the Eastern District of Louisiana, 150, 183

U.S. District Court for the Eastern District of Michigan, 233

U.S. District Court for the Northern District of Illinois, 125

U.S. District Court for the Northern District of Oklahoma, 124

U.S. District Court for the Southern District of Mississippi, 158

U.S. District Court for the Southern District of New York, 84

U.S. District Court for the Western District of Kentucky, 124–25

U.S. District Court for the Western District of Texas, 10, 96, 101, 104, 106, 117, 167–68, 173, 188, 195–96, 226, 279

U.S. District Court for the Western District of Virginia, 105
USA Today, 147, 257–58

V

Vanderbilt University Law School, 4, 21, 88, 117, 131–32, 167, 216, 286, 310, 312
Vanguard Award, 135, 284
Vasquez, Rick, 46
Veltman, Hap, 22, 27
Verrilli, Donald, Jr., 207, 226, 241, 243, 245–47
violence against gays and lesbians, 19, 28–29, 37–38, 46, 229. *See also* Shepard, Matthew
Virginia Declaration of Rights, 218, 318

W

Wahlberg, David, 192
Walker, Shannon, 278, 308
Walker, Vaughn, 175
Wallace, George, 15, 95
Wallace, Mike, 268
Walsh, Mark, 265
Warbelow, Sarah, 232, 297, 300, 302
Warning, Tim, 258
Warren, John, 267
Washington Blade, 200, 257
Washington Post, 6, 213, 215–16
Watch What Happens Live with Andy Cohen, 135–37
Waxman, Seth P., 220–21
WDSU, 146
Webb, Carla, 147, 257
Webber, Andrew Lloyd, 319
Weisel, Jessica, 177
Weld, William, 77
Wenke, Lorence, 267
West Virginia v. Barnette, 120
Westboro Baptist Church, 138
Westin Stonebriar Hotel, 278, 308, 310
Westminster College, 4, 20–21, 262, 265, 304, 310

White, Byron, 65

White, Molly, 300

Whitman, Walt, 108–9

Will and Grace, 212–13

Williams, Daniel, 298–300

Williams, Peter, 265

Williams Institute

Willis, Britton, 4

Willis, Tish, 264

Willkie Farr & Gallagher, 221–26, 285

Wills, Jesse, 112–13

Winchell, Barry, 37

Windsor, Edith, and Thea Spyer: lawsuit filed, 83, 87, 212; Mark and Vic borrow from their wedding vows, 320; marriage in Canada, 83; Windsor signs Brief of the Human Rights Campaign, 218. See also *United States v. Windsor*

"Winning Marriage: What We Need to Do," 83

Wisdom, John Minor, 153

Wolfson, Evan.142, 232; co-counsel in *Baehr*, 73–74, 201; founds Freedom to Marry, 201; hosts reception at Holland & Knight, 200–3; Mark's Facebook homage to, 207; note to Mark and Vic on their wedding, 317; op-ed with Julian Castro, 125; press release after district court decision in *DeLeon*, 128–29; reaction to *Obergefell* decision, 255, 269, 278; reaction to post-*Obergefell* backlash in Texas, 297; reaction to Sixth Circuit loss in *DeBoer*, 190; thesis at Harvard Law School, 71–72; 2003 conference on the future of marriage equality, 83

Wray, Diana, 153

Wright Smith, Kali, 269

Y

Yentl, 22–23

Yorksmith, Pamela, 265

Z

Zablocki v. Redhail, 90, 107

Zahrn v. Perry, 101–4, 106

Zahrn, Shannon and Catherine, 101

Zirillo, Jeff, 142